THE BIBLICAL PRESENCE IN
SHAKESPEARE, MILTON, AND BLAKE

The Biblical Presence in Shakespeare, Milton, and Blake

A COMPARATIVE STUDY

HAROLD FISCH

CLARENDON PRESS · OXFORD

OXFORD

UNIVERSITY PRESS

Great Clarendon Street, Oxford OX2 6DP

Oxford University Press is a department of the University of Oxford.
It furthers the University's objective of excellence in research, scholarship,
and education by publishing worldwide in

Oxford New York

Athens Auckland Bangkok Bogotá Buenos Aires Calcutta
Cape Town Chennai Dar es Salaam Delhi Florence Hong Kong Istanbul
Karachi Kuala Lumpur Madrid Melbourne Mexico City Mumbai
Nairobi Paris São Paulo Shanghai Singapore Taipei Tokyo Toronto Warsaw

and associated companies in Berlin Ibadan

Oxford is a registered trade mark of Oxford University Press
in the UK and in certain other countries

Published in the United States
by Oxford University Press Inc., New York

ISBN 0-19-818489-1

Printed in Great Britain
on acid-free paper by
Bookcraft (Bath) Short Run Books
Midsomer Norton

For Geoffrey and Renée Hartman

Preface

His little throat labours with inspiration; every feather
On throat & breast & wings vibrates with the effluence Divine
(William Blake, Milton, Pl. 31)

This is a book about literary influence as it relates to the work of three poets. One would almost want to say, *the* three poets, because Shakespeare, Milton, and Blake may be seen as representing three basic poetic possibilities: centrifugal, centripetal, and mythical. The first poet projects himself outwards so as to construct a universe, indeed many universes, all of which retain a certain autonomy. The second takes as wide a sweep almost as the first, but power is introjected towards the centre, into the arena of the poet-speaker's own subjectivity; there the drama is played out. In the third option there is ultimately neither centre nor circumference; such geometrical relations are annulled, power being directed rather at the abolishing of all boundaries whatever—those separating subject and object, male and female, outer and inner, earlier and later. The person of the poet also merges into the totality of the myth-world, as selfhood and identity become increasingly problematical. A later myth-maker, who owed not a little to Blake, was to ask: 'How can we know the dancer from the dance?'

These different modes also characterize the hermeneutic encounter of the three poets with the powerful texts from the past by which they were influenced. I shall be concerned primarily with the way my chosen authors incorporate biblical paradigms into their work. This will be taken not as an example of influence in the narrow sense but as a key to their poetic practice—a claim that will be more readily granted in reference to Milton and Blake than to Shakespeare. However, I will argue that Shakespeare draws on biblical sources to an extent not generally recognized. Merely to point to these sources is not to say very much; what is of particular interest is the tension set up between these and other cultural influences which had likewise acquired a new intensity in the period when Shakespeare wrote. The resulting *agon* is not the play that we see on the stage so much as a contest for the control of that play—and the outcome of the contest is by no means determined in advance. With that *agon* we shall be concerned.

Milton's posture *vis-à-vis* the biblical texts that he sets himself to interpret in his poems is likewise marked by extreme dialogic tension, but the poet-narrator is himself the battleground; he confronts the ancient source, struggling for the saving word for himself and his audience, aware at the same time that a poet charged as he is and elected as he is to a high destiny, is also beset by many competing forces. From time to time, as in the Proem to Book VII of *Paradise Lost,* he will turn for help to his heavenly mentor: 'still govern thou my Song.' Without such help and without such control there is the danger of flying too high like Bellerophon or of sinking too low like Orpheus who, after descending into the underworld, is torn to pieces by the Maenads. He constantly runs the risk, like his hero Samson, of succumbing to alien influences. Indeed Samson the Nazirite, who is both bound and free, granted power and at the same time constrained by the terms of his contract, becomes, as I will argue, a primary reflexive image of the poet himself in the hermeneutic relation.

Of the three poets under discussion, Blake's indebtedness to his precursors is the most clearly foregrounded. In his epic prophecy *Milton,* he dramatizes the relation between himself and his great seventeenth-century forerunner as a visionary encounter in his garden at Felpham in the course of which Milton enters Blake through his left foot to become one with him. He uses the Miltonic term 'effluence' to designate a coming together which is more than mere influence. The Lark in the passage quoted at the head of this Preface labours with inspiration. It has listened silently to the voice of the Nightingale, but now it takes a higher flight, mounting upon the wings of light to lead the choir of day. This is Blake being seized by the power of Milton's poetry as symbolized by the Nightingale. But it is also Blake asserting his own lyric supremacy over Milton. Effluence works both ways. Blake is not only inspired by Milton; he incorporates and rewrites Milton's poems so as to render them into an instrument of the true spiritual revolution!

Blake sees it as his task to incorporate and rewrite the Bible also. In an episode parallel to his encounter with Milton, the poet-narrator is met by Los who likewise becomes one with him: 'And I became one man with him, arising in my strength.' Los, the god of time and history, is also the spirit of biblical prophecy, in this resembling Urania, the Muse of Milton's divine poetry. But Blake sees himself to be even more authentically inspired than Milton. Whereas Milton addresses Urania in the I–Thou of a covenantal dialogue, Blake unites with Los to become an indistinguishable God-Man incarnation. Such unions or incarnations have their shadow side also. Ololon, a central figure in the second book of the poem, represents what may be termed hermeneutic despair, a questioning of literary continuities of any kind. And in keeping with this the poem concludes with an account of the self-annihilation of Milton as well as the symbolic death and resurrection of the poet-narrator himself.

There is thus no unitary model of influence, as some critics have claimed, no single universal way to represent the intertextual relations of poets and poems. Nor is this only a matter of fundamental differences in poetic orientation; if these three poets react differently to their sources it is also because of changes in the world around them. The hermeneutic question cannot be separated from the changing historical context. Blake experienced the full impact of the Enlightenment with its rebellion against received norms and beliefs. Milton did not—at best he was able to see it as a cloud like a man's hand. As a result, the two poets related differently to the authority of the past and the texts in which that authority was encoded. Inevitably, therefore, a study devoted to the poetics of influence becomes a study of the spiritual history of the West, its revolutions, and conflicts.

Chapter 5 of this book first appeared (in a slightly abbreviated form) in *Summoning: Ideas of the Covenant and Interpretive Theory*, edited by Ellen Spolsky (Albany, NY: State University of New York Press, 1993). It is reproduced here by kind permission of the editor and publishers. The remaining chapters are new but I have from time to time built on and reworked ideas first set out in earlier publications. Readers of my work on biblical poetics (*Poetry With a Purpose: Biblical Poetics and Interpretation* (Bloomington, Ind.: Indiana University Press,

1988)) will recognize echoes of that study at several points in the discussion. For the Shakespeare chapters I draw upon *Hamlet and the Word: The Covenant Pattern in Shakespeare* (New York: Ungar, 1971) as well as '*Antony and Cleopatra*: The Limits of Mythology', *Shakespeare Survey*, 23 (1970), and ' "Debbo io ricordare?" L'arte e la negazione della memoria', trans. Francesco Paolo Vertova, in *Iride: Filosophia e discussione pubblica*, anno VIII, no. 14 (Jan.–Apr. 1995). In Chapter 6 I have incorporated some thoughts from 'Hebraic Style and Motifs in *Paradise Lost*', in *Language and Style in Milton*, edited by Ronald D. Emma and John T. Shawcross (New York: Ungar, 1967), and also from 'Creation in Reverse: The Book of Job and *Paradise Lost*', in *Milton and Scriptural Tradition*, edited by James H. Sims and Leland Ryken (Columbia, Miss.: University of Missouri Press, 1984). Some of the ideas on Blake and Milton in the Blake chapters were first set out in 'Blake's Miltonic Moment' in *William Blake: Essays for S. Foster Damon*, edited by Alvin H. Rosenfeld (Providence, RI: Brown University Press, 1969).

For references to *Hamlet* and *Richard II* I have used the New Cambridge Shakespeare; for other plays of Shakespeare, except where noted otherwise, I have used the Arden edition. Citations from Milton's poetry are from the edition of Merritt Y. Hughes (*John Milton: Complete Poems and Major Prose* (New York: The Odyssey Press, 1957)). The Blake quotations and references are from *The Poetry and Prose of William Blake*, edited by David V. Erdman (New York: Doubleday, 1970). Blake's Job illustrations are reproduced from the magnificent set of the engravings in the possession of Mr William Margulies of London. I am much indebted to Mr Margulies for his kind assistance and courtesy in this matter. Two additional works of Blake in water-colour are reproduced here by courtesy of the Fogg Art Museum of Harvard University (Fig. 2) and the Tate Gallery (Fig. 7).

In 1988–9, during the preparation of the early chapters of this book, I benefited from a fellowship at the Institute for Advanced Studies in the Humanities of Edinburgh University. Similarly, during the year 1991–2 I was able to profit from a visit to Yale University as the Horace W. Goldsmith Fellow in Judaic Studies. My thanks are due to the governing bodies of both institutions for their timely invitations and their many courtesies.

I have profited from the comments of several colleagues, particularly Sanford Budick, Marcel Mendelson, Murray Roston, Aaron Stavisky, and Aaron Streiter, all of whom saw drafts of one or more of the chapters whilst the work was in progress. In addition, I owe important references to Moshe Idel, Edna Sharoni, Ilona Treitel, and Oded Irshai. Finally, and not least, my thanks are due to several generations of students both in Israel and America who have over the years patiently followed my attempts to trace the intertextual web which links these three authors to their predecessors and to one another; more importantly, they have on numerous occasions helped me to find the thread I was seeking. Psalm 119: 99 reads in most translations, 'I have more insight than all my teachers, for thy testimonies are my study.' With a finer and modester sense of their place in the intellectual economy, the Rabbis of the Talmud read the first half of this verse as: 'From anyone who had anything to teach me, I have gained understanding' (Mishnah, *Aboth* 4: 1). That would be about right for the preparation of this book.

H. F.

Contents

List of Figures   xiv

PART I. SHAKESPEARE   1

1. *Julius Caesar*: Stones or Men?   3

2. *Antony and Cleopatra*: Soldering up the Rift   35

3. *Hamlet*: Thy Commandment All Alone   66

4. *King Lear*: Organized Incoherence   116

PART II. MILTON   151

5. Samson and the Poetics of Covenant   153

6. *Paradise Lost*: Subtext and Supertext   179

PART III. BLAKE   207

7. Mock on Voltaire Rousseau   209

8. Cognition and Re-cognition   235

9. The Golden Sandal of Hermes   259

10. The Poetics of Incarnation   288

Index   327

List of Figures

1. Job and his Family   292
   (Job Series, Plate 1)

2. By the Waters of Babylon   293
   (By courtesy of the Fogg Art Museum, Harvard University Art
   Museums, Bequest of Grenville L. Winthrop)

3. Job and his Family Restored to Prosperity   295
   (Job Series, Plate 21)

4. Job's Evil Dreams   297
   (Job Series, Plate 11)

5. When the Morning Stars Sang Together   298
   (Job Series, Plate 14)

6. Behemoth and Leviathan   299
   (Job Series, Plate 15)

7. Elohim Creating Adam   302
   (By courtesy of the Tate Gallery, London/Art Resource,
   New York)

8. The Lord Answering Job out of the Whirlwind   309
   (Job Series, Plate 13)

9. The Vision of Christ   311
   (Job Series, Plate 17)

10. Job and his Daughters   316
    (Job Series, Plate 20)

PART I

SHAKESPEARE

CHAPTER 1

Julius Caesar: Stones or Men?

When the conspirators meet in *Julius Caesar*, Act II, scene i, to plan the assassination, Brutus shows a commendable degree of high-mindedness and delicacy. Caesar must be killed for the sake of Rome, but there must be no unnecessary bloodshed. To kill Antony as well would be 'to cut the head off and then hack the limbs'. Ideally, one would want to get at Caesar's life by a kind of spiritual laser-surgery:

> We all stand up against the spirit of Caesar,
> And in the spirit of men there is no blood.
> O, that we then could come by Caesar's spirit,
> And not dismember Caesar!
>
> (II. i. 167–70)

But along with the moral fastidiousness, the seeming aversion to bloodshed, there is another rather different strain of imagery in this speech, namely, that of a ritual. Brutus proposes to Cassius that the killing of Caesar be undertaken as a sacrifice: 'Let's be sacrificers, but not butchers, Caius'—a procedure that would evidently not be quite so immaculate in its effects as the laser-surgery, for he goes on to say:

> Let's carve him as a dish fit for the gods,
> Not hew him as a carcass fit for hounds.
>
> (II. i. 172–4)

The parisonic balance of these two lines emphasizes the fact that the amount of cutting and bleeding involved would be much the same if the dish was being carved for the gods or hewn for hounds, the only difference being in the more exalted state of mind of those engaged in the former activity.

Like a number of other critics, A. D. Nuttall remarks that these lines with their 'oddly "aesthetic" vision of carving another human being' create an 'off-key impression'. We find them slightly weird, he says.[1] We might overlook this momentary lapse except that in Act III, after dealing Caesar the death-blow with his sword, Brutus calls once again for a ritual performance.

> Stoop, Romans, stoop,
> And let us bathe our hands in Caesar's blood
> Up to the elbows, and besmear our swords . . .
>
> (III. i. 105–7)

Cassius promptly seconds the proposal and the conspirators crouch over the body in order to daub the blood plentifully on their hands and their weapons. Whereafter, Brutus and his friends, their bloodied swords held aloft, their arms covered with blood *up to the elbows*, congratulate themselves on being 'the men that gave their country liberty'. Nuttall properly points out that in this 'wild ceremonial' we have an inversion of the normal rituals associated with blood-guilt. One would expect rather an attempt, like Lady Macbeth's, to wash away the blood with water. Nuttall finds a psychological explanation for this anomaly. Being out of touch with reality, Brutus comes to see the murder itself as an act of cleansing. It is something like a study in schizophrenia.[2]

This, however, seems not to be the point. The scene lights up not the individual quirks of Brutus but the frightful moral chasm between the Roman world and our own. It is no longer a matter of strange language; it is not that Brutus is off-key, momentarily out of touch with reality. It is that we, the audience, have suddenly become aware of reality—a reality of the most shattering kind and different from our own. In Act II the ritualizing of murder had been a matter of poetic imagery— 'Let's carve him as a dish fit for the gods,' Brutus had said. Now we see the carving and the bleeding going on before our eyes with Brutus taking the lead in the bloody performance. There is a great distance here between sign and signified, between the gesture as called for and the reality which we actually witness. As Pegeen says in *The Playboy of the Western World*, when she becomes convinced that her lover has in reality killed his

---

[1] A. D. Nuttall, *A New Mimesis: Shakespeare and the Representation of Reality* (London: Methuen, 1983), 179.

[2] Ibid. 180.

father—'There's a great gap between a gallous story and a dirty deed.' What we see on the stage is the ultimate deed of horror; we experience shock—one which no fine-spun scruples on the part of Brutus can serve to mitigate. Leo Kirschbaum has made the point with great cogency:

That the dignified and gentle Brutus should propose the ghastly procedure of the conspirators bathing their hands in the blood of Caesar's body wrenches the mind . . . We see the noble Brutus suddenly turn into a savage.[3]

In this connection he points to a kind of cover-up on the part of critics and editors who have tended to confine their comments to Brutus' sincerity or his noble commitment to the republican cause, at the same time ignoring the bloodbath. There has been, he remarks, 'some kind of turning away from the unseemly. None of them [the critics and editors] appears willing to face the scene on its own maculate terms.' Moreover, the lines about stooping and washing and the actions that go with them were regularly omitted in eighteenth- and nineteenth-century productions of the play.[4]

There is clearly something profoundly disturbing about this moment in the play, something that the audience would rather hide itself from. Romanism is not after all frozen in the past and done away with; it is an enduring part of the cultural and literary inheritance of Shakespeare and his audience. At the same time there is a 'great gap' between literary culture—the charm of Ovid, the noble, swelling line of Virgil—and the savagery which is Rome. Shakespeare does not fill in that space for us; it remains for us a stage on which to mount our own *agon*, our own response to the world of the play.

2

To understand both the special horror, the fascination, as well as the evident embarrassment which this scene arouses, it is necessary to define the kind of ceremony which Brutus and his

---

[3] Leo Kirschbaum, 'Shakespeare's Stage Blood and its Critical Significance', *Publications of the Modern Language Association of America*, 64 (1949), 524.
[4] Ibid. 522.

friends are conducting. It is of course a ritual of human sacrifice. In this most ancient and most persistent mode of propitiation, a particularly valued member of the tribe or family is offered up to guarantee the well-being of the rest. Brutus' purpose is to guarantee the political well-being of his society. The shedding of the victim's blood had therapeutic value—'we shall be called purgers, not murderers'. We are reminded of the myth of Osiris, who was carved in pieces by his brother Typhon. This evidently goes back to a sacrificial ritual in which a human body was dismembered and the pieces were then scattered over the fields to ensure fertility.[5] The likeness to the imagery used by Brutus in Act II is patent.

Kings (or in the case of Caesar, a would-be king) are favoured candidates for this ritual. The priest of Diana, who was regularly slain by his successor in the grove at Nemi, was also a king.[6] The assassin knows no personal cause to seek the life of the incumbent priest-king. He acts for the general good. It is a necessary killing—necessary for the orderly succession of the seasons—or, as in the case of Brutus, for the stability of the political order. These purposes obviously transcend the fate of the individual.

This is the position taken explicitly by Brutus and it is one to which the audience, whilst not consciously condoning human sacrifice, can nevertheless respond. In some hidden recess of its collective psyche, it understands the grave exigencies which give rise to this ritual. Hence the cover-up to which Leo Kirschbaum drew attention. Instead of simply registering shock, critics are drawn to speak of Brutus' 'terrible sublimity' or his 'deep sincerity' as he bids his friends stoop and wash.[7] We are clearly speaking of still-active forces in our minds and in the world we live in. We are shocked by what we see on the stage, but we are also powerfully moved. Rituals of this kind, especially in the form of a foundation-sacrifice, marking the building of a city or some other important structure, were widespread in

---

[5] See J. G. Frazer, *The Golden Bough: A Study in Magic and Religion*, abridged edn. (London: Macmillan, 1941), 378.

[6] Ibid. 1–9.

[7] Charles Knight, as cited in *Julius Caesar*, ed. H. H. Furness, New Variorum edn. (Philadelphia: Lippincott, 1913), 145–6; and see Harley Granville-Barker, *Prefaces to Shakespeare* (London: Batsford, 1963), ii. 227.

the ancient world; the victim would often be buried under the foundation-stone.[8] But they have been practised in relatively recent times also. In the German city of Oldenburg children are said to have been buried alive as late as the seventeenth century as a way of guaranteeing that the dykes would hold.[9] Christ's Kingdom was not of this world; his was a building not built with hands; nevertheless, the same imagery of a foundation-sacrifice is evoked, when, no fewer than six times, the authors of the New Testament apply to him the verse in Psalms which declares: 'The stone which the builders rejected, is become the headstone of the corner' (Psalm 118: 22).

But necessary though such killings are for the establishment of a new world, or a new political order, or for the purpose of founding a city (we recall that Romulus, the founder of Rome, first slew his brother Remus), the performance of such an act nevertheless involves guilt. The executioner is both a hero and a transgressor. He is a hero because he has performed an act necessary for the well-being, perhaps even the survival, of the community but he is a transgressor because he has blood-guilt. 'In any expiatory human sacrifice,' says Hyam Maccoby, 'the community wants the victim to die, but also wants to be free of all responsibility for his death.'[10] The Sacred Executioner will thus have to be cast out; he will be tragically marked, like Cain. He is a figure of radical ambiguity, arousing at the same time our profound thankfulness and our utter condemnation. We are drawn to him and yet we must at all costs distance ourselves from him.

All this sounds very much like Aristotle's definition of tragedy, which he says typically arouses in us pity and fear, sympathy and also horror (*Poetics*, chapter 14). We may suspect that behind the typical myths which formed the subject-matter of so much ancient tragedy was the buried memory of actual deeds of human sacrifice. This makes the Sacred Executioner something like the quintessential tragic hero. In the story of the House of Atreus, Agamemnon slays his daughter to propitiate Artemis and, later,

---

[8] See Hyam Maccoby, *The Sacred Executioner: Human Sacrifice and the Legacy of Guilt* (London: Thames and Hudson, 1982), 12–24, 97.
[9] L. Strackenjan, *Aberglaube aus dem Herzogtum Oldenburg*, 2nd edn. (Oldenburg: G. Stalling, 1908), 127 f. (cited by Maccoby, *The Sacred Executioner*, 187).
[10] Maccoby, *The Sacred Executioner*, 129.

Orestes slays his mother with the connivance of Apollo. *Julius Caesar* is from this point of view the most classically *contrived* of Shakespeare's tragedies. Significantly, the blood-ritual here enacted in the murder-scene is one of a very small number of crucial episodes in the play not derived from Plutarch but invented by Shakespeare.[11] Shakespeare's purpose, it may be suggested, is not so much to reconstruct the circumstances of Caesar's death as to display for our critical judgement the phenomenological core of ancient tragedy.[12] What we see on the stage as Brutus and Cassius and the rest bathe their hands in the blood of their victim, whom they have just carved as a dish for the gods, is what we may term the 'primal scene' of tragedy. And as befits a primal scene, it was not usually performed in public; in the ancient Greek theatre it would be decently hidden from the spectators' eyes. Shakespeare not only puts the 'savage spectacle' on centre stage at the very climax of the play, but has all the main characters comment on it. He clearly demands that we give it our attention. There is a reflexive movement here as the characters take cognizance of the scene as expressive of the very

[11] See Brents Stirling, *Unity in Shakespearian Tragedy* (1956; New York: Gordian Press, 1966), 52.

[12] See Theodor H. Gaster, *Thespis: Ritual, Myth and Drama in the Ancient Near East* (New York: Harper and Row, 1966), 325. Earlier studies by Gilbert Murray and F. M. Cornford also stressed the killing and dismemberment (*sparagmos*) of the god (Osiris or Adonis) as an essential element of the myth-pattern underlying Greek tragedy. For recent discussion, see Richard Seaford, *Reciprocity and Ritual: Homer and Tragedy in the Developing City-State* (Oxford: Clarendon Press, 1994), 340, 369–71. There is little doubt that the festival of Dionysus, from which tragedy takes its origin, at some times and places included orgiastic ceremonies in which a human being might be torn in pieces and even devoured. Richard Wilson in his recent, new-historicist study, *William Shakespeare: Julius Caesar*, Penguin Critical Studies (Harmondsworth: Penguin Books, 1992), suggests the carnival tradition as an alternative key to the understanding of *Julius Caesar* (see pp. 48–61), the killing of Caesar in Act III corresponding to the killing of the carnival king or Lord of Misrule, whether in pantomime or *in propria persona* (as a cover for political assassination). It is an intriguing theory and, what is more, it puts the ritual murder where it belongs—at the centre of the play. But against this argument it must be insisted that Caesar is very unlike a carnival king and the play (in spite of the off-stage account of the Lupercalia) is as far removed as can be from the atmosphere of the world of carnival. I have the same difficulty with Michael D. Bristol's claim that, in *Hamlet*, Claudius is also a kind of carnival king: whilst he 'does not directly acknowledge himself as a Lord of Misrule, his language is a "transformation upward" of Carnival'. (*Carnival and Theatre* (London: Methuen, 1985), 208). Carnival-related festivities, going back to the Roman saturnalia and still continuing in Shakespeare's time and beyond, surely belong more to the background of comedy, cf. C. L. Barber, *Shakespeare's Festive Comedy* (Princeton: Princeton University Press, 1959), *passim*.

nature of the theatre, indeed as a dramatic protoype. Cassius remarks:

> Stoop then and wash. How many ages hence
> Shall this our lofty scene be acted over,
> In states unborn, and accents yet unknown!
>
> (III. i. 111–13)

When Antony enters there is a similar foregrounding of the ritual itself and its high dramatic possibilities. Pointing at the 'purpled hands' and at the 'swords made rich | With the most noble blood of all this world', Antony seems to acknowledge the aesthetic grandeur of the occasion. Brutus responds by speaking of 'this our present act' and points out that, in spite of appearances, his heart and those of his friends are full of pity for the man they have killed and full of brotherly love for Antony. Ritual executioners at any time would claim no less. Brutus adds that the multitude are 'beside themselves with fear'. Pity and fear then, as Brutus here claims, mark the 'lofty scene' which he has just stage-managed. Antony thereupon performs his own little ritual coda by asking each of the killers to 'render me his bloody hand' which he will then shake as a sign of love. But it is characteristic of the ironic distance which Shakespeare here creates that, as soon as the others have gone, Antony reverses his attitude in soliloquy and in effect demolishes with the word 'butchers' the ritual in which he has just taken part:

> O, pardon me, thou bleeding piece of earth,
> That I am meek and gentle with these butchers.

Brutus earlier on had declared, 'Let's be sacrificers, but not butchers.' Sacrificers or butchers—these represent two ways of looking at the same scene. They also involve a choice between opposed world-views. By poising the alternatives before us in this fashion, without resolving the issue, Shakespeare demonstrates a remarkable degree of detachment. If we are shocked here by this scene, it is because Shakespeare meant it to shock us. His mind and art are not here in thrall to the modalities of ancient myth and ritual. These are rather the subject of the drama. We are invited to participate, indeed to become involved as fascinated spectators, but we are also invited to judge and weigh what we see. Shakespeare leaves us to conduct that *met-agon* for ourselves. And this will involve a judgement not merely of this particular episode and its ritual accompaniments, but of the ancient art of tragedy as such, of which this play and this scene constitute a singular paradigm.

I have spoken of a gap or critical space, the parameters of which are marked out for us by the antithesis of 'sacrificers' and 'butchers'. But this in the end is too simple and too stark a formulation in that it fails to do justice to the multiple ironies as well as the poetic suggestiveness of this scene. If Shakespeare were writing a thesis-drama in the manner of Bernard Shaw, the opposing concepts might be neatly labelled in this fashion. Instead of this, he indicates, through resonances in the language of the scene, the need to seek points of reference outside the Roman world of the play. It is a technique akin to perspectivism; whilst Shakespeare does not actually step outside the world of Rome, as brilliantly depicted for him in Plutarch, he nevertheless creates a multiple perspective from which we may view Rome in relation to other cultural legacies. The alternatives are not spelled out but behind the ceremony and the ritual as performed we may detect the shadowy presence of other ceremonies and other rituals.

3

One such presence is Christian. On seeing the strange and hor-rifying actions of Brutus and his friends, Shakespeare's audience would inevitably call to mind a contrary ritual, of which this might seem to be a caricature, namely, that related of Pontius Pilate who had washed his hands before the multitude, saying he was innocent of the blood of the crucified Saviour (Matthew 27: 24). In fact this washing ritual is recalled in an earlier play of Shakespeare, when Richard II, deposed and forced to abdi-cate, casts his enemies in the role of Pilate:

> Though some of you with Pilate wash your hands,
> Showing an outward pity, yet you Pilates
> Have here delivered me to my sour cross
> And water cannot wash away your sin.
>
> (IV. i. 238–41)

If in the case of Brutus there was a gap between the language of blood and the actual deed of blood enacted on the stage, in the case of Richard and his enemies there is a like gap, but sign and signified here point different ways. As Richard declares in the lines just quoted, the language used by the assembled lords is deferential, respectful ('showing an outward pity') but their intent is murderous. Indeed, in the next act, Richard will be put to death at Bolingbroke's request. Pilate is the emblem of such duplicity; he is after all an ambiguous figure in the crucifixion story, 'showing an outward pity' whilst actually delivering his prisoner to the soldiers for execution. The washing of the hands in water, whilst it represents a moral advance on the washing in blood, thus becomes a metonym for hypocrisy. It is an empty ritual, unlike the washing in blood which in *Julius Caesar* expresses precisely the inner character of the occasion.

But the charge of hypocrisy involves Richard also; far from being an innocent victim or Christ-figure, he too is a figure of guilt. In an earlier scene, Gaunt, Richard's uncle, then near death, had spoken of the kindred blood that Richard had savagely shed, indeed *drunk*!

> That blood already, like the pelican,
> Hast thou tapped out and drunkenly caroused.
>
> (II. i. 126–7)

Thus in spite of the profound semiotic contrast between the two ritual modes—washing with water as against 'washing' in blood—the Christian world of Richard seems to share with the Pagan world of Brutus a propensity for deeds of blood, or at least seems unable to rid itself of the taint, however hard it tries. The water evidently does not help.

And perhaps the reason is that both orders, the medieval Christian order reflected in *Richard II* and the Roman order in *Julius Caesar*, retain a mythology based on human sacrifice. In Christianity a man is killed in order that his blood might cleanse the world from sin (1 John 1: 7 and 2: 2). Again it is a necessary killing, exhibiting the same disturbing combination of guilt and blessing. But here the figure of the Sacred Executioner splits in two; the disciples are the immediate beneficiaries of the promise of salvation arising out of the 'savage spectacle', but only one of their number, namely, Judas, is seen to bear the guilt of betrayal and he is accordingly eliminated (Matthew 27: 5). But the chief device employed for the removal of guilt is the ritual washing of the hands performed by Pilate.[13]

Bolingbroke shares something of this double perspective. If Richard sees himself as a sacrificial victim, Bolingbroke sees him in the same way but seeks to shift the guilt of his murder from himself, retaining only the benefits. Thus when Exton, after carrying out the execution, comes to Bolingbroke to claim the thanks due to his loyalty, Bolingbroke articulates the precise combination of gratitude and horror which the Sacred Executioner typically arouses in us:

> Though I did wish him dead,
> I hate the murderer . . .
>
> (v. vi. 39–40)

This whole speech of Bolingbroke with which the play ends represents in fact a kind of summing up of our argument so far:

> Though I did wish him dead,
> I hate the murderer, love him murdered.
> The guilt of conscience take thou for thy labour,
> But neither my good word nor princely favour.
> With Cain go wander through shades of night
> And never show thy head by day nor light.
> Lords, I protest my soul is full of woe
> That blood should sprinkle me to make me grow.
> Come mourn with me for what I do lament,
> And put on sullen black incontinent.
> I'll make a voyage to the Holy Land
> To wash this blood off from my guilty hand.
>
> (ibid. 39–50)

The blood-guilt associated with human sacrifice had always been a problem, but in the Christian order this guilt became intolerable and needed at all costs to be purged away or shifted

---

[13] As a parallel to the Pilate story, we may cite another episode likewise involving the symbolic conjoining of blood and water, namely, the piercing of Christ's side as related in the Gospel of John: 'But one of the soldiers with a spear pierced his side, and forthwith came there out blood and water' (19: 34). This became the basis later on for the most famous of eighteenth-century hymns, Augustus Toplady's 'Rock of Ages': 'Rock of ages, cleft for me, | Let me hide myself in Thee! | Let the Water and the Blood, | From thy riven Side which flow'd, | Be of sin the double cure; | Cleanse me from its guilt and pow'r.' The 'double cure' well conveys the ambiguities with which we are here concerned (and see also 1 John 5: 6, 8).

to others. Pilate shifts it on to the Jews, who are sent to wander over the face of the earth as in the medieval legend of the Wandering Jew. Bolingbroke takes this line with Exton—'with Cain go wander through the shades of night'—at the same time maintaining his own princely dignity. The figure of Cain was often conflated in later literature with that of the Wandering Jew. But the burden of his own complicity proves too heavy for Bolingbroke. His soul is full of woe at the thought of his hands stained with blood; nor can any blood-ritual such as that practised by a Brutus or a Cassius bring him relief. 'That blood should sprinkle me to make me grow' is altogether too shocking and repellent a thought, a kind of grotesque parody of baptism! Instead he will seek a different ritual solution, a pilgrimage to the Holy Land where, symbolically, he would 'wash this blood off from my guilty hand'. Like Lady Macbeth he thinks that 'a little water clears us of this deed' but the water-cure it seems will not help him, nor will he ever get to Jerusalem. Bolingbroke will be haunted through his life by the memory of Richard's blood shed on Pomfret stones. He has it seems, like Macbeth and Lady Macbeth, a Christian conscience but a Pagan set of instincts.

What then is the water good for? Does it have any potency? To answer that we have to look behind the Pontius Pilate episode in Matthew to a more ancient scene to which the Pilate story clearly has reference. In Deuteronomy 21 we learn that when the body of a slain man or woman was found in the open field, the murderer or murderers unknown, the elders of the town nearest to the corpse were to carry out a rather strange public ceremony of absolution. They would first sacrifice a young heifer in a wild and uncultivated ravine; then they would ritually wash their hands in water, at the same time declaring that they were innocent of shedding human blood and praying that any blood-guilt be accordingly removed from them and their city:

And [they] shall testify and say, Our hands have not shed this blood, neither have our eyes seen it. O Lord, be merciful unto thy people Israel, whom thou hast redeemed, and lay no innocent blood to the charge of thy people Israel, and the blood shall be forgiven them. (Deuteronomy 21: 7–8)[14]

---

[14] This and other biblical passages cited in reference to Shakespeare are from the Geneva Bible.

It is clear that the effectiveness of the water-ritual ('and the blood shall be forgiven them') is dependent on the truthfulness of the prior declaration ('our hands have not shed this blood, neither have our eyes seen it'). A murderer or an accessory to murder could gain no immunity by means of this ritual. More than that, it appears, like several other Old Testament *loci*, to be actually directed against human sacrifice and its fascinations. The heifer in the ceremony, like the ram in the story of the Binding of Isaac (Genesis 22), calls attention to a religious norm based upon the sacrifice of animals rather than human beings. The insistence on the 'stony valley' which would be left waste after the ceremony[15] seems also to be levelled against the practice of the foundation-sacrifice, in which the body of the victim would mark the spot for some new constructive endeavour. The elders of the city visibly renounce any intention of benefiting in this way from the murder. In general it is clear that murder could not bring any blessing whatsoever to the community, but only defilement and danger. Far from human sacrifice (the Oblation) guaranteeing fertility, or 'redemption, propitiation, and satisfaction', in the words of the Anglican Articles of Religion, the taint of it was likely to jeopardize the redemption already promised: 'O Lord, be merciful unto thy people Israel, whom thou hast redeemed.' Only by sincerely disavowing any part in the crime —even that of passive spectators ('neither have our eyes seen it') could the people hope for divine favour! In short, it was urgently necessary, *for the sake of the community's well-being*, that the stain of bloodshed be removed from the city and its environs.

This then is the original context of the hand-washing ritual in Matthew as well as of the references to it in *Richard II* and *Macbeth* and is among the perspectives suggested by the travestied version in *Julius Caesar*. Pilate, the Roman prefect of Judea, who is elsewhere reported as having actually mingled human blood (presumably that of Jews whom his soldiers had killed) with the Temple sacrifices (Luke 13: 1), is seen here in

---

[15] Deuteronomy 21: 4 speaks of a 'stony valley which is neither ploughed nor sown'. The imperfect tense of the verbs in the Hebrew could indicate past or future. The Mishnah rules, however, that the future is intended, the land being thereafter prohibited for working, except as a quarry or as a place for combing flax. (See *Sotah* 9: 5 in *The Mishnah*, trans. H. Danby (Oxford: Clarendon Press, 1933), 304.)

Matthew as using a ritual of absolution from Deuteronomy in order to roll the guilt of the Crucifixion on to the Jews! Indeed the situation we are describing is characterized by multiple displacements. Bolingbroke, holding fast to the benefits which the killing of Richard has brought him, will, as I have noted, dream of a pilgrimage to Jerusalem and of a cleansing by water as in the Deuteronomic legislation. But in *Henry IV, Part I*, this has become a plan for a crusade in which many enemies of Christ would be destroyed (I. i. 24–7)! We are evidently back to something more like purgation through blood. Bolingbroke, like Richard, Macbeth, and Lady Macbeth, is here trapped in the contradictions of two opposed ethical systems. These characters can no more withstand the fierce temptations of murder and usurpation than can a Nero or a Catiline, but by now, their image-world, irremediably changed by the Bible, they can no longer glory in deeds of blood. Lady Macbeth will seek to cleanse her hands of blood but they will remain as stained as those of any Roman murderer. In the end her evil will destroy her—the cherubins horsed upon the sightless couriers of the air (from Psalms 18 and 104) will see to that.

4

There are thus two primal scenes, not one. To set against the scene of ritual murder in which Brutus and Cassius brandish the murder weapons in their bloody hands, crying 'peace, freedom, and liberty', we have the wild ravine, the washing of the hands, and the absolute rejection of human sacrifice. What we may ask is the implication of this alternative scene for the Western literary tradition, in particular for Shakespearian tragedy? Clearly Deuteronomy 21 gives us the polar opposite of the sublimity and terror which belong to Agamemnon or Orestes, and of the grandeur and pathos which belong to Othello as, priest-like, he approaches Desdemona's couch in the fifth act, at the same time uttering his magnificent lines. Othello fears that if the grand progress of this ceremony is disturbed, it will turn that 'which I thought a sacrifice' into mere murder (v. ii. 66). In that scene, as also in the 'sacrifice' of Julius Caesar in the third act of that play, is to be found the quintessence of the tragic. By the same token, we must conclude that the scene in Deuteronomy 21 represents the ultimate refusal of the tragic. It strips the glory and the nobility from Macbeth and Othello and Brutus, and from Caesar and Antony also, reducing them to butchers. Such an uncompromising rejection of the ethic of human sacrifice,[16] involves inevitably a break also with the aesthetic of tragedy and of much else in our classical inheritance. The tragic hero stripped of his nobility and honour is no longer a tragic hero. But Shakespeare's heroes, no matter how dreadful their crimes, remain magnificent in their defiance to the end. Macbeth and Brutus are obvious examples. How then can the scene of the hand-washing in Deuteronomy be regarded as a presence, however shadowy, in *Julius Caesar*? If it reduces the ritual of sacrifice which the conspirators enact on the stage to no more than a 'dirty deed' what possible relevance can it have to our response to the play which Shakespeare wrote, or to Shakespeare's theatre in general?

First it must be said that the reduction of which we speak is already to be found as a subtext in the plays themselves. Shakespeare writes tragedies, but they are tragedies which to a significant degree subvert their own structure. If he builds up the scene of Desdemona's murder into an elaborately staged ritual, he also overturns that ritual through the homely directness of Emilia who sweeps aside the 'gallous tale' and names the 'dirty deed':

> O gull, O dolt,
> As ignorant as dirt; thou hast done a deed . . .
> I care not for thy sword . . .
> The Moor has kill'd my mistress, murder, murder!
>
> (v. ii. 164–6, 168)[17]

---

[16] On the other side, Israel J. Yuval has recently argued that the readiness with which Jews living in the Rhineland at the time of the Crusades took their own lives, sometimes killing their wives and children first—this to avoid forced conversion or simply by way of anticipating a coming massacre at the hands of the crusaders— suggested something like a cult of 'human sacrifice'. ('Vengeance and Damnation, Blood and Defamation, etc.', *Zion*, 58: 1 (1993), 33–90 [Hebrew], English Summary, vi–viii). In these extreme situations, the line between voluntary martyrdom and ritual murder (or self-murder) could become somewhat indistinct. Other scholars in subsequent issues of *Zion* have disputed both Yuval's evidence and his conclusions.

[17] On the effect of Emilia's intrusion, see Brents Stirling, *Unity in Shakespearian Tragedy*, 202–3.

Antony does much the same when he dismisses the whole ceremony we have witnessed as simple butchery and announces that
'this foul deed shall smell above the earth | With carrion men,
groaning for burial'. But before long Antony will prove to be
as murderous as his opponents, as in Act IV he cold-bloodedly
agrees to the liquidation of his nephew Publius in the general
purge agreed upon by the triumvirate: 'Look, with a spot I
damn him.'

The presence we are talking about is indeed shadowy; there
is no character in the play to represent the biblical ethic. That
order would seem to be absent. Like the omen which surprised
the augurs on the day of Caesar's death, the whole Roman world
seems to be 'a beast without a heart'. ('Our hearts you see not;
they are pitiful', says Brutus to Antony as he holds up his weapon
in his bloody hands, but we wonder whether there is a heart
there and where the pity he speaks of has fled—perhaps to brutish
beasts?) This is in fact the exact image for the kind of absence
we are seeking to define. A beast without a heart is an image
of gaping absence; but it suggests a void which absolutely
demands to be filled. Not to fill it will result in mere absurdity.
And Shakespeare does in a manner fill it. The shock which the
audience experiences on witnessing the scene of blood is, we
have insisted, an essential dimension of understanding. And that
shock enables us to discern something like the outline of an
antithesis—the cavity if you like to which the heart belongs. The
result will be akin to what Bradley termed 'the intestinal war-
fare of the ethical substance'—in this case, the clash between
the visual imagery set forth on the stage and the biblical values
and images which the audience brings with it to the theatre. It
may be argued that in the play viewed as a text over there no
such clash is present—it exhibits a monolithic Roman world,
complete and self-enclosed—but in the play as a transaction
involving audiences, as well as author and actors, such a clash
is not only conceivable but practically inevitable. What we have,
in short, when the play is sensitively produced, is a Pagan text
and a biblical-Christian subtext.

Once this is recognized we shall easily discern this subtext
in other episodes and other aspects of the play. We might consider some of the play's typical, or iterative images. References
to metal tools and objects, for instance, recur with obsessive

frequency.[18] We are again and again made vividly conscious of the daggers which hacked one another in Caesar's body; and there is also the cobbler's awl with which the play opens and the stylus with which Antony pricks the names of those who are to die. People themselves are in a sense made of metal or flint, like the instruments they use. Thus Cassius remarks in Act I that he is glad 'that my weak words have struck but thus much show | Of fire from Brutus', whilst Brutus remarks that 'since Cassius first did *whet* me against Caesar | I have not slept'. Here the concealed metaphor of a metal instrument which has to be whetted or sharpened identifies Brutus with the knife with which he will later stab his friend. These images clearly come with a certain ironic shading. Men are not made of metal, though other people may use them as if they were and though they may often try to represent themselves as being tough and unbending like metal. In particular, we may note the frequent punning on metal/mettle. Cassius notes that Brutus' 'mettle may be wrought | From that it is dispos'd'. Both meanings are present here: 'metal', signifying strength and rigidity, and 'mettle', signifying temperament and thus, pliancy and malleability. Cassius is the blacksmith who can bend the metal of Brutus any way he wishes. The same irony attaches itself to Casca ('What a *blunt* fellow is this grown to be! | He was quick *mettle* when he went to school' (I. ii. 292–3)) and to the plebeians: 'see where their basest mettle be not mov'd.' In spite of their having the solidity and insensitivity of base metal, their emotions are easily roused and they can be swayed from one position to another—as will be vividly demonstrated again in Act III. Again, Casca's 'metal' will crumble to become the most pliant 'mettle' in the terror of the storm.

Closely related to this group of images is another even denser concentration of references to stone objects and, in particular, statues. A central visual feature of the murder scene was the statue of Pompey 'which all the while ran blood'—drawn, like the many other references to statues, from Plutarch. This image of the bleeding statue becomes a key to the play's essential dialectic. From it there seems to extend outwards a system

[18] See *Julius Caesar*, Arden Shakespeare (London: Methuen, 1955), ed. T. S. Dorsch, p. lxvii.

of opposed and yet interconnected references to metal, stones, flints on the one hand and to tears, blood, and feelings on the other. G. Wilson Knight drew attention to the rather surprising emphasis on weeping in the play; nearly all the characters—Brutus and Cassius included—weep at some time or other.[19] They also bleed. There is a paradox here since the weepers seem not to be the weeping type, and the bleeders seem to be peculiarly blood-less, like veritable statues. Supremely, Caesar himself (whom Cassius associates ironically with the greatest statue of all, namely, the Colossus at Rhodes, I. ii. 133-6) notes immediately prior to his death that other men are flesh and blood, whilst he is 'unshak'd of motion', i.e. a veritable statue! He even seems to claim that he has ice in his veins instead of blood:

> Be not fond
> To think that Caesar bears such rebel blood
> That will be thaw'd from the true quality
>
> (III. i. 39-41)

Thirty-five lines on, and Caesar will be on the ground, dead from a dozen stab-wounds. The statue visibly bleeds; the ice visibly thaws.

Again, Antony exposes the absurdity of this Roman obses-sion with statuary. Just as he had spat out the reductive term 'butchers' after the ceremony of the ritual slaying, so now he rouses the people in a few minutes of acting time to a violent counter-revolt, at the same time telling them, 'You are not wood, you are not stones, but men' (III. ii. 144). But again Antony will not serve as the spokesman of a non-Roman standard, one which will take into account our human limitations as well as the greatness and wonder which we can attain in our flesh and blood condition. For Antony himself, even at the moment of pronouncing these words, has ice in his veins; he is making a coldly calculated assault on the emotions of his audience, using his words like veritable metal instruments. But those words nevertheless open up for us the ironical space between the Roman ethic and that which lies beyond it. In that space the words of Antony reformulate themselves as a question which we address

---

[19] G. Wilson Knight, *The Imperial Theme* (1931; London: Methuen, 1965), 43-4; and see Nuttall, *A New Mimesis*, 103.

to each and every figure in the play: 'Are you stones or men?'
It is a question that we are also driven to put to ourselves as
the residuary legatees of that Roman civilization so powerfully
re-created in the play. Can this paradoxical image of mettle/
metal, of emotional turbulence combined with cold-blooded ferocity, serve as a model for breathing men and women? The play
does not offer us an ethical alternative to Romanism, but whilst
remaining within that world, Shakespeare also lights up its para-
doxality. That is his original contribution, his fundamental
departure from Plutarch. Everywhere we behold men and women
with hearts of stone, but eventually it becomes impossible to
conceive this as other than an absurdity. And the consciousness
of that absurdity causes us instinctively to desire that some divine
hand will 'take the stony heart out of their bodies, and will give
them an heart of flesh'.

5

The verse from Ezekiel (11: 19, 36: 26) just cited is not in the
play. And yet it is somehow buried in the text. The move from
Marullus addressing the citizens in Act I as

> You blocks, *you stones*, you worse than senseless things!
> O *you hard hearts*, you cruel men of Rome—
>
> (I. i. 35–6)

to Antony's speech in Act III:

> You are not wood, *you are not stones, but men*;
> And being men, hearing the will of Caesar,
> It will inflame you, it will make you mad—
>
> (III. ii. 144–6)

can be read as a kind of charade illustrating that verse in
Ezekiel. The verse would then lie hidden in the play as text and
performance.

We have in short an absence which is really a presence, as in
the example of the beast without a heart. The absence of that
telling verse is a conspicuous absence; it cries out from the vacant
space. I would now like to go one step further and argue that
such a dialectic is not an incidental feature of the play. The play

is centrally concerned throughout with things that are denied, with the absent which is also present and the seeming present which is none the less absent.

We may take the case of Pompey. The power struggle between Caesar and Pompey the Great and the battles fought between them, culminating in the deaths of Pompey and his older son Gnaeus, had dominated Plutarch's *Life of Caesar*. Shakespeare seems to ignore this, picking up the story at a point four-fifths of the way through the *Life*, where Pompey is dead and Caesar is the sole dictator. But in fact in this most political of his plays, Shakespeare does not ignore it, nor could he easily do so, seeing that the struggle between the two leaders constituted the essential background to the conspiracy itself, Brutus and Cassius having both been supporters of Pompey who were later pardoned by Caesar. What Shakespeare does is to reinstate the power struggle by means of a technique whereby the absent Pompey is also powerfully present. The opening scene of the play features a eulogy by Marullus in the epic style, beginning 'Knew you not Pompey?' It is a set piece of a dozen lines of the kind that, could he have known it, Longinus might have used as an example of the Sublime:

> Many a time and oft
> Have you climb'd up to walls and battlements,
> To towers and windows, yea, to chimney-tops,
> Your infants in your arms, and there have sat
> The livelong day, with patient expectation,
> To see great Pompey pass the streets of Rome:
> And when you saw his chariot but appear,
> Have you not made an universal shout,
> That Tiber trembled underneath her banks
> To hear the replication of your sounds
> Made in her concave shore?

There is no other passage in the play of comparable 'height' and magnificence. In particular, there is no comparable exalting of Caesar during his lifetime. Whilst the dead Pompey is given heroic honours, what we chiefly learn about the living Caesar is that he is deaf in one ear, that he suffers from the falling-sickness, and that Cassius had to save him from drowning! It is only after his death that we hear for the first time of his 'conquests, glories, triumphs, spoils'—the superhuman achievements for which Caesar had gained eternal fame. Plutarch does justice to all this in the detailed account he gives of Caesar's military prowess, his personal bravery, and his self-sacrificing consideration for his soldiers during the campaign in Gaul and elsewhere. But Shakespeare inverts Plutarch's procedure. Like Pompey, Caesar is given the credit due to his heroic qualities, but only when he is reduced to clay, i.e. when he is essentially absent:

> O, mighty Caesar! dost thou lie so low?
> Are all thy conquests, glories, triumphs, spoils,
> Shrunk to this little measure?

(III. i. 148–50)

In this ironic technique the living hero is diminished, even, in a manner, extinguished; he achieves his full presence as hero only when he is dead. The eulogy pronounced by Antony in Act III—beginning with 'Thou art the ruins of the noblest man | That ever lived in the tide of times' and continuing intermittently through his speech to the citizens—is exactly parallel to Marullus' epic account of Pompey's past glory in the opening scene of the play and has a like function. It is in these retrospective speeches of praise that the *agon* between the two leaders is conducted. The power struggle between Pompey and Caesar is thus a struggle between phantoms, absences. It is a competition for *post mortem* poetic tributes. We might add that it is also a competition between lifeless statues. The people in the first scene are being rebuked for adorning Caesar's images with festive scarves. Flavius and Marullus who remove the scarves in a demonstration of support for Pompey, will be put to death by Caesar's orders. Caesar had a shrewd sense of the importance of statues.[20]

Pompey's statue set up in the Capitol will get its 'just revenge' (in Plutarch's words) when it presides over the scene of blood in Act III, Caesar actually collapsing in his blood at the base of the statue. Pompey so to speak wins that round. But Caesar will win the next as, after his death, he triumphs over his enemies

[20] Plutarch records a number of Caesar's acts of clemency after his final victory over Pompey. Among these, he notes that 'where Pompey's images had been thrown down, he caused them to be set up again: whereupon Cicero said then, that Caesar setting up Pompey's images again he made his own to stand the surer' ('The Life of Julius Caesar', in *Plutarch's Lives . . . in North's Translation*, ed. R. H. Carr (Oxford: Clarendon Press, 1932), 98). Caesar carried on the struggle with Pompey it seems, after the latter's death, but did so by setting the statues against one another!

who are also Pompey's friends. Both Brutus and Cassius will acknowledge this. 'Caesar, thou art revenged,' Cassius concedes before his death, whilst Brutus declares, 'O Julius Caesar, thou art mighty yet' (v. iii. 45, 94). In the ironic structure of the play, therefore, Pompey's triumph over Caesar in Act III is balanced by Caesar's triumph over Pompey in Act V. Both of them are dead. These are contests where funeral speeches, statues, and ghostly memorials take the place of living protagonists.

Absence is thus a central phenomenon. The play explores a no-longer-existing world, foregrounding that non-existence by its ironic selection of events and images. Rome as a whole retains a phantom existence for Shakespeare's audience in 1600; it is still with them in remembered poems, records, philosophical ideas, even political systems which continue to have some meaning. But there are no Romans left; they are absent. This is the fundamental datum of the play. And Shakespeare, far from seeking to deceive us by the power of his imagination into thinking otherwise, as he perhaps does in the other Roman plays, keeps the fact of that absence steadily before us. He does not lull us with the dream of some Roman Arcadia into which we may escape or of a *polis* (like Hamlet's Denmark) in which we might see reflected the form and pressure of our own times and places. We are held and fascinated but we remain in a deep sense detached from the Roman world of *Julius Caesar*, disturbed by its strangeness and its moral voids. We maintain a critical distance.

It would seem then that we may, without doing violence to the play, reverse our earlier notion of the relation of text to subtext. It is not the world of medieval Christianity and the new, open Bible of the Reformation which are absent. Rome itself is absent. By contrast, the audience brings into the theatre ways of thinking and feeling coloured by the Book of Common Prayer, by the sermons it had heard at Paul's Cross and, above all, by the vernacular Bible. These sources were more immediately available to them than the records of Roman history, closer even than the writings of Seneca and Plutarch, though these were enjoying a new vogue at this time. The washing of the hands in blood in Act III would strike the audience as an upside-down version of what was said of Pilate in the Gospel reading for the Sunday before Easter. It was not a matter of bringing some remote analogue to bear on a scene from Shakespeare. It was rather the other way round; the scene from Shakespeare was unfamiliar, those from Matthew and Deuteronomy were near at hand. The latter could help us to understand the former.

6

There is a point in the play where the biblical-Christian anti-thesis to the world of Rome becomes explicit. This is at the penultimate moment, i.e. the phase preceding the battles at Philippi with which the play ends. We shall see that in other plays there is a moment of like significance occurring at the same point in the action, i.e. at the end of Act IV or early in Act V. In this instance, it is important to note that the three mini-scenes to which we shall be giving our attention are again to an important degree Shakespeare's invention. As with the sacrificial ritual in Act III, he is at this moment seemingly detaching himself from his source in order to exhibit the spiritual economy of Rome in relation to other cultural modes and options.

At the end of his Life of Brutus, Plutarch had mentioned the strange death of Portia who, according to two contemporary reports, had committed suicide by swallowing fire. Shakespeare, taking his hint from that source, shows us Brutus reacting to the news. It is a textbook example of stoic *apatheia*: 'Why, farewell, Portia. We must die Messala.' Messala, who had brought the report, is duly impressed: 'Even so great men great losses should endure,' he declares. Cassius likewise pays his tribute of admiration: 'I have as much of this in art as you | But yet my nature could not bear it so' (IV. iii. 189, 192, 193–4). Actually, Brutus is cheating, because he had already mentioned the news to Cassius, as something he had heard earlier.[21] But even if we are to think of him as only pretending to this extraordinary degree of self-possession, our reaction as an audience is surely going to be sharply different from that of the Roman characters on the stage.

[21] The two separate reports have been taken by recent editors as a case of authorial revision, Shakespeare's intention being to replace version 1 (the report of Messala, lines 180–94) with version 2 (Brutus' own report to Cassius, lines 146–57). If we omit version 1 and retain only version 2 we get a slightly more human image of Brutus. The textual evidence for revision is, however, far from being conclusive.

Like existentialism in the earlier part of our own century, stoicism was fashionable at the time of Shakespeare, popularized,
for instance, in the *Two Books of Constancy* by the somewhat
inconstant Justus Lipsius. But again this was largely an intellectual fashion. An Elizabethan stoic might say with Cassius that
he had it 'in art' as well as Brutus; but it was a different matter
to see this *apatheia* brutally translated into practice, with Brutus
dismissing the subject of his wife's horrible death with 'Speak
no more of her. Give me a bowl of wine.' This unwillingness
even to speak was calculated to shock the audience and to awaken
for it the long-standing Christian debate with the stoics, going
back at least to Lactantius in the fourth century, and vividly revived
in the seventeenth century. At the same time that Shakespeare's
major drama was being produced, Bishop Joseph Hall, a professed admirer of Seneca, was arguing that the stoic way as set
out in Seneca's *De Tranquillitate Animi* was a model the Christian could emulate. But limited as it was by the forms of Nature,
it could not in the end provide true mental peace. 'Not *Athens*
must teach this lesson, but *Jerusalem*,' he pithily declared.[22] In
particular, the stoic lacked the key to happiness which came from
dialogue with the Other. For the Christian this meant

a daily renuing of heavenly familiaritie ... by talking with him in our
secret invocations; by hearing his conference with us; and by mutual
entertainment of each other in the sweet discourse of our daily meditations. He is a sullen and unsociable friend, that wants words. God
shall take no pleasure in us if we be silent. The heart that is full of
love, cannot but have a busie tongue. ... We speak familiarly, we are
heard, answered, comforted.[23]

'The heart that is full of love, cannot but have a busie tongue'
might almost be a comment on Brutus' refusal to speak of his
wife's death. The missing factor in his personality, according
to Hall, would be love. Milton in his criticism emphasized the
stoic's essential egoism. '[They] in themselves seek vertue, and
to themselves | All glory arrogate, to God give none' (*Paradise
Regained*, IV. 314–15), a point made even more forcefully by
Henry More, writing at about the same time:

[22] 'Heaven Upon Earth' (1606), sect. I, in *The Works of Joseph Hall* (London, 1634), 65.
[23] Ibid., sect. XXII, 82–3.

For this Kingdome of the *Stoicks* is the Kingdome of *Selfishness*, and *Self-love* sways the Sceptre there and wears the Diademe: but in the Kingdome of God, God himself, who is that pure, free, and perfectly *unselfed love*, has the full dominion of the soul, and the ordering and rule of all the Passions.[24]

The well-ordered mind of the stoic, his invulnerability to pain and pleasure, his self-sufficiency, and above all the concern he has for his honour—all of which are so central to Brutus' personality —are defined in the play for the most part as virtue ('I know that virtue to be in you, Brutus'). Here in the passage from More they are reduced to one word, Selfishness. When the audience observes Brutus' reaction to Portia's death, they are likely to sum all this up as Hall and More had done; also to agree with them that what is missing in all this supposed virtue is simply, love.

We have then once again a Christian subtext emerging as a function of the audience's shocked reaction to the Roman behaviour displayed on the stage. But Shakespeare does not leave it at that. There will be a representation of the alternative also, even though it may be suggested by only one or two minimal strokes. Brutus' monologue of the Self will ultimately alienate the audience not only from Brutus but from the play! It is not as though there is anyone else in the play to make good this fearful lack, this absence of 'unselfed love', as More termed it. Antony and Cassius are capable of strong bonds of affection but these are combined with so much cold-blooded policy that it is difficult for the reader to identify with them. Dialogue may not be for Shakespeare a theological necessity as it is for Hall, but it is evidently an artistic necessity. And dialogue is not only a mode of discourse between characters, but also a necessary relationship of complementarity between text and audience, between our world and the represented world on the stage.[25] There must in short be someone for us to love.

It is not easy to imagine Shakespeare writing a play in which the principal protagonist (let us not even call him the tragic hero) would die like Chapman's Bussy D'Ambois propped up on his

---

[24] Henry More, *Divine Dialogues* (1668), Dialogue IV.

[25] Cf. M. M. Bakhtin, *The Dialogic Imagination: Four Essays by M. M. Bakhtin*, trans. Caryl Emerson and Michael Holquist, ed. Michael Holquist (Austin, Tex.: University of Texas Press, 1981), 280, and id., *Esthétique de la création verbale*, trans. Alfreda Aucouturier (Paris: Gallimard, 1984), 150–4.

sword in imitation of the Emperor Vespasian to demonstrate his philosophical indifference—'the equal thought I bear of life and death'—at the same time announcing the triumph of stone over flesh:

> Here like a Roman statue I will stand,
> Till death hath made me marble.[26]

And indeed Shakespeare does not end the play in this fashion. His chief protagonist, as we have seen, exhibits these same extremes of *ataraxia* and *apatheia* (though with some ironic shading) in the confrontation with Cassius and the receipt of the news of Portia's death, but then there is a swerve. In the continuation of that same scene, Shakespeare proceeds to humanize Brutus at least to the extent of enabling us to feel for him a modicum of pity and fear. For that to happen he has to show himself likewise capable of pity and fear. This he now does.

The breaching of Brutus' monologic isolation is achieved in the two final episodes of Act IV which take place in his tent at night. In the compressed time of the drama, this is the night before the final battles at Philippi. In the first of these sequences we are given Brutus' conversation with his servant-boy, Lucius. This character and Brutus' relationship with him are entirely Shakespeare's invention. Lucius had made three brief appearances, earlier in the play, but only now does he become of central importance. In the expressions of tenderness and love for Lucius we have the first real breach in the iron-clad armour of Brutus' self-sufficiency. ('I am armed so strong in honesty', he had declared earlier to Cassius.) Now we see him without his armour, as he gently asks Lucius to play him 'a strain or two' on his instrument.

> I trouble thee too much, but thou art willing.
> LUC. It is my duty, sir.
> BRU. I should not urge thy duty past thy might;
> I know young bloods look for a time of rest.
> LUC. I have slept, my lord, already.
> BRU. It was well done, and thou shalt sleep again;
> I will not hold thee long. If I do live,
> I will be good to thee.
> *Music and a song*

[26] George Chapman, *The Tragedy of Bussy D'Ambois*, v. iv. 85–6.

But the song ceases after a few bars as Lucius falls asleep over his lute and Brutus gently takes it out of his hand, quietly wishing him good night before he settles down to read his book. G. Wilson Knight points out that Brutus here shows 'a more spontaneous love than any he shows to other people'. He draws attention also to the combination of love, music, and sleep that often marks Shakespeare's major drama.[27] (There is for instance the reunion of Cordelia and King Lear in Act IV of that tragedy.) It is a combination of high spiritual significance.

This clearly is a paradisal moment, but does it have anything of the Christian significance of the analogous scene in Act IV of *King Lear* with its echoes of the parable of the Prodigal Son and its powerful religious emphasis on blessing and forgiveness? The episode as we have noted is not in Plutarch, but in another way it is in Plutarch. After all, Plutarch had noted that Brutus 'loved Plato's sect best'[28] and we might argue that we have here a celebration of *eros* in line with Plato's *Symposium*, with a strong suggestion of the homoerotic which for Plato is the ideal form of love. Again, Plato had (in the speeches of Eryximachus and Agathon) emphatically joined the harmony of music to that of love.[29] Thus, even if there is a crack here in Brutus' stoic armour, in terms of our *met-agon* we are arguably still in the spiritual zone of Athens rather than Jerusalem.

But a closer look at the dialogic exchange between Brutus and Lucius reveals a more fundamental shift than that provided for in Plato's writings. The Platonic *eros*, whether in the cruder definitions of Aristophanes or in the more ideal version expressed by Socrates, ultimately aims at the reunion of the divided parts of the Self, and through that the discovery of the soul's essence.[30] It gives us the higher knowledge of the Good and the Beautiful which we had conceived before in memory.[31] In other words we repossess that which had always been part of ourselves. From this point of view, both the heavenly and the earthly *eros* have in them an element of that narcissism which More had condemned. The lovers desire to fuse, 'so that being two you shall

---

[27] Knight, *The Imperial Theme*, 77.
[28] 'The Life of Marcus Brutus', in *Plutarch's Lives*, 113.
[29] 'The Symposium' in *The Works of Plato*, trans. B. Jowett (New York: The Dial Press, n.d.), iii. 311, 323.
[30] Ibid. 317, 339–40.   [31] Ibid. 340–3.

become one . . . and after your death in the world below still be one departed soul instead of two'.[32] Here is evidently one of the grounds for the homoerotic bias of Greek culture. The oneness of the lovers is already affirmed by the identity of gender, the distinction between the One and the Many being thereby in a manner abolished.

This, however, does not really capture the transformation in the essential posture of Brutus as reflected in the brief scene we are examining. His primary discovery is not the Platonic *eros*, but something else. That something else we can I think arrive at by considering the characteristic grammar of Brutus' discourse in the play, and the change that this grammar undergoes. Thus a sensitive interpretation of Brutus' role by a skilled actor should draw our attention to the extraordinary frequency of the first-person pronouns in Brutus' earlier and later speeches. We may consider one typical passage of nine lines from Act I which contains ten such self-references:

> That you do love *me*, *I* am nothing jealous;
> What you would work *me* to, *I* have some aim:
> How *I* have thought of this, and of these times,
> *I* shall recount hereafter. For this present,
> *I* would not (so with love *I* might entreat you)
> Be any further mov'd; what you have said
> *I* will consider; what you have to say
> *I* will with patience hear, and find a time
> Both meet to hear and answer such high things.
>
> (I. ii. 160–8)

In the same scene Cassius had subtly exploited this weakness of Brutus, by offering to illuminate (in a suitably flattering light) those parts of himself which even so consummate an egoist as Brutus could not actually observe. This he did by an equally concentrated use of second-person pronouns, thus shoring up his friend's ego even more:

---

[32] Ibid. 318. On the narcissistic trend in Plato's doctrine of *eros*, see Jean-Pierre Vernant, 'One . . . Two . . . Three: Eros', in David M. Halperin, John J. Winkler, and Froma I. Zeitlin (eds.), *Before Sexuality: The Construction of Erotic Experience in the Ancient Greek World* (Princeton: Princeton University Press, 1990), 465–77. Vernant differentiates between the narcissism of Aristophanes and that expressed by Socrates; the latter involves a yearning for immortality (pp. 471–2).

> And since *you* know *you* cannot see *yourself*
> So well as by reflection, I, *your* glass,
> Will modestly discover to *yourself*
> That of *yourself* which *you* yet know not of.
>
> (I. ii. 66–9)

Brutus' speech to the people in Act III is self-involved to a like degree: 'Believe *me* for *mine* honour, and have respect to *mine* honour, that you may believe.' This will give Antony the opening he needs to turn Brutus' great reputation for honour into mere pretension, as in the mounting irony of the repeated line: 'And Brutus is an honourable man'.

From this point of view the brief conversation with Lucius cited earlier marks a decisive shift. It will be seen that instead of the first-person pronouns, we now have a new and equally concentrated use of the second-person pronouns: thou, thee, and thy. This change is not merely grammatical, but ontological. Brutus has moved from a fundamentally I-centred to a Thou-centred existence; he is no longer the centre of his own world. Like King Lear in the storm, he has discovered the other. This is the new note that is struck also in the continuation of the quoted passage:

> O murd'rous slumber!
> Layst thou thy leaden mace upon my boy,
> That plays thee music? Gentle knave, good night;
> I will not do thee so much wrong to wake thee.
> If thou dost nod, thou break'st thy instrument;
> I'll take it from thee; and good boy, good night.
>
> (IV. iii. 266–71)

Here are tenderness, pity, and, above all, love. This new orientation is not a matter of Platonism or of stoicism; it is in line rather with what is taught by the contemporary philosopher, Emmanuel Lévinas. The fundamental precept of Western philosophy, Lévinas tells us, is that of the Delphic oracle: Know thyself! Its fundamental ontology is that of Descartes: I think, therefore I am. Both start from and return to the Self.[33] By contrast Lévinas's fundamental starting-point will be not

---

[33] Emmanuel Lévinas, *Difficult Freedom: Essays on Judaism*, trans. Sean Hand (Baltimore: Johns Hopkins University Press, 1990), 10.

self-awareness but the face of the other ('le visage de l'autre').
'Responsibility for the others', he maintains, 'precedes any relationship of the ego with itself.' Nor is the other in any sense a
reflection of the self. The discovery of the face of the other is
a discovery of his absolute alterity. Between the self and the other
there subsists a relationship of proximity and separateness. The
two do not fuse.[34] It is the end of that harmonious world of
fused identities which Athens had authorized and the affirmation of a world founded rather on difference and separateness.[35]

Here likewise in the scene between Brutus and Lucius is the
end of monologue and the beginning of dialogue, the symbolic
suspension for the moment of what Henry More called 'the
Kingdome of *Selfishness*'. In the confined and shuttered space
of Brutus' selfhood a window has been opened 'to let the warm
love in'. In the final episode of this scene a second window is
opened; but this one will let in terror:

> [*Enter the Ghost of Caesar*
> How ill this taper burns! Ha! who comes here?
> I think it is the weakness of mine eyes
> That shapes this monstrous apparition.
> It comes upon me. Art thou anything?
> Art thou some god, some angel, or some devil,
> That mak'st my blood cold, and my hair to stare?
>
> (IV. iii. 274–9)

Knight regards this episode as shattering the 'momentary heaven'
created by the dialogue with Lucius and the accompanying song,
and bringing back 'the opposing hell'.[36] This is not the way I
read these lines. On the contrary, their effect seems to me to
be rather that of completing and confirming the humanizing of
Brutus begun in the exchange with Lucius. The other side of
softness and warmth is vulnerability; and his reaction to the Ghost
expressed in these lines shows him to be essentially vulnerable.
If in the first of these two scenes he shows pity for a boy, in

[34] Id., *Otherwise Than Being Or Beyond Essence*, trans. Alphonso Lingis (The
Hague: Martinus Nijhoff, 1981), ch. 1, sects. 5, 6; ch. 4, sect. 5; ch. 5, sect. 1 (d),
pp. 9–14, 119, 135.

[35] These notions have had a significant impact on the thinking of Jacques Derrida.
See, Derrida, *Writing and Difference* (London: Routledge and Kegan Paul, 1978),
79–153.

[36] Knight, *The Imperial Theme*, 77.

the second we, the audience, are moved to pity for Brutus. In general the effect is to bring him down from the high ground of stoic pride, sometimes called 'virtue' or 'honesty', and to realign him, if only for a moment, with our everyday humanity.

But this does not exhaust the Ghost's function. It is not a matter simply of Brutus' rating as a tragic hero; the Ghost is there to question through the terror of his presence the viability of the Roman ethic and the Roman metaphysic. This is in fact something of a type-scene in Shakespeare. Shortly after writing *Julius Caesar*, Shakespeare was to show us Hamlet's friend, the stoical Horatio, similarly confronted with a visitor from the other world. Horatio ('more an antique Roman than a Dane') was to be shaken in the same way as Brutus; 'it harrows me with fear and wonder,' he would declare. Hamlet later on, after his own meeting with the Ghost, would explicitly draw the conclusion which in *Julius Caesar* is left unspoken: 'There are more things in heaven and earth, Horatio, | Than are dreamt of in your philosophy.' *Hamlet* may be regarded in this and other respects as the sequel to *Julius Caesar*. In particular, the confrontation between the biblical and the Pagan worlds, which, as I have suggested, constitutes the undeclared matter of *Julius Caesar*, is, as we shall see in Chapter 3, built continuously into the fabric of the later play. It is no longer an absent dimension which we supply; it is much rather the actual subject of Hamlet's meditations.

Here in *Julius Caesar* this conflict, central though it is, is for the most part hidden. However, in this meeting between Brutus and his supernatural visitor, what we have termed the subtext becomes for that moment visible. We see on the stage the confrontation between the natural and the spectral, between a world that is harmonious and rational and one that is radically discontinuous, no longer reflecting the structure of the well-ordered mind. Here we may say is the meeting of the Self with the absolute Other; it is dialogue with a vengeance! Brutus confronts the mystery that had been absent in the Roman world, now become present, even frighteningly present. There are of course ghosts and other supernatural manifestations in the classical drama also, but their function is chiefly to indicate the fatal hap or doom about to befall the hero—a function not essentially different from that of the soothsayer who warns Caesar to beware the Ides of March. Their task is to keep the wheels of the plot turning. Here Caesar's Ghost comes to overwhelm Brutus with thoughts beyond the reaches of his soul.[37]

There had been one other, earlier moment of the same kind. I am referring to the ghastly storm in Act I, scene iii, when, as in this ghost scene, the natural order is ripped aside and the mystery momentarily asserts itself. Storms have a revelational function in Shakespeare. It is not just a matter of disorder in the cosmos reflecting disorder in the state by a kind of sympathetic magic, as we used to be taught. Rather it is that a Word is spoken amid thunder and lightning—a message of salvation or judgement. This will become explicit in *The Tempest* where, as Alonso testifies, the thunder 'did bass my trespass'. Here in *Julius Caesar*, Casca, when exposed to the terrors of the storm, its prodigies and portents, undergoes, like King Lear and Alonso, a moral awakening; his stoic-cynic self-possession (so marked in his earlier appearance in scene ii) now deserts him and he bears witness in fear and trembling to a new and shocking reality:

> It is the part of men to fear and tremble
> When the most mighty gods by tokens send
> Such dreadful heralds to astonish us.

> (I. iii. 54–6)

Casca in these lines had been brushed by the same numinous terror which would so appal Brutus in Act IV. Brutus we recall was to express himself in similar fashion:

> I think it is the weakness of mine eyes
> That shapes this monstrous apparition.
> It comes upon me. Art thou anything?
> Art thou some god, some angel, or some devil,
> That mak'st my blood cold, and my hair to stare?

[37] Again, Shakespeare's relative independence of his source should be noted. The accounts given in Plutarch do not explicitly identify the 'monstrous shape' as the Ghost of Caesar as Shakespeare does in his stage-direction. Moreover, Brutus is essentially unafraid. In one version ('Life of Brutus', in *Plutarch's Lives*, 145), Plutarch twice speaks of Brutus' boldness and lack of fear. In the 'Life of Caesar' (ibid. 110), when the 'horrible vision' appears, it 'at the first made him marvellously afraid' but he seems to regain his self-possession immediately. In Shakespeare, the fear is more strongly stressed, as in the quoted lines, and Brutus only recovers from this fear at the end of the episode: 'Now I have taken heart thou vanishest.'

When these two passages are set side by side we shall make a further discovery, namely, that the mystery we speak of is a biblical mystery. Taken together, they constitute a sequential and close echoing of a famous text in Job. It is the account given by Eliphaz the Temanite of 'the visions of the night, when sleep falleth on men'.

> *Fear came upon me*, and dread,
> which made all my bones *to tremble*.
> And the wind passed before me,
> *and made the hairs of my flesh to stand up*.
> *Then stood one, and I knew not his face*;
> an image was before *mine eyes*.
>
> (Job 4: 14–16)

As so often in Job, the otherness which we encounter is an eerie, even demonic otherness. But, extraordinarily, it speaks to us. Eliphaz's apparition has a voice and the storm in chapter 38 has a voice. If the answers that they give us are in fact questions, they are nevertheless, amazingly, addressed to us. And being thus addressed, we are seized and changed. Job, in face of that shattering word, loses his composure, his nobility, any pride and honour which belong to the role of tragic hero. 'I abhor myself', says Job, 'and repent in dust and ashes.' Eliphaz says that his bones shake and his hair stands on end. The same happens in the play to Casca and Brutus. At that moment they know that they are not heroes but mere mortal men who 'dwell in houses of clay, whose foundation is in the dust, which shall be destroyed before the moth' (Job 4: 19). But dust though they are, they are also liberated—if only for a moment—from the enclosed, monologic world of myth from which tragedy derives its form and compulsions and are granted 'a difficult freedom'.

CHAPTER 2

Antony and Cleopatra:
Soldering up the Rift

As if to confound the image of the Roman world as a beast without a heart, a world, as we argued in connection with *Julius Caesar*, all but incapable of love, Shakespeare gives us in *Antony and Cleopatra* one of the great love-stories of all times. And the partners are the Queen of Egypt and the Roman Antony, hero of Philippi and vanquisher of Brutus. Rome and its values are again central; the reliance on Plutarch is no less in this play than in *Julius Caesar*, yet the emphasis on luxury and sensuality and the sudden, violent lurches of mood from despair to ecstasy, from fury to torpor, create an emotional atmosphere as far removed as may be imagined from that of *Julius Caesar*. And as though to give structural expression to this difference, Shakespeare here replaces the classical economy of *Julius Caesar*, in which, as in Aristotle's formula for tragedy, every part is necessary to the whole, with a wildly veering dramatic technique involving vast spaces and 'great gaps of time'. He seems deliberately to explode the unities, as the action shifts from land to sea and back again, taking in Syria, Egypt, Rome, the Bay of Naples, and the Greek islands—virtually the whole eastern Mediterranean basin—as in the epic voyages of Odysseus or Aeneas.

This epic sweep and extravagance are matched moreover by a sustained poetic abundance rarely attained in *Julius Caesar*, indeed rarely aimed at, except in one or two set passages. In this, *Antony and Cleopatra* would seem to affirm a deliberately non-Roman, Asiatic standard.[1] The opening speech of Philo in Act I, scene i, indeed has abundance, or rather superabundance, as its subject:

[1] See Rosalie L. Cole, 'The Significance of Style', in *William Shakespeare's Antony and Cleopatra: Modern Critical Interpretations*, ed. Harold Bloom (New York: Chelsea House, 1988), 59–65 (hereafter *Interpretations*, ed. Bloom).

Nay, but this dotage of our general's
O'erflows the measure: those his goodly eyes,
That o'er the files and musters of the war
Have glow'd like plated Mars, now bend, now turn
The office and devotion of their view
Upon a tawny front.

(I. i. 1–6)

Antony and Cleopatra, who now enter, proceed likewise to discuss the antinomy of measure and measurelessness:

CLEO. If it be love indeed, tell me how much.
ANT. There's beggary in the love that can be reckon'd.
CLEO. I'll set a bourn how far to be belov'd.
ANT. Then must thou needs find out new heaven, new earth.

(i. 14–17)

If Rome stands for measure and self-control and yields a correspondingly restrained, forensic language of exposition, then this more abundant and overflowing language of hyperbole, which in this passage actually explores the paradoxes of abundance and excess, would seem to represent the antithesis of Romanism.

In *Julius Caesar* we argued also that there was an antithesis to Rome and its values, but this antithesis was asserted largely through its absence—it was a matter of a subtext created through voids and silences. Here it would seem that we have instead a poetics of vivid presence. Moreover the contrary Roman system of values is likewise given sharper expression through the need felt by its spokesmen—as in this scene—to articulate their response (positive or negative) to the seductive challenge of Egypt. The measureless power of love is verbally realized in the line, 'Then must thou needs find out new heaven, new earth.' Later in the same scene it is contrasted with the opposite fascination, namely, the power and grandeur of empire, as Antony magnificently exclaims:

Let Rome in Tiber melt, and the wide arch
Of the rang'd empire fall. Here is my space.

The four words, 'Here is my space', with their deictic force and inclusiveness may stand as the perfect example of the poetics of presence.

The simple explanation for this poetics is that Plutarch in his Life of Antony had supplied the materials for a full account of Egypt and the sumptuous way of life of Cleopatra and her court. Plutarch was himself clearly fascinated by the barbaric splendours of Egypt, its religious and artistic forms, and Shakespeare, in this instance, needed to look no further than his source to supply the antithesis to the Roman world. It was not a missing dimension to be supplied by the audience. Enobarbus' famous description of Cleopatra setting out on the river Cydnus for her first meeting with Antony ('The barge she sat in, like a burnish'd throne . . .', II. ii. 190–218) is in fact pure Plutarch, as magnificently rendered by North:

the poop whereof was of gold, the sails of purple, and the oars of silver, which kept stroke in rowing after the sound of the music of flutes, howboys, citherns, viols, and such other instruments as they played upon in the barge. And now for the person of herself: she was laid under a pavilion of cloth of gold of tissue, apparelled and attired like the goddess Venus commonly drawn in picture . . .[2]

When Shakespeare found anything as good as this, he made free use of it. In this case, he took the passage over almost word for word. Nevertheless, this descriptive abundance of Plutarch is essentially a matter of epideictic rhetoric. There is no poetic *surrender*, no suspension of disbelief. Plutarch never sees the world through Egyptian eyes; he remains fascinated but detached. Cleopatra was seen by Plutarch for the most part as Antony's evil spirit, 'the last and extremest mischief of all other':

and if any spark of goodness or hope of rising were left him, Cleopatra quenched it straight, and made it worse than before.[3]

So that whilst Plutarch provided Shakespeare with the materials for a poetic reassessment of the Egyptian world, he himself did not make that reassessment; its system of values did not, for him, challenge those of Rome and Athens. In all of Plutarch's rich and colourful account of Antony's involvement with Cleopatra, there is no phrase which conveys the inwardness of 'Here

[2] 'The Life of Marcus Antonius', in *Plutarch's Lives . . . in North's Translation*, ed. R. H. Carr (Oxford: Clarendon Press, 1932), 185.
[3] Ibid. 184.

is my space'. Plutarch gives us no access to that space—he shows no acknowledgement of its spiritual geography. Instead, he presents their passion in terms of Plato's judgement of the lower *eros*:

And in the end, the horse of the mind, as Plato termeth it, that is so hard of rein, (I mean the unreined lust of concupiscence), did put out of Antonius' head all honest and commendable thoughts: for he sent Fonteius Capito to bring Cleopatra into Syria.[4]

Shakespeare here then corrects Plutarch's cultural bias;[5] he uses his prodigality of language as a way of reaching out to a realm beyond language, to a love that can be pointed to (as in the deictic 'Here is my space') but not really defined. Plutarch achieves abundance, but Shakespeare, echoing that, enables us to achieve superabundance, an ever-moving and never-attained horizon of meanings. He uses Plutarch's opulent imagery to show the ultimate inadequacy of all images, even the most opulent. This direction is already clear in the opening lines of the play already quoted which, as we noted, speak of the unmeasured and the undefinable. There is Philo's cynical 'this dotage of our general's | O'erflows the measure' and, following that, Antony's enraptured exclamation—'there's beggary in the love that can be reckon'd'. The same term is echoed in the Cydnus passage (in a phrase which Shakespeare did not owe to Plutarch): 'For her own person, | *It beggar'd all description.*'

Again and again in the play we encounter this region of hyperbole.[6] Hyperbole is invariably paradoxical, a figure inviting deconstruction. Paradoxically, one speaks of infinity and at the same time declares that it cannot be spoken of; it is a celebration and at the same time a declaration that the object celebrated is beyond our apprehension and thus beyond celebration. The noteworthy departures from Plutarch's superb language in the Cydnus passage seem all to have to do with such beyondness, suggesting

[4] Ibid. 195–6.

[5] See Herbert B. Rothschild, Jr., 'The Oblique Encounter: Shakespeare's Confrontation of Plutarch with Special Reference to *Antony and Cleopatra*', *English Literary Renaissance*, 6 (1976), 404–29 (see especially, pp. 417–18).

[6] Cf. Maurice Charney, 'Style in the Roman Plays', in Maurice Charney (ed.), *Discussion of Shakespeare's Roman Plays* (Boston: D. C. Heath, 1964), 22–5; Janet Adelman, *The Common Liar: An Essay on Antony and Cleopatra* (New Haven: Yale University Press, 1973), 114–21; Cole, 'The Significance of Style', 73.

a region beyond all known signifieds. Where Plutarch had said that Cleopatra was 'attired like the goddess Venus, commonly drawn in picture', Enobarbus speaks of her as '*O'er-picturing that Venus* where we see | The fancy *outwork nature*'. Here unsignifiability is addressed in both half-lines. Cleopatra is beyond any picture of Venus and at the same time any true picture of Venus is beyond nature. We remain within the poetics of presence (note again the deictic 'where we see' joining the two half-lines) but there is throughout the passage a pull in the direction of transcendence.

Enobarbus ends his speech with perhaps the most memorable of all Shakespearian hyperboles, again in a striking addition to Plutarch's text. Plutarch, as rendered by North, had remarked that as Cleopatra made her progress down the river in her barge,

> there ran such multitudes of people one after another to see her, that Antonius was left post alone in the market-place in his imperial seat to give audience: and there went a rumour in the people's mouths, that the goddess Venus was come to play with the god Bacchus, for the general good of all Asia.[7]

The notion of Venus consorting with Bacchus (Dionysus) is used here to give a little extravagant colouring to the occasion. Shakespeare will pick up these mythological patterns and use them in a more fundamental way, as we shall see presently. At this moment I am more concerned with the image of Antony 'left post alone in the market-place in his imperial seat'. North's brilliant balancing of the homely 'post alone' against the dignity of 'his imperial seat' gives us the comic reduction of Antony from conqueror to an unregarded block of wood. Shakespeare marvellously extends the comic possibilities of North's language:

> The city cast
> Her people out upon her; and Antony,
> Enthron'd i'the market-place, did sit alone,
> Whistling to the air; which, but for vacancy,
> Had gone to gaze on Cleopatra too,
> And made a gap in nature.
>
> (II. ii. 213–18)

---

[7] 'The Life of Marcus Antonius', in *Plutarch's Lives*, 186.

Antony 'enthron'd' as befits the 'triple pillar of the world', is here left alone to whistle to himself like a schoolboy whose friends have run off. Not only the people but the whole world has gone to gaze on Cleopatra and, 'but for vacancy', the air itself would have joined them 'and made a gap in nature'. This is not merely magnificent hyperbole; it is more like a condensed discourse on hyperbole. Hyperbole is almost inevitably meta-poetic. It here speaks of itself as a figure of astonishment, one which, if pressed to its logical conclusion would make a gap in nature. It gazes at the limits inherent in any signifying system and seeks to surpass them ('it beggar'd all description'), know-ing at the same time that it is itself bound by those same limits. To signify is to define, but the gesture of transcendence here seems to enable the speaker and his audience to overleap the merely natural and the definable. To use language in this way is to perform a most difficult balancing-act. One risks absurdity on the one hand ('whistling to the air') and dissociation on the other ('and made a gap in nature'). But it is nevertheless the most powerful of figures for, when the balancing-act is successfully performed, then the world that we know, that to which our signs necessarily have reference, is raised to the power of infinity. Thus Cleopatra's (and Antony's) lips, eyes, brows, and 'parts' remain vividly present in the act of love though the lovers are turned into gods:

> Eternity was in our lips, and eyes,
> Bliss in our brows' bent; none our parts so poor,
> But was a race of heaven.

> (I. iii. 36–9)

2

We have spoken so far as though hyperbole, expressing, accord-ing to George Steiner the farthest reach of language—'the unboundedness of discursive potentiality'[8]—belongs to the non-Roman dimension of the play, Alexandrian unrestraint balancing Roman self-control. This corresponds broadly to Plutarch's thesis;

[8] George Steiner, *Real Presences* (Chicago: University of Chicago Press, 1989), 57.

for him the square Roman virtues are contrasted with Alexandrian excess. And many critics have adopted this binary contrast as a kind of master-key to the play's meaning. 'Egypt is itself hyperbolical,' declares Janet Adelman. Everything there overflows its bounds like the Nile itself, whilst in Rome and for the Romans 'shall all be done by the rule' (as Antony promises Octavia in II. iii. 7). The Roman ideal she says is someone like Sir Guyon, the knight of Temperance, in Spenser's epic.[9] But I would want to argue that in this respect too Shakespeare departs from his source. Whilst seeming to keep this simpler antithetical scheme in place, he in fact undermines it and shows us the two orders as linked together by a web of analogies. At the deeper levels of the play, empire and love, military power and uncontrolled sensuality function not as contraries but much rather as reciprocal forces which join together under the same signs and images.

This appears in the opening speech of the play already glanced at earlier. Philo strikes the typical note of hyperbole at once, speaking of Antony's love of Cleopatra in terms of an excess which defies measurement: 'this dotage of our general's | O'erflows the measure.' But if boundaries are breached, it becomes apparent in the continuation of that speech that they are breached no less by the measureless desire for glory in war. Antony is depicted as the supreme and absolute warrior, the incarnation of Mars himself:

> those his goodly eyes,
> That o'er the files and musters of the war,
> Have glow'd like plated Mars . . .
> .   .   .   .
> his captain's heart,
> Which in the scuffles of great fights hath burst
> The buckles on his breast . . .
> .   .   .   .
> Take but good note, and you shall see in him
> The triple pillar of the world transform'd
> Into a strumpet's fool . . .
>
> (I. i. 2–13)

In an image of explosive violence Antony's heart is said to have 'burst the buckles on his breast'—his power is not to be restrained. Here too we have the deictic 'take but good note'

---

[9] Adelman, *The Common Liar*, 121–8.

—a phrase which governs both the epiphany of the war-god as 'the triple pillar of the world' and his sorry lapse into 'a strumpet's fool'. War and the virtues it inspires are as immediate a presence in the play as love.

At the risk of stating the obvious, it should be added that the Antony whom Cleopatra loves and worships is above all the commander of armies and the conqueror of territories. For Cleopatra, unlike the flower-children of the 1960s, warriors made the best lovers. Mars, as the play reminds us (I. v. 17–18), was the natural consort of Venus. Accordingly, in her speeches Cleopatra combines the hyperboles of war and empire with those of love and its delights. In the following speech in praise of the dead Antony, the two in fact flow in and out of one another by a kind of osmosis:

> His legs bestrid the ocean: his rear'd arm
> Crested the world; his voice was propertied
> As all the tuned spheres, and that to friends:
> But when he meant to quail, and shake the orb,
> He was as rattling thunder. For his bounty,
> There was no winter in't: an autumn 'twas
> That grew the more by reaping: his delights
> Were dolphin-like, they show'd his back above
> The element they lived in: in his livery
> Walk'd crowns and crownets: realms and islands were
> As plates dropp'd from his pocket.

(v. ii. 82–92)

Common to both these universes, that of war and love, of Rome and Egypt, and very prominent in this speech, is a particular kind of hyperbole—that having reference to cosmic space and celestial bodies. Antony is here seen as bigger than life, in fact, bigger than the world; like Vulcan, he 'shakes the orb'. Whilst attention is often given to these many references to the cosmos,[10] it is again not always recognized that this iterative image is common to empire and to love, constituting what S. L. Bethell calls a 'deliberate equation' between the two.[11] As

[10] See Caroline F. E. Spurgeon, *Shakespeare's Imagery and What It Tells Us* (Cambridge: Cambridge University Press, 1935), 352; W. H. Clemen, *The Development of Shakespeare's Imagery* (London: Methuen, 1951), 160, 162–3.

[11] S. L. Bethell, *Shakespeare and the Popular Dramatic Tradition* (Durham, NC: Duke University Press, 1944), 146.

'triple pillar of the world' Antony naturally stands astride the ocean in the manner of Colossus. In this, Cleopatra's testimony in Act V coincides precisely with Philo's in Act I. By the same token, as the world's supreme lover, his voice is tuned to the music of the spheres. In fact it is more than an equation; there is convergence. In the lines immediately preceding the above quoted lines, Cleopatra had declared:

> His face was as the heavens, and therein stuck
> A sun and moon, which kept their course, and lighted
> The little O, the earth . . .

Here it is not possible to assign the celestial quality to one side of Antony's life and personality rather than another. He is simply like the sun, and that being so, he will (as we learn elsewhere) 'shine on those | That make their looks by his' (I. v. 55–6). Cleopatra too touches the heavens. Antony addresses her as 'thou day o'the world' (IV. viii. 13) and as her death comes upon her, Charmian cries out 'O eastern star' (V. ii. 307). Again the quality of transcendence implied in these figures is not differentiated. At this level, we are too far out in space for us clearly to discern the boundary line between Rome and Egypt.

But this does not mean that the play totally supports this line of imagery, or that the audience unequivocally surrenders to it. For one thing, the bombardment is so heavy, or, as Bethell says, deliberate, that the text becomes self-parodying. The constant inflation of the characters and their doings, their repeated elevation to the celestial sphere, seem to produce an almost inevitable reaction—they are almost as constantly brought down to earth.[12] Thus Enobarbus early on comments on the 'storms' of Cleopatra's passions:

> We cannot call her winds and waters sighs and tears; they are greater storms and tempests than almanacs can report. This cannot be cunning in her; if it be, she makes a shower of rain as well as Jove. (I. ii. 145–9)

Enobarbus here momentarily reduces Cleopatra's astral pretensions to barrack-room banter. Nor is such deflation simply a

---

[12] See Charney, 'Style in the Roman Plays': 'the hyperboles of the play are constantly undercut' (28); Brents Stirling, *Unity in Shakespearian Tragedy* (New York: Gordian Press, 1966), 167; Adelman, *The Common Liar*, 116–18.

matter of Rome versus Egypt as might appear from this example. It would seem to occur equally when Romans and Egyptians discuss their own people. Thus in Act I, scene iv, Lepidus sums up Antony's shortcomings in macrocosmic terms: 'His faults in him, seem as the spots of heaven, | More fiery by night's blackness', but Caesar promptly counters this with a vision of Antony 'tippling with a slave . . . reel[ing] the streets at noon, and stand[ing] the buffet with knaves that smell of sweat' (I. iv. 11–13, 19–21). We have descended from the superhuman to the subhuman. This lurch or its reverse seems to be a fundamental feature of the play. In her final scenes Cleopatra lurches upwards, so to speak, from an unedifying slanging-match with her servant Seleucus, in the course of which she tries to scratch out his eyes, to sublime gestures of timelessness—'I have nothing of woman in me . . . now the fleeting moon | No planet is of mine' (v. ii. 237–40)—in which she expressly puts aside the merely human, at the same time pointing to the outer limits of an expanding universe.

It would thus appear that the cosmic images, whilst carrying much of the play's meaning, are nevertheless under question. Moreover, this undermining or reduction is not a matter of occasional ironic touches; it is clearly an intrinsic feature of the spectacle and the language. The play is in this respect similar to *Julius Caesar* where we noted a dialectical combination of stone and blood as a constant feature (going back to the primary symbol of the bleeding statue of Pompey in the Capitol). There was an emphasis throughout that play on stone statues and metal instruments but an equal though opposing emphasis on tears and blood. The tension between these two interconnected image-systems gave us a key to the play's meaning. I will suggest that *Antony and Cleopatra* works in the same way. In addition to the imagery of heavenly bodies and cosmic space and in dialectical opposition to it, we have numerous low references. Enobarbus' enraptured account in Act II of Cleopatra's first meeting with Mark Antony on the river Cydnus, for instance, is framed by two snatches of conversation in which we are given a far less sublime glimpse of Egypt and its Queen. In the first of these the subject is the vast quantity of food and drink consumed at the feasting in Egypt:

MAEC. You stay'd well by't in Egypt.

ENO. Ay, sir, we did sleep day out of countenance; and made the night light with drinking.

MAEC. Eight wild-boars roasted whole at breakfast, and but twelve persons there; is this true?

ENO. This was but a fly by an eagle: we had much more monstrous matter of feast, which worthily deserved noting.

(II. ii. 176–83)[13]

And at the end of the scene Enobarbus defines Cleopatra's extraordinary sexual fascination again in terms of feasting:

> Age cannot wither her, nor custom stale
> Her infinite variety: other women cloy
> The appetites they feed, but she makes hungry,
> Where most she satisfies.

(II. ii. 235–8)

Nor is this reduction from the sublime to the gastronomic simply a Roman military perception of Egypt and its wonders, a view from the officers' mess. Cleopatra too has a preoccupation with the alimentary canal. Trying to console herself for Antony's absence she shores up her vanity by boasting of her earlier conquests: 'Broad-fronted Caesar, | When thou wast here above the ground, I was | A morsel for a monarch' (I. v. 29–31). At the end of that scene, in a characteristic about-face, she dismisses her affair with Caesar as an adolescent folly committed in 'my salad days, | When I was green in judgement' (ibid. 73–4). Antony subsequently picks up the same language to express his anger with Cleopatra after he sees her flirting with Octavius Caesar's messenger: 'I found you as a morsel, cold upon | Dead Caesar's trencher' (III. xiii. 116–17). But a few lines further on he has leapt once again into outer space. Cleopatra is 'our terrene moon' which 'is now eclipsed' (ibid. 153–4).

This strain of imagery in the play reaches its stunning climax in the final scene of Cleopatra's life when, having immortal longings in her, she throws off the baser elements, namely, earth and

---

[13] Cf. J. Leeds Barroll, 'Antony and Pleasure', *Journal of English and German Philology*, 57 (1958), 708–20.

water, to become pure air and fire. Charmian sees her already apotheosized as the eastern star, but her final words give us instead an image of primal ingestion as she applies the aspic to her flesh:

> Dost thou not see my baby at my breast,
> That sucks the nurse asleep?

(v. ii. 308–9)

Here, acting the part of a mother suckling her infant, we may say that she truly makes hungry where most she satisfies! Constance Kuriyama does well to remind us in this connection of the oral level of sexual development in the Freudian scheme. Here in this final episode we have the archetypal conjunction of food, sexuality, and death, a '*Liebestod* fantasy' in which 'the closely allied oral and genital desires are limitlessly fulfilled'.[14] In this ultimate image of mother-love, Mark Antony we may say once again 'in Egypt sits at dinner' whilst Cleopatra is being gently eased into death. The 'baby at my breast' is of course the serpent which is to be the instrument of that death, but proleptically it is also the bridegroom whom she is about to join, whilst Antony is momentarily visualized as restored to the maternal embrace. This moment is indeed 'deeply regressive';[15] we are not merely back at the oral or Oedipal stage, we are being drawn rather into a prenatal, indeed prehuman zone of instinct. Here it is suggested is the dark desire for death along with the return to the womb which is what the characters (and by implication, the audience) most desire.[16]

This perspective is undoubtedly present in the play but such a Freudian reading scarcely does justice to the dialectical structure of the imagery that we have been attempting to describe. In particular it does not account for the tension between these oral fantasies and the frequent images of infinite aspiration and power. Ms Kuriyama brushes aside such cosmic aspirations and gestures as evidence merely of the romantic and mystical leanings of some of the critics.[17] But they are not to be dismissed.

---

[14] Constance Brown Kuriyama, ' "The Mother of the World": A Psychoanalytic Interpretation of Shakespeare's *Antony and Cleopatra*', *English Literary Renaissance*, 7 (1977), 328, 339.
[15] Ibid. 339. [16] Ibid. 349–51 and *passim*. [17] Ibid. 325–6.

The characters, both Egyptian and Roman, are reaching out for more than one kind of gratification. If the food imagery brings us back to the threshold of the prehuman, then there is, as we noted earlier, an opposing pull in the direction of the superhuman. Could it not be the case that Shakespeare is in possession here of the symbolic union of food, sex, and death as it would later be developed in Freudian doctrine but is here displaying this complex before us with a certain critical reserve, in the context of other more dialectical systems?

Even in regard to the food-images themselves, we should note once again the deliberate equation between Rome and Egypt. Food and drink (as well as excrement) are archetypally associated with love and sex, but the play shows that they are no less archetypally associated with war and empire. The earth from which we draw our nourishment is the earth for which, and over which, we fight and which we manure with our blood. It is the material object for which war is waged. For the honour of gaining possession of a piece of land 'which is not tomb enough and continent | To hide the slain', twenty thousand men, says Hamlet, will 'go to their graves like beds' (*Hamlet*, IV. iv. 62–5). Here Hamlet touches on the point where Ares and Eros meet—love and war both drawn by a kind of *Liebestod* to the earth itself. But there is a difference. Here in the case of war we encounter not the passive surrender to sleep and death and with it the return to the womb, but the restless and urgent desire for glory on the stage of history.

In the first scene of the play, Antony renounces this latter fascination. 'Kingdoms are clay,' he declares, 'our dungy earth alike | Feeds beast as man.' But of course Antony only seems to be renouncing the glories of war and conquest. To speak as he does in this same speech of 'the wide arch of the rang'd empire' is to betray the irresistible attraction that they still have for him. Like love, empire operates at the superhuman, cosmic boundary; but again like love, it also operates at the lower limits of our nature where the foundations of empire are laid in 'dungy earth' which 'feeds beast as man'. For that is his 'space' also—in spite of his seeming rejection—as Caesar testifies a little later on in the same act, vividly recalling Antony's warrior-like affinity for the diet, as well as the excrement, of animals.

> Thou didst drink
> The stale of horses, and the gilded puddle
> Which beasts would cough at: thy palate then did deign
> The roughest berry, on the rudest hedge;
> Yea, like the stag, when snow the pasture sheets,
> The barks of trees thou browsed.

> (I. iv. 61–6)

The frequent animal references in this speech and elsewhere ('the baby . . . that sucks the nurse asleep' in Act V is of course a snake) serve to reinforce the food images, forming a single code common to the Egyptian and Roman sides of the play. For both these societies the food and animal images point to the area of the less than fully human. 'What is a man,' Hamlet asks, 'If his chief good and market of his time | Be but to sleep and feed?' The answer he gives is 'A beast, no more' (*Hamlet*, IV. iv. 33–5). All the main characters in *Antony and Cleopatra* would come under this stricture at one time or another. While the feasting and wassailing so fundamental to the Egyptian lifestyle are commented on critically by the Romans from time to time in the play, the fact is that the one great feast actually performed on stage, thus giving visible substance to this line of imagery, is that given by Pompey on board his galley and attended by all three pillars of the world! It is they, not the Egyptians, who sing the hymn to Bacchus as the 'gaudy night' draws to its end. By then one of the 'pillars' is under the table and another is barely able to speak. The talk is of crocodiles. Asked by Lepidus 'What manner o' thing is your crocodile?', Antony confides to his colleague in the empire of the world the ultimate mystery of that animal, and indeed of all the other animals which inhabit the planet, including Lepidus and Antony himself: 'It lives by that which nourisheth it, and the elements once out of it, it transmigrates' (II. vii. 43–5).

Does this emphasis on the feeding of animals, on their body waste and copulation, leave room for more human possibilities? Many critics, especially in the first half of this century, argued that the poetic magnificence of the verse itself somehow constitutes, or implies, human value, the action of the imagination itself having a kind of saving function—as Blake would later maintain. Thus D. A. Traversi maintained that the play enacts

a process of 'poetic redemption'. He saw this redemptive movement as particularly marked in the great, final love-speeches
'in which irony and criticism . . . are dissolved into transcendent
poetry'. 'Transcendent' is indeed a favourite adjective in such
discussions: it is not simply that the poetry makes a gesture
of transcendence; it *is* transcendent! But such belief in achieved
transcendence can only be maintained by denying or failing to
notice the dichotomy of the celestial and the earthly, the superhuman and the less than human which is so central a mark of
this play. Instead, Traversi rather pointedly insisted on gradu-
alness and harmony. He spoke of 'the gradual ascent of the love
imagery from earth and "slime" to "fire and air" '.[18] But gradu-
alness and harmony are precisely what seem to be absent. There
is, to use Octavia's phrase, 'no midway | 'Twixt these extremes
at all'.

I am arguing that in spite of its unparalleled poetic abundance,
the play does not display a world redeemed and in harmony
with itself, but one marked essentially by absence and division.
A critical perspective similar to that which I noted in *Julius Caesar*
here embraces both Rome and Alexandria in a design of great
subtlety. In this critical perspective the two are seen to be riven
by the same basic split. Pitched beyond the human at one end
of the scale and among the beasts who sleep and feed and manure
the earth at the other, both societies fail to define for us the
vacant middle-ground of the human. This is where the dialectical structure of the play is really tending. In spite of the
vivid and sharply drawn differences between them, Rome and
Alexandria are from this point of view properly to be seen as
interchangeable paradigms. They share the same lack and pro-
voke in us the same question. If the manifest but unspoken question of *Julius Caesar* is: 'Who shall turn these hearts of stone
into hearts of flesh?', then the great but unspoken question of
Antony and Cleopatra is: 'How shall the "gap in nature" be
filled? How shall a man whose head is raised to the stars and
whose body is planted in the dung, yet remain Man, whole and
indivisible?'

---

[18] D. A. Traversi, *An Approach to Shakespeare* (1938; New York: Doubleday,
1956), 249, 254, 260. For a similar Romantic approach, see G. Wilson Knight,
The Imperial Theme (London: Methuen, 1965), 245, and J. Middleton Murry,
Shakespeare (London: Jonathan Cape, 1936), 357, 377, 378.

3

A fundamental strategy which men have developed for managing these contradictions is myth.[19] Myth serves to connect us to the gods on the one hand and to the earth on the other. It links our animal condition with the heavens—that at least is its implicit claim. 'None our parts so poor,' Cleopatra says, 'but was a race of heaven.' The earliest type of myth, it is generally thought, was simple animism. Before the Olympian gods emerged as individuals possessed of characters and a history, mana or divine potency was found in animals, men, the things that grow in the earth, indeed in the earth itself.[20] All these had a common soul. Hence the Pythagorean doctrine of 'transmigration' which Antony jokingly alludes to in his conversation with Lepidus. The crocodile might be inhabited by the soul of Lepidus' grandam (as Feste would say) or vice versa. The higher and lower levels of consciousness are thus in principle undifferentiated.

Later the gods achieve names and distinct personalities with stories attached to them. Instead of intimations of immortality, we now have what may be termed institutionalized hyperbole expressing itself in stabler forms such as allegory and personification which are less liable to deconstruction. With such we can conduct a more everyday commerce. Nevertheless, even in the later stages of mythology, hyperbole and the astonishments that go with it are always there—in reserve; the great poets can always reanimate the names of the gods and with them those transcendental imaginings as well as the darker impulses which gave them birth. In the Cydnus passage, as we saw, Cleopatra was linked with Venus-Aphrodite as she prepared to meet with Mars-Bacchus. Elsewhere we are told that she customarily gave audience 'in the habiliments of the goddess Isis' (III. vi. 17). Isis is the Egyptian version of the Great Mother; like Demeter she

[19] Recent studies have stressed the dialectical factors in mythology, as expressing basic contradictions. (See especially, Richard Seaford, *Reciprocity and Ritual: Homer and Tragedy in the Developing City-State*, (Oxford: Clarendon Press, 1994) 60–5.) Tragedy gave a particularly vivid representation of these paradoxes (ibid. 363–7 and *passim*).

[20] See Gilbert Murray, *Five Stages of Greek Religion* (New York: Doubleday, 1955), 12–31 (from the chapter entitled 'Saturnia Regna').

is a vegetation goddess with a story and a formal ritual, but in a simpler as well as a profounder sense she is the ripening corn itself, or, like Persephone, she is the seed of the new crop which dies and goes underground in the winter and is reborn in the spring. Gilbert Murray notes that in the early mana stage of the Greek religion, the fertility of the earth and the fertility of the tribe are felt as one. 'The earth is a mother: the human mother is *aroura*, or ploughed field.'[21] Agrippa is thus close to the mark when he sums up the mating of Julius Caesar and Cleopatra with the words: 'He plough'd her and she cropp'd' (II. ii. 228).

Isis in fact is not merely a fertility goddess, but the principle of fertility itself, not merely the goddess of love, but love itself —love, so to speak, carried to the infinite degree. Of Cleopatra in her role as Isis it may thus truly be said that 'age cannot wither her, nor custom stale | Her infinite variety' (II. ii. 235–6). She is in principle changeless and timeless—characteristics clearly marked in her own speech where she asserts her antiquity, her immortal, fixed and absolute quality:

> Think on me,
> That am with Phoebus' amorous pinches black,
> And wrinkled deep in time.
>
> (I. v. 27–9)

But as well as her universal aspect, she also has a distinct local connection with the Nile waters, the slimy, fertile ooze which, through the annual rise and fall of the Nile, guarantees sustenance to man and beast, thus joining the human with the less-than-human. Cleopatra explicitly makes this connection. She swears by 'the fire | That quickens Nilus' slime' (I. iii. 68–9)— the verb suggesting fertile life but also a swarming and insalubrious abundance, breeding produced by putrefaction.

Antony for his part is likewise descended from immortals, being the offspring of Hercules, as we are often reminded in the play. Hercules is not merely the sun-god but in a more primary sense the undying sun itself.[22] (Hercules is well connected:

[21] Ibid. 27.
[22] Cf. Robert Graves, *The White Goddess* (New York: Vintage Books, 1958), 133.

he gets to be identified with Dionysus who is of course no other than Bacchus, the consort of Venus!) All this not only helps to explain Antony's god-like status in the play ('His face was as the heavens, and therein stuck | A sun and moon . . .'), but also his association with animals—the stale of horses, the stag, the bull, the mallard. For among the labours of his great ancestor had been the cleaning of the stables of Augeas with their thirty-year accumulation of animal excrement! Likewise Hercules is regularly pictured, dressed in the hide of the many animals and monsters whom he had confronted and overcome. This is not something hidden in the play's texture. The references to Hercules are explicit and the stories related to Hercules too well known to the audience for their force to be missed.

Antony and Cleopatra is from this point of view the most mythological of Shakespeare's plays. This is not to say that he shared the mythological vision of the world; the play is not mythologically determined, any more than it is determined by Freudian categories. But Shakespeare here shows enormous understanding for this mode of creativity. This would make *Antony and Cleopatra* one further example—perhaps the best there is —of his centrifugal relation to prior texts and influences. He is able to enter into and share different modes of experience and belief but without any authorial commitment to one system rather than another. Here the mythological mode is set to work within a larger dramatic context which has yet to be defined. What he gives us is a profoundly sensitive reflection of mythological patterns with enough distance to permit an occasional burlesquing of those same patterns, as in Cleopatra's conversation with the eunuch Mardian:

> CLEO.   I take no pleasure
>   In aught an eunuch has: 'tis well for thee
>   That being unseminar'd, thy freer thoughts
>   May not fly forth of Egypt. Hast thou affections?
> MAR. Yes, gracious madam.
> CLEO. Indeed?
> MAR. Not in deed, madam, for I can do nothing
>   But what indeed is honest to be done:
>   Yet have I fierce affections, and think
>   What Venus did with Mars.
>
>   (I. v. 9–18)

And if mythology is the subject of the play rather than its source of inspiration, then it is clear that the audience too stops short of complete identification. We are, so to say, being taken on a conducted tour: we ascend with our poet into the upper reaches of the cosmos where we may catch a glimpse of Antony-Hercules in a fit of hyperbolic fury:

> teach me,
> Alcides, thou mine ancestor, thy rage.
> Let me lodge Lichas on the horns of the moon
>
> (IV. xii. 43–5)

But as part of the same tour package we get an arranged view of Antony-Bacchus tippling in the streets with knaves that smell of sweat. Whilst the spectator thereby gains a sympathetic insight into the workings of Pagan mythology—perhaps more insight than he would gain from the writings of Joseph Campbell, C. G. Jung, and Otto Rank all together—he is also in effect being invited to view the shortcomings and contradictions of the system. What is borne in on him in particular is the sudden drop from the cosmic image of Antony, to the image of Antony holding up a lamppost after closing-time at the pub. This is again the lurch, the fundamental dichotomy which the myths of the ancient world had sought to overcome. But they are not easily overcome. We look for a word, an image, an alternative myth which might serve to 'solder up the rift'. But the mythic vision and the amazing poetry which supports it give us instead, clearly foregrounded so that we cannot ignore them, the unresolved extremes of the superhuman and the less than human.

The contradiction which above all others the mythologies and rituals of the ancient world (particularly Egypt) sought to resolve was that of death and immortality. The Isis/Osiris myth which in a manner dominates the latter half of the play is of special importance in this regard.[23] Osiris is the dying sun-god, slain by his brother Set; Isis, goddess of Nature, is by the same token goddess of all things that die. Her task is to gather together the mangled remains of Osiris. At the centre of the myth is this celebration of death. And in the play too there is

---

[23] See M. Lloyd, 'Cleopatra as Isis', *Shakespeare Survey*, 12 (1959), 88–94; H. Fisch, '*Antony and Cleopatra*: The Limits of Mythology', *Shakespeare Survey*, 23 (1970), 59–67.

a like ceremony of dying as the 'bruised pieces' (IV. xiv. 42) of the mortally wounded Antony-Hercules-Osiris, are brought to Cleopatra-Isis, who cherishes him, saves him from his 'brother' Octavius, and eases his passage to the kingdom of death.[24]

But death was only one side of the coin; the other and sunnier side was the active attainment of eternal life, for it was the peculiar achievement of the ancient Egyptians that for them death was swallowed up in immortality. Osiris is a dying god who dies into eternity. Isis, by gathering the scattered parts of the dead body of Osiris, guarantees that he becomes immortal and reigns as king of the underworld. The myth celebrates death and with it, paradoxically, the resurrection to immortal life—the ritual expression of this dialectic being the practice of mummifying the remains of the dead man who would thereby live forever in the 'field of peace'. This is the pattern dramatized in the play from the middle of Act IV to the end. In these scenes Antony and Cleopatra seem not so much to prepare for death as to celebrate their translation to an immortal existence. 'I come, my queen,' Antony declares. And he adds, 'Stay for me, | Where souls do couch on flowers' (IV. xiv. 50–1).

Shakespeare here enacts a ritual of apotheosis which is also a marriage ceremony. His hero and heroine will in the most ceremonial fashion put off mortality and announce their union as god and goddess living on eternally among the stars. It is Cleopatra, in her great final speeches, who realizes the mythic combination most completely:

> Give me my robe, put on my crown, I have
> Immortal longings in me
>
> .   .   .   .
>
>   Husband, I come:
> Now to that name my courage prove my title!
> I am fire and air; my other elements
> I give to baser life.
>
>   (V. ii. 279–80, 286–9)

---

[24] Shakespeare would most probably have learned about the myth from Plutarch's own *Of Isis and Osiris* translated by Philemon Holland in 1603 as part of his edition of Plutarch's *Morals*. And it is likely too that he knew *The Golden Ass* of Apuleius translated by William Adlington in 1566, which relates the epiphany of the goddess Isis and the god Osiris as experienced in Lucius' dreams at the end of the book.

It is an amazing piece of virtuosity, this latter-day dramatiza-
tion of the most powerful of myths, the one which holds in itself
a key to the entire system of nature religion, striving to link the
inner drives of the flesh with the varying seasons of the year
and seeking by magic ceremonies and rituals to overcome the
most dreadful of all terrors—death itself, uniting its most disgusting aspects with the most alluring dream of which man is
capable, namely, the dream of eternal life.

We hardly need to be reminded that death and resurrection
(another name for immortality) not only belong to the core
beliefs of the ancient world; they also lie close to the origins
of tragedy itself as an art form.[25] In *King Lear*, as we shall see,
the image of the circle is notably foregrounded ('the younger
rises, when the old doth fall'). And in *Hamlet*, the revenge cycle
is seen to be based on the order of the seasons. *Romeo and Juliet*
seems to interpret the fate of the heroine in terms of the myth
of Proserpine who becomes the bride of Dis—god of death—
in the underworld, enacting in this the disappearance of the
flowers as a result of the winter frost. Thus Old Capulet:

> Death lies on her like an untimely frost
> Upon the sweetest flower of all the field
>
> .   .   .   .
>
> O son! the night before thy wedding-day
> Hath Death lain with thy wife. There she lies,
> Flower as she was, deflowered by him.

> (*Romeo and Juliet*, IV. v. 28–9, 35–7)

And of course, in almost parodic obedience to the myth pattern, Juliet will come back to life in the tomb, but only to die
again, as the ritual repeats itself. This rhythm of implied recurrence is even more evident in the myth of Isis and Osiris whose
cult was meant to assure the rise and fall of the Nile waters. In
such models, as in the myth of Dionysus-Bacchus from which
tragedy took its rise, are to be found the shadowy outlines of
a master narrative comprising the descent, death, and rebirth

---

[25] The early classic discussions are those of Jane Harrison, *Themis* (Cambridge:
Cambridge University Press, 1912), *passim*, and Gilbert Murray in his essay,
'Ritual Forms in Greek Tragedy', appended to the same volume. For a more recent
discussion see Seaford, *Reciprocity and Ritual*.

of the hero and with that the completion of the cycle which guarantees the eternal renewal of the life of Nature.

In other words, Shakespeare's depiction of this ritual of death and apotheosis in *Antony and Cleopatra* has an archetypal relation to the art which is here being practised. And Shakespeare seems to have had an uncanny awareness of this. If the sacrificial murder of Julius Caesar is, as I have said, a kind of primal scene, taking us back to one of the ritual beginnings of tragedy, then here in the dying and anticipated rebirth of the hero and heroine in the world to come, is another primal scene. It seems to call attention to itself as the latter-day re-enactment of a foundation-narrative; it is again tragedy reminding us of the origins of tragedy. In keeping with this tendency, these scenes, like the assassination scene in *Julius Caesar*, are conspicuously theatrical. 'Observe this scene,' Shakespeare seems to say, 'here the mythological ground of tragedy is displayed for your appreciation and judgement.' The characters are consciously acting. There is a high degree of reflexivity in these scenes. Not only do the characters perform a ritual, but they emphasize the fact that they are doing so.[26] Cleopatra, ceremoniously putting on her robe and crown, seems to stage her own pageant, a kind of Masque of Queens.[27] She tells her women: '*show* me . . . like a queen: go fetch | My best *attires*.' The language of theatrical performance is here very prominent. She seems to see Antony 'rouse himself | To praise my noble *act*'. And as we saw earlier she goes on almost playfully to mime another part, that of a mother suckling her infant. Dolabella uses the same language of the theatre as Octavius arrives on the scene a little later:

> thyself art coming
> To see perform'd the dreaded act which thou
> So sought'st to hinder.
>
> (v. ii. 329–31)

The notion of performance (as of a ritual or as an action upon a stage) is central to the play as a whole. The love scenes between the hero and the heroine are essentially performances. John

[26] See Rothschild, 'The Oblique Encounter', 426.
[27] Ruth Nevo interestingly points out elements of the pageant and the masque in Cleopatra's great speeches in Act V. (See 'The Masque of Greatness', *Shakespeare Studies*, 1 (1967), 115–18.)

Holloway perceptively remarks that the two lovers always seem to require an audience.[28] Unlike Shakespeare's other great lovers they are never seen on the stage alone with one another, engaged in the dialogue of heart and heart, of soul and soul. This I would suggest is bound up with the formal character of those appearances and with the tendency to emphasize that formal character. They are engaged in a ceremony rather than in the communion of lovers. Consequently they are inclined to public gestures rather like those of Blake's Zoas and their Emanations. This gives them nobility, height, even erotic power. But the softer human shading, the selfless concern for the other, tends to be lost in the harsh stage lighting which goes with such performances.[29]

But there is a paradox. The moment of Antony's death becomes the occasion for a dialectical reversal of these public gestures and rituals. The moment of separation becomes, ironically, the only occasion of true meeting, of dialogue. As Antony draws his last breath, Cleopatra ceases to perform for the gallery and temporarily abandons her grand style. She becomes (to use a phrase from a later speech) 'no more but e'en a woman'. There is a brief passage of extraordinary tenderness:

> Noblest of men, woo't die?
> Hast thou no care of me, shall I abide
> In this dull world, which in thy absence is
> No better than a sty? O, see, my women:
> The crown o' the earth doth melt.
>
> (IV. XV. 59–63)

---

[28] John Holloway, *The Story of the Night* (London: Routledge and Kegan Paul, 1961), 102; see also Laura Quinney, 'Enter a Messenger', in *Interpretations*, ed. Bloom, 160.

[29] Stanley Cavell (*Disowning Knowledge: In Six Plays of Shakespeare* (Cambridge: Cambridge University Press, 1987), 18–37), whilst recognizing the theatrical nature of this scene, reads it, and indeed much else in the play, very differently. He proposes that the play dramatizes the modern crisis of scepticism and with it the loss of all assured knowledge. This is expressed by Antony's withdrawal from the world of action, or, more correctly by 'the withdrawal of the world from Antony'. Cleopatra in her vision of transcendence at the end of the play redeems this loss. 'Returning the lost world as her dowry', she offers 'a ceremony of single intimacy' climaxed in the words, 'Husband, I come!'—suggesting total female gratification. Cleopatra thus invents or reinvents marriage, as 'proof of the continued existence of the human'. I welcome and share Cavell's view that *Antony and Cleopatra* should be read as a history play, but the scheme of sexual and philosophical history that he proposes is surely irrelevant to Shakespeare's reconstruction of Roman and Egyptian antiquity in this play.

It will be seen that this expression of personal loss with its utterly simple diction and its human depth, lasts for only three lines. It gives way again in the fourth line to the more typical need of an audience ('O, see, my women') and to the more customary language of cosmic hyperbole ('The crown o' the earth doth melt'). Paradoxically, the possibility of simple dialogue, of communion, is here glimpsed as death takes Antony away from her forever, thus rendering dialogue impossible.

There is perhaps a way of explaining this paradox. The mythologies of Rome and Egypt seem to have death as their subject, but in fact they are built on the negation of death, on the Shangri-La dream of an immortal afterlife in a super-Egypt, or a super-Rome. Or else they feed our nostalgia for a lost paradise, a prehuman state without responsibility, a return to the womb. To face death without these seductions is, we may say, the beginning of wisdom of another, more human kind. To that point we also arrive in the play, however briefly and however late.

4

The entry of the Clown with his basket of figs at the penultimate point of the play and the subsequent conversation in vulgar realistic prose between him and Cleopatra (v. ii. 240–78) represent the comic deflation of the whole mythic hyperbole on which the play had been based. But it does more than that; like the Gravedigger scene in *Hamlet*, it provides the biblical perspective, bringing a biblical realism to bear on the dream-world of Paganism. Significantly, this moment belongs to what Erich Auerbach characterized as Shakespeare's mixed mode, his non-classical mingling of high and low, comic and tragic, aristocratic and bourgeois. This mode had expressed from the early Middle Ages onwards the Christian challenge to the literary culture inherited from Greek and Latin antiquity. In keeping with this, the everyday prose or *sermo humilis* of the 'simple countryman' introduces into the play that subversive mixture of styles authorized originally by the Bible which, from the time of Augustine, had implicitly challenged all classical decorums.[30] Here the Countryman, belonging to real time in Shakespeare's own world, calls into question Cleopatra's high, aristocratic ceremony of dying as well as the mythic archetypes on which it is based. In this respect, the Clown functions like the Fool in *Lear*, or like Edgar when disguised as a bedlam-beggar, or like the Porter in *Macbeth*, or like the Gravediggers in *Hamlet*. And like the Gravediggers he makes death real, showing it to us in a handful of dust. His opening words reverse the Egyptian myth of immortality as expressed in the Isis-Osiris legend:

CLEO. Hast thou the pretty worm of Nilus there,
  That kills and pains not?
CLOWN. Truly I have him: but I would not be the party that should desire you to touch him, for his biting is immortal: those that do die of it, do seldom or never recover.

The finality of death as in Psalms ('shall the dust give thanks unto thee?' (30: 9)), Ecclesiastes (3: 19–20), and other places in the Old Testament, is here given a comic form: 'those that do die of it, do seldom or never recover'; and through the mal-apropism of 'his biting is immortal', the whole notion of immortality, whether in the Egyptian form of a pastoral idyll or in the Roman form of an eternity of glory, is ironically reduced. It is the death-bringing worm which becomes immortal. We are reminded of the disastrous end of history as foreseen in the last verse of Isaiah:

And they shall go forth and look upon the carcases of the men that have transgressed against me: for their worm shall not die, neither shall their fire be quenched; and they shall be an abhorring unto all flesh

a verse which would be thrice echoed in the Gospel of Mark (9: 44, 46, 48). Perhaps this passage was also in Shakespeare's mind when he has Cleopatra speak of herself as lying dead in the Nile mud as the water-flies 'blow' her 'into abhorring'. The Clown's worm also takes us back to the garden of Eden. Like

---

[30] See Erich Auerbach, *Literary Language and its Public in Late Latin Antiquity and in the Middle Ages*, trans. Ralph Manheim (New York: Bollingen Foundation, 1965), 34–58; on the mixed style in Shakespeare, see id., *Mimesis: The Representation of Reality in Western Literature*, trans. Willard Trask (New York: Doubleday, 1957), ch. 13 *passim*.

the Gravedigger, Cleopatra's visitor takes in the biblical reach of time from Adam to doomsday. Only yesterday, he tells her, he had heard of 'a very honest woman but something given to lie, as a woman should not do . . . how she died of the biting of it, what pain she felt'. And he goes on:

truly, she makes a very good report o' the worm: but he that will believe all that they say, shall never be saved by half that they do: but this is most falliable, the worm's an odd worm.

The man who believed the good report that the woman brought of the worm but could not be saved by what she had done, is of course Adam; just as Cleopatra is Eve, no longer the eternal feminine principle, goddess of love and nature, but the erring female who sins and consequently forfeits the gift of immortality. Even the fig-leaves fit into place in the new pattern.[31]

The Clown's comic patter, like that of the Porter in *Macbeth*, glances at some of the main metaphoric concerns of the play, not only at the notion of immortality but also at the imagery of food as a way of referring to the concupiscence of the flesh. Cleopatra had described herself earlier on as 'a morsel for a monarch'. She now asks the Clown whether the asp, when hungry, is likely to eat her! The Clown replies:

You must not think I am so simple but I know the devil himself will not eat a woman: I know that a woman is a dish for the gods, if the devil dress her not. But truly these same whoreson devils do the gods great harm in their women: for in every ten that they make, the devils mar five.

The serpent, from being a fertility symbol, possessing, like Cleopatra herself ('serpent of old Nile'), the cthonic potency or mana of the Nile mud, has now become the Tempter of Genesis, chapter 3, whilst Cleopatra is momentarily transformed into a figure in a morality play, a woman who might have been a dish for the gods but who has been unfortunately marred by the devil. The Clown makes fun of womankind but at the same time, rejecting her own self-definition as 'a morsel for a monarch', he addresses Cleopatra as a responsible moral agent. She is no longer a mere sex-object.

---

[31] Cf. Roy W. Battenhouse, *Shakespearean Tragedy: Its Art and Its Christian Premises* (Bloomington, Ind.: Indiana University Press, 1969), 167.

Above all the whole ritual of apotheosis is in this scene overturned, if but for a moment. We have instead the middle-ground of the human and with it a reversal of values, a sudden refocusing of the whole dream within an archetypal frame entirely different from that which the Isis-Osiris-Set legend had provided. Here man is tested and found wanting within the limits of his brief span of three-score years and ten. Those who die of the worm—that is the whole race of man—do seldom or never recover. A cold, sharp, but morally bracing wind of realism blows through this dialogue. At the end we have Cleopatra reduced to size as she and Antony, beheld in this new perspective, become for a moment actors in the Christian drama of salvation and damnation. Here we glimpse not only a different ideological perspective, but a different artistic perspective also —a departure from the archetypal model for tragedy suggested by the myths of Osiris and Dionysus. Indeed one might even want to say that there is here an implicit questioning of tragedy itself!

Situated strategically just before Cleopatra takes her own life, this scene has thus a function similar to the scene in Brutus' tent on the night before the battle of Philippi. There a new Brutus had been disclosed in the dialogic exchange with Lucius and, following that, in the terror and wonder inspired in him by the Ghost of Caesar. In both plays a biblical perspective is introduced at approximately the same moment, i.e. immediately before the catastrophe. If I am not mistaken, we have here something like a recurring pattern. In *Hamlet* too, as we shall see, the encounter with the Gravediggers provides the clearest biblical commentary on the action and that too takes place at the beginning of Act V before the fatal rapier contest. Again, the scene of love and forgiveness between Lear and Cordelia with its recollections of the parable of the Prodigal Son comes, like the Gravedigger scene, some five hundred lines from the end of the play. There is in short a common strategy. The biblical path of redemption and atonement, or of sin and punishment, is briefly but sharply defined for us at this penultimate moment.

There are other pointers in the same direction. Ethel Seaton noted many years ago that Cleopatra reminds us through several verbal echoes of 'the great Whore [of Babylon] that sitteth upon many waters, with whom have committed fornication the

Kings of the earth' from Revelation 17: 1–2.[32] But these are merely undertones, as Seaton makes clear. Even when coupled with the powerful reversal of values effected by the Clown's speeches, they do not constitute *Antony and Cleopatra* into a Christian drama.[33] What we have is rather a biblical counterplot, the addition of an important new perspective to the action of the play. The myth of the dying god who dies into eternity is not thereby overthrown, but the effect of this dialectical posing of different possibilities is to bring about a subtle refraction of that myth. As a result there will be no final identification between us and the displayed mythic forms, or between the author and his characters in their mythic personalities.

Immediately after the comic scene introducing the Countryman with his basket of figs, Cleopatra will proceed to the final and most ceremonial stage of what I have termed her ritual of apotheosis, beginning with the lines, 'Give me my robe, put on my crown, I have | Immortal longings in me.' But these gestures of immortality are now seen—in the Old Testament perspective created by the Clown—as no more than theatrical gestures. They are what she says they are, 'longings'. *If only* we could rest in such beliefs in the same unquestioning fashion as the ancient Egyptians who supplied their dead kings and queens with robes and precious ornaments to furnish their onward journey in the other world! But it is now too late in the day for such

---

[32] '*Antony and Cleopatra* and the Book of Revelation', *Review of English Studies*, 22 (1946), 219–24. This is the moment to pay tribute to the late Ethel Seaton, my supervisor at Oxford, 1946–8. In addition to her wisdom and 'judgement ever awake', she had a capacity for elegant and meticulous scholarship in the best traditions of that University.

[33] As maintained for instance by Battenhouse, *Shakespearean Tragedy*, 161–83. Battenhouse argues for a typological reading of Shakespeare's major drama, according to which there is a two-level mode of representation, the actions of the characters being a dark parody, or 'upside-down version' of Christian beliefs and doctrines. Howard Felperin ('Mimesis and Modernity in *Antony and Cleopatra*', in *Interpretations*, ed. Bloom, 88 f.) likewise sees the play as offering a displaced or parodic version of Christian salvation. But for Felperin this is just one of several competing perspectives. A more straightforward Christian reading is that of John F. Danby ('The Shakespearian Dialectic', *Scrutiny*, 16 (1949), 196–213). He sees the play as developing a Christian condemnation of both Rome and Egypt; they are 'the opposed halves of a dis-creating society'. There is such a dichotomy in the play, but I would argue that Shakespeare situates himself (and his audience) imaginatively and spiritually on both sides of the dividing line at once. He refrains from a final judgement which would reveal what Danby terms 'the Christian core of his thought'—but then perhaps there is no such core!

imaginings. This sense of *if only* defines the audience's response to these 'immortal longings'. It is very different from a true suspension of disbelief. Cleopatra's language is no more than a way of expressing the tension between the desire for immortality and the knowledge that such desires are unattainable. Here is the play's final deconstructive turn, its supreme hyperbole. It is the victory of language, not that of life over death. There is no transcendence here, but only the poetic echo of a would-be transcendence. If Cleopatra triumphs in any other sense, it is in having beaten Octavius to the draw. In taking her life she makes him appear an 'ass unpolicied' (v. ii. 306–7).[34] The tone of the ending is set by this quasi-Machiavellian achievement, rather than by a more tragic catharsis or a more complete fulfilment of mythic promises.

Paradoxically, whilst the play, as I have argued, foregrounds the myth of the dying and rising god, seeming to point to it as a tragic paradigm, a kind of primal scene, the truth is that the play does not in its structure actually mirror such myths of circularity. It is a very impure tragedy. The play as a whole, as is notorious, bursts the last fetters of classical restraint; it lacks the rounded, satisfying, self-contained form of ancient tragedy —the form to which we still respond in *King Lear* or even in *Romeo and Juliet*. The latter example is for one thing infinitely more concentrated than *Antony and Cleopatra*. In its simpler fashion it remains focused from beginning to end on the two young lovers driven by tragic necessity to their deaths.

By contrast, *Antony and Cleopatra* belongs to a more radically mixed mode. The very notion of tragedy is here in conflict with other notions. In addition to the struggle between the characters on the stage, there is a *met-agon*, a struggle for control of the play itself. The final player in this enclosing drama, this play-without-the-play, was introduced through the entry of the Clown with his basket of figs. The play had up to that point taken in the ancient worlds of Rome and Egypt with their sharp differences and their surprising analogies. We judge, we compare, we make our choice, as the epic sweep of the drama lights up first one of these ancient cultures and then the other. But

---

[34] As skilfully argued (perhaps over-argued) by Harold C. Goddard, *The Meaning of Shakespeare* (1951; Chicago: University of Chicago Press, 1965), ii. 199–205.

there was a third ancient civilization belonging to the eastern Mediterranean at the time of Cleopatra and very visibly represented in the Rome of Octavius. I refer of course to the Judaic system. Needless to say, this was more immediately and powerfully present to Shakespeare's audience than the myth-world of Egypt or the imperial memory of Rome. Indeed Plutarch himself had, in his *Morals* as translated by Philemon Holland (the book from which Shakespeare had evidently drawn his knowledge of the myth of Isis and Osiris), given considerable (if somewhat disdainful) attention to the Jews and their practices. In particular, with his penchant for comparative studies, he had attempted a number of dubious parallels between the Jewish festivals and the Feast of Dionysus.[35] In brief, it would have been surprising if Shakespeare had not included the legacy of ancient Israel (which for the period covered by the play meant Christianity also) in his vast canvas. And of course he did include it. Moreover, unlike in *Julius Caesar*, where the audience supplies a factor which is for the most part absent from the text of the play, here in *Antony and Cleopatra*, in keeping with the poetics of presence, it is not absent. The Clown visibly and audibly expresses the biblical antithesis, echoing the words of the Bible which peasants and great ones alike would hear from the pulpit every Sunday. He voices a cultural option, opposed not only to the ethical standards of both Rome and Egypt but to their artistic norms also. For the critical perspective which the play establishes takes in the aesthetic claims of tragedy itself, as the Clown in his comic intrusion implicitly questions the formalities of the tragic order.

---

[35] 'Table-Talk' (*Of Symposiaques*), Book Four, Question Five, in *The Philosophie, Commonlie Called, The Morals, Written by . . . Plutarch*, trans. Philemon Holland (London, 1603), 710–11. Jews were very much on Plutarch's mind here and in other places. Shakespeare would very likely have noted in this connection Philemon Holland's vigorously worded *Summarie* prefixed to his translation of Plutarch's essay 'Of Superstition' (ibid. 258) in which he reproves Plutarch for his 'mockerie and derision of the Iewes', and especially for comparing 'the feast of the Tabernacles ordeined by the eternall and almightie God, with the Bacchanalles and such stinking ordures of idolators; thinking verily that *Bacchus* was the god of the Iewes.' Holland felt obliged to speak up on this because he well understood that in effect Plutarch's comments were an aspersion on Christianity also. For Plutarch and for most of his contemporaries Christians would have figured as just one more obnoxious Jewish sect.

Such a *met-agon* repeats itself in Milton's writings and those of Blake. There we shall find likewise a contest between the Hebraic and the non-Hebraic components of Western art and belief. In Milton's case it is not merely an *agon* but an *agony*— a struggle in which he is himself always personally involved. Shakespeare for the most part leaves the contestants free to engage one another in a kind of Bakhtinian dialogue. He contents himself with giving them a voice and setting them to work. They will fight out the issues between themselves and he will leave it to the spectators to judge the outcome.

CHAPTER 3

Hamlet: Thy Commandment All Alone

There is one further dialectical feature of the ending of *Antony and Cleopatra* that we have yet to consider. Both the Egyptians and the Romans pursue a cosmic delusion; for the Egyptians it is that of an immortal feast of love, for the Romans it is an immortal feast of power. But there is a sharp difference in what may be termed the dynamics of these two modes. The one world is timeless, the other is time ridden. Cleopatra seeks escape from time; she proposes to 'sleep out this great gap of time | My Antony is away' (I. v. 5–6). Her preferred rhythm is biological, governed by the order of Nature—birth, copulation, and death. There is no advance. When in Egypt Antony adopts this mode, but when in Rome he catches the Roman sense of urgency, the Roman obsession with time and opportunity. On the need to confront the power of Pompey, Lepidus remarks:

> Time calls upon's,
> Of us must Pompey presently be sought,
> Or else he seeks out us.
>
> (II. ii. 158–60)

Antony responds in the same spirit:

> Haste we for it,
> Yet ere we put ourselves in arms, despatch we
> The business we have talk'd of.
>
> (ibid. 164–6)

The little business that has to be dispatched before the triumvirs make their hasty departure for Misenum is of course the arranged marriage between Antony and Octavia which will be formalized and consummated in haste between this scene and the next. We are reminded that it was a Roman poet who wrote 'Carpe diem', a love-ditty composed by a man with one eye on the clock. Octavius Caesar does not write love-poems, but like

Pompey he has a finger on the trigger. At Actium he declares, 'Our fortune lies | Upon this jump' (III. viii. 5–6). Pompey has the same sense of opportunity; when the moment is missed it cannot be recalled. Menas makes his infamous proposal to liquidate Pompey's enemies whilst they are in his power but Pompey tells him that it is already too late: 'Ah this thou shouldst have done | And not have spoken on't' (II. vii. 73–4). Brutus had a more meditative cast of mind but he too shared the same Roman awareness of the critical moment which has to be seized, the 'tide in the affairs of men, | which, taken at the flood, leads on to fortune' (*Julius Caesar*, IV. iii. 217–18). Here is perhaps the reason that led Shakespeare to commit the famous anachronism in that play (at II. i. 192 and II. ii. 114)—if there were no clocks in Rome, well then, perhaps there should have been!

Yet of course it is precisely by adopting this Roman mode of existence that Cleopatra in the final scenes turns the tables on Octavius. Through the shouting-match with Seleucus she deceives Octavius into thinking that she is only interested in the treasure needed for continuing her indolent lifestyle. At the end of this episode, Octavius, taking the bait, bids her 'feed and sleep'—the Alexandrian recipe for oblivion—but she has other plans as she and her maids synchronize watches in the count-down to her final move:

> IRAS. Finish, good lady, the bright day is done,
>   And we are for the dark.
> CLEO.   Hie thee again,
>   I have spoke already, and it is provided,
>   Go put it to the haste.
>
>   (V. ii. 192–5)

Iras, her maid, steals a march on her by applying the aspic to herself first. With a sense of immediacy which sounds like a fantastic parody of the very point we are now making, the race is on to determine which of them will be the first to meet and kiss 'the curled Antony'! Charmian, skilfully timing her own demise for the Guard's entry a moment later, can taunt Caesar with having sent 'too slow a messenger'.

What does this dialectic seem to show? It shows for one thing that many of the critics have been wrong. It is not true to say that 'the strong necessity of time may command Antony's Roman services, but Cleopatra will offer an escape from the necessity of time itself.'[1] At the end of the play we have something like the reverse of this. Clearly, in so far as we rejoice at Cleopatra's triumph over Octavius, we recognize that this has been made possible by her giving up (at least as a tactical measure) the dream age of mythology with its recurring cycles and adopting in its place a more immediate, less enchanted sense of reality, that of the here and now. Mythological time has been to that extent superseded by a more modern awareness of time and history. But this is not a victory for Romanism either. In fact there are no winners. The Romans for all their careful attention to timing have missed the boat, whilst Cleopatra, who has learned to adapt the Roman style for her purposes, is very dead at the end. Those that die of the worm—and this includes all the Romans and all the Egyptians as well—do seldom or never recover. In spite of Octavius' prediction in Act IV that 'the time of universal peace is near' (IV. vi. 5), the ending of the play does not create any strong sense of historical continuance or promise.[2] When the insubstantial pageant fades it leaves not a rack behind, only the echo of its marvellous poetry.

We may wonder why this should be? The play creates a powerful image of Octavius urging his active star; indeed, it is hardly an exaggeration to say that the Roman world which Shakespeare displays for us has discovered time as the medium in which the human will is exercised. Why then does the play not seem to reward them for this achievement, this advance in existential awareness? One would have thought that this propensity for acting in the heat would have made a strong appeal to the men of the Renaissance. But instead of being privileged in the economy of the play, this aspect of Romanism is beheld in the same critical and ironic perspective as other Roman characteristics that we have considered. Again and again the Romans in the play seize occasion by the forelock (a Roman emblem of course) but, one after another, they are seen to blunder. Pompey strikes a deal with the triumvirate, but he will pay for it with his life.

---

[1] Janet Adelman, *The Common Liar: An Essay on Antony and Cleopatra* (New Haven: Yale University Press, 1973), 152.

[2] But see Frank Kermode, Introduction to *Antony and Cleopatra* in *The Riverside Shakespeare* (Boston: Houghton Mifflin, 1974), 1344–5.

Antony's marriage of convenience brilliantly conceived by Agrippa as a way of sealing the union between the two leaders, misfires; in the end it will turn out to be a cause of aggravated tensions. Enobarbus shrewdly judges that the moment has come to abandon the leaky vessel of Antony's declining fortunes. But no good will come of it; he fails to reckon with Antony's greatness of mind and the strength of his own feelings. Antony's own end in Act IV is a case of double misprision: he is not only deceived by false information about Cleopatra's death, but bungles the suicide itself. And of course, Octavius, the greatest tactician of them all, is outmanœuvred by Cleopatra. All these masters of time and opportunity are seen to stumble in one way or another. Why should this be?

We may find the hint of an answer in Aristotle's closely reasoned discussion of time in the *Physics*. Unlike Plato in the *Timaeus*, Aristotle separates time for all practical purposes from eternity. Moreover, he lays his stress on the now; the present moment is fundamental, and it would seem to be the sole reality to which our experience of time reduces itself. The only immediate awareness we have of the passage of time is through the difference between one now and another, the instants by which time is constituted being singular and discrete. The problem therefore is that of continuity. What, if anything, connects the separate nows with one another? Being non-spatial, time cannot properly be conceived as a line; even the terms before and after are spatial analogies and therefore do not tell us of anything that can be truly said to exist. Time does not move from point A (the past) to point B (the future) because the now itself is the only point from which measurement is possible.[3] Before and after come to have meaning only because the 'now' defines their limits, marking off the instant that has just passed from the instant that is still to come. Indeed, there is a sense in which before and after only exist at this point of intersection.[4] It would seem to follow that time past and time to come have no firm independent status; nor do we owe them anything; they are merely the trace created by the movement of the now as it defines the ever-changing boundary between the no-longer and the not-yet.

[3] Aristotle, *Physics*, iv. 9, trans. P. H. Wicksteed and F. M. Cornford, Loeb Classical Library (1929; Cambridge, Mass.: Harvard University Press, 1980), i. 389–93.
[4] Ibid., iv. 13. 409.

It will be seen that this model goes a long way towards elucidating the sense of time in Shakespeare's Roman plays. If the Romans seize the moment, they also deny to the moment any compelling link with the past and future. Once the moment has gone it would seem no longer to obligate. Antony marries Octavia; this 'act of grace' binds him to Octavius giving them the hearts of brothers (II. ii. 147–8). Immediately after the marriage, he makes a show of declaring his loyalty to Octavia, at the same time dissociating himself from the past and giving an undertaking regarding the future:

> I have not kept my square, but that to come
> Shall all be done by rule.
>
> (II. iii. 6–7)

Thirty lines on—say, two and a half minutes of acting time—and he is saying

> I will to Egypt:
> And though I make this marriage for my peace,
> I'the east my pleasure lies.
>
> (ibid. 37–9)

In the next act, now still with Octavia in Syria, he reaffirms his loyalty to her (III. ii. 33–6) but a few lines later, in Athens, he is sending her on a diplomatic mission to her brother from whom he is now estranged. As soon as she is out of the way he will hie back to Alexandria. Alliances are formed and broken with dizzying rapidity. Lepidus is still an active power-sharer in Act III, scene ii; eighty lines further down he is overthrown and under arrest at Caesar's command. It is not merely that people betray their friends and violate oaths and promises. There is something more fundamental involved here than simple political cynicism and self-seeking. Rather what we have is inconstancy raised to a principle of action; it has become the only constant. There is a lack of connection between past and present. Decisions taken in the instant have their life and meaning in that instant. Undertakings, relationships, and desires belonging to the past do not obligate in the present and will not reverberate in the future. In a word, it is a world without memory; instead we have, as in Aristotle's concept of time, a succession of nows, each singular and distinct from the other.

In fact, we have what might almost be termed a culture of forgetfulness. Oblivion is privileged, sought out. Cleopatra courts oblivion, trying to abolish the empty spaces between desired nows, to sleep out the gaps of time. Whilst memory is a peculiarly human endowment (or handicap, depending on the point of view), oblivion would seem to link us to the animal kingdom. Hamlet calls it 'bestial oblivion'. Here is perhaps the ultimate significance of *Antony and Cleopatra*'s many animal images. The worm will do its kind, not obedient to memory but to instinct. In the same way Cleopatra will do her kind—which means fleeing from the battle at Actium 'like a cow in June' that has been stung by gadfly, whilst Antony will fly after her 'like a doting mallard' (III. x. 14, 20). The many food images are also relevant: as noted earlier, the recipe for oblivion is food and sleep. Pompey makes the connection, hoping that Antony will stay in Egypt where

> Epicurean cooks
> Sharpen with cloyless sauce his appetite,
> That sleep and feeding may prorogue his honour,
> Even till a Lethe'd dulness.
>
> (II. i. 24–7)

But the preferred gateway to oblivion for Romans and Egyptians alike is wine. The cult of Bacchus in the play is no incidental feature; it is not a matter of social habit merely, like the frequent recourse to the cocktail cabinet in some televison series depicting modern lifestyles. Drink in the play is dramatically functional; it serves to inhibit any disturbing intrusions of memory, to rub out any inconvenient thoughts about the future. Pompey's response to Menas who is concerned about what will happen tomorrow, is 'desist and drink'. Pompey would have done better to have followed the system which Tacitus attributes to the Germans: before making their decisions, he tells us, they considered each problem twice: once when sober and once when drunk. To drink is to exist in an eternal and unbroken present which is the realm of Bacchus. Responsibility for past and future is abolished. The river Lethe in this context becomes almost a synonym for wine: 'Come let's all take hands,' says Antony, 'Till that the conquering wine hath steep'd our sense | In soft and delicate Lethe' (II. vii. 105–7). Later, to drown the memory of his disastrous and shameful defeat at Actium, Antony, now reconciled to Cleopatra, calls for 'Some wine within there, and our viands' (III. xi. 73). And finally, his life ebbing away, after being drawn up into Cleopatra's monument, he asks for wine, seeking to extend thereby the moment he would still spend in Cleopatra's arms. Cleopatra herself does not seem to need the help of Bacchus in her last moments but her farewell to life is also significantly a farewell to wine:

> Now no more
> The juice of Egypt's grape shall moist this lip.
>
> (V. ii. 280–1)

Wine had not only made life endurable, it had given it its meaning, extending to infinity the possibilities of the Aristotelian now.

The god of wine,[5] we need hardly add, is also the god who presides over the beginnings of tragedy and comedy. The cult of Bacchus-Dionysus is no incidental part of tragedy as a whole. As Nietzsche points out in the first chapter of *The Birth of Tragedy*, intoxication is the key to the understanding of Dionysiac rapture and Dionysiac rapture (modified by Apollonian harmony) is the key to tragedy. Under that influence, the barriers which separate men from one another are abolished and 'nature itself . . . rises again to celebrate the reconciliation with her prodigal son, man'.[6] This loss of individuality in the merging of Man with Nature is expressed by the Dionysiac chorus. The chorus which bears witness to the sufferings of Dionysus and the wonder of his renewal becomes the 'symbol of an entire multitude agitated by Dionysus'.[7] It is important to note that Nietzsche speaks of

[5] On Dionysus as the wine-god see Walter F. Otto, *Dionysus: Myth and Cult*, trans. R. B. Palmer (Bloomington, Ind.: Indiana University Press, 1965), 55, 56, 100–1, 143–51 (ch. 12). Mention has already been made of the association between Dionysus and Hercules (with whom Antony identifes himself). By way of analogy, it may be noted that a very fine 3rd-century mosaic was recently uncovered in Sepphoris in Galilee depicting scenes from the life of Dionysus, among them a drinking competition between Dionysus and Hercules. Dionysus is drunk but controlled, whilst Hercules is seen prostrate, supported with difficulty by a maenad and a satyr and vomiting into a bowl (reproduced by Zeev Weiss and Ehud Netzer in *Sepphoris* (Jerusalem: Israel Exploration Society, 1994), 32, 34; in Hebrew). For further comment on these floor decorations, and their resemblance to details found in the *Dionysiaca* of the late epic-writer, Nonnus, see G. W. Bowersock, *Hellenism in Late Antiquity* (Cambridge: Cambridge University Press, 1990), 48–9.

[6] Friedrich Nietzsche, *The Birth of Tragedy*, ch. 1, in *The Birth of Tragedy* and *The Genealogy of Morals*, trans. Francis Golffing (New York: Doubleday, 1956), 23.

[7] Ibid., ch. 8 (p. 57).

this loss of Selfhood in the merging of the Self with the law of Nature as a 'self-forgetting'.[8] Oblivion is not a mere side-effect of the artistic experience, according to Nietzsche; it is much rather its aim and essence:

While the transport of the Dionysiac state, with its suspension of all the ordinary barriers of existence, lasts, it carries with it a Lethean element in which everything that has been experienced by the individual is drowned. The chasm of oblivion separates the quotidian reality from the Dionysiac.[9]

Here we have one of the essential modes celebrated in *Antony and Cleopatra*. Nor is it a matter only of an exploration of the philosophy of oblivion; the Bacchic-Dionysiac mode finds direct dramatic expression in the overt scene of Bacchus worship (complete with a hymn to Bacchus!) on board Pompey's galley. Here again we have a scene which exhibits for our critical attention something fundamental to the origins of ancient drama itself.

But the system of myth and ritual which Nietzsche was later to define in such ecstatic terms is here both displayed and questioned, and so is the typical art form whereby that system is represented. *Antony and Cleopatra* compels us to reconsider the Nietzschian formula. Can we truly expunge memory and remain in the enchanted realm of art and oblivion? Can we deny that 'quotidian reality' where men and women labour under the burden of the past and in expectation of the future? Or does not the greatest art at some point require us to come to terms with this more everyday scene of human responsibility also? Such a necessity is just hinted at in *Antony and Cleopatra*—again in that little exchange between Cleopatra and the Countryman. It transpires that he is the one character in the play who truly remembers; and he remembers a great deal:

> CLEO. Remember'st thou any that have died on't?
> CLOWN. Very many, men and women too ...

In contrast to the Dionysiac cult of oblivion and the aesthetic which it yields, the Countryman takes a long retrospective view of the generations of men and women, their trials and failures, together with a long prospective view of the end of days, with its undying worm and also, we may suppose, the 'new heaven

[8] Ibid., chs. 1 and 4 (pp. 22, 35).   [9] Ibid., ch. 7 (p. 51).

and the new earth' (Isaiah 66: 22, 24) which the lovers had vainly aspired to in the first scene of the play. All this is a mere hint, indeed an absence. However, there are other plays in which Shakespeare wrestles more openly and unremittingly with the contradictions of art and memory. One of these is *Hamlet*.

2

'Must I remember?' Hamlet cries out in his first soliloquy. Why can he not forget the death of his father and his mother's marriage to his uncle? That is the way of the world: a king has died; two months or so later he has been forgotten, his wife has remarried, and the kingdom is now competently ruled by a new monarch. The past has buried the past. Nothing could be more natural than such oblivion; it is a guarantor of order and stability. Oblivion for Nietzsche is not only a necessary ingredient of art, it is also necessary for life; it 'represents power, a form of strong health'. Without what he calls 'active forgetfulness', there can be no happiness, no serenity, no hope, no pride.[10]

As against such pride and health—the characteristics incidentally of the regime instituted by Claudius—Hamlet in his black dress, seeking his noble father in the dust, represents sickness and melancholy. Such obstinate perseverance is, according to his mother Gertrude, a violation of Nature. 'All that lives must die,' she tells him, 'passing through nature to eternity.' Claudius urges the same connection between Nature and oblivion. To remain fixated on the past, is, he says, 'a fault to nature, | To reason most absurd, whose common theme | Is death of fathers.'

Claudius, we should note, is, like the Egyptians and the Romans in *Antony and Cleopatra*, a prominent worshipper of Bacchus. The first scenes of the play strongly emphasize this. Expressing his joy at what he calls Hamlet's 'unforced accord' with his mother's wishes, he announces a drinking ritual for the rest of that day:

> No jocund health that Denmark drinks today
> But the great cannon to the clouds shall tell,
> And the king's rouse the heaven shall bruit again,
> Re-speaking earthly thunder.

> (I. ii. 125–8)

---

[10] *The Genealogy of Morals*, essay 2, trans. Francis Golffing, 189.

No wonder that almost the first remark Hamlet makes to Horatio when they meet shortly afterwards is: 'We'll teach you to drink deep ere you depart' (ibid. 175). In the fourth scene the sound of the cannon, the drum, and the trumpets, added to the noisy revelry in the feasting chamber as the King 'drains his draughts of Rhenish down', provide an ironical accompaniment to the action on the battlements in the course of which Hamlet will receive his charge from the Ghost, a charge which will culminate in the words, 'Remember me!'

Again, the drinking in this play is not a mere background feature; it is dramatically functional. Claudius is the Dionysiac man, living in the now of achievement and decisive action, unburdened by memory or conscience, adapting himself to the natural course of things. The constant 'draughts of Rhenish' enable him to live in this continuous present tense. He really does not seem to be aware of himself as the murderer of his brother until Hamlet forces him to face the image of that deed. Hamlet himself is by contrast a melancholy figure, weighed down with a past of which he cannot be entirely certain, burdened with responsibility for a future which he cannot wholly control. The association between Claudius and drink is maintained to the end of the play. Hamlet resolves in Act III to delay the assassination attempt until Claudius is 'drunk, asleep, or in his rage, | Or in th'incestuous pleasures of his bed . . .' Hamlet jokes about it. 'The King', says Guildenstern,

> Is in his retirement marvellous distempered.
> HAMLET. With drink sir?
> GUIL. No my lord, rather with choler.
>
> (III. ii. 273–5)

In the final scene we are offered another Bacchanalia. The stage direction in the folio gives prominent attention to the table with 'flagons of wine on it'. Claudius now institutes another, even more elaborate drinking ritual. If and when Hamlet scores a hit, the King will drink, the cannon will fire, the drums and trumpets will sound; at the same time, Claudius will drop a pearl (but actually a poison-pellet) into the wine cup—which Hamlet will then drink off in response to the King's toast. The rapier play is thus punctuated by the King's drinking, with the trumpets, drums, and cannon sounding off each time. The Queen drinks the final toast to Hamlet from the poisoned goblet. The excitement of the players, giving way to violence and frenzy as they become incensed, creates a kind of *Walpurgisnacht* atmosphere; it is precisely in the spirit of the Dionysiac *orgia*. The scene reaches its climax with the Queen's cry: 'the drink, the drink—O my dear Hamlet— I The drink, the drink—I am poisoned.' At this, Hamlet slays his uncle with the envenomed rapier but—what is symbolically more important—he forces the remainder of the poisoned wine into his mouth. What we have here is not only the final vivid realization of the Dionysiac mode in the inevitable oblivion of death, but also a symbolic gesture of repudiation. There is a metapoetic statement here: Hamlet in destroying Claudius, also seeks to overthrow the Nietzschian mode which Claudius had so well exemplified. He affirms an alternative mode whose key terms are memory, trial, and survival.

From this point of view, there is a structural correspondence between the final scene of the play and the scene on the battlements in Act I. There, whilst the court was given over to drunken revelry, Hamlet had received a 'commandment' from beyond the grave. An obligation had been laid upon him to remember, to bring the record of the past to bear upon the present. He feels it as a painful, almost unbearable responsibility. That responsibility will remain with him to the end—not so much the need to kill his uncle as the need to set the record straight, to forge a meaningful bond between times past and to come.

At the end of the play amid the spilt wine and blood, the litter of weapons and overturned tables, Hamlet, now near death, lays a similar charge on Horatio. Horatio wishes to drink the remaining poison, thus joining his friend in the feast of death. But he is denied this aesthetic satisfaction, this felicity, this oblivion, and is commanded instead to live on to tell the story of Hamlet's life and death:

> Absent thee from felicity awhile,
> And in this harsh world draw thy breath in pain
> To tell my story.

> (v. ii. 326–8)

In effect Hamlet is saying to Horatio what the Ghost had said to him: 'Remember me!' The story has to go on being told. That matters more than closure and the perfection of form. As the play ends, Horatio announces that he is about to commence his narration, and Fortinbras prepares to hear it. In a sense, therefore, the story does not end; rather it finds its meaning in the telling and retelling. Beside this scene in which Hamlet commands his unwilling friend to go on telling his story for the future time, we might set such a text as Coleridge's ballad of 'The Ancient Mariner'. The Mariner seizes the arm of the Wedding Guest and then he 'holds him with his glittering eye', forcing him to listen to his tale of wonder and terror, a moral history involving sin, trial, suffering, and repentance. He must go on telling it compulsively and the auditor, for his part, 'cannot chuse but hear'.

A narrative governed by the imperatives of memory, with the emphasis on survival and witness rather than death and oblivion, is clearly in an important sense, anti-tragic, anti-Nietzschian, and also anti-Aristotelian. Shakespeare is here reaching out towards a different category, or rather a different set of categories— towards an art based not on synchrony and the unity of time ('a single circuit of the sun' in Aristotle's formula) but on a genuine diachrony. If we seek a philosophical foundation for this art we shall not find it in Aristotle's *Physics* with its exclusive stress on the reality of the present moment, nor in Plato's *Timaeus* with its notion of time as an image of eternity, aspiring to the same unchanging perfection and order. We shall find the beginning of an answer rather in another foundation document in Western man's search for the meaning of time, this time a Christian source from later antiquity.

Augustine in his *Confessions* begins like Aristotle from a sense of the difficulty of attributing any certain existence to the past and the future. 'Nothing surely can be, but that which now is,' he states and later: 'Clear now it is and plain, that neither things to come, nor things past, are.'[11] But in spite of this ontological difficulty, which would rob the past and future of any objective existence, Augustine is haunted by the mystery and power of memory. His reflections on this subject occupy a large part of the *Confessions*. Where are the images of memory lodged? How do we come to know things which 'are not'? How does

[11] Augustine, *Confessions*, XI. 18, 20, trans. William Watts, Loeb Classical Library (Cambridge, Mass.: Harvard University Press, 1951), ii. 249, 253.

it come about that we conceive of things which are still to come as though they were present? Sometimes memory obeys our will; at other times memories come unbidden and undesired. 'These I drive away with the hand of my heart from the face of my remembrance,' Augustine declares.[12] It is like Hamlet trying to drive away the thought of his mother's remarriage—'must I remember?'

Augustine comes to the conclusion that memory, whether of the future or the past, is a power of the soul; we have that within which passeth show. And yet whilst the images of the past and future are produced by the mind from its inward store, they are in a way independent of us and indeed transcend the limits of the mind. They come to us charged with a certain mystery. Here are heaven, earth, the sea, and a great deal more besides. He is filled with astonishment at the force and range of memory.

Great is this force of memory, exceedingly great, O my God; a large and an infinite inner room: who can plummet the bottom of it? Yet is this a faculty of mine, and belongs to my nature: nor can I myself comprehend all that I am. Therefore is the mind too strait to contain itself: so where could that be which cannot contain itself?[13]

It would seem that our memory of the past and our foreknowledge of the future have greater force and thus greater reality, than the now of Aristotle. The Ancient Mariner, Hamlet, and after him Horatio, are not merely haunted by the images of the past, they are possessed, demon driven. The record of the past lives within them and gives them no peace. And yet there is always an edge of uncertainty as well, a question about its origin and status. 'Look now, whence and which way got these things into my memory? I for my part know not how,' says Augustine.[14] Hamlet says much the same thing. He declares after the performance of the Mousetrap that he will take the Ghost's word for a thousand pounds; but at other times he is not so sure; perhaps he is subject to delusions induced by his weakness and melancholy. Power and uncertainty are anomalously joined. For Hamlet throughout the play the great summons is always there, the memory of the encounter on the battlements. It lives in him more strongly and more persistently than the passing

---

[12] Ibid., x. 8 (Loeb edn., ii. 95).   [13] Ibid. 99.   [14] Ibid., x. 10 (ii. 105).

moment of which Aristotle speaks. And yet it is not an absolute *given*, it can be lost sight of; he can be distracted by random
circumstances—a cry of players, other memories, a meeting with
friends from the University. This is not the inverted U of tragedy of which Northrop Frye speaks,[15] but something more
open-ended, more like time and history as men endure them. It
is significant that Augustine rejects the notion that the movement
of the sun, the moon, and stars constitutes time.[16] Time is a function of the soul, discovered by turning inwards in meditation
rather than by gazing outwards at the cosmos as in so much Greek
philosophy.[17] We might want to say in our modern fashion that
for Augustine time is relative—its measure is subjective rather
than objective.

3

The kind of memory that we are seeking here to define and
the kind of dramatic discourse to which it gives rise should be
differentiated from what might be termed the automatic memory of the protagonist in a Senecan revenge play. The revenger
is driven to exact payment in kind for a crime committed in
the past against his near kin. The remembrance of that crime
drives him inexorably on a predetermined course. But this is
remembrance almost in the sense of a natural reflex; we have
it in common with the animals, many of which bear gratitude
to friends and settle accounts with their enemies in the same
fashion. In fact it would be unnatural for the revenger to forget. The Ghost makes this point when he says to Hamlet, 'If thou
hast nature in thee bear it not!' The key term here is Nature.
From this perspective, Hamlet's task is really nothing more

---

[15] Northrop Frye, *The Great Code* (New York: Harcourt Brace, 1982), 176.
[16] *Confessions*, XI. 23 (ii. 259).
[17] See John F. Callahan, *Four Views of Time in Ancient Philosophy* (New York:
Greenwood Press, 1968), 160–4; Arnaldo Momigliano has some reservations as to
the weight that should be given to Augustine's perception of Greek views of time as
determined by the movement of the heavenly bodies; he comes to the conclusion
that 'Augustine is a valid witness only for himself' and that 'Greek philosophers often
thought in terms of cycles, but Greek historians did not' ('Time in Ancient Historiography', in *History and Theory: Studies in the Philosophy of History*, Beiheft 6
(1966), 7, 13).

than to follow his instinct which will lead him to do what his ancestors have done and what his successors will continue to do in their turn, namely, to kill, usurp, and then to be himself killed by the next usurper. Hamlet (both the play and the character) are here governed by the circle of retaliation, its inevitable rising and falling movement determining that every successful revenger becomes himself a victim. To use a formula of Lévi-Strauss in reference to 'cold' societies characterized by recurrent rituals, 'history is subordinated to system'.[18] It may even be claimed that at this level the Ghost's message does not differ basically from that of Claudius. What Claudius had urged upon Hamlet in their first interview was the necessity of obeying the natural rhythm of recurrence:

> But you must know, your father lost a father,
> That father lost, lost his, and the survivor bound
> In filial obligation for some term
> To do obsequious sorrow.
>
> (I. ii. 89–92)

What we have here again is automatic memory—human beings programmed like computers to remember according to patterns printed on their neurons. No moral categories are involved.

The call to remember, however, urged upon Hamlet at the end of the Ghost's speech and in close proximity to it the warning, 'Taint not thy mind, nor let thy soul contrive | Against thy mother aught', intimates something different—a history unsubordinated to system, a truer diachrony. History is where we are tested; we may succeed but we may fail. As against the rhythm of eternal recurrence we have that of the test or pilgrimage—a time marked by discord and discontinuity. Sudden and shocking gaps are revealed.

> The time is out of joint: O cursed spite,
> That ever I was born to set it right.
>
> (I. v. 189–90)

Either the present appears to have become meaningless—'an unweeded garden that grows to seed'—in contrast with the past,

---

[18] Claude Lévi-Strauss, *The Savage Mind* (Chicago: University of Chicago Press, 1966), 233, 236.

or else the past seems to be nullified, of no further consequence
in light of the startling challenges of the present. That indeed
is the effect of the Ghost's message on Hamlet:

> Yea, from the table of my memory
> I'll wipe away all trivial fond records,
> All saws of books, all forms, all pressures past,
> That youth and observation copied there,
> And thy commandment all alone shall live
> Within the book and volume of my brain,
> Unmixed with baser matter.

> (I. v. 98–104)

How much easier it would be to ignore these breaches and dis-
locations in time and to live in the eternal present of mythology
with its recurring circles, a dream age as the Australian tribes-
men call it.[19] But this option it seems is no longer available.

The obligation to remember which Hamlet here undertakes is
thus something more than the accustomed, involuntary response
to natural stimuli. The speech just quoted suggests that he is
not merely going to replace the trivial fond records previously
stored in his memory with new data. It is rather that memory itself will operate differently. To start with, it will involve
a second-order awareness, an awareness of the pastness of the
past. Hamlet will not merely be subject to past pressures and
to present disclosures; he will place them side by side and interpret the result. 'Look here upon this picture, and on this,' he
will say. 'This was your husband . . . Here is your husband.' To
remember in the fully human sense, as against the remembering of the revenger, or of homing-pigeons, or of the green sea-
turtle,[20] is to become aware of oneself as remembering.

The phenomenology of true memory in short incorporates
the hermeneutic act. Paul Ricoeur speaks of certain fictions
such as Virginia Woolf's *To the Lighthouse*, Thomas Mann's *Der
Zauberberg*, and above all Proust's *À la recherche du temps perdu*

---

[19] Ibid. 237.
[20] Archie Carr, a distinguished zoologist, has described the habits of a family of
green sea-turtles (of the genus *Chelonia*) which, guided by the memory of their ancestors, find their way generation after generation across the Atlantic ocean from their
pastures on the coast of Brazil to their breeding-grounds on the distant island of
Ascension (*So Excellent a Fishe: A Natural History of Sea Turtles* (Garden City,
NY: The American Museum of Natural History, 1967), 200–7).

as 'projecting an experience in which time as such is thematized'; they are tales about time.[21] I am arguing that memory as understood in the passage we are considering involves such a process —it involves seeing the light and shade together and being aware of the contrast. Such memorializing does not only occur with the 'refiguration' (to use Ricoeur's term) of events for the purpose of fictional or historical description. The hermeneutic moment antedates refiguration; it is already present in the very exercise of memory. To truly remember is to observe the intersection of past, present, and future and to draw the necessary conclusions— conclusions which might take the form of guilt, responsibility, hope, regret. The past is not simply given, it comes fraught with ironies, metonymies, antitheses. It is already marked by the signs of identity and difference. Whenever we re-encounter something or someone we have known in the past, we perform Hamlet's interpretive gesture: 'Look here upon this picture, and on this.' We write our own book and interpret our own text.

The metaphor of writing which I have just used in trying to say something about memory is itself of course basic to *Hamlet*. In responding to the Ghost's command, Hamlet speaks of wiping from 'the table of my memory' ('table' here in the sense of writing-tablet) all earlier records and inscriptions. And he goes on to say

> thy commandment all alone shall live
> Within the book and volume of my brain,
> Unmixed with baser matter.

Not surprisingly, Augustine gives us an early intimation of this essentially verbal character of memory. Things or events are not themselves stored in the memory, nor yet, strictly speaking, the images of things, but rather the verbal signs conceived from those images—'ex memoria proferuntur non res ipsae, quae praeterierunt, sed verba concepta ex imaginibus earum'.[22] He says much the same of our perceptions of things yet to come, what we might term future memory: it is not the things themselves

---

[21] 'Narrated Time', trans. Robert Sweeney, *Philosophy Today*, 19 (Winter 1985), and 'Time Traversed: Remembrance of Things Past', trans. K. McLaughlin and David Pellauer, in Paul Ricoeur, *Time and Narrative*, ii. (Chicago: University of Chicago Press, 1985), both reprinted in *A Ricoeur Reader*, ed. Mario J. Valdes (London: Harvester, 1991), 350, 356.

[22] *Confessions*, XI. 18 (ii. 248).

that we perceive but the signs of those things—'cum ergo videri dicuntur futura, non ipsa, quae nondum sunt . . . sed eorum causae vel signa forsitan videntur, quae iam sunt'.[23]

This semiotic model clearly supports the notion of memory as an active, interpretive process. It would follow from Augustine's formulation that we are engaged not in passively recording and retrieving information, but in coding and decoding, in reading signs. Polonius likewise, who is something of a parody of Hamlet, links memory to written texts. A certain effort of understanding is required—'And these few precepts in thy memory | Look thou character' (I. iii. 58–9)—we note the prescriptive 'Look thou'. Textuality is here more than a metaphor. The play in fact constantly foregrounds the link between remembering and writing. Remembering inevitably suggests writing and actually stimulates that act, as when Hamlet writes down his notes of the meeting with his father. Like Montaigne and so many cultivated men of the sixteenth century, Hamlet carries around with him a notebook (his 'tables') in which he jots down his chance thoughts and recollections. As the Ghost disappears he reaches in his pocket for that notebook:

> My tables—meet it is I set it down
> That one may smile and smile, and be a villain.
>
> (I. v. 107–8)

This interaction also works in the opposite direction: written texts become the recommended means of activating the memory within us, the book within finding confirmation in the book without. Thus Hamlet determines to catch the conscience of the King by means of a play designed to awaken his 'occulted guilt'. And for this purpose he composes some sixteen lines for the actors to insert in their performance in Act III. Hamlet, the man who is commanded above all things to remember, is also at every turn of the play seen to be engaged in writing or reading.

4

It requires no great perspicacity to determine the particular cultural influence at work in bringing about this emphasis on

[23] Ibid.

the supreme importance of memory and this association between memory and textuality. The new factor that had interposed between the earlier Greek philosophers and Augustine was the Hebrew Scriptures and the Gospels. This is clear not only from his discussion of the concept of memory, but from the actual reflections on his own spiritual history which constitute the bulk of the *Confessions*. The encounter with the biblical text, in particular the Book of Psalms, was decisive both as remembered experience in itself and as a model by which other remembered events in his life might be organized and interpreted. Thus in Book IX, chapter 4, he recalls the period of his life when he gave up his lectureship in rhetoric, abandoning Cicero as he discovered the greater power of the Psalms:

What cries made I unto thee in those Psalms! Oh, how was I inflamed towards thee by them! Yea, I was on fire to have resounded them, had I been able, through all the world, against the pride of mankind.[24]

The memory of his conversion experience ('thou hast enlarged me in my distress') and of his zeal against the false doctrines of the Manichees ('who yet love vanity and seek after leasing') takes the form of a verse-by-verse encounter with the fourth psalm. The dialogue with the biblical text becomes a spur to memory and by the same token the recalling of the details of his own past life becomes a way of reading and interpreting that text. In short the encounter with the Bible gives new moral force and urgency to the exercise of the memory.

Unlike Augustine Shakespeare evidently did not undergo a conversion experience. Nevertheless, it seems clear that the radical shift in the consciousness of time and memory which marks off Shakespearian tragedy from that of the Greeks and Romans, has something to do with the revolutionary impact of the Bible in the intervening centuries and especially in Shakespeare's own time with the rise of Reformation biblicism. From this point of view *Hamlet* is a crucial example. Arnaldo Momigliano in a thoughtful essay on ancient historiography might almost have been speaking of Shakespeare's *Hamlet* when he remarked that

[24] Ibid., IX. 4 (ii. 17).

The Jew has the religious duty to remember the past. The Greeks and Romans cherished the example of their ancestors and derived inspiration from it. Isocrates and other rhetoricians made this one of the main reasons for writing history. But as far as I know, no Greek ever heard his gods ordering him to 'remember': 'Thou shalt well remember what the Lord thy God did unto Pharaoh, and unto all Egypt' (Deuteronomy 7: 18).[25]

Likewise no Greek hero was ever charged like Hamlet with the commandment to 'Remember me!' Nor did the hero of ancient tragedy see it as a moral obligation to hand on his burden of memory to a successor. The prototype here is the command placed on the Children of Israel to hand on from one generation to the next the saving narrative of the Exodus from Egypt (Exodus 10: 2, 13: 8). Harold Bloom has made the point that 'Hamlet is biblical rather than Homeric or Sophoclean'.[26] I will claim further that the biblical paradigms are here decisive and that in this play Shakespeare confronts the challenge of Hebraism more openly than in any other play, with the possible exception of *King Lear* (to be considered in the next chapter). It becomes a working alternative to those classical models to which the tragic stage had owed its form and tendency.

Moreover, as we have already remarked, there is the specific association between memory and textuality. This again is biblical. Jan Assmann, a distinguished Egyptologist, has recently described the sense of the past cultivated by three great civilizations of antiquity: Egypt, Israel, and Greece. Whilst in all three cultures written records are important as a means of bringing the past into relation with the present, it is Israel which first privileged and canonized a body of writing as the vessel of its collective memory. With the destruction of the Temple, the locus of such memory was no longer the temple cult with its ritual enactments, ceremonies, and recitations but the foundational texts of the Torah (such as the account of the departure from Egypt and the Book of the Covenant) which were kept alive through constant reinterpretation. To remember the words and

---

[25] Momigliano, 'Time in Ancient Historiography', 19–20.

[26] Harold Bloom, *Ruin the Sacred Truths: Poetry and Belief from the Bible to the Present* (Cambridge, Mass.: Harvard University Press, 1991), 61, though I find Bloom's explanation of what makes him biblical by turns obscure and wide of the mark.

to meditate on them day and night was a supreme obligation laid on the people by solemn oath.[27]

From this point of view Hamlet's revelational encounter with his father's ghost in Act I may count as another primal scene corresponding to the assassination scene in *Julius Caesar* and the ritual of apotheosis in *Antony and Cleopatra*. Here on the battlements we view the biblical alternative to those archetypal enactments which, as we argued earlier, had reference to the ritual origins of tragedy, and which accordingly drew attention to their special importance by reflexive gestures and tropes. Hamlet's meeting with the spirit of his dead father in which a command is given and a charge accepted is bracketed in the same fashion and has a similar centrality and comparable dramatic power. Behind it, we discern the outline of such biblical scenes of revelation as that at Mount Sinai (Exodus 19 f.). There too a Father had appeared to lay his command on his people. Only one of their number is called to ascend the mountain (ibid. 19: 20) whilst the others stay below in terror and seek to distance themselves from the alarming sounds and sights (ibid. 20: 18–19). From now on the People of Israel are chosen, burdened with a task which they will forget or try to forget but which will never forget them. Hamlet has the same sense of being chosen, and the same recoil from such chosenness:

> The time is out of joint: O cursed spite,
> That ever I was born to set it right.
>
> (I. v. 189–90)

Hamlet's encounter with the Ghost recalls the biblical scene in many ways, but above all by the imagery of writing, so prominent in this biblical pericope. As in the sequel to the assembly at Sinai (Exodus 24: 4, 12), here too the scene on the battlements in Shakespeare's play is marked by the writing down of the commandment in a book ('And thy commandment all alone shall live | Within the book and volume of my brain') and by the inscribing of the record upon 'tables' ('My tables, meet it is I set it down'). More impalpable than such particular echoes but perhaps even more striking is the biblical resonance of this scene;

---

[27] Jan Assmann, *Das Kulturelle Gedächtnis: Schrift, Erinnerung und politische Identität in frühen Hochkulturen* (Munich: C. H. Beck, 1992), 87, 296, and *passim*.

we are impressed with the momentous quality of the encounter and with the sense it creates of entering upon a new path of life whereby all previous bonds and loyalties ('all forms, all pressures past') are wiped away. This is entirely in accord with the biblical paradigm.

The scene which I am proposing as Shakespeare's model here enacts, according to the Bible's own definition, the entry into a Covenant or *berit* (Exodus 19: 5, 24: 7). There are several such scenes in Genesis also—the so-called covenants with the Patriarchs: Abraham, Isaac, and Jacob. These are likewise transforming encounters, scenes of high drama. In covenant scenes persons and places often receive new names to indicate the new path on which history is launched. Abram becomes Abraham, Luz becomes Bethel, Jacob becomes Israel (Genesis 17: 5, 28: 19, 35: 10). (Traditionally, the entry into the covenant of Abraham is the moment when the male child receives his name and, in effect, his identity.) They are moments of solemn dedication—commands are given and promises made by one side; solemn obligations are undertaken by the other (Exodus 24: 3, 7). All this serves to emphasize the break between the past and the present.

Thus, whilst a covenant signifies a joining together for common purposes, it also implies a break or rupture. In biblical Hebrew one cuts a covenant; the ritual of covenant-cutting might include the severed body of a sacrificial animal (Genesis 15: 9–18). This says something about the biblical sense of time and memory. Israel's story begins with Abram leaving his birthplace and his father's house and going to a Land which he has not known (Genesis 12: 1). There is a radical break with the past, and the future is essentially unknown. Such rupture inheres deeply in the folk-memory of the Israelites. The covenant does not eliminate such breaks; it embodies them rather in a pattern of belief and action, enabling us to turn them to purposeful ends. As Jan Assmann acutely observes, the book of Deuteronomy, a text dominated by the command to remember and by warnings against forgetfulness, institutes a mnemonic principle and method whereby, when in Zion, the people would, paradoxically, remember the exile and, when in exile, they would remember Zion![28] This two-way memory provides the groundplan for that most

---

[28] Ibid. 212–13.

haunting of all memory-poems, namely, Psalm 137, beginning with the words:

> By the rivers of Babylon, there we sat,
> and there we wept, when we remembered Zion.

The author of the poem, writing after the Return, vividly recalls the scene of the exile and its bitterness whilst the figures in the poem sitting by the famed canals of Babylon tenaciously hold on to their memories of Zion.

Older Bible critics, following the lead of O. Cullman's 1946 study, *Christus und die Zeit*, argued that whilst the Greek concept of time was cyclical, that of the Hebrews was linear, history proceeding in a straight line from Creation to the End of Days. It is a model which students of Shakespeare have also made use of from time to time to distinguish the biblical element in Shakespeare's plays.[29] More recent scholarship, however, in particular James Barr's important corrective study, *Biblical Words for Time*, has questioned this distinction. Whilst Greek philosophers inclined (though not invariably) to circular models of time, Greek historians rarely used them. The authors of the Hebrew Bible and the New Testament, for their part, never spoke of time in terms of lines.[30] It may be added that lines are by definition continuous, whilst as we have noted the biblical sense of time and memory is profoundly discontinuous.

We nevertheless need metaphors of integration. If lines will not serve, are there other models which can express the unifying power of memory and at the same time do justice to the splits and tensions which mark our historical experience? Wordsworth expressed a basic spiritual need when he wrote:

> And I could wish my days to be
> Bound each to each by natural piety.

But how can that binding be brought about? The poem from which those lines are taken begins with the words:

---

[29] For instance, Tom F. Driver, *The Sense of History in Greek and Shakespearean Drama* (New York: Columbia University Press, 1960), 19–25.

[30] James Barr, *Biblical Words for Time* (1962; London: SCM Press, 2nd rev. edn., 1969), 62–5, 145, and *passim*; Momigliano, 'Time in Ancient Historiography', 10–14.

> My heart leaps up when I behold
> A rainbow in the sky;
> So was it when my life began;
> So is it now I am a man;
> So be it when I shall grow old.

The rainbow is of course a primary memory-symbol, taking us back to the first of the biblical covenants, that made with the human race after the Flood (Genesis 9: 14–17). The nature of this sign is that it spans contradictory states: rain and sun, loss and renewal, warning and hope. It carries the memory of catastrophe, but it also carries a promise that no such catastrophe will occur again, that 'the waters shall no more become a flood to destroy all flesh'. In this way the covenant binds our days each to each. Rupture is not denied; the antinomies remain, but they have been brought together under an arching or bridging structure. Moreover, the rainbow has reference to time and its changes, its marvellous ephemerality being the very sign of change.

The rainbow is one symbol or metaphor which helps us to come to terms with time and history. There are others. The covenant is often spoken of with the use of stage metaphors. Stephen Toulmin and June Goodfield have remarked that the Israelites took history seriously, more seriously than other ancient peoples. This is because they saw the historical process as 'a divine drama in which they themselves had been cast in an important role'.[31] They were concerned with history as the site of an encounter with God. There the drama of the covenant was played out.[32]

Thus, though the Israelites knew nothing of the stage and did not actually use this language, one unavoidably finds oneself using these terms in discussing their sense of time. The covenant it would seem is a dramatic model imposed on the flow of time. It visualizes a challenge thrown out, a promise given, followed by the tense expectation involved in awaiting the fulfilment of that promise. This is the plot of history, conducted under providence like a vast morality play. Nor is it only modern students

---

[31] Stephen Toulmin and June Goodfield, *The Discovery of Time* (London: Hutchinson, 1965), 56.
[32] Cf. Barr, *Biblical Words for Time*, 150, citing Walter Eichrodt, 'Heilserfahrung und Zeitverständnis im Alten Testament', *Theologische Zeitschrift*, 12 (1956), 103–25.

of the subject who tend to connect covenant history with the art of the theatre. It was a commonplace notion in Shakespeare's time also. Thus Sir Walter Ralegh in the Preface to his great *History of the World* (1614):

For seeing God, who is the Author of all our Tragedies, hath written out for us, and appointed us all the Parts we are to Play: and hath not, in their distribution, been partial to the most mighty Princes of the World . . . why should other Men, who are but as the least Worms, complain of wrongs?[33]

Here, as in the engraved frontispiece to his *History*, the eye of providence supervises the doings of men in this 'great Theatre'. Bishop Joseph Hall writing in 1605 makes much the same point: 'The World is a stage: every man an actor, and plaies his part, here, either in a Comedie, or Tragedie.' The trouble is that we cannot know which it is going to be; for that, he says, we must 'stay till the last act'.

Thou seest a wicked man vaunt himself on the stage: stay till the last act, and looke to his end (as *David* did) and see whether that be peace.[34]

The outcome of the play—whether it will have a happy ending or not—depends to a great extent on our actions. Time is to that extent open, undetermined, unlike the closed time of Greek tragedy. Henry More later in the century uses the same trope. The whole created universe is the stage for a divine drama. There is providence in the fall of a sparrow. We are, he says, to observe

the admirable windings of Providence in her Dramatick Plot which has been acting on this Stage of the Earth from the beginning of the World.

Like Joseph Hall he acknowledges an edge of uncertainty about the outcome of that plot: 'we cannot judge the tendency of what is past or acting or present.' But again like Hall he adds that we should attend patiently for 'the entrance of the last Act, which shall bring in righteousness in triumph'.[35] Eventually the promise of the covenant will be fulfilled.

[33] Walter Ralegh, *The History of the World* (edn. of 1687), p. xxi.
[34] Joseph Hall, *Meditations and Vowes*, Centurie II, ii. 30, in *Works* (1634), 22.
[35] Henry More, *Divine Dialogues* (1688; edn. of 1713), 172.

The posture of attentiveness which characterizes this model makes it in some ways a more powerful option than those other dramatic models that Shakespeare had inherited from classical antiquity. It has the tensions of real dialogue. Hamlet in the scene on the battlements is confronted, challenged, summoned. He is given a crippling burden of responsibility. But whilst he is trapped, he is not trapped in the same way as Orestes or Oedipus in the Greek drama, or like the characters in a Senecan revenge play. In their case the shape of the plot is predetermined for them. Hamlet is, by contrast, being tested; he will have a share in determining the shape of the plot. There is here a dialectic of coercion and free will which is reflected in the stage imagery so pervasive in *Hamlet*. Like Macbeth, Hamlet steps on to a stage already set for him by his very theatrical visitor. This is underlined for us by a good deal of self-reference to the art of the theatre. Hamlet speaks of the Ghost's 'questionable shape'; Horatio addresses him as a 'fantasy' and an 'illusion'. Like the Weird Sisters in *Macbeth* (though in an opposite sense), the 'fellow in the cellarage' functions as the manager of a supernatural stage-play in which Hamlet becomes an unwilling actor. This is what may be termed the play-without-the-play—which as Henry More said 'has been acting on this stage of the Earth from the beginning of the World'.

But Hamlet also mounts his own play. He is so to speak a character in search of an author. In keeping with the covenant paradigm, he is free, responsible for writing his own script as he goes along. He tells his friends that he will put on an 'antic dispositon'—in other words, act a part. And this he does with great verve whenever he meets Polonius, or Claudius, or Rosencrantz and Guildenstern. And he does in fact write part of the script for the Mousetrap and stage-manages that performance. There the theatre-image becomes explicit in the action on the stage like the myth and ritual of Bacchus-Dionysus in the drinking scene on Pompey's barge! In short, the imposing of a covenant-task and the response to it by the human partners to the covenant are not merely high drama, but high drama bracketed so as to draw our attention to its dramatic character. Nor is this surprising. Indeed it would have been surprising if Shakespeare had overlooked so powerful a dramatic model and one which, no less than the myth of the death and rebirth of Dionysus, had its origins in one of the ancient Mediterranean civilizations which had shaped the spiritual history of the West. And of course he did not overlook it—*Hamlet* is the evidence for that.

But though the scene on the battlements demands to be understood as a metaphysical encounter, a covenantal moment, as in some medieval morality, the total effect is very different from that of a morality play. In *Hamlet* the covenant-type drama is evoked, beheld, and even acted out, but it is not unambiguously embraced. In relation to this scene as to the other primal scenes that we have examined in other plays, there is a certain critical reserve. For one thing, it has a tonal ambiguity; the scene is not entirely solemn. As often noted it also has a certain theatrical, self-parodying character—when for instance the Ghost assures Hamlet that if he could tell the secrets of his prison-house, his son's hair would stand up 'like quills upon the fretful porpentine'. The audience could be relied on to laugh at these familiar evocations of the atmosphere of the Senecan melodrama. This is especially so at the end of the scene where 'this fellow in the cellarage' spookily echoes Hamlet's words, whilst the actors on the stage above keep moving their ground to get away from the 'Ghost' as he bumps around under the boards in full view of the audience.[36] These comic touches indicate the phenomenological duality of the scene: it is a set piece of traditional fustian which the audience expected to see and enjoy; it is what they had paid their money for.

But when all that has been said, the scene also has an unmistakable religious charge. The audience in 1603 could be expected equally to respond to that, for that too is what they had paid their money to see. The simplified, one-dimensional religiosity of the bad quarto of that year is a sign of it. The religious ideas were not only there; they were getting across to unsophisticated members of the audience. Here too the frequent theatre-images helped. They have in them an element of parody but they also carry a serious message. They are a way of saying to the audience: 'attention must be paid to this scene; we all know that it is no more than a scene in a play but it is only by dramatic devices that we can represent the high design of providence, the supernatural order which shapes our ends.'

[36] Cf. William Empson, *Essays on Shakespeare*, ed. David B. Pirie (Cambridge: Cambridge University Press, 1986), 85–7.

5

The weight of biblical-Christian allusion in *Hamlet* is not confined to one scene; it is felt throughout the play. The Christian
order of sanctity is invoked early on by Marcellus in his speech
on the 'crowing of the cock'—itself a potent New Testament
image:

> It faded on the crowing of the cock.
> Some say that ever 'gainst that season comes
> Wherein our Saviour's birth is celebrated,
> This bird of dawning singeth all night long,
> And then, they say, no spirit dare stir abroad
> . . . .
> So hallowed and so gracious is that time.
>
> (I. i. 157–64)

This idyllic note will not be picked up again until the end of
the play when Horatio bids farewell to his friend with the words
'Good night sweet prince, | And flights of angels sing thee to
thy rest'. But if the harsher scenes in between have little room
for Christmas gladness and heavenly choirs, they are weighted
with biblical reference just the same, with a strong prejudice
in favour of the Genesis narratives. Claudius on his knees links
his crime of fratricide with Cain's murder of Abel—'it has the
primal eldest curse upon't' (III. iii. 37). This grim chapter of
Genesis is again recalled when Hamlet, observing the gravedigger shovelling a skull out of the ground, remarks:

How the knave jowls it to th' ground, as if 'twere Cain's jawbone,
that did the first murder. (V. i. 64–6)

Claudius not only kills his brother—he takes his brother's wife
to his bed, thereby making them both guilty of incest.[37] Critics
have tended to take the incest theme lightly, giving an enormous
amount of attention instead to the Freudian implications of
Hamlet's obsession with his mother's remarriage. But the Ghost,
who presumably has no hidden Oedipal motives, refers to the

---

[37] This question had been much debated by canon lawyers in the previous century in connection with the marriage of Henry VIII with Catherine of Aragon. Com-
plicating the clear prohibition against a union with a brother's wife in Leviticus
18: 16 was the directive in Deuteronomy 25: 5 enjoining such a marriage when the
brother dies without issue. Hamlet of course was the living evidence that in this
case such a situation had not arisen.

crime of incest twice and with great emphasis. The Everlasting had fixed his canon against that deed also and consequently no one in the play takes it lightly. God's presence as creator and lawgiver is constantly invoked in this play, more so than in other plays of Shakespeare with the possible exception of *Measure for Measure*. If he is 'he that made us' (IV. iv. 36), we owe him something in return. Part of Hamlet's problem—and not the least part—is to discover what that something is.

One evident obligation is to preserve the life thus given to us. This is not always a simple matter, especially if you find yourself cast as a tragic hero. Dying is then very much your business. The first lines of Hamlet's first soliloquy show him complaining (like John Donne some years later in *Biathanatos*) about the biblical prohibition against suicide, derived from Genesis again, this time the first of the biblical covenants—that made with Noah and the survivors of the Flood:[38]

> Or that the Everlasting had not fixed
> His canon 'gainst self-slaughter.
>
> (I. ii. 131–2)

People like Hamlet, suffering from melancholy (we would nowadays call it depression), are notoriously liable to suicide and suicidal thoughts, as Burton emphasized in his *Anatomy of Melancholy*.[39] Hamlet returns to brood on the problem of self-slaughter in the third soliloquy; inhibiting that stoic self-sufficiency which would enable him to put an end to his troubles with 'a bare bodkin', is the 'conscience' that makes cowards of us all.[40] This, at the simplest level of understanding, is the issue debated in that soliloquy: 'To be or not to be', that is to say,

---

[38] Genesis 9: 5; see also Exodus 20: 13 and Wisdom of Solomon 1: 12. All these are debated by Donne in *Biathanatos* (printed 1647), Part 3.

[39] Robert Burton, *Anatomy of Melancholy*, Part I, sect. 4, member i (London: B. Blake, 1836), 284–90.

[40] Not everyone agrees. Eleanor Prosser (*Hamlet's Revenge* (London: Oxford University Press, 1967) 159–60) argues strongly that the speech is not about suicide; Harold Jenkins, (*Hamlet*, Arden Shakespeare (London: Methuen, 1982), 485–7) argues that the choice of ending one's life with a bare bodkin is an incidental feature of the speech introduced at line 70 only to be dismissed. Philip Edwards, on the other hand, (*Hamlet*, New Cambridge Shakespeare (Cambridge: Cambridge University Press, 1985), 48–50), adopts the more traditional position of critics from Warburton onwards and sees suicide as the issue from the beginning of the speech. Irving Ribner, another recent editor, concurs. The debate continues.

to live or to die. It is Job's problem. His wife urges him to 'curse God and die', to end his sore distraction, his torments, with a bare bodkin. Irrationally, he makes the harder choice of living and bearing witness, even though his hope is gone and, with it, his health and dignity. It is precisely here that biblical man parts company with Brutus and Antony and their admirers among the stoics of the Renaissance. 'Choose life that thou mayst live' the Deuteronomist had said (Deuteronomy 30: 19). The limit of logical understanding is here marked by a tautology that would have been incomprehensible to the Greeks and Romans. Life it declares is simply an ultimate value; as such it obligates in spite of everything.

The issue of suicide is at the cutting edge of the argument between stoicism and Christianity down the ages and, not surprisingly, it becomes a central moral and philosophical question for the men of Shakespeare's time and later. Not only Donne but Milton too in *Samson Agonistes* is troubled over the question of self-inflicted death. He characteristically seeks an accommodation between the two opposite drives by concentrating attention on the last day of Samson's life. At that point it would appear that his hero finds a satisfactory balance between the stoic readiness for death and the dynamic code of the Puritans expressed in the biblical verse, 'Up therefore and be doing, and the Lord will be with thee' (1 Chronicles 22: 16). But this is only a theoretical accommodation. Although Milton observes the formal rules for tragedy, the essential downward curve is in fact missing. Death, that ultimate goal of the stoic, the consummation he so devoutly wishes, is, we might say, swallowed up in victory! It hardly touches us. As a result, Samson fails to convince as tragic hero. Shakespeare does better with *Hamlet*. That play maintains the *agon* throughout. The biblical model which commands life and redemption struggles against the powerful downward drag of death which governs the fate of the tragic hero.

Of course the conflict is not so simple. The debate is not simply between ancient tragedy and stoicism on the one hand and the Bible on the other. The Christianity that Hamlet was heir to itself harboured contradictions. As against the good Ghost of the Catholics who would normally be doing time in Purgatory, there was the Protestant Ghost who almost certainly was a goblin damned. That was one of Hamlet's problems. But on the question of life or death as set out in the third soliloquy, the thinking of the Church, whether Protestant or Catholic, was marked by deeper tensions and anomalies. Whilst Job's decision and the Deuteronomic imperative to 'choose life' represent an important strand, there was also to set against that a strong evangelical bent to otherwordliness. Paul says very simply 'I am crucified with Christ' (Galatians 2: 20). The figure on the Cross is the supreme model for imitation. In that sense not life but death is the ideal. Since 'flesh and blood cannot inherit the kingdom of God', it follows that the other world is a better place than this one. And Paul goes on to say, 'We shall not all sleep, but we shall all be changed' (1 Corinthians 15: 50–1). These thoughts surely lurk behind Hamlet's third soliloquy.

> To die, to sleep—
> No more; and by a sleep to say we end
> The heartache and the thousand natural shocks
> That flesh is heir to—'tis a consummation
> Devoutly to be wished

Here the stoic death-wish, far from clashing with Christian principles, comes to strengthen the faith in an otherwordly destiny. To die is to sleep no more but to be translated into a more blissful state. Hamlet is here also echoing the burial service as set out in the Elizabethan Book of Common Prayer which speaks of the death of the elect as 'our perfect consummation and bliss'. But the word 'consummation', in the sense of a consuming away, has also been remembered from Florio's translation of Montaigne's essay 'On Physiognomie' where he remarks

If it [death] be a consummation [anéantissement] of ones being, it is also an amendment and entrance into a long and quiet night. Wee finde nothing so sweete in life, as a quiet rest and gentle sleepe, and without dreames.[41]

Death for the secular-minded Montaigne, a latter-day stoic, is the end of all, the dissolving of the Self in the *mundus*, the passage into a dreamless and unending sleep. For the author of the Prayer Book it is the entrance into bliss. But for both it is a

---

[41] Michel de Montaigne, *Essays*, iii. 12, trans. John Florio (London: Oxford University Press, 1906), iii. 351.

'consummation devoutly to be wished'! Hamlet in short, in facing the choice of being and not being was poised not only between a biblical and a Pagan option, between stoical suicide and the example of Job, but between different and conflicting possibilities within the Christian dispensation itself, consisting as it did of a not-wholly-resolved antithesis between Old Testament activism and New Testament pietism. Suicide was ruled out by the canon law of the Church, but in focusing on it as he does in this play, Shakespeare has touched a deep nerve in Western culture as a whole. It was a problem which Christians in the seventeenth century and later would debate without finding a wholly satisfying solution.

It sometimes seems in fact that the fundamental issue in *Hamlet* is suicide, not revenge. It is in relation to suicide that the real *agon* is played out. Likewise, it becomes a major issue in the scenes between Gloucester and Edgar in the fourth act of *King Lear*. Edgar, a survivor like Lot, or Noah, or Isaac, or Jacob, here spells out the biblical-Hebraic option more explicitly than anyone in *Hamlet*. But in *Hamlet* the debate, starting with the first soliloquy, is more interior, more intense, and, also, more continuous. We return to it in the conversation of the Gravediggers where, in a comic inversion (of the same kind as 'his biting is immortal'), Ophelia is described as one who 'wilfully seeks her own salvation'—a phrase which catches both opposed Christian attitudes. But in principle their comic exchange, like the comments of the Countryman in *Antony and Cleopatra*, articulates the fundamental biblical criticism of what we see going forward on the stage—in this case the death of Ophelia illustrating in its shocking inevitability that suicide is the norm of tragedy. Their reaction is to treat this phenomenon in the way that contemporary moralists treated the cult of personal revenge, namely, as part of the heritage of Pagan, in particular, Graeco-Roman culture, preserved in the upper-class code of honour. This sociological aspect is comically glanced at in the conversation of these (literally) down-to-earth clowns:

OTHER. Will you ha'the truth on't? If this had not been a gentlewoman, she should have been buried out o' Christian burial.

CLOWN. Why, there thou sayst—and the more pity that great folk should have countenance in this world to drown or hang themselves more than their even-Christen.

The Clowns here, like the Countryman in *Antony and Cleopatra* and the Gatekeeper in *Macbeth*, do not merely supply comic banter; they represent a levelling Christian point of view. And this point of view (as in Augustine's writings) is ultimately subversive not only of social rank and distinction, but also of received literary standards, in this case, of the high mode of tragedy itself. The Countryman, by comically exploding Cleopatra's immortal longings, had in effect questioned the myth pattern which governed that play; likewise, the Gravediggers here, in linking suicide with upper-class privilege and in condemning both in the name of a Christian ethic, are undermining one of the foundations of Shakespeare's theatre. For if they had their way we would be left not only without the Roman plays but also without *Othello*, *Romeo and Juliet*, *Hamlet*, and a good deal else besides. Thus if Hamlet is faced with the existential choice of being and not being, it would be true to say that on this issue Shakespeare too, as tragic author, also confronts the choice of 'to be or not to be'! The scene is loaded in the end in favour of Ophelia and the pathos of her 'virgin crants', but the two Clowns are admirably impartial in their judgements, making no allowance for tragic heroines and their right to die.

This question of suicide persists to the end of the play when Horatio, who has consistently represented the stoic option, makes ready to accompany his dying friend in the accepted Roman manner by drinking what is left of the poisoned cup, declaring at the same time 'I am more an antique Roman than a Dane'. Hamlet passionately commands him to desist.

> If thou didst ever hold me in thy heart,
> Absent thee from felicity a while,
> And in this harsh world draw thy breath in pain
> To tell my story.

> (v. ii. 325–8)

Death he says is the easier option. To survive to tell the tale is the harder course. Here again is the accent of Job. Job in chapter 3 wishes to be dead, but that wish must be withstood. Hamlet says the same. Survival and witness matter more than such 'felicity'. In enacting this debate between the Bible and an important strand of pre-Christian ethical doctrine, Hamlet and Horatio are completing a conversation which began with the words:

There are more things in heaven and earth, Horatio,
Than are dreamt of in your philosophy.

(I. v. 166–7)

These two admonitory speeches, one coming at the end of the
play, the other near its beginning, not only serve as an *inclusio*
to frame the whole actions on the stage but give us a key to its
central dilemma, that expressed more oracularly as 'to be or
not to be'.

The density of biblical echo and reference is impressive. It
becomes most pointed in the Gravediggers' scene in Act V. This
occupies the same strategic position in relation to the play's ending as the corresponding episodes which we noted in *Julius Caesar*
and *Antony and Cleopatra*. There a kind of biblical counterplot could momentarily be glimpsed. Here in *Hamlet* there had
been a higher degree of explicitness all along. But now in the
scene in the graveyard at the beginning of Act V, the biblical
notion of time and memory receives direct and unambiguous
emphasis. It is a comic scene but this comedy does not render
it of less consequence for the understanding of the play as a
whole. On the contrary, the comic characters with their London
accents (like the Countryman bearing his basket of figs in *Antony
and Cleopatra*), are here a bridging device connecting the action
on the stage with the lives of the audience in the theatre. When
they speak of Christian burial and the need of salvation they
speak of matters which are nearer to that audience than the
Senecan revenge cycle.

The scene is among other things a comic exercise in biblical
hermeneutics. The two Clowns engage in a discussion regarding the Bible: 'How dost thou understand the Scripture?' asks
the First Clown and proceeds to a witty interpretation of the
verse in Genesis 3 which speaks of Adam as a tiller of the soil.
Adam must have been, among other things, the first gravedigger and a gravedigger builds houses that will last till doomsday. Here is the biblical span of human history from Adam to
doomsday; but graves, he suggests, are the only houses that last
that long. When Hamlet enters, he takes up the conversation.
Holding a skull in his hand, he ponders on time and memory. How long will a man lie in the earth till his body decays?
Alexander the Great in a physical sense is now no more than

a piece of clay with which one might stop up a beer-barrel; but this would be to ignore the memory of him which still endures. Which is more real? Can memory measure itself against death? On being told that the skull he has picked up is that of Yorick, the King's jester, he brings Yorick back to life in a marvellous passage of imaginative recall. Life affirms itself against death, the *then* of a past which still, incredibly, lives, against the *now* of our immediate apprehensions:

I knew him Horatio, a fellow of infinite jest, of most excellent fancy, he hath borne me on his back a thousand times—and now how abhorred in my imagination it is! My gorge rises at it. Here hung those lips that I have kissed I know not how oft. Where be your gibes now? your gambols, your songs, your flashes of merriment that were wont to set the able on a roar? Not one now, to mock your own grinning? Quite chop-fallen? (v. i. 156–63)

Hamlet is in effect again saying, 'Look here upon this picture, and on this.' There is the stench of death, the *now* represented by the skull, but there is also the ongoingness of memory which reaches back to Adam and forward to doomsday. Are we bound by the finalities of Nature, according to which all that lives must die? Or do we gain a ground beyond Nature through memory, through those narratives which are communicated to us from the past and which we in turn transmit to the future?

6

What is involved in the memory-type drama which I am seeking to define is not merely a different set of ideas and a different plot structure but a mode of discourse which has no equivalent in the rhetoric inherited from the classical stage. This mode owes something to the religious meditation as practised on the Continent by Ignatius of Loyola and Luis de Granada and in the England of Shakespeare's time by Joseph Hall in prose and by Donne, Southwell, and others in verse. Hamlet's 'meditation' on Yorick's skull just quoted would serve as a good example. L. L. Martz has remarked that in Luis de Granada's *Of Prayer and Meditation*, first published in English in 1582, we may note 'the very poise of Hamlet in the graveyard scene'.[42] The skull which describes its present bare and empty state while reflecting ironically on past glories is a commonplace of this devotional tradition. Some of the practitioners actually kept a skull in their rooms to meditate upon.

Hamlet touches on the same themes and adopts the same poses as these devotional writers. But he does more than that; his typical discourse seems often to display the same rhetorical structure as the religious meditations of his time. The typical meditation would begin with a descriptive thesis or act of memory, called in the manuals of meditation, the 'composition of place' or *protasis*. This could be an account of a skull in a graveyard, or it could be the motion of the heavens as in Psalm 8 or the opening of Psalm 19.[43] Indeed that psalm, which actually speaks reflexively of 'the meditation of mine heart', was regarded as a particular model for the soul in meditation. But almost any occurrence or sight which came one's way—all occasions in fact—would serve to start off the meditative process —the sight of a spider in the window, a flower in the garden, or (as in one of Hall's early meditations) 'a harlot carted'. But random though the starting-point might be, this was no idle musing. The second part or *apodosis* consisted of an act of understanding, the scene, or event, or memory presented in the first part being here analysed and interpreted by the meditating subject so as to bring it into relation with his major interests and responsibilities. In the final part, the speaker reaches his conclusion in the form of a vow, or resolution, or prayer. This procedure integrated three functions of the mind, memory, reason, and will, in a purposive movement. Wit was involved but it was wit of a serious kind.

One of Hall's later 'Occasional Meditations', for example, starts with the sight of a beggar in the street:

---

[42] L. L. Martz, *The Poetry of Meditation* (New Haven: Yale University Press, 1954), 137–8, 324; cited also in Prosser, *Hamlet's Revenge*, 220–30.
[43] Cf. Robert Bellarmin, *The Mind's Ascent to God by a Ladder of Created Things*, trans. Monialis (London: Mowbray, 1925), 92; Hall, *The Art of Divine Meditation* (1606), ch. 3, in *Works* (1634), 96; id., *Occasional Meditations* (1630), no. 1 in *The Works of Bishop Joseph Hall*, ed. P. Wynter (Oxford: Oxford University Press, 1863), x. 121.

With what zeal does this man sue! with what feeling expressions! with how forcible importunity. When I meant to pass by him with silence, yet his clamour draws words from me.[44]

In the ratiocinative passage which follows he reflects on, and interiorizes, this remembered scene, applying the beggar's situation analogically to his own:

Why do I not thus to my God? I am sure I want no less, than the neediest: the danger of my want is greater: the alms I crave is better; the store and mercy of the Giver, infinitely more.

He is then in the posture of prayer and can carry the exercise to its proper conclusion.

Hamlet's great soliloquies are not exactly religious meditations, but they follow this same rhetorical pattern. Indeed his second soliloquy, inspired by the sight of the weeping actor, has more than a slight resemblance to Hall's discourse on the importunate beggar. Hamlet begins by recalling the scene he has just witnessed:

> Is it not monstrous that this player here,
> But in a fiction, in a dream of passion,
> Could force his soul so to his own conceit
> That from her working all his visage wanned.
> Tears in his eyes, distraction in's aspect,
> A broken voice, and his whole function suiting
> With forms to his conceit?
>
> (II. ii. 503–9)

In the *apodosis* Hamlet applies the lesson in argumentative fashion to himself and his present situation.

> What would he do,
> Had he the motive and the cue for passion
> That I have?

And he ends with an act of will, namely, the decision to mount the play:

> I'll have these players
> Play something like the murder of my father
> Before mine uncle.

[44] *Occasional Meditations*, no. 138, ibid. 186.

The last of Hamlet's formal soliloquies—'How all occasions do inform against me'—displays the threefold pattern with even greater clarity. The 'occasion' is the sight of the army of Fortinbras marching across the stage on their way to fight in Poland. In the dialectical passage he tries to analyse his own very different behaviour:

> Now whether it be
> Bestial oblivion, or some craven scruple
> Of thinking too precisely on th'event—
> A thought which quartered hath but one part wisdom
> And ever three parts coward—I do not know
> Why yet I live to say this thing's to do,
> Sith I have cause, and will, and strength, and means
> To do't.

(IV. iv. 39–44)

Having argued himself into a desire to emulate the Fortinbras-model, he ends with the vow or act of will: 'Oh from this time forth, | My thoughts be bloody or be nothing worth.'

This last line, it will be noted, turns sharply to the future ('from this time forth') just as the preceding argument focuses on the present ('I do not know | Why yet I live to say this thing's to do . . . | How stand I then . . .'). Indeed, instead of speaking of memory, reason, and will, we could more properly define the tripartite structure of this mode of discourse in terms of past, present, and future. This is already clear in the first of Hamlet's soliloquies where he is first tormented by the felt discontinuity between past and present ('Must I remember?'), whilst at the end he looks to the dangers ahead—'It is not, nor it cannot, come to good'—and decides on an appropriate response: 'But break, my heart, for I must hold my tongue.' This dynamic movement is the key also to the form practised by the meditation-writers. Recollected experience is interiorized, translated into the present tense of the meditating subject, and then used as an instrument for shaping a future.

Again, when considering this particular mode of discourse, it may be noted that in this regard too Augustine's contribution was fundamental. His *Confessions* were amongst the earliest and most influential models for the meditation-writers in England and elsewhere.[45] They have inwardness, intensity, and the determination to derive spiritual profit from the remembered experiences of his life. In the chapter quoted earlier (Book IX, chapter 4), he recalls a period when he had suffered terribly from the toothache. His recovery from that ordeal strengthened his faith and, at the same time, the memory of his vulnerability guarded him from spiritual complacency for the future. In all the passages of his life starting with the earliest memories of his infancy when he first began to use articulate speech,[46] he traces the dealings with him of his God and his Saviour. He is thus writing a kind of sacred history or drama, potent for his salvation and that of others who might read his book:

For the confessions of my past sins . . . whenas they read and hear, they stir up the heart that it may not sleep in despair, and say: I cannot . . .[47]

As with Hamlet, such remembering (guided in this instance by Psalm 51) sharply underscores the break between past and present: 'This is the fruit of my Confessions, not of what I have been but of what I am.' But it is also directed towards a future when the meaning of this internal drama will be played out and its promise fulfilled: 'and no ways giving over what thou hast begun in me, finish up what in me is imperfect.'[48] Such memory-writing is thus teleologically poised, past, present, and future being bound purposefully together. It is dramatic discourse of a special and urgent kind.

One other dramatic feature of this meditation-discourse must be pointed out. Augustine's *Confessions* like the meditations of Hall and Donne are personal, reflective, concerned with the life of the soul and the sufferings of the body, but they are not monologic. They are in essence dialogic. Everywhere, even in the midst of abstruse philosophizing, Augustine will turn to his God in debate, in contrition, in anguished supplication:

And I confess to thee, O Lord, that I yet know not what time is; yea, I confess again to thee, O Lord, that I know well enough, how that I speak this in time . . . How then come I to know this, seeing I know

---

[45] Cf. Helen C. White, *English Devotional Literature [Prose]* (Madison, Wis.: University of Wisconsin Studies in Language and Literature, 1931), 75–8.

[46] Augustine, *Confessions*, I. 8 (i. 25).   [47] Ibid., x. 3 (ii. 79).

[48] Ibid., x. 4 (ii. 83).

not what time is? . . . Woe is me, that do not so much as know, what
that is which I know not!⁴⁹

Characteristically, he ends with a verse from Psalm 18: 'Thou
shalt light my candle, O Lord my God, thou shalt enlighten
my darkness.' Hamlet does not engage in such colloquy; he
does not address God directly in this manner, and yet, in their
anguished tone and in their question-and-answer form, Hamlet's
soliloquies (and, we may add, those of Angelo in *Measure for
Measure*) remind us not a little of Augustine's *Confessions*. They
are only monologues in a formal sense; they may more correctly
be defined as interior dialogues. In this Hamlet's soliloquies
are essentially different from the familiar essay as practised by
Montaigne—to which they are sometimes compared. Montaigne's
essays are the work of the secular imagination, and of a man
who is happy to be alone. It is his own picture he draws, he
tells us; he is the subject of his book. Hamlet is not given the
same opportunity to cultivate his own garden; his privacy is
constantly invaded ('Who calls me villain, breaks my pate
across, I . . . who does me this?'); he is charged with a task. As
a result he does not write familiar essays; his soliloquies are
more intensely dramatic than that—and more tormented. Thus,
whilst he has, like Montaigne, undergone the crisis of modernity, he is haunted by presences. He does not actually engage
in prayer, but he makes that gesture from time to time. At the
end of his third soliloquy, he turns to Ophelia with the words:
'Nymph, in thy orisons I Be all my sins remembered.'

The primal scene on the battlements in which Hamlet receives his task is of course the most shattering of all dialogues.
In the course of that scene a supernatural visitor addresses his
quaking son and lays on him a commandment ending with the
words, 'Remember me!' We would surely not be wrong to view
Hamlet's meditative discourses, involving as they do the discipline of memory, reason, and will, as the response to that command. His quest for enlightenment which continues through
the play would then stem from that originary covenant-moment.
And yet, dialogic though they are, it is necessary to say that
these discourses are not directly related to the dialogue then

⁴⁹ Ibid., XI. 25, 9 (ii. 265).

inaugurated. On the contrary, there is a manifest disconnection between the soliloquies and the scene on the battlements. During these passages of reflection and self-questioning, Hamlet seems sometimes to forget about his meeting with the Ghost altogether! Notoriously, after being granted an interview with a visitor from the other world, he speaks in his third soliloquy of the life beyond as 'the undiscovered country from whose bourn | No traveller returns'! And it is not only the Ghost that he forgets; he seems to forget the business of the play altogether and why he is in it. William Empson speaks of 'the collapse of interest in the story'.[50] It is as though there is a dislocation of the interior drama represented by the soliloquies from the external action of the play. Thus, after determining in the first soliloquy to keep silent about his mother's hasty second marriage, he takes up the subject almost immediately afterwards in conversation with Horatio. Similarly, after determining at the close of the fourth soliloquy that his thoughts from now on will be bloody or be nothing worth, he immediately embarks for England at the King's behest!

This relative disconnection between Hamlet's inner drama and the outer action to which he finds himself driven would seem to be bound up with two factors: the first is the essential duality of that very encounter with the Ghost. Whilst the Ghost's command launches Hamlet on his quest ('Now to my word: | It is "Adieu, adieu, remember me"'), he cannot serve Hamlet as a guide to the spiritual life. He is too much like the ghost of Thyestes in Seneca's tragedy of *Agamemnon*, calling for blood and vengeance by his descendants against his brother and his brother's descendants in an unending cycle of retaliation, to serve as a spiritual model. And, what is more, Hamlet's father has, as he himself tells us, a pretty heavy prison record to live down. It is rather like Magwitch trying to tell Pip how to become a gentleman. Like Magwitch the Ghost can blindly point the way, but Hamlet will have to learn the integrated meaning for himself. He will have to do what the Ghost cannot do—namely, to transform revenge into justice, to combine Nature with Grace. This is the quest that he conducts in the great soliloquies.

The second factor which makes for a certain disjunction between the soliloquies and the revenge plot has to do with the

---

[50] Empson, *Essays on Shakespeare*, 87, 98.

nature of this new mode of interior discourse and its place in the total economy of the drama. The function of such discourse is almost exactly the opposite of that provided for in Aristotle's *Poetics*. There speech and thought had served the ends of the plot. The *mythos* was the controlling factor; language and thought were obedient to that.[51] Here in this covenantal mode there is a new balance between thought and action. The most vital movements of the drama take place not on the boards of the theatre but in a more interior space. But it is not simply a question of interiority versus exteriority. Brutus in *Julius Caesar* is an introspective figure, yet his monologues, unlike those of Hamlet, are locked tightly into the plot: they serve its interests, leading on from what has gone before and preparing us for what is to come. His speech beginning 'It must be by his death' (II. i. 10), and concluding with 'And kill him in the shell', is the hinge on which the plot of the conspiracy turns. In *Hamlet* the interior discourse is much more open-ended, yielding something more like a counter-drama only loosely connected to the predetermined, classical design of the revenge plot. This spiritual activity, set in motion by random events or circumstances, will in the end come to shape the outer action of the plot but it will do so in ways that cannot be precisely anticipated. In the end the inward moral changes will be reflected in outer events with the former proving to be the crucial dramatic factor. The plot will ultimately come to serve the interests of the discourse; the action of the mind will shape and govern action in the world—this is the novelty of *Hamlet* and indeed of much of Shakespeare's mature dramaturgy.

Under the stress of the changes enacted in the meditative process, then, Hamlet will emerge from what I have termed the interior dialogue of the soliloquies into a dialogic engagement with history in the course of which he will not only meditate, but act and be acted upon. Till now Hamlet had not always seemed to know which play exactly he was in. Now in the fifth act he knows. From now on, inner consciousness and outer experience will beat in time. This is the significance of the events enacted in Act V and the line of meditation which begins in the graveyard.

[51] *Poetics*, VI. 16, and XIX. 1–3.

7

We thus return to Hamlet's meditation in the graveyard which opens with a typical composition of place or act of memory —namely, the vivid evocation of the figure of Yorick whom he remembers from his infancy and who has been dead for twenty-three years. It is his skull that Hamlet now holds in his hand. This meditation is not conducted in soliloquy form but in the form of a conversation with Horatio. The dialectical part which follows likewise consists of a series of questions addressed to Horatio: 'Why may not imagination trace the noble dust of Alexander, till a find it stopping a bunghole?' Horatio responds by expressing a doubt about the weird logic of such a proposition: ' 'Twere to consider too curiously to consider so.' But Hamlet goes on to prove his thesis in a series of rigid syllogistic steps:

as thus: Alexander died, Alexander was buried, Alexander returneth to dust, the dust is earth, of earth we make loam, and why of that loam whereto he was converted may they not stop a beer-barrel? (v. i. 171–9)

The all-inclusive reality of death which dominates the now of this scene, would seem to have obliterated not only the past glory of Alexander the Great but all other human achievements whatever. To this favour we must come.

The resolution or act of will completing his meditation on the skull, comes in the next scene, after an interval of some 300 lines.[52] Hamlet, invited by the King to undertake a bout with Laertes, using rapiers, has a sense of uneasiness. Death is in the air. But he comes to the conclusion, again in conversation with Horatio, that the future cannot be escaped:

We defy augury. There is special providence in the fall of a sparrow. If it be now, 'tis not to come; if it be not to come, it will be now; if it be not now, yet it will come—the readiness is all. (v. ii. 192–5)

'The readiness is all' encapsulates the dynamic thrust of these meditations. They are not general reflections on life and death

[52] Eleanor Prosser demonstrates the close connection between the meditation in the graveyard and Hamlet's speech on the fall of a sparrow in the following scene, supporting her argument by an analogous instance from Luis de Granada's meditation on graveyards and corpses (*Hamlet's Revenge*, 223, 225, 230).

but exercises in facing the future. From a recollection of past experience and an analysis of the bearing of that experience on the present, we move forward in this example also to a confrontation with the future. Readiness in this context signifies a tense expectancy and also a readiness for action when the moment presents itself. Hamlet is after all going to act decisively and vigorously in the course of this scene. Readiness here is the stance recommended by the psalmist when he speaks of those who 'wait on the Lord' (Psalm 37: 34). Such readiness is far from being a state of disinterestedness—as Harold Bloom has suggested.[53] It is more like the awaiting of a sign; when that sign comes, one acts.

Providence and its workings are very much in Hamlet's mind during this final act of the play. Here providence is said to take a hand in the fall of a sparrow, as the Gospel had taught—'Are not two sparrows sold for a farthing? and one of them shall not fall on the ground without your Father' (Matthew 10: 29). If that is so, it follows that 'Heaven' is no less 'ordinant' in determining Hamlet's affairs and those of the Danish kingdom. He is called upon to respond accordingly, i.e. to 'wait upon the Lord'. He is now acutely conscious of being guided, challenged, and admonished from moment to moment. In short he is in a dialogue situation and providence is his partner in this dialogue. This awareness was especially strong on board ship when, like Augustine in many passages of his life, he was persuaded that 'there's a divinity that shapes our ends, | Rough-hew them how we will'. Such notions are often scoffed at today. They were not scoffed at in Shakespeare's time. Witness most of the historiography of the period, including Ralegh's *History of the World* and witness also the fact that the Pilgrim Fathers, Shakespeare's direct contemporaries, were upheld by precisely such an awareness.

Providentially unable to sleep, Hamlet had crept into the cabin where Rosencrantz and Guildenstern were sleeping; there he 'fingered their packet' and discovered the design on his life. Providentially also, he had his father's signet-ring in his purse and was able to rewrite the commission with orders for the execution of Rosencrantz and Guildenstern, seal it, and put it back in its place. In all these transactions he felt himself guided by

---

[53] Bloom, *Ruin the Sacred Truths*, 58–9.

heaven. As a result the deaths of the two spies are he says 'not near my conscience'. Agnostic critics generally conclude that such guidance can only be misguidance or self-persuasion. That being so, they persuade themselves that Shakespeare could not possibly have intended his hero to share such primitive beliefs or that they are signs of an early draft that Shakespeare had not finished tidying up! Shakespeare's own beliefs, even if they were accessible to us, are not our concern; Hamlet's are. And Hamlet was surely no agnostic either in this scene or anywhere else in the play; nor was he squeamish on the matter of judicial execution.

The meditation in the graveyard, leading up to these remarks on special providence, signifies therefore Hamlet's new and heightened sense of being addressed by events and circumstances. His typical discourse now expresses a responsiveness of the self to that which is outside the self. World and Word have joined; he feels himself to be acting in concert with providence. This change is also defined for us by means of a particular kind of trope which we have already briefly looked at, namely, the theatre-trope. In Act V this serves to explicate Hamlet's dialogic situation and the new ground of existence that it implies. Up to the fifth act, we find two separate, and alternate, uses of the trope. There are on the one hand the theatre-images associated with the melodramatic appearance of the Ghost; on the other hand, there are the references to Hamlet's own play-acting, especially after the revelation on the battlements. This is climaxed by the actual production which he organizes and stage-manages ('the play's the thing | Wherein I'll catch the conscience of the king'). The two do not combine; they are even in a manner in conflict. Hamlet unwillingly steps on to a stage which this 'fellow in the cellarage' (like the Weird Sisters in *Macbeth*) has set up for him; afterwards he mounts his own performance out of a suspicion that he may have been tricked by the histrionics of the Ghost ('the spirit that I have seen | May be a devil').

But now, instead of seeking to manage his own play, Hamlet will humbly co-operate with the metaphysical order—what I have termed the play-without-the-play. It will be a joint dramatic production; there will be neither constraint nor the arrogant assertion of a self-conceived design. He expresses this sense of a collaborative proceeding in speaking of the sea-voyage:

> Our indiscretion sometimes serve us well,
> When our deep plots do pall, and that should learn us
> There's a divinity does shape our ends,
> Rough-hew them how we will.
>
> (v. ii. 8–11)

The word 'plots' keeps the image of the theatre before us; the deep plot by which Hamlet had earlier sought to catch the conscience of the King is here abandoned; and instead there will be a more indirect and hesitant kind of dramaturgy. A little further down he represents his thwarting of the design of the two spies by another group of theatre references:

> Being thus benetted round with villainies,
> Or I could make a prologue to my brains,
> They had begun the play.
>
> (v. ii. 29–31)

His brains are here working almost independently of his will, 'the play' as he calls it being written in a kind of spontaneous collaboration between himself and the divinity that shapes our ends.

Here is a further connotation of the phrase 'the readiness is all'. It comes to reinforce the theatre-trope. It suggests the readiness to respond to the signs which come to one from this larger play, the readiness, in a word, to come in on one's cue and perform one's part. Osric, to whose message Hamlet is here reacting, represented one such sign. His theatrical gestures and antics had given us a kind of comic version of the Ghost's fustian in Act I. Fantastic though this visitation is, it is Hamlet's cue and he will respond more readily than he responded to the Ghost's summons in Act I and Act III: the readiness is all. The rapier contest itself which follows has clear theatrical overtones; the word 'play' is prominent. The Queen sends a message to Hamlet asking him to 'use some gentle entertainment to Laertes, before you fall to *play*' (v. ii. 180–1); Hamlet accordingly makes friendly overtures to Laertes, saying he will 'this brother's wager frankly *play*' (v. ii. 225). The scene as a whole matches the Mousetrap scene in Act III. Some producers wisely emphasize this by similar seating and lighting arrangements.

But the similarity underlines the conspicuous difference; for the King is now stage-manager, taking over that function from Hamlet. It is he who now seeks to catch Hamlet by means of a carefully staged performance of his own. There is thus an exchange of roles; Hamlet will react to Claudius's initiatives, letting events take their own course until his moment comes. Claudius is the active, scheming figure, the masked actor, pursuing his own 'deep plot'. But in the course of the play which Claudius has so cunningly set up, the metaphysical powers will put on their instruments. It turns out not to be the play that Claudius had designed. Not only does providence take a hand, adapting Claudius's plot for its own very different purposes but the human figures, instead of behaving like puppets, display an unexpected degree of autonomy. Gertrude, Laertes, and Hamlet himself all fail to keep to their assigned roles in Claudius's play. That is why things go wrong. A greater power than he can contradict thwarts Claudius's intents, but that power paradoxically allows for a broad area of human freedom. That is part of the dialectic conveyed by the theatre-images. This particular image-complex indeed becomes the nearest thing we have to a key for the understanding of this, the subtlest and richest of Shakespeare's plays. In his final summarizing use of the theatre-image, Hamlet addresses the 'audience to this act'—the reference being both to the audience on the stage and that in the theatre—

> You that look pale and tremble at this chance,
> That are but mutes or audience to this act,
> Had I but time, as this fell sergeant death
> Is strict in his arrest, oh I could tell you—

> (v. ii. 313–16)

'This act' is first to be understood as Hamlet's final action in taking charge of the play and executing the King; it is also the 'act' that Claudius had planned and to which the assembled courtiers are 'mutes', i.e. actors with walk-on parts; and finally it is the 'act' being managed by providence on the theatre of the world and which, according to Sir Walter Ralegh, governs the destinies of 'the most mighty princes of the World'.

But we have yet to speak of one other important dimension, perhaps the most important of all. 'This act' is also in a more specific sense, the horror of the tragic stage, with its many dead. Three figures are already lying dead when these words are uttered and Hamlet will soon become the fourth. They have been preceded earlier in the play by four others all directly or indirectly slain by Hamlet. The 'act' referred to is thus that of 'this fell sergeant death' who presides over tragedy. Let there be no mistake about it. Death and supremely the death of the hero, are the centre and circumference of the tragic world; death occupies the whole stage and it has the last word. Moreover, we are satisfied that this should be so, but it is the satisfaction of a different wish from that which leads us to desire the triumph of righteousness in the world. It is more like the death-wish, the desire to loosen the bonds, to sink into the grave. Hamlet shares this desire. It is for him a consummation devoutly to be wished. He will embrace the 'felicity' which he denies to Horatio. Here is the final ironic distribution of roles: Horatio, the latter-day stoic, will obey the biblical imperative to live and testify; Hamlet who, in a biblically loaded scene of revelation had been chosen to put the world to rights, will perform the archetypal descent of the tragic hero into Hades. He will witness to the triumph of death.

And here too is the final and also perhaps the decisive implication of the phrase 'the readiness is all'. For if that phrase implies as I have argued a readiness to act, as well as the tense expectancy of the psalmist awaiting the promise of salvation in historical time, the phrase also implies almost the very opposite of that, namely, a passive readiness for death. This meaning is clearly required also by the context: 'there is special providence in the fall of a sparrow. If it be now 'tis not to come . . .' The 'it' refers to death which will come sooner or later; we must patiently attend to the will of providence in this as in everything else. Moreover, the phrase echoes the Gospels where Jesus, in anticipation of his approaching death, bids his followers be ready for his second coming at the end of time: 'Therefore be ye also ready: for in the hour that ye think not will the Son of man come' (Matthew 24: 44 and cf. Luke 12: 40).[54]

[54] It should be noted that the verse in Luke occurs in the same chapter as a variant of the passage on the fall of the sparrow already cited from Matthew 10: 29. Luke 12: 6 reads: 'Are not five sparrows bought for two farthings, and yet not one of them is forgotten before God?'

In short we have here an essential and crucial ambiguity. The words 'the readiness is all' bring together the legacies of the Hebrew and Christian testaments. They point to the *eschaton* and at the same time to historical vindications. In fact, the phrase that we are considering, and with it the whole pattern of the ending of this play, bring many contraries together. They seem to reconcile the forces which lead in the direction of death and tragedy with other, more life-affirming forces no less central to our culture. They seem to combine closure with openness in a seamless unity, to do justice simultaneously to the circular predetermined shape of the Senecan revenge plot and the more untidy but more challenging models of the quest and the pilgrimage. But of course this is all achieved by something akin to *trompe-l'œil*. In this amazing fifth act Hamlet carries out his revenge as the Renaissance man of honour and also by the same 'act' he discharges his high moral responsibility as the elected instrument of providence. It is a difficult balancing-act. And that in fact is what it is—a balancing-act, an illusion sufficient for the theatre and its needs. Opposites are not truly reconciled. It is only that the questions, the tensions, the ambivalences have been concealed in the richness of the texture. A well-nigh perfect example of this ambivalence is to be found in the phrase, 'There's a divinity that shapes our ends.' The 'ends' have been much argued about. Does that word in its context signify purpose or fate? The answer is that it signifies both. The first meaning points to a Hebraic perception of human life on earth as witnessing to a divine purpose still to be accomplished (cf. Isaiah 46: 9–13); the second meaning points to the 'end of the matter' in a different sense, i.e. the terminal point, the 'promis'd end' to which we all come at last and on which tragedy bids us gaze with horror and fascination:

> O proud death,
> What feast is toward in thine eternal cell!
>
> (v. ii. 343–4)

The tragic hero matches his pride against that of 'proud death'. He is gloriously defiant to the last. But he is lost. Death is total, the end of all. It is the end beyond which nothing is, only oblivion. Dionysus we must remind ourselves is essentially and above all things the god of death, 'the lord of dying and of the dead'.[55] That is why he presides over tragedy. But Shakespeare in this phrase—and indeed in this play more than any other of his plays—keeps alive the other option, ends in the other sense. There are ends beyond the end which tragedy exhibits. What matters is the future time when the story will continue to live in the world. Memory will then have gained its victory over death, openness over closure, and testimony over art. The options are left open and in the end we make our own choice.

[55] Otto, *Dionysus: Myth and Cult*, 196. Otto points out that, unlike Osiris, Dionysus is destroyed in the flower of his youth (195); he is strictly the god of death rather than of vegetation; see Otto, chs. 11 and 17 *passim*.

CHAPTER 4

King Lear: Organized Incoherence

The New Critics in their day were fond of drawing attention to the kind of paradoxes and multiple meanings that we have noted in the last act of *Hamlet*, in such phrases as 'the readiness is all' or 'a divinity that shapes our ends'. Another example would be 'the rest is silence' (v. ii. 337) where 'rest' signifies simultaneously a terminus, an eternal rest (as in Horatio's farewell a moment later—'And flights of angels sing thee to thy rest') and also the rest of the story which will go on in spite of the fact that Hamlet himself will now be silent, the phrase thus suggesting a dialectic of closure and openness. Dialectical elements of this kind were fashionably sought and found especially in seventeenth-century metaphysical lyrics of which the New Critics were especially fond. But the very term 'dialectical' as used in such contexts signified a reconciling of opposites, a logical contradiction which was due to be resolved. There would ultimately be unity, fusion, a happy, though hard-wrought, balance of conflicting parts. But I am arguing for something more radical than this, namely, an essential duality of structure not resolvable into some higher unity. Hamlet is really two plays at once. In one of these, the revenger and his victim are swept around in the same vicious circle of retaliation—there is no room for any significant moral advance, just the satisfaction of the completed circle, reflecting the order of Nature itself and its fulfilment in the death of the hero. In the other, there is set up a different, non-cyclical movement, that of the quest or pilgrimage. Here Hamlet is embarked on a voyage of self-discovery; he is the man with a burden on his back, a seeker after salvation. There is thus a metaphysical disjunction at the heart of the play. Such a disjunction is represented also by the positions taken by the critics who have sharply disagreed on the essential character of the play and its hero—one group, including Irving Ribner, Sister Miriam Joseph, and C. S. Lewis, seeing it as a play of redemption with Hamlet as a saviour-figure, another, seeing it 'as a study in degeneration from first to last'.[1] Nevertheless each maintains that its reading enables one to see the play as a coherent whole. What does not normally occur to either group is the possibility that the play may not be a coherent whole and that thus both readings may be right (and wrong).

It is of course the extraordinary richness of the texture which conceals the rift, thus creating an illusion of unity. The result is an achievement akin to medieval and Renaissance harmonistics. Jerome claimed (and no doubt believed) that the Hebrew Bible was written in Greek hexameters; humanists of the sixteenth century constructed an (apparently) seamless combination of heroic and Christian virtues which found its ultimate literary expression in Spenser's *Faerie Queene*. Here too the chasms and contradictions which separate Aristotle's Ethics from the Sermon on the Mount are deeply buried in the texture. But there is a difference. Spenser, unlike Shakespeare, not only persuades the reader; he persuades himself. He has an ideal of Christian humanism which he proceeds to represent in such figures as Britomart and the Redcrosse Knight. Shakespeare I would argue is not self-deceived. He creates an illusion of unity sufficient to hoodwink the spectators (and the critics too) but this too is a matter of artistic cunning. Unlike Spenser he does not have an integrated ideology to sell. What he has is rather an extraordinarily clear perception of the issues involved, of the unresolved conflicts which have beset Western Christianity from its beginnings, and which in the new radical phase of the Renaissance and the Reformation can no longer be glossed over. This is the *agon* which *Hamlet* enacts.

From this point of view, *King Lear* is of particular interest. There, the conflict of which we speak is not buried in the texture but is clearly exhibited for the audience. It becomes the very matter of the drama. As with *Hamlet* and the other plays we have considered, there is here too at the penultimate stage of the tragedy a scene powerfully loaded with Christian-biblical meaning. I refer, of course, to Act IV, scene vii, in which Cordelia, having found her father, provides him with healing and refuge

---

[1] John Vyvyan, *The Shakespearean Ethic* (London: Chatto and Windus, 1959), 55.

after his terrible ordeal in the storm. At that point father and daughter are clearly functioning in a biblical-type drama as they kneel to one another in tranquil restoration. The ritual of kneeling (drawn from *The True Chronicle Historie of King Leir*) is central to this scene. It suggests atonement and consecration,[2] whilst the presence (in the Quarto version) of the doctor and the sound of music likewise marks this as a redemptive moment. The religious charge is as clear as in the Gravedigger scene in *Hamlet*, the entry of the Countryman with a basket of figs in *Antony and Cleopatra*, or 'Enter a Doctor' towards the end of Act IV of *Macbeth*—scenes which in those plays also occur shortly before the catastrophe. It is this scene in *King Lear* on which the Christian school of critics chiefly dwell in arguing their case for Lear's play as a drama of salvation. And as far as that scene goes, they are right; it is a moment inconceivable in ancient tragedy. It gives us a true dialogue of soul and soul, a true mutual offering of unconstrained love which redeems the language of sale and barter in the love-test of Act I when Lear had given his lands to the highest bidder who said she loved him most. Now there is no sale; love itself, freely offered, is its own reward.

Behind this about-turn, as many critics have noted, is the parable of the Prodigal Son from Luke 15. Cordelia welcoming her father after his fearful exile, asks:

> And wast thou fain, poor father,
> To hovel thee with swine and rogues forlorn,
> In short and musty straw?
>
> (IV. vii. 38–40)

D. G. James notes that the roles of parent and child are reversed, the father now having returned and having been welcomed home is the returning prodigal.[3] However, a truer view sees this as a mutual process of love and forgiveness. Cordelia too has come a long way from her stoic immobility in Act I when she could

---

[2] See by the present author, 'Shakespeare and the Language of Gesture', *Shakespeare Studies*, 19 (1987), 239–51 (242). Kneeling is important throughout the play. In IV. vi, before throwing himself off the imaginary cliff, Gloucester kneels to the 'mighty gods', calling down their blessing upon Edgar (see below, section 5). In II. iv, the meaning of the sign is inverted as Lear kneels with an ironical plea to the absent Goneril, 'that you'll vouchsafe me raiment, bed, and food'.

[3] *The Dream of Learning* (Oxford: Oxford University Press, 1951), 120.

say nothing to gain her father's affection. She too is a kind of returning prodigal, bountiful now in her expressions of love and honour, as if to make good her earlier refusal of speech:

> Restoration hang
> Thy medecine on my lips, and let this kiss
> Repair those violent harms that my two sisters
> Have in thy reverence made!
>
> (IV. vii. 26–9)

Whoever is the returning prodigal, a new curve is here set up, not the downward fatal curve of tragedy but the upward curve of salvation-history. After his long estrangement from his daughter, Lear discovers a reason for living. We would expect him to express that discovery in a determination to endure. And that in fact is what he declares in his second and last meeting with Cordelia in Act V. 'So we'll live, and pray and sing', he declares and goes on to say

> we'll wear out,
> In a wall'd prison, packs and sects of great ones
> That ebb and flow by th'moon.
>
> (V. iii. 11, 17–19)

Not the ritual cycle of death and rebirth—the ebb and flow of the moon—as performed by 'great ones' but the harder trial of survival and witness is what he promises to them both.

This it would seem is where the play is going. But now comes the surprise: the upward and onward curve is sharply reversed. Shakespeare puts Lear back on the 'wheel of fire', thus snatching defeat out of the jaws of victory! There is no attempt at harmonizing as Shakespeare now substitutes his tragic ending for the far-off divine event to which the play had seemed to be moving. Our hopes are sharply and violently disappointed as in some Hardy novel where a fatal mischance—say a letter pushed accidentally under the carpet and thus failing to reach its addressee—governs the ending. Here Edmund, meaning to do some good, remembers too late that his writ is on the life of Lear and Cordelia. Consequently the messenger sent to countermand these orders fails to prevent the hanging of Cordelia. The tragic ending is in keeping with the atmosphere of storm and savagery established early in the play, but from another point

of view—one no less clearly established in the play—it is gratuit-
ous. We should note that it is moreover entirely Shakespeare's
invention and not required by any of his sources. In all the
previous versions of the story, Leir/Leyr died naturally of old
age.[4] Nor is Cordelia ever executed.[5] If we take Act V as a whole
from the 'gilded butterflies' speech at the beginning of scene iii
to the deaths of Cordelia and Lear at the end, Shakespeare
appears to weigh the merits of two alternative endings and to
choose the grimmer of the two. Or else, we could say that in
the sequence of events from the reunion of Lear and Cordelia
in Act IV, scene vii, until their deaths at the end of Act V, he
gives us thesis and antithesis but no synthesis, not even the illusion of a synthesis as in *Hamlet*. The only hint of a concession
is in the extra line and a half added in the Folio version of Lear's
final speech:

> Do you see this? Look on her, look, her lips,
> Look there, look there!

> (V. iii. 310–11)

Bradley, basing himself on these words, proposed that Lear dies
of joy, believing Cordelia to be alive.[6] But even if there is a hint
of consolation here for the dying Lear (a point we shall discuss
later) there is no consolation whatever for the audience. It knows
when one is dead. And this cruellest of all tragic deaths, that
of Cordelia, is not mitigated for us in any way. Shakespeare has
set before us life and death, good and evil—and he has chosen
death! Death is the sovereign event. And tragedy here pays to
it its dark tribute. This ending expresses a powerful current in
the play and yet there is a contrary and equally powerful movement which resists it. Hence Nahum Tate's version with its happy
ending which, wooden though it is, held the stage for 150 years
as the more acceptable version of the play. Tate, as well as the

---

[4] Thus in all the sources adduced by Geoffrey Bullough (*Narrative and Dramatic Sources of Shakespeare*, vii (London: Routledge and Kegan Paul, 1973)). Hereafter Bullough.

[5] However, in Geoffrey of Monmouth, Holinshed, and Spenser (*Fairie Queene*, II. x. 32), she is said to have slain herself in prison. But this occurs several years later as a result of harassment by her nephews, and without reference to her part in Lear's ordeal (Bullough, 315–16, 319, 334).

[6] *Shakespearean Tragedy* (London: Macmillan, 1949), 291.

producers and audiences who went along with his version, were also employing categories of understanding and response which have their basis in the play that Shakespeare wrote.

I am arguing in short that the play is to a certain degree incoherent. It was for long a shibboleth of criticism, especially Shakespearian criticism, that great works of art must have a unified tendency or structure. It is this Aristotelian assumption which needs to be questioned. It underlies much of the more traditionalist criticism of *King Lear*. Thus Irving Ribner speaks of *King Lear* as a 'neatly unified whole'.[7] R. B. Heilman finds plenty of thematic paradoxes in the play—nakedness and dress, sight and blindness, etc.—but beneath are the everlasting arms. There is he says 'an order and an underlying reality'.[8] Governing all is the process of spiritual rehabilitation undergone by the tragic hero. In a briefer study Heilman remarks that 'Lear weaves Gloucester into his brilliant synthesis of the world and the play'.[9]

From this point of view there is practically a consensus regarding the symphonic or musical character of the action of *King Lear*. It goes back to Coleridge and to Harley Granville-Barker who speaks of 'orchestration' and 'harmony'. An orchestral image dominates much *Lear* criticism and has even been made the focus of special studies.[10] E. E. Stoll speaks of the 'musical method' of the play.[11] Among more recent critics, Stanley Cavell relates the play to the tonal mode of the sonata,[12] whilst Jonathan Miller has referred to *King Lear* as 'a complicated symphony'.[13] Daniel Seltzer makes the musical analogy the cornerstone of his essay on the play.[14]

It cannot be denied that the orchestra is, in reference to *King Lear*, a very useful and persuasive trope. There is a marvellous

[7] *Patterns in Shakespearean Tragedy* (London: Methuen, 1960), 116.

[8] *The Great Stage: Image and Structure in King Lear* (Seattle: University of Washington Press, 1963), 285-7.

[9] 'The Unity of *King Lear*', *Sewanee Review*, 56 (1948), 170.

[10] George F. Kernodle, 'The Symphonic Form of *King Lear*', in *Elizabethan Studies and other Essays in Honor of George F. Reynolds* (Boulder, Col.: University of Colorado Press, 1945), 185-9.

[11] *Art and Artifice in Shakespeare* (London: Methuen, 1963), 142.

[12] *Disowning Knowledge* (Cambridge: Cambridge University Press, 1987), 91-3.

[13] Heather Neill writing in *The Times*, 24 Mar. 1989.

[14] 'Lear in the Theater', in Lawrence Danson (ed.), *On King Lear* (Princeton: Princeton University Press, 1981), 165, 171-2, 180, 184-5.

blending of different types of discourse especially in the storm scenes and the musical metaphor does help us to define that. But there has been a more particular reason for privileging the musical metaphor in the criticism of *King Lear*. Musical compositions can tolerate an almost infinite variety of contrasts in tone, mood, and tempo without the unity of the composition being impaired. That is what makes the trope so welcome to the critics of the harmony-at-all-costs school. At the same time musical compositions do not make statements, ideological or otherwise, which are subject to proof or refutation; literary texts do. In the use of the musical trope by critics of *King Lear* this distinction tends to be lost; it often becomes a strategy for ignoring contradictions and treating them instead as tonal contrasts. Seemingly jarring notes and discontinuities are presented as somehow blending into a single organic whole. The word 'organic' (going back to Coleridge and Goethe) is another word which begs the question. If *Lear* is an organic whole or a symphony, all contradictions become seeming contradictions. The subplot, different though it may be from the main plot, will only intensify the effect of the main plot, reinforcing the same idea. For a great work of art is, by definition, a unified whole.

This is not the position which I will take with regard to *King Lear*. I subscribe rather to the views of a group consisting mainly of more recent critics who have shown themselves less committed to the notion of organic unity. John Reibetanz sees the end of the play as controlled by 'the two threads of hope and despair'.[15] Derek Peat likewise maintains that '*King Lear* forces every spectator to choose between the contrary possibilities it holds in unresolved opposition'.[16] Howard Felperin argues that the play ends in *aporia*. It 'represents the very negation of the possibility of unity, coherence and resolution . . . [there is a] dizzying fluctuation between contradictory meanings.'[17] Norman N. Holland holds that in *King Lear* the problem of values is unresolved. In the final scenes, we witness the opposing pulls of belief and disbelief and he concludes that 'Shakespeare does not attempt to resolve the pull of these two demands'.[18] This is

[15] *The Lear World* (London: Heinemann, 1977), 114–15.
[16] 'And That's True Too', *Shakespeare Survey*, 33 (1980), 43.
[17] *Shakespearian Representation* (Guildford: Princeton University Press, 1977), 105.
[18] *The Shakespearian Imagination* (New York: Macmillan, 1964), 258.

well said but, unlike Mr Holland, I am not sure whether Shakespeare did or did not attempt to resolve the contradictions. Maybe he tried but failed. Perhaps the opposing myths are managing him, not he them! All that we have is the finished product. And the finished product is both strongly Christian and strongly Pagan. The two are not harmonized. However, I will argue that, having found himself and his play thus impaled on the horns of a dilemma, he exploited that very situation for all it was worth, lighting up for us the discontinuities to which the dilemma gave rise and creating a super-*agon* which overshadows the *agon* enacted between the characters on the stage. We may express this super-*agon* in shorthand form as a contest between Job and Prometheus.

2

It is by now a commonplace of Lear-criticism to speak of the king as a Job-figure. This is not surprising. It would seem that no writer in the West can begin to explore extreme suffering, in particular, unmerited suffering, and the posture of rebellion against its author or cause, without the Job model powerfully asserting itself. Even when not directly invoked, it is there. Here it would seem to be directly invoked. Jan Kott sees *King Lear*, Acts II–IV, i.e. the middle sections from the scenes in the storm leading to the reunion with Cordelia, as an attempt to write a new Book of Job.[19] Harold Bloom likewise sees these middle sections as 'designedly Joban . . . Shakespeare intended his audience to see Job as the model for Lear's situation'.[20] But he also regards the Lear of the earlier and later parts of the play as quite unlike Job.[21] Frank Kermode shrewdly remarks that Shakespeare 'makes Lear like Job, but denies him divine compensations; Lear's sufferings seem to end and are then renewed'.[22]

[19] *Shakespeare Our Contemporary* (New York: Doubleday, 1964), 104.
[20] From his Introduction to Harold Bloom (ed.), *William Shakespeare's King Lear: Modern Critical Interpretations* (New York: Chelsea House, 1987), 1–2.
[21] Ibid. 2.
[22] From his Introduction to F. Kermode (ed.), *King Lear: A Casebook* (London: Macmillan, 1969), 18.

The truth is that Lear's personality at the beginning of the play, as he utters ferocious curses on all who cross his path, is very markedly un-Joban. He is most like Job in the scenes in the storm where he is tried through suffering, seeing himself as 'a poor, infirm, weak, and despis'd old man'. In the two scenes of mutual forgiveness between Lear and Cordelia, we await the consummation of the Job pattern according to which storm is followed by reconciliation, and reconciliation is followed by restoration and blessing (Job 42: 10–17). Instead of this there is, as we have noted, a sharp swerve as Shakespeare deliberately dashes the hopes which the play itself had encouraged. For if the evocation of Job is, as Bloom says, designed then the rejection of the Job model is just as surely designed. We are left with an essential contradiction.

It may be argued that the *aporia* or contradiction we are speaking of is not peculiar to Shakespeare; it belongs to the deepest levels of our culture.[23] If Job rebels against God, writers have rebelled against Job! It seems nearly always to be crossed with another, adversary text, thus creating an inevitable swerve from the direction taken by the biblical book in its received form. Milton in *Samson Agonistes* structured the debate between the blind and suffering hero and his three visitors on the Job model, but chose to ground his subsequent conduct on a stoical readiness for death. As we shall see in a later chapter, Blake, whilst finding in Job his supreme model of the Sublime, turns the biblical *fabula* upside down. Job's perfect rectitude and fear of God are condemned as Urizenic; he must learn not submission, but the worship of the Divine Humanity as manifested in the Imagination of the artist.

The crucial difficulty has of course always been the ending. Job after hearing God's 'answer'—or rather his questions—out of the storm wind, submits to the authority of the divine voice; he 'repents in dust and ashes' (42: 6). God subsequently vindicates him and restores his fortunes. If the self-abasement of Job is a scandal to the Greeks who expected pride and defiance from their heroes especially at the end of their careers, the happy ending is a scandal to both Greeks and Christians. How can God

---

[23] For additional comment on this see, by the present writer, 'Being Possessed by Job', *Literature and Theology*, 8 (1994), 284–7.

both subject his servant to the most appalling sufferings and then without any explanation 'restore his captivity' providing him with a new family as well as fourteen thousand sheep and two thousand head of cattle? The ending would seem to be unrelated to the beginning or the middle—in contradiction to the Aristotelian notion of the proper management of a work of art. The issue is not the integrity of the text of Job—this scarcely concerns any of the writers who have responded to the Job archetype. And perhaps the questions raised by biblical scholars about the authenticity of the final chapter are themselves the effect of the same uneasiness which led writers to swerve from the happy ending.[24] Job forces on us a fundamental choice, a choice between the untidiness and ongoingness of the pilgrimage and the artistic demand for closure. It defeats the dark desire for death which is so powerful a motif in Western mythology and with it the aesthetic perfection of the downward curve of tragedy; it denies us the logical fulfilment of Job's suffering, that consummation devoutly to be wished which would have made it consistent with the Crucifixion and a great deal else besides.

King Lear thus situates itself at an eminent point of intersection in Western culture. The hero testifies in his moral history to the force of the Job archetype but he dies in fulfilment of the laws of tragedy and there is a hint also, as many critics have noted, of a sacrificial death, a kind of crucifixion, in Kent's lines:

> he hates him
> That would upon the rack of this tough world
> Stretch him out longer.

> (v. iii. 313–15)

Death thus wins in the end. Dionysus, the god who presides over tragedy, is as we noted the god who dies. This is the dark

---

[24] There is not one shred of real evidence to support the view that at some stage the book of Job lacked the frame-story, as maintained by a majority of present-day critics. On the contrary the oldest manuscript evidence—that of the Aramaic paraphrase found in Qumran—suggests that as early as the third pre-Christian century the book of Job was known essentially in the form in which we have received it. (See Michael Sokoloff, *The Targum of Job from Qumran Cave XI* (Ramat-Gan, Israel: Bar-Ilan University Press, 1974), 103). It would seem that just as there have been revisers like Nahum Tate who felt that *King Lear* ought to end like Job, so there are revisers of Job, who feel that Job ought to end like *King Lear*!

side; the other side is defiance. Even as the tragic hero goes to meet his death, he shows his pride of life. Othello makes his grandest gesture, performing in fact his one and only act of heroism when, recalling a deed of blood performed in Aleppo to vindicate the honour of the state of Venice, he draws his sword to end his own life. In his death, the tragic hero is one with all mortal men, but in his pride he is a Titan. The tragic hero's magnificent, final gesture of defiance is one which the biblical-type drama cannot, or rather, will not, endorse. Job has his own special kind of moral courage: he too is a kind of rebel. Claiming the right to a hearing, he demands to meet God face to face and state his case. It is an astonishing demand. But what we have at the end of *Lear* is something different—a Promethean defiance, an assertion of Lear's undiminished royalty. We see this when Lear enters 'with Cordelia in his arms'. He has killed Cordelia's murderer with his own hands! He is now no longer the pathetic figure he was in the reconciliation scene in Act IV, when he had said, 'Pray you now, forget and forgive—I am old and foolish'. Now he dominates the scene as never before. He is truly a figure of power. The moment of death is the moment of maximum heroic self-assertion. That is the ironic achievement of ancient tragedy and that is the quality with which Shakespeare finally endows his hero.[25] Lear does not end in Christian fashion; he ends with a gesture of pride and defiance. The imagination of Western man is stirred by this glory and magnificence even as we deplore the need for such terrible conclusions.

3

So far we have considered the Job paradigm only in relation to the figure of Lear himself. But in fact it is distributed among three characters: Gloucester, Lear, and Edgar. The play as a whole becomes very much a study of the Job model and its applicability to tragedy. Edgar's total abasement in the role of poor Tom—'a poor, bare, forked animal'—reminds us of Job's total abasement:

[25] Cf. James Ogden, 'The Ending of *King Lear*', *The Aligarh Journal of English Studies*, 8 (1983), 182–4; and see Barbara Everett, 'The New *King Lear*', in Kermode (ed.), *King Lear: A Casebook*, 197.

I have sewed a sackcloth upon my skin,
and have abased mine horn unto the dust.
My face is withered with weeping,
and the shadow of death is upon mine eyes.

(16: 15–16)

Naked, helpless, and demanding our pity, and at the same time innocent of any wrongdoing, Edgar as the bedlam beggar is the most obviously Job-like figure in the play. His situation also conspicuously matches the Job story. In clear contrast to Lear, his 'captivity is restored'; he suffers the ultimate degradation and the ultimate injustice, but he is finally vindicated and lives to tell the tale. Edgar is the survivor and witness, a role most clearly emphasized in the Folio recension where he is given the summarizing words of the play.[26] From this point of view, he would seem to belong to a Hebrew-type narrative and in keeping with this he is also a figure of memory—he takes us back to the conceiving of Edmund—'the Gods are just, and of our pleasant vices | Make instruments to plague us' (v. iii. 170–1)—and forward to a future time of sad recollections—'we that are young | Shall never see so much, nor live so long'. But clearly he would not do as the hero of a tragedy. If he distinguishes himself in personal combat twice in the play, thus proving his nobility, he is nevertheless no Titan. He is essentially Job on his dunghill, never 'Prometheus tied to Caucasus', in Shakespeare's own phrase (*Titus Andronicus*, II. i. 17). In fact we might say that his function is to show us the non-Titanic option—to suggest the outline of the play that *King Lear* would have become if Shakespeare had chosen the alternative ending which seems to be called for after the pathos and wonder of the reunion in Act IV.

In the figure of Edgar Shakespeare's play thus provides a Joban contrast to the Promethean model. But it does more than that: it directs our attention to that contrast and to the nature of the incompatibility of the two roles—the one tragic, the other, antitragic. This is even more apparent in the deliberate twinning of Lear and Gloucester, the third of the Joban characters in the

---

[26] Elizabeth Freund suggests that Edgar's witness role reflects that of the spectator and reader 'in an interminable chain of witnessing'. ' "Give the Word": Reflections on the Economy of Response in *King Lear*', *Hebrew University Studies in Literature*, Special Issue in Honour of A. A. Mendilow (Jerusalem, 1982), 211–14 (213).

play. The great lesson that Gloucester must learn is survival. Edgar performs a charade to divert him from the path of suicide, the path taken by half of Shakespeare's tragic heroes and heroines. He carefully sets up for his father an imagined scene of the cliffs of Dover, whereupon the blind man jumps and is 'miraculously' preserved. The lesson:

> Men must endure
> Their going hence, even as their coming hither:
> Ripeness is all.
>
> (v. ii. 9–11)

This last phrase in this quotation is not, as often thought, a commendation of the stoic readiness for death. Edgar is telling Gloucester in this context that life is to be endured. Even if all hope and dignity are gone, the time of the end may not be wilfully anticipated. It is Job's reply to his wife when she urges him to suicide ('Curse God and die!'). His response:

What? shall we receive good at the hand of God, and not receive evil? (2: 10)

Here in fact is the Joban alternative to tragedy. This speech of Edgar, ending with the phrase 'ripeness is all', is often compared to Hamlet's 'fall of a sparrow' speech in Act V:

If it be now, 'tis not to come; if it be not to come, it will be now; if it be not now, yet it will come—the readiness is all. (v. ii. 193–5)

As we noted in the previous chapter, this speech has many varied meanings, but first and foremost Hamlet is speaking of death ('yet it will come'), of the need to be ready for the moment, which providence will appoint, to kill and be killed. When that moment arrives later in this very scene, he must be ready to seize it. Edgar is saying something else, almost in fact the direct opposite. Just as we have no control over our birth, so we must not claim control over our death. The 'ripeness is all' in the sense that the fruit will fall from the tree when it is ready. This is not an echo of Hamlet's speech, but rather its non-tragic antithesis. And it points to a different kind of denouement, one in which tragic closure is denied in favour of an ongoing and undetermined course of trial and endeavour.

The Job paradigm thus works not simply as a source of attitudes and ethical ideas, but as a structural principle with profound implications for the ordering of the plot. If, reduced to its simplest terms, the tragic mode requires a precipitate fall (like that of Lear or like that of Julius Caesar who is Olympus at one moment and a moment later is struck down and levelled with the least of mortals), then the anti-tragic model of Job requires a persistent onward struggle in spite of odds, a pilgrimage through the wilderness of this world. Job asks

> Wherefore is light given to him that is in misery,
> and life unto them that have heavy hearts,
> Which long for death, and if it come not,
> they would even search for it more than treasures?
>
> (3: 20–1)

The power of the longing for death is here only exceeded by the strength of the conviction that that longing is not to be gratified. The form of the sentence makes it clear that light is given. Light and not darkness is the fundamental datum, much as Job would like it to be otherwise. Incredibly, life is given to the bitter in soul—and it obligates. We must endure our going hence even as our coming hither.

This structural opposition between the fall and the pilgrimage is not left for us to discover by a laborious process of interpretation. Shakespeare explicitly defines it for us, by graphically representing the two options on the stage in the scene of Gloucester's attempted suicide. In this scene the figure of perpendicularity is powerfully invoked in Edgar's description:

> half way down
> Hangs one that gathers sampire, dreadful trade!
> Methinks he seems no bigger than his head.
> The fishermen that walk upon the beach
> Appear like mice, and yond tall anchoring bark
> Diminish'd to her cock, her cock a buoy
> Almost too small for sight
>
> .   .   .   .
>
> I'll look no more,
> Lest my brain turn, and the deficient sight
> Topple down headlong.
>
> (IV. vi. 14–24)

Gloucester, in a kind of burlesque version of the quintessential mode of tragedy, throws himself over the supposed edge. But this is a tragic fall to end all such falls. Instead of falling down a cliff, Gloucester falls flat on the boards to be picked up by his son Edgar and gently persuaded to continue his journey through further trials. He must not wilfully seek his own salvation.

> EDGAR. Hadst thou been aught but gossamer, feathers, air,
>   So many fathoms down precipitating,
>   Thou'dst shivered like an egg; but thou dost breathe,
>   Hast heavy substance, bleed'st not, speak'st, art sound.
>   Ten masts at each make not the altitude
>   Which thou hast perpendicularly fell:
>   Thy life's a miracle. Speak yet again.
> GLOUC. But have I fall'n or no?

(IV. vi. 49–56)

Gloucester's question precisely defines the structural irony of the whole play: 'Have I fall'n or no?' In one sense he must fall; this is the hellenic myth pattern. But in another sense such a tragic fall is denied him, for his 'life's a miracle'. As well as having a part in the tragedy of *King Lear*, he is indeed also in something more like a miracle play.

Closely related to perpendicularity is the image of circularity and this too is sharply foregrounded both as an idea and as a structural principle in *King Lear*. The image of the wheel is central; it reflexively defines for us half at least of the play's structure. Thus Lear speaks of being bound upon 'a wheel of fire' (IV. vii. 47). The reference is not only to the torments of the damned, but also to the wheel of Ixion, suggesting the wheel of fortune and also the circuit of the sun. Kent, resigning himself to a night in the stocks, declares: 'Fortune, good night; smile once more; turn thy wheel' (II. ii. 173). The fool in this respect as in others intuits a major theme in the play, for he too speaks of the King as a great wheel running down a hill: 'Let go thy hold when a great wheel runs down a hill, lest it break thy neck with following' (II. iv. 71–3). The shape of the play may be understood under this figure. Lear at the beginning, mounted high on his throne, commands his followers, demands love and obedience. In the storm in Act III he is 'a poor, infirm, weak, and despis'd old man' (III. ii. 20). In Act I he imperiously banishes Cordelia from his presence; in Act IV he kneels and begs her forgiveness. The play is governed by images of circularity, the fall of the characters being foredoomed from the beginning of the play. Thus Edmund declares: 'The younger rises when the old doth fall' (III. iii. 27). We realize even as he says this that the alternate rise and fall of the generations carries with it the inevitable implication of his own foreordained descent when the wheel shall have 'come full circle' (V. iii. 174).

We hardly need to be told that such images owe their force to the archetypal rhythms of nature as in the regular movements of the heavenly bodies. Lear links his existence emphatically to the natural cycle as he swears by

> the sacred radiance of the sun,
> The mysteries of Hecate and the night,
> By all the operations of the orbs
> From whom we do exist and cease to be.
>
> (I. i. 109–12)

If he is a great wheel running down a hill, we know why this must be. There is a necessity at work here as ancient as the most ancient of myths and rituals.

As we noted earlier, such myth cycles are also present in *Antony and Cleopatra* and in *Hamlet*. Gilbert Murray long ago pointed out that the Hamlet myth is ordered ultimately by the cyclical movement of the seasons. Old Hamlet had been a winter god: he 'smote the sledded Polacks on the ice' (I. i. 63). Claudius is a summer god, the usurper who comes along in high summer when old Hamlet is sleeping in his orchard in the afternoon. When the play opens, some months have passed (according to one passage, two months, according to another, four) and it is again winter. In the first scene and again in the fourth, we are told how bitter cold it is. Young Hamlet, dressed in black, is the winter god all over again and he will be unseated by another spring god who comes at the turn of the year.[27] But this image of circularity, unlike that in *King Lear*, is only implied. It does not become explicit as a focus for discussion in the play (except perhaps in the flattering speech of Rosencrantz to Claudius on 'the cess of majesty'—which hardly carries the weight of the play.) In *King Lear* by contrast Shakespeare metapoetically defines his procedure and intentions through such figures as that of the

---

[27] 'Hamlet and Orestes' (The British Academy, 1914; revised 1920), *passim*.

wheel. It is as though he is not only writing a dramatic master-piece but is also conducting a seminar on the application to his play of the mythic patterns drawn from ancient tragedy. As part of the same seminar, he also makes explicit the antithesis to these mythic patterns of circularity. The opposed pattern is that of the trial or pilgrimage. This latter term which defines the more open, less determined order of existence characteristic of biblical man, is also introduced into the play as a key term when Edgar, speaking of Gloucester's final moments relates how he 'ask'd his blessing, and from first to last | Told him my *pilgrimage*' (v. iii. 195–6).

We are thus speaking of a phenomenological duality clearly defined for us in the play in a series of opposed key terms as well as in graphic form in the 'cliffs of Dover' scene where Gloucester enacts the shift from fall (or wheel) to pilgrimage in a kind of dumb show. It will be seen that Lear shifts in the oppo-site direction—from the redemptive movement in Act IV to the precipitous tragic fall in Act V. These examples highlight the fundamentally opposite tendencies of the two plots and indeed raise the whole question of the double-plot structure, a unique feature of *King Lear*. I will argue that the two plots, the one fea-turing Gloucester and his sons, the other, Lear and his daughters, offer a tonal and functional contrast in keeping with the duality we are speaking of. Through this contrast Shakespeare exhibits for our attention the opposition between the Hebraic pattern of the pilgrimage and the pattern of inevitable doom which belongs to the Hellenic mode of tragedy. Nor is this a case of a dialectical pattern of contrast yielding to some higher sym-metry. As A. C. Bradley long ago perceived, the twin plots rep-resent 'competing interests'.[28] What we have is not a harmony or a symphony, but rather an essential duality. It is a case of organized incoherence.

4

The two plots are linked by many parallels and cross-references. This is immediately evident. But what makes us suspicious of

[28] Bradley, *Shakespearean Tragedy*, 255.

this apparent symmetry is the fact that the chief characters on both sides constantly harp on it, as though to say to the audience: you see this is really the same play we are in. Thus Edgar at the end of Act III, scene vi, in the Quarto version:

> But then the mind much sufferance doth o'erskip,
> When grief hath mates, and bearing fellowship.
> How light and portable my pain seems now,
> When that which makes me bend makes the king bow;
> He childed as I father'd.[29]

These couplets are a little too neat, and what is more, the parallel is wrong: Lear's plot is not like the one that Edgar is in; that which makes him bend is *not* that which makes the King bow. The audience knows, as Edgar does not, that Gloucester has been cozened by Edmund. He has not suddenly taken it into his head to drive Edgar from his door as an act of natural insurrection in the manner of Goneril and Regan. Moreover, there is a moral history behind the events in Gloucester's household going back to the birth of Edmund and the imbalance in the family consequent upon the jealousy of the illegitimate son for his legitimate brother. Such a background, so central to the Gloucester plot, is lacking in Lear's situation, the essence of which is that it is inexplicable—an act of Nature! Just as his initial division of the kingdom is left basically unexplained (especially so in the Quarto), so no motives are offered for the behaviour of the cruel daughters; it is treated more like a natural cataclysm. In the typical imagery of the play, the trouble in Lear's family is like the effect of a sunspot or an earthquake, or like the roaring sea (III. iv. 10). No moral aetiology is involved.

Gloucester also ponders the parallelism. Already in Act I, he seems to subscribe to the orchestral theory of the play:

These late eclipses in the sun and moon portend no good to us ... love cools, friendship falls off ... This villain of mine [meaning Edgar] comes under the prediction; there's son against father: the king falls from bias of nature; there's father against child. (I. ii. 107–17)

But we are only taken in for a moment. We soon realize (even before Edmund makes the point brutally and coarsely) that

---

[29] On the significance of the omission of this passage in the Folio, and other differences between the two versions, see below, sect. 6.

Gloucester himself bore some responsibility for his troubles; whereas no such background is provided to explain the amazing differences between the behaviour of the three daughters of Lear. In contrast to *The True Chronicle Historie*, there is no obvious motivation given in Shakespeare's play for Cordelia's 'nothing' and little motivation for the King's decisions to divide the kingdom and submit his daughters to a love-test in the first place. These moves are arbitrary—they do have something of the character of eclipses of the sun and moon.

In short, we are suspicious of the parallelism that Gloucester makes the moment we hear it—he is it seems trying to evade responsibility by saying to the audience: 'You see the main plot is about storms and eclipses; if the King is more sinned against than sinning, well then so am I.' But we are not deceived. The King himself also tries his hand at this analogy. When he first sees Edgar in his nakedness and misery, he cries out, 'What! has his daughters brought him to this pass?' and a minute later he tries one of his famous curses:

> Now all the plagues that in the pendulous air
> Hang fated o'er men's faults light on thy daughters!
>
> (III. iv. 67–8)

Kent's response 'He hath no daughters, Sir' is not only an attempt to move Lear away from his obsession and to try to make him conscious of other people's very different dilemmas. It is also a dismissal of the parallelistic view of the play: Kent is saying that in spite of the skilful interweaving of the two plots, their moral and existential ground remains radically distinct. Edgar has no daughters; Lear has no father. Lear is trying to get Edgar into his play and Kent is saying in effect that it will not work. At other times, Lear tries to get himself into Gloucester's play. This is the force of his speech on adultery in Act IV:

> Let copulation thrive; for Gloucester's bastard son
> Was kinder to his father than my daughters
> Got 'tween the lawful sheets.
>
> (IV. vi. 117–19)

We could translate this speech to read: 'If I had been chosen for a role such as that of Gloucester in his play I would be better off than being the sort of tragic hero that I am.' Gloucester's bastard son Edmund treats Gloucester better than my daughters treat me. Of course, the audience knows and Gloucester, who is present, by now knows also, that Edmund is the villain of the subplot. Lear is mistaken about Edmund. He is not kinder to his father than Goneril and Regan are to theirs. He is just as bad as they are, but his evil belongs to a different kind of moral history. Lear's obsession with lechery and adultery at this point shows him trying to mitigate the harsh incomprehensibility of his situation for which no moral or psychological explanations will work.

In short, the constant underlining of the parallelism by the characters themselves has two functions—it serves to tie the two plots together but it also serves to keep them apart. If the parallel has to be so strenuously worked out again and again, it shows us that there is something that does not fit, that there are 'competing interests' in the play represented by the twin plots. Critics who have recognized this have also occasionally sought to identify the nature of these competing interests. Howard Felperin for instance shrewdly noted that the parallelism is constantly called in question by the Christian atmosphere of the subplot.[30] And that is the real point.

Indeed, I am not the first to argue that the subplot has a moral pattern which, in contrast to the main plot, is specifically biblical. Edgar, attending Lear in the storm in the character of Tom a' Bedlam, refers the world's troubles not to a nature mythology but to the biblical code of moral judgement:

Take heed o'th'foul fiend. Obey thy parents; keep thy word's justice; swear not; commit not with man's sworn spouse; set not thy sweet heart on proud array. (III. iv. 80–3)

Here in this brief summary of the second table of the commandments and the echoing of the catechism we have the entry into the play of the Judeo-Christian categories. And they govern the subplot as a whole. For Gloucester is no king, no Nature god. He is—to stretch a point—a bourgeois citizen functioning in a domestic moral fable. His past bears down on his future as in some novel by Dickens or George Eliot. The morality play aspect of the subplot has been noted by several critics but with a

---

[30] Felperin, *Shakespearean Representation*, 92.

certain pejorative emphasis. Thus Bridget Gellert Lyons declares that the subplot 'evokes a medieval legal morality with its direct translation into modes of justice of biblical injunctions and metaphors'.[31] Felperin speaking of the 'conventional Christian design' of the subplot, adds that 'it smells of morality'.[32] These critics and others tend to see the subplot as dramatically weaker than the main plot. Terms like 'conventional', 'didactic', 'simplified' abound. It is taken for granted that the subplot with its underlying structure of biblical morality shows up by contrast the greater force of the main plot. Might there not be some prejudice at work here of the same kind as that which inhibits so many present-day critics from accepting a straight reading of such lines as Hamlet's 'there's a divinity that shapes our ends, | Rough-hew them how we will'?

What we can say is that the subplot is to a significant degree non-tragic, even anti-tragic. But Shakespeare clearly felt that justice had to be done to that mode also. And if we wish to do justice to the play that Shakespeare wrote, we will have to suspend our disbelief to the extent of giving the kind of attention to the subplot that it demands. If we do this we will find that it is no more conventional and contrived than are Lear's grandiloquent gestures in the tragic main plot. On the contrary, the biblical images which it evokes carry some of the subtlest of the play's meanings and, what is more, they overflow into the main plot. In fact it sometimes seems that we would do better to speak of parallel plots rather than main and subplot. It is a matter of undecidability rather than of subordination; sometimes the Gloucester-Edgar-Edmund triangle seems to dominate and sometimes the story of Lear and his daughters. There is a double focus. Just as the fall and the wheel invade Gloucester's world, so the various biblical motifs and influences penetrate the Lear plot and momentarily transform it. The power and pathos of such moments are by no means inadequate to Lear's experience—as claimed by Bridget Lyons.[33] It would be truer to

---

[31] Bridget G. Lyons, 'The Subplot as Simplification in *King Lear*', in Rosalie L. Colie and F. T. Flahiff (eds.), *Some Facets of King Lear: Essays in Prismatic Criticism* (London: Heinemann, 1974), 23–38 (p. 28).

[32] Felperin, *Shakespearean Representation*, 93–4.

[33] Lyons speaks of the 'recognizably structured perceptions and values' of the subplot as 'obviously inadequate' to Lear's experience ('The Subplot as Simplification', 25).

say that the modern reader's sensitivity to these image patterns is often inadequate for a full appreciation of Shakespeare's play and of the oppositions which it strives to contain.

5

We have already considered the use of the Job model in both plots. But there is another biblical pattern no less important for this play to which I wish to draw attention, and that is the story of Isaac's blessing of his two sons, Esau and Jacob, from Genesis 27. Here is what may be termed the biblical subtext of *King Lear*. Isaac like Gloucester is blind. His two sons had been in competition for the birthright which Jacob had earlier wrested from Esau. They are now in competition for their father's blessing. There is a close and subtle pattern of analogy linking the biblical text with Shakespeare's play: the blind Gloucester cries out to his supposedly absent son Edgar:

> Might I but live to see thee in my touch,
> I'd say I had eyes again
>
> (IV. i. 23–4)

recalling the words of the blind Isaac to his son Jacob in Genesis 27: 21: 'Come near, now, that I may feel thee, my son.'[34] In both cases a blind father speaks of touching his son; in both cases the 'good' son is actually present though his identity is concealed from his father. Clothing and disguise are important in both stories. Jacob like Edgar is disguised—he presents himself to his father in 'skins of goats'; only his voice belies his rough dress—'the voice is Jacob's voice, but the hands are the hands of Esau' (27: 22). Similarly, Gloucester is puzzled by Edgar's altered voice and his 'better phrase and matter' (IV. vi. 8). As for Edmund, like Esau he has murderous designs on his brother (Genesis 27: 41) but, as with Jacob and Esau, there will be a final reconciliation between the two brothers (33: 4). Fleeing from the dangers posed by his brother's hatred, Jacob, like Edgar,

[34] The link was first brought home to me by Abraham Shlonsky's Hebrew translation of the play (1956)—translated incidentally not from the original but intermediately from the Russian. In rendering this passage, Shlonsky uses a verb-form, *amushekha*, which at once recalled to his Hebrew-speaking audience the words of Isaac in Genesis 27: 21.

will go into exile, a penniless beggar, couching out of doors upon the rough stones of Luz—to be renamed Bethel because it will become in the future the house of God (28: 10–11).

All these are details which have an interesting but incidental bearing on the play. There is, however, one feature of the analogy which has more than incidental importance. I refer to the great emphasis placed on the blessing—'the bounty and the benison of heaven'—which the disguised Edgar wins from his blind father in Act IV (IV. vi. 226). At two earlier points Edgar had been the recipient of his father's bounty and blessing (at IV. i. 64 and at IV. vi. 27–30). On both occasions Gloucester gives Edgar a purse, at the same time calling down on him divine favour; the second occasion is the most emphatic:

> Here, friend's another purse; in it a jewel
> Well worth a poor man's taking: fairies and Gods
> Prosper it with thee!

And this episode concludes with Gloucester kneeling to give extra force to the blessing which he now calls down on (the supposedly absent) Edgar with the words: 'O you mighty Gods . . . If Edgar live, O, bless him!' (IV. vi. 34, 40). In Act V, Edgar reports his final conversation with his father before his heart 'burst smilingly'. Again, the essential feature of that conversation was the matter of blessing: 'I ask'd his blessing, and from first to last | Told him my pilgrimage' (V. iii. 195–6). It would not be an exaggeration to say that to gain his father's blessing becomes a primary aim of what Edgar speaks of here as his 'pilgrimage'. The trial he has undertaken is not only that of taking care of his father—he is seeking to assure a certain kind of continuity by means of the blessing bestowed by a father on his son. For the sake of that blessing Edgar will undergo immense hardship and danger. All this is clearly in accordance with the letter and spirit of Genesis 27 in which the disguised Jacob presents himself to his father with the sole purpose of winning his blessing, appropriating it by stealth from his more favoured brother, Esau. That blessing included material benefits—'the dew of heaven, and the fatness of the earth, and plenty of wheat and wine' (verse 28)— but also moral and spiritual gifts—'blessed be he that blesseth thee' (verse 29). These are momentous blessings and their power will shape the subsequent history of Jacob and his offspring.

We are here in the realm of salvation-history and something of this quality attaches itself to the subplot of *King Lear*. Like Jacob, Edgar is a survivor. Lear and his daughters are doomed by the laws of tragedy, but Edgar will carry a blessing from his father into the future. Here the biblical notion of history ruled by covenant promises enters into the play.

Paradoxically the blessing motif, whilst going back to Genesis 27, seems to have been suggested to Shakespeare's mind in the first place by *The True Chronicle Historie of King Leir*—the source of the main plot. This old Lear play has a strong biblical flavour throughout. Two passages are directly relevant to our present discussion. In scene 13, Cordella, married now to the King of Gallia, is on her way to church to pray that she may be restored to her father's favour. She tells us that the loss of that is the main cause of her grief and to regain it, the main object of her endeavours:

> I would abstain from any nutryment
> And pyne my body to my very bones;
> Bare foote I would on pilgrimage set forth
> Unto the furthest quarters of the earth,
> And all my life time would I sackcloth weare,
> And mourning-wise powre dust upon my head:
> So he but to forgive me once would please.[35]

In scene 24, the scene of the reunion, Cordella kneels to beg her father's blessing:

> But I will never rise from off my knee,
> Untill I have your blessing, and your pardon
> Of all my faults committed any way,
> From my first birth unto this present day.

Leir who had earlier knelt to ask forgiveness of Cordella and has just been persuaded to rise from his knees, now solemnly declares:

> The blessing which the God of *Abraham* gave
> Unto the trybe of *Juda*, light on thee,
> And multiply thy dayes, that thou mayst see
> Thy childrens children prosper after thee.
> Thy faults, which are just none that I do know,
> God pardon on high, and I forgive below.[36]

---

[35] Bullough, 363–4.   [36] Ibid. 394.

It is probable that, for all its sentimentality and exaggeration (all the characters excepting Perillus constantly kneel and rise throughout), this scene prompted Shakespeare to turn the blessings in Genesis to dramatic account. (The old play is evidently referring to Jacob's blessing of Judah from Genesis 49: 8–12.) The first of the quoted passages seems to have given him also the key term 'pilgrimage'. But Shakespeare has deftly transferred the weight of these biblical suggestions to the subplot. It is Edgar who undertakes a pilgrimage and it is Edgar who throughout seeks his father's blessing. As far as the main plot is concerned, the motif of blessing is confined to the reunion itself (IV. vii) and to the briefer 'birds i'th'cage' passage in Act V, scene iii. Shakespeare wisely cuts down the multiple kneelings in the old play to just one prominent instance of Lear kneeling and Cordelia's remonstrance—'No, Sir, you must not kneel.'[37] Shakespeare thus, by what is without doubt a conscious contrivance, performs a neat switch, eliminating or reducing the morality play elements (or turning them upside-down) in his reworking of the Lear story and transferring them instead to the Gloucester plot. In the same way he omits the detailed motivation for Lear's division of the kingdom as given in the old play. He clearly has other plans for the Lear plot. It will testify not to a rational moral order ruled by cause and effect and responsive to the pieties of prayer and blessing but to a harsher and more pitiless order —more like that presided over by the Ironic Spirits of Hardy's *Dynasts*. After a paradisal moment of blessing and mutual forgiveness, Lear and Cordelia will resume the fatal course marked out for them by the inexorabilities of the tragic mode.

Indeed if blessing is the supreme sign of the biblical-type subplot, then the Lear plot both at the beginning and at the end essentially demonstrates the opposite principle, namely, the power of the curse. Here the typology of Isaac and Jacob in Genesis 27 is precisely reversed: Lear is the antitype of Isaac; he sends his younger daughter into exile 'dower'd with our curse, and stranger'd with our oath' (I. i. 204). In bidding farewell to

---

[37] As Kenneth Muir points out, 'in the old play Leir and Cordella keep on kneeling and rising until the scene topples over into absurdity'. Shakespeare avoids the absurdity but he 'realized the inherent pathos of the scene and transmuted it for his own purposes'. Introduction to *King Lear*, Arden Shakespeare (London: Methuen, 1952), p. xxx.

Cordelia and her chosen husband, the King of France, he explicitly negates the words of blessing which Edgar later wins from his father:

> therefore be gone
> Without our grace, our love, our benison.
>
> (I. i. 265)

Later on he directs his curses at Goneril calling upon Nature to smite her with sterility:

> Into her womb convey sterility!
> Dry up in her the organs of increase,
> And from her derogate body never spring
> A babe to honour her!
>
> (I. iv. 287–90)

These are formidable utterances and they are as potent as blessings, if not more potent. The word once spoken will act like a spell. Goneril and Regan will die childless. Nor will Cordelia escape the disastrous force of her father's terrible words. As Geoffrey Hartman does well to remind us in connection with this play, 'Curse is primary, blessing secondary.'[38] Words wound; they can even wound mortally. Over the house of Atreus in the ancient Greek tragic cycle of Aeschlyus culminating in 'The Eumenides', broods the dark power of the curse:

> We are the everlasting children of the Night,
> Deep in the hall of Earth they call us curses.

There will be sunny intervals of achievement, even of blessing. Cities will be founded and children born but death has the last word as the curse inexorably fulfils itself for generation after generation.

It is here in this region of blessing and cursing that words most powerfully shape reality, thus raising misgivings about W. H. Auden's view that 'poetry makes nothing happen'. Whether or not this is true of poetry in general, it seems peculiarly inapplicable to spells, curses, and blessings. These have always made things happen. Perhaps Auden would say that such utterances are

---

[38] *Saving the Text: Literature/Derrida/Philosophy* (Baltimore: Johns Hopkins University Press, 1981), 131.

not strictly poetry. But they certainly seem to be an ingredient in dramatic poetry. Here language enters into direct commerce with events. There is a necessary interaction beween speaker and interlocutor, and between them and the world around them. Even a word as seemingly empty of significance as Cordelia's 'Nothing' becomes something like a curse, a 'decreating word' from which the whole lamentable history of Lear and his daughters may be seen to follow.[39]

In short, in setting up these two options, the blessing which Edgar wins in the subplot against the curse which no one escapes in the main plot, Shakespeare is again testing the limits of two alternative and ultimately irreconcilable modes of imagining. He understood and responded to tragedy and with it the power of the curse, but he understood also that a world like Edgar's, governed ultimately—in spite of exile and immeasurable suffering —by blessing and promise, meant a refusal of the tragic. Here was the dilemma.

Shakespeare, as we have seen, sharpens and foregrounds this very dilemma through the mechanism of the twin plots. There are of course significant cross-references. The motif of blessing and the kneeling gesture which accompanies it spill over into the Lear–Cordelia plot, in the scene of reunion, momentarily realigning it as a drama of redemption, just as, in the scene of the attempted suicide, Gloucester momentarily pursues the option of the tragic fall. But these are diversions which ultimately confirm the essential ideological difference between the two plots. Just as Gloucester, tempted to curse God and die, has to be gently redirected and persuaded to take the harder path of trial and pilgrimage, so Cordelia and Lear cannot be allowed to escape the fascination of *thanatos* and its dark curses. We have in effect two plays, not one. The marvel is that Shakespeare gets away with it!

6

It has been increasingly recognized in recent years that *King Lear* is in a very literal sense two plays rather than one. I refer of course to the two distinct versions of the play, that of the Quarto

---

[39] Ibid. 130, 131.

publication of 1608 and that of the Folio of 1623. Following the work of Michael Warren, Steven Urkowitz, Peter W. M. Blayney, and others, it is now agreed by most of the textual scholars that the two versions are both authentic, the Folio reflecting Shakespeare's own revision of his play with significant changes of emphasis.[40] The two texts should therefore be considered separately, each on its own merits. Editors for over two hundred years have been in the habit of fusing the two, making their own selection among the variant readings as though there was some unitary text to be recovered by skilful editing. The recent one-volume Oxford edition of Shakespeare's *Complete Works*[41] abandons this approach and sets out the two texts separately and in full, exhibiting them as two independent recensions of the same play—both authentically Shakespearian but as distinct from one another as the two different versions of *The Prelude*.[42] They both deserve our attention and, more than that, the shifts in focus revealed by a comparison of the two versions deserve our attention.

Many of the changes are, as we might expect, simply a matter of second thoughts, arising out of the experience gained in rehearsals and performance during the interval of four years or more which evidently separates the two versions,[43] and not involving questions of principle: 'the trend of the Folio revision

---

[40] See Michael J. Warren, 'Quarto and Folio *King Lear* and the Interpretation of Albany and Edgar', in D. Bevington and Jay L. Halio (eds.), *Shakespeare: Pattern of Excelling Nature* (Newark, Del.: University of Delaware Press, 1978), 95–107; Steven Urkowitz, *Shakespeare's Revision of* King Lear (Princeton: Princeton University Press, 1980), *passim*; Peter W. M. Blayney, *The Texts of 'King Lear' and their Origins*, 2 vols. (Cambridge: Cambridge University Press, 1982), *passim*. These views are ably summarized by Stanley Wells, 'The Once and Future *King Lear*', in Gary Taylor and Michael Warren (eds.), *The Division of the Kingdoms: Shakespeare's Two Versions of* King Lear (Oxford: Oxford University Press, 1983), 1–22. Hereafter *Division*.

[41] William Shakespeare, *The Complete Works*, ed. Stanley Wells, Gary Taylor, John Jowett, and William Montgomery (Oxford: Oxford University Press, 1986).

[42] The analogy is proposed by Stanley Wells in 'The Once and Future *King Lear*', *Division*, 18.

[43] Gary Taylor in a well-reasoned essay concludes that the earlier text of *King Lear* was finalized in late 1605 to early 1606 and that the Folio version reflects a revision by Shakespeare himself probably in 1609–10. ('The Date and Authorship of the Folio Version', *Division*, 429). Taylor and his colleagues have advanced similar arguments regarding the independent status of the folio and quarto versions of other plays, notably *Richard II* and *Hamlet*, but the differences there do not reveal so clear a direction and pattern. (See Stanley Wells and Gary Taylor, *William Shakespeare: A Textual Companion* (Oxford: Oxford University Press, 1987), *passim*.)

is towards streamlining and simplification.'[44] An example of this would be the omission of the mock trial of Goneril and Regan by the mad Lear in Act III, scene vi. The author may have concluded that, powerful though the scene is, much the same effect is achieved by the second mad scene (IV. vii) where again Lear imagines he sees 'Goneril with a white beard' and where his ravings are again concerned with justice and the administration of justice. Tightening of this kind accounts for many of the passages (some 300 lines) from the Quarto which were not included in the Folio. But other changes, in particular lines and passages only to be found in the Folio, represent a more radical rethinking. And here a pattern emerges of more than local or technical interest. The two recensions seem to disclose a certain uneasiness about the direction that the play should take, an uneasiness generated I believe by that selfsame contradiction that we have been examining so far, or something very like it. The two versions of *King Lear*, when set side by side, express the principle of undecidability; they seem to give a formal confirmation to the deep cultural division, the rift that is the subject of these chapters. But here in the case of *King Lear* we are not seeking by indirections to find directions out, not trying to conjure up the lurking absences and ambivalences out of the text by a process of interpretation; rather, we are observing Shakespeare in his workshop as he manifestly shifts his ground, first emphasizing the fatal movement of tragedy and then trying a movement of a different kind, one which has more in common with the values of the morality play. And we are left feeling by no means certain which was the greater fascination.

There can be little doubt that the later Folio version strives to mitigate the starkness and grimness of the Lear plot in favour of something more rationally motivated, in fact more like the Gloucester plot. Thus whilst the Quarto text leaves Lear's decision to divide the kingdom totally unexplained, 'the folio provides Lear with something of a motive for his division of the kingdom, namely "that future strife | May be prevented now" '. And other explanatory phrases are introduced at this point lacking in the Quarto.[45]

---

[44] Roger Warren, 'The Folio Omission of the Mock Trial: Motives and Consequences', *Division*, 45–57 (p. 53).
[45] Thomas Clayton, ' "Is this the promis'd end?" Revision in the Role of the King', *Division*, 121–41 (p. 125).

The basic contradiction between the norms of the Lear plot and those of the Gloucester plot remain in the Folio version but there is a certain tilting of the balance in favour of the Gloucester–Edgar situation with its morality atmosphere. Likewise, the subordination of the subplot to the main plot, taken for granted in the Quarto, is here less marked. As an example of this, we may consider Edgar's rhymed couplets from the end of Act III, scene vi, discussed earlier ('How light and portable my pain seems now, | When that which makes me bend makes the king bow', etc.) Edgar would seem here to be subordinating his story to that of Lear and his daughters, seeing his troubles as secondary to the mightier griefs of the King ('When we *our betters see* bearing our woes'). These fourteen lines of Edgar's speech occur in the Quarto but not in the Folio.

Indeed the Folio significantly enhances the authority of the Gloucester–Edgar plot and the norms which govern its structure. As we move from the earlier to the later version (or as many of the textual scholars would say, from the earlier to the later play) we note that Edgar is now given a more central and independent role. This is not only brought about negatively through the elimination of his self-effacing speech in Act III, scene vi; it is brought about through giving him centre stage and through a corresponding diminution in the roles of Albany and Kent. These figures, who belong essentially to the Lear plot, are in the Folio repeatedly upstaged in favour of Edgar.[46] This tendency can be discerned in many touches throughout the play but it is most noticeable in the long closing scene (v. iii). Michael Warren concludes from his rigorous and cautious analysis of these changes that Edgar in the Folio text is 'a stronger, more commanding figure'. 'The Folio', he says,

focuses on Edgar as the youth of the realm, not as does the Quarto, on Albany and the generation that has already known power; it concentrates upon Edgar's survival in disguise and on the relative success of his revelation of his identity to his father, presenting Edgar as the inheritor of reponsibilities in the shattered realm. The parallels in Kent's behaviour are played down, to emphasize Edgar's triumph.[47]

[46] As demonstrated by Michael Warren in his two important essays: 'Quarto and Folio *King Lear* and the Interpretation of Albany and Edgar', in Bevington and Halio (eds.), *Shakespeare: Pattern of Excelling Nature*, 95–107; id., 'The Diminution of Kent', *Division*, 59–73. See also Taylor, 'The Date and Authorship of the Folio Version', *Division*, 424–9.

[47] 'The Diminution of Kent', *Division*, 70.

But what finally makes the enhancement of Edgar's role absolute in the Folio text is the change in the assignment of the four last lines of the play.

> The weight of this sad time we must obey,
> Speak what we feel not what we ought to say,
> The oldest hath borne most; we that are young
> Shall never see so much, nor live so long.

In the Quarto these lines are given to Albany, but in the Folio they are given to Edgar. The lines in themselves are not of great significance and perhaps they are little more than a formal way of marking the ending but, taken in conjunction with the other evidence in the Folio and taken in conjunction also with the disappearance of Lear and Cordelia, the imminently expected death of Kent ('I have a journey, sir, shortly to go') and Albany's explicit abdication of authority in favour of Edgar, the reassignment of this closing speech becomes enormously significant. 'Edgar . . . becomes by default the play's prime medium of moral continuity, the most important agent and witness of the denouement.'[48] This final speech establishes the role of Edgar as survivor and witness. He is, so to speak, the spokesman of the future, a kind of combination of Horatio and Fortinbras. But what has to be insisted upon is that, unlike those two survivors of Hamlet's tragedy, here the figure of continuity is the prime representative of an alternative mode of drama. If it is Edgar 'who finally articulates Lear's own great struggle',[49] then we should be aware that that struggle has now been realigned to match that of the wayfaring hero of a pilgrim's progress who bears witness not to the fatal curve of tragedy which had required the deaths of Lear and Cordelia, but to the processes of redemption.

In this connection, the final and even more decisive change is in the manner of Lear's dying.[50] In the Quarto Lear's life ends on a note of despair; he dies of heartbreak:

---

[48] Taylor, 'The Date and Authorship of the Folio Version', *Division*, 424.
[49] Seltzer, 'Lear in the Theater', in *On King Lear*, 185.
[50] On this see Clayton's valuable essay, ' "Is this the promis'd end?" ', *Division*, 128–38.

O thou wilt come no more, neuer, neuer, neuer, pray you vndo this button. thanke you sir, O, o, o, o.[51]

In the Folio the long-drawn-out groan ('O, o, o, o') is omitted and a new line and a half are added to his last speech:

> Do you see this? Looke on her? Looke her lips.
> Looke there, looke there.

> *He dies*

There can be no doubt that here the Folio has introduced a note of consolation not found in the Quarto text. Lear dies but in his last moment he fancies that Cordelia may still be alive. There is also no doubt as to where this consolation has come from— it has spilled over from the Gloucester plot. Lear's death now strikingly approximates to that of Gloucester as described by Edgar earlier in this very scene:

> but his flaw'd heart,
> Alack too weak the conflict to support!
> 'Twixt two extremes of passion, joy and grief,
> Burst smilingly.

> (v. iii. 196–9)

Lear, imagining from her lips that Cordelia breathes and then turning in wonder to those present with his final 'looke there', clearly dies in the same fashion as Gloucester (and in the same fashion too as the King of Paphlagonia in the story by Sir Philip Sidney from which the Gloucester plot is taken[52])—namely, 'twixt two extremes of passion, joy and grief'. His heart too, we might say, 'burst[s] similingly' in the Folio version. Lear's death is thus 'prepared for by the manner and details of Gloucester's death'.[53] This momentary assimilation of the Lear plot to the Gloucester plot is of a piece with the enhancement of Edgar's role in the Folio version of the play. It is Edgar who reports the manner

---

[51] In the Quarto Lear is given an additional line which actually speaks of his heart breaking ('Breake hart, I prethe breake'). In the Folio this line is assigned to Kent. No great weight should, however, be attached to this line—the assignment to Lear may even be an error in the Quarto—Lear's total desolation being made clear by the thrice repeated 'neuer' and by the cry of pain ('O, o, o, o') which follows.

[52] See Bullough, 407.

[53] Clayton, ' "Is this the promis'd end" ', *Division*, 136–7.

of his father's dying and it is Edgar who is given the final summarizing word on the passing of Lear.[54]

Stanley Wells has concluded from all this that in the Folio Lear 'is, if we wish to use the theological term, redeemed'.[55] This is a stronger term than I would care to use. Lear is not redeemed but he sees the phantom of redemption, he hears the echo of a different myth. It is like the delusive last moments of Kafka's hero in *The Trial*. Joseph K. on his way to his execution looks out for vindication, a last-minute rescue. A moment before his death he imagines that he sees the figure of such a rescuer framed in the window of a house near the quarry to which his executioners have brought him:

Who was it? A friend? A good man? Someone who sympathized? Someone who wanted to help? Was it one person only? Or was it mankind?[56]

Here too is a great work of the imagination profoundly influenced, like *King Lear*, by the Book of Job;[57] but Kafka too, like Shakespeare, is unwilling or unable to go along with the redemptive promise of Job. The happy ending is aborted; what remains is the phantom of such an ending and such a promise. Shakespeare's play, in fact, features two such phantoms, for its two opposing models of dramatic action, the biblical and the Pagan, are each shadowed by the phantom of the other. Lear in his last moment sees himself, in fantasy, escaping the harsh inevitabilities of tragedy and the Nature myths which sustain it. Gloucester for his part, in what he perceives as his last moment, feeds his imagination on the perpendicular horror of the tragic fall. That is the end that he desires but it will be denied him, just as the opposite hope will be denied to Lear.

---

[54] Another change made in the Folio which makes easier the assimilation of the Lear plot to the Gloucester–Edgar plot is the omission of Edgar's lines on his last meeting with Kent (v. iii. 214–18). The reference here to Kent's imminent death from heartbreak ('His grief grew puissant, and the strings of life | Began to crack') would have given the wrong kind of signal, whilst the omission of this report leaves the death of Gloucester, reported by Edgar a moment earlier, as the sole model and prefiguration of the death of Lear.

[55] Stanley Wells, '*The Taming of the Shrew* and *King Lear*', *Shakespeare Survey*, 33 (1980), 65.

[56] *The Trial*, trans. Willa and Edwin Muir (New York: Schocken Books, 1968), 228.

[57] See Harold Fisch, *New Stories for Old: Biblical Patterns in the Novel* (London: Macmillan, 1998), 89–99.

There are thus no simple answers. To paraphrase Keats, Shakespeare reveals a capacity for being in uncertainties and contradictions without any irritable reaching after unity. *King Lear*, like the other plays that we have examined, maintains a dual focus. The result is a work of art that is neither pure tragedy nor pure salvation-history; it testifies rather to the phenomenological duality that is at the heart of our culture. This is the *agon* behind the *agon*—not the dramatic conflict that Shakespeare invented, but one which was thrust upon him and which he marvellously utilized, thereby giving shape to our innermost dilemmas.

PART II

MILTON

CHAPTER 5

Samson and the Poetics of Covenant

Shakespeare owed as much to earlier writers as any author can decently permit himself to owe, but he recognized no obligation. He showed no anxiety about their prior claims or about his belatedness; he simply raided the larder whenever he felt there was something there that he could use. He exercised total freedom. To Plutarch he owed the incidents, the characters, and much of the imagery and language of *Antony and Cleopatra*, but he did not set himself up as his pupil or interpreter. To the contrary, he also turned Plutarch upside down, investing Cleopatra with a power and inwardness which threaten those very Roman values which Plutarch so admired. Likewise in *Julius Caesar* there is scarcely a detail or episode which cannot be traced back to Plutarch's *Lives*. Nevertheless, the general thrust of the presentation is often very non-Plutarchian.

Shakespeare, we may say, availed himself of that prior text completely, feeding his imagination with its images of power and valour; he also deconstructed it. The Roman virtues as set out by Plutarch are celebrated and they are at the same time exploded. This source, a fundamental shaping force for Shakespeare's imagination, is there to be utilized in the dramatic *agon*, to be set free in a field of force. In drawing upon his sources what interested Shakespeare was not the exposition of the text of Plutarch or the Bible but rather the field of force, the dramatic possibilities that they might yield. He might have said that a source is but a cheveril glove to a good wit; how quickly the wrong side may be turned outward.

The inclusive Elizabethan term for such a free use of sources is in fact wit. Wit is the quality whereby different sources are nimbly combined with, and set off against, one another (e.g. *The Chronicle Historie* and the episode of the Paphlagonian king from Sidney's *Arcadia* in *King Lear*) and it is also the quality which determines the total freedom of action which the author implicitly claims with regard to these sources. A synonym for wit in this connection could be irresponsibility. Shakespeare is not answerable to his source, it is not set over and against him as an authority. If Shakespeare has appropriated the power of a biblical paradigm, he has also discarded it. There is no question of submitting himself to its authority. Having been integrated into the dramatic pattern, that paradigm has done its work. Shakespeare is always in that sense free or imagines himself to be so; he ranges freely within the zodiac of his own wit. It is a mark of his greatness.

Here precisely is a fundamental point of difference between Shakespeare and Milton. Milton too owes as much as any poet decently can owe to his sources. There is scarcely an image or idea or episode in *Paradise Lost* which has not been traced to one or more forerunner texts. The industry of scholars has, as in the case of Shakespeare, enabled us to see Milton in his workshop. We have been made aware of his mastery of the poetic resources of Shakespeare, Spenser, the Italian poets, of Ovid, Homer, and Virgil, and of his own English and European contemporaries. Above all, we are aware of what he owed to his prime text, the books of the Bible together with much of the literature of commentary and paraphrase in Hebrew, Aramaic, Latin, and Greek which had accumulated around that text over the centuries. And we are aware too of the amazing virtuosity with which, like Shakespeare, he wove all this together into the tapestry of his poems. But if he owed so much to his sources he also acknowledged an obligation. He does not range only within the zodiac of his own wit but stands before his forerunner in a posture of grave attentiveness.[1] He strictly meditates his muse. There is freedom to be sure; Milton like Shakespeare reveals his greatness in the originality of his selection, in the daring of his invention. His song pursues things *unattempted yet* in prose or rhyme. And yet the text before him commands, it retains its

---

[1] Such a posture hardly fits Harold Bloom's notion of an Oedipal struggle between Milton and his precursors. (See *The Anxiety of Influence* (New York: Oxford University Press, 1973), 22, 32–4, and *A Map of Misreading* (New York: Oxford University Press, 1975), 125–43.) Bloom recognizes the importance of the dense echoing of precursor poets in Milton but treats this as a 'transumptive strategy' aimed at affirming his own priority.

authority. It is there not simply to be utilized but to be echoed and, above all, to be interpreted.

Part of the pleasure that Milton implicitly promises his reader is the joy of recognition—the recognition of the familiar stories of Genesis and Judges, the familiar invocations from Virgil's epic, the familiar topos of the descent of Hermes as in Homer, but newly and marvellously applied to the visit of Raphael to Adam in Book V of *Paradise Lost*. And this in turn marvellously reminds the reader (and is supposed to remind him) of the visit of the angels to Abraham in Genesis 18. To the joy of such recognitions is added the pleasure of novelty. If we respond to an anterior voice still audible in the text we respond also to the new voice which both echoes and answers it. The intensest pleasure comes from the mingling of those voices. In Shakespeare's case our attention is not thus directed. Other joys are promised us, but the recognition of the source and the acknowledgement of its power are not usually among those joys.

We have now seemingly reversed Coleridge's position on what he terms Milton's egotism. He maintains that

in the Paradise Lost—indeed in every one of his poems—it is Milton himself whom you see; his Satan, his Adam, his Raphael, almost his Eve—are all John Milton; and it is a sense of this intense egotism that gives me the greatest pleasure in reading Milton's works. The egotism of such a man is a revelation of spirit.[2]

Shakespeare he declares is absent from his poetry; he is 'the Spinozistic deity',[3] whereas Milton's selfhood constitutes both the centre and the circumference of his writing. His is the sole voice that we hear. He has evidently become for Coleridge, in this respect, the true prototype of all Romantic poets. That is why 'the egotism of such a man' as he terms it gave him such intense pleasure. Like Wordsworth's solitary reaper—'breaking the silence of the seas | Among the farthest Hebrides'—or like Shelley's skylark, Milton sings by himself and the whole universe is filled with the ecstasy of his single song.

---

[2] *Specimens of the Table Talk of S. T. Coleridge* (London: John Murray, 1851), 278–9 (entry for 18 August 1833).
[3] Ibid. 71 (entry for 12 May 1830).

Now if what I have claimed is true, there is here a fundamental Romantic misreading of Milton. Milton, we could say
is least alone when he is alone. His is not the monologue of the
poet who utters his word in a universe evacuated of other presences—one might much rather speak of Shakespeare's relation
to his sources in those terms. Milton is to the contrary always
and intensely dialogic. We have to do with his Satan, his Eve,
his Adam to be sure, but they are there to be related to the Satan,
the Eve, and the Adam whom we have already known and who
speak to us from within Milton's text and also from beyond it.
They are not 'single in the field', nor does the poet in presenting them to us pour out his profuse strains of unpremeditated
art. They are both meditated and unpremeditated, newly invented
and also echoed from the past.[4] The excitement of Milton's poetry
is bound up with the mutual tensions, the dialogic encounter,
we may say, between these two modes.[5]

'Unpremeditated' is in fact the term that Milton uses about
his verse in his proem to Book IX of *Paradise Lost*. Urania, he
says,

> dictates to me slumb'ring, or inspires
> Easy my unpremeditated Verse.

The line may have been in Shelley's mind when he wrote about
the skylark's 'unpremeditated art'. The term 'easy' in this context carries great force. As adverb, it suggests the essentially
relaxed mode of guidance practised by his muse; as adjective it
points to the unconstrained, spontaneous nature of the verse itself.
The use of this term 'easy' suggests that Urania's part is to release
his poetic gift; far from imposing herself upon him, she enables
him to discover his own intensely individual voice. And yet she
is also said in this selfsame sentence to *dictate* to him—she 'dic-
tates to me slumb'ring'. Elsewhere he speaks of submitting to her

---

[4] Cf. Michael Lieb, *The Dialectics of Creation: Patterns of Birth and Regeneration in* Paradise Lost (Amherst, Mass.: The University of Massachusetts Press, 1970),
46–7.
[5] I am using the term dialogic here in the Bakhtinian sense. Cf. *The Dialogic
Imagination: Four Essays by M. M. Bakhtin*, trans. Caryl Emerson and Michael
Holquist, ed. Michael Holquist (Austin, Tex.: University of Texas Press, 1981), 69,
280.

governance: 'still govern thou my Song', he declares (VII. 30). If she grants him his freedom, she also governs him.[6]

To understand this paradox we must understand the dual role of Urania. She is the muse of divine poetry, i.e. of poetry inspired by the Bible, and that is because she herself is no other than the spirit of biblical prophecy. It is she, he tells us, who inspired

> That Shepherd, who first taught the chosen Seed,
> In the Beginning how the Heav'ns and Earth
> Rose out of *Chaos*.
>
> (*Paradise Lost*, I. 8–10)

She is thus the authority behind the text that he is expounding and to that authority he submits. But a little further down in the same passage (ibid. 17–22), Urania seems to slip into another role, that of the agent of world creation. She is there all but identified with the spirit which in Genesis 1: 2 brooded on the vast abyss and made it pregnant. She is therefore not only the author of the text that Milton is interpreting, she is also the author of the poet and thus the source of the power and freedom which the poet finds in himself.[7] That is her gift.

From this point of view, the several invocations to Urania are no mere epic formality; they are the very dramatic ground of the poem which may be read under the sign of an unremitting dialogue between the 'ephebe' to use Bloom's term and the greatest precursor poet of all, namely, the voice which addresses him from the biblical text and is, in turn, addressed by him in the poem. Both sides to this dialogue retain their independence.

---

[6] Noam Flinker seems to be pointing in the same direction when he speaks of 'the narrator's . . . simultaneous attraction towards and fear of Urania' ('Courting Urania: The Narrator of *Paradise Lost* Invokes His Muse', in Julia Walker (ed.), *Milton and the Idea of Woman* (Urbana, Ill.: University of Illinois Press, 1988), 90). However, unlike Flinker, I am not persuaded as to the psychosexual origins of this relationship with Urania.

[7] Cf. John T. Shawcross ('The Metaphor of Inspiration in *Paradise Lost*', in Amadeus P. Fiore (ed.), *The Upright Heart and Pure* (Pittsburgh: Duquesne University Press, (1967)) who identifies the source of inspiration invoked by the poet as the *anima*—the creative force in the universe—'the poet's creation thus inspired . . . will be an emblem of God's own creation' (75). See also Regina M. Schwartz's interesting discussion of *Paradise Lost* as a creation analogous to the creation of the cosmos in *Remembering and Repeating: Biblical Creation in* Paradise Lost (Cambridge: Cambridge University Press, 1988), 60–1 and *passim*.

Urania is the sign of a power supremely independent of the poet, one he tells us who converses with eternal Wisdom in the presence of the Almighty—and is thus independent in a sense even of those august partners. Yet her name is also one of the titles of Aphrodite and she thus stands for pure invention and impulse, for a spontaneous generation of poetic images.

Urania is thus more than a muse in the traditional sense. She is the key to Milton's inventive procedure, personifying the link between the two parties to the dialogue: the voice of the anterior text and that of the new poet who addresses it and is addressed by it. She signifies the hermeneutic encounter between them. Now if text and reader can come together in this encounter, it is because there is a prior bond between the two. It is not just a matter of a book which happened to come Milton's way in the library. There is for Milton a prestabilized relationship, a bond between them predating his own existence. And again Urania bears witness to that bond. That is one of her functions:

> Thou from the first
> Wast present, and with mighty wings outspread
> Dove-like satst brooding on the vast Abyss
> And mad'st it pregnant: What in me is dark
> Illumine . . .

The 'heavenly muse' who first inspired 'that shepherd', that is to say Moses, to write a scripture relating the beginning of things, will now guide the poet's pen in his poetic interpretation of that same scripture:

> What in me is dark
> Illumine, what is low raise and support;
> That to the highth of this great Argument
> I may assert Eternal Providence,
> And justify the wayes of God to men.

2

In pondering the nature of interpretation carried out under such conditions of prior relationality, we are naturally reminded of the category of midrash. Gerald Bruns has spoken of midrash as 'a dialogue between text and history' founded on a 'mutual belonging of the text and those who hear it':

The key to midrash lies in this reciprocity between text and history. Midrash is a dialogue between text and history in which the task of giving an account—giving a midrash—does not involve merely construing a meaning; it also involves showing how the text still bears upon us, still speaks to us and exerts its claim upon us even though our situation is different from anything that has gone before. The task of midrash is to keep open the mutual belonging of the text and those who hear it. There is a common accord between ourselves and what is written, and the task of midrash (indeed the task of any biblical interpretation that is hermeneutically informed) is to bring this accord into the open.[8]

The phrase 'mutual belonging' catches the sense of an unwilled relationship, one which is almost a condition of our existence; but 'common accord', the second phrase Bruns uses to define this relationship, suggests a voluntary turning towards the text, an agreement freely undertaken. We might more properly call such a belonging and accord and the readings to which they give rise covenantal hermeneutics. From the point of view of the Rabbis, indeed, the possibility of midrash is grounded in covenant.[9] Whilst the Written Law was public, the ongoing interpretive dialogue with the Torah, the so-called Oral Law, was the task of a covenant community, bound to one another and to the text they had received by bonds originating at Sinai, i.e. going back to the same event from which the written text itself arose.

Milton conceives himself as having precisely this same covenantal relationship to the text that he was interpreting. And Urania is the person or the agency who comes to express this mutual

[8] Gerald L. Bruns, 'Midrash and Allegory', in Robert Alter and Frank Kermode (eds.), *The Literary Guide to the Bible* (Cambridge, Mass.: Harvard University Press, 1987), 633–4.

[9] Cf. R. Yohanan's statement that God's covenant with Israel is solely on account of the Oral Law (Babylonian Talmud, tractate *Gittin*, 60b, and parallels). His proof text is Exodus 34: 27. On the other hand, Alon Goshen-Gottstein has argued vigorously that there was a 'general decline in the position of the covenantal concept in rabbinic literature' ('The Promise to the Patriarchs in Rabbinic Literature', in Alviero Niccacci (ed.), *Divine Promises to the Fathers* (Jerusalem: Franciscan Printing Press, 1995), 60–97). This thesis carries weight in regard to theology—the Rabbis of the Talmud did not much concern themselves with the covenant as theological notion nor did they particularly emphasize the covenantal promises made to the patriarchs. But they implicitly (and explicitly too, for that matter) formed their concept of the Oral Law—i.e. midrashic exegesis—on the awareness of themselves as a privileged body of interpreters bound by covenant to the text they were interpreting. That is the force of R. Yohanan's statement.

accord. She stands for an authority to which the poet has already voluntarily submitted. It is thus accepted rather than imposed. On the other side, his imaginative freedom, that spontaneity which will find its expression for a later age in images of Romantic flight and Romantic individualism is fully preserved. Yet it is not, for Milton, a matter of simple autonomy. He is not self-created or self-inspired; his freedom also is granted within the framework of a covenantal transaction. It is this dialogic, coven-antal aspect of the discourse which the Romantic reader and critic of Milton missed—the bringing together of a personal con-text with an ancient source whereby the two enter into a rela-tion of reciprocity without forfeiting their independence. There is a kind of exchange of pledges. If the poet's part is to submit to the authority of his divine source, then the muse of divine poetry for her part will inspire and raise him to ever greater heights; she is called upon to guarantee his freedom:

> whose Voice divine
> Following, above th' *Olympian* Hill I soar,
> Above the flight of *Pegasean* wing.
>
> (*Paradise Lost*, VII. 2–4)

The elan and vertiginous wonder of this flight will communicate themselves later to Coleridge, Shelley, and Byron, sometimes in the form of fantasies of space travel, but the covenantal ground of such imaginings, the dramatic exchange of vows, the recipro-city will be lost sight of. Dialogue will give way to monologue.

The special relationship of which we speak also involves enorm-ous risks. It is after all not a mechanism but a freely under-taken partnership. As such, it can be forfeited by betrayal. What is said of Adam applies to the poetic vocation as well as to the moral life:

> I made him just and right,
> Sufficient to have stood, though free to fall
>
> (III. 98–9)

The poet is also 'free to fall'. If he is lifted up 'above the flight of *Pegasean* wing', he can also be 'carried away', tempted to a wanton exercise of his spontaneity. That is a danger which Milton vividly represents for his reader in the proem to Book VII and from which he begs to be protected:

> Lest from this flying Steed unrein'd, (as once
> *Bellerophon*, though from a lower Clime)
> Dismounted on th' *Aleian* Field I fall
> Erroneous there to wander and forlorn.

(VII. 17–20)

3

These passages are from *Paradise Lost* where Urania, as I have suggested, is the agent of covenantal hermeneutics. But I would wish to argue that *Samson Agonistes* provides us with an even better model of covenantal discourse or midrash. There is first the sustained dialogue with his source. The original account of Samson's life and death in the book of Judges remains an active point of reference throughout the poem, its authority unsubverted, its voice never silenced. Joseph Wittreich is surely correct in insisting that Milton in this dramatic poem is everywhere guided by the biblical framework. The additions and changes that he introduces, the interviews, for instance, with Manoa, Dalila, and Harapha, are designed 'not to obscure but to reveal the implications of Milton's original'—the original being the story of Samson's life and death as set out in Judges 13–16.[10] To this text he is in voluntary bondage. He could leave it behind and do his own thing—but he chooses not to do so. 'His objective', says Wittreich, 'is to wring from scriptural history its highest truths.'[11] If the poem is an aesthetic exercise, it is no less—and perhaps more—an exegetical exercise.

The phrase that Wittreich uses to define this mode is 'interpretive fiction'.[12] He borrows it from Frank Kermode's *Genesis of Secrecy* which is mainly concerned with the authors of the Gospels and the way they refashion and reinvent their stories and parables, each one making his own changes and additions. But as Kermode shows, this mode of invention or reinvention goes back to the Rabbis in their interpretive homilies on the Hebrew Scriptures.[13] This, says Kermode, was the method of

[10] J. A. Wittreich, *Interpreting Samson Agonistes* (Princeton: Princeton University Press, 1986), 60.
[11] Ibid.   [12] Ibid. 61.
[13] Frank Kermode, *The Genesis of Secrecy: On the Interpretation of Narrative* (Cambridge, Mass.: Harvard University Press, 1979), 81 f.

midrash. So that what Wittreich is really saying, though he does not use the term, is that *Samson Agonistes* is a kind of midrash on the Samson story in Judges.

Milton of course was familiar with traditional midrash and employed many actual rabbinical glosses in *Paradise Lost*.[14] *Samson Agonistes* contains fewer direct borrowings from the Rabbis,[15] but Milton's essential procedure may without distortion be termed midrashic. The added material, such as Samson's bitter meditations on his blindness, his reflections on the justice or injustice of God's dealings with him (with frequent echoing of Job), Dalila's renewed attempt to attract him back to her and his new-found capacity to resist her allurement, the introduction by association of Harapha, a giant mentioned in 2 Samuel 21: 22 as belonging to Gat—all these are metonymic extensions of the biblical story itself as Milton found it in the Hebrew Scriptures. And the same applies to the evocation of other Old Testament episodes and texts such as the story of Elijah on Mount Carmel (1 Kings 18) evoked in the confrontation with Harapha (ll. 1145–55). These serve to enrich and fill out the story of Samson as set forth in Judges by associating it with other places of Scripture. From this point of view the drama he develops is continuous with the biblical narrative as he understood it in its Old Testament context. It has not been radically removed from that context.

But it seems to me that *Samson Agonistes* is not merely an example of midrashic discourse; it is also a reflection on the nature of such discourse. One would almost want to say that such discourse is the subject of the poem. If Urania in *Paradise Lost* is the agent of covenantal hermeneutics then I will suggest that *Samson Agonistes* provides us with an even better model in Samson himself. William Kerrigan has shrewdly observed that Samson's conflict is that of the poet in the act of composition: 'given a source of strength and forbidden to reveal his source of strength—the dilemma of Samson could be taken as a parable

---

[14] Discussed by several scholars; Golda S. Werman has illustrated the considerable use Milton made of an 8th-century midrash, *Pirke D'Rabbi Eliezer*, which had been translated into Latin by Vorstius. See 'Midrash in *Paradise Lost*: *Capitula Rabbi Elieser*', *Milton Studies*, 18 (1983), 145–71.

[15] An exception to this is the notion, nowhere mentioned in the text of Judges, that Samson was married to Dalila. Cf. S. S. Stollman, 'Milton's Samson and the Jewish Tradition', *Milton Studies*, 3 (1971), 189.

about this artistic conflict.'[16] But instead of seeking, as Kerrigan does, a Freudian key to this conflict, I would argue that Samson gives us a reflexive image of the poet who is both bound and free, liberated and, at the same time, controlled by the terms of his contract. And for that contract there is a biblical model near at hand.

Samson is of course held to his vocation by his Nazirite vow or pledge—this is the central theme of his meditations and debates, and as such the very hinge on which the drama turns. This vow, binding a particular individual to God by a special relationship, may also stand as a microcosm of the covenant structure in general as it might apply to larger groups and societies.[17] It was of particular service because it caught, as perhaps no other image might, the antinomy of constraint and power which Milton was seeking to define. He was reaching towards this in the figure and function of Urania; in Samson it is even more cogently articulated:

> I was his nursling once and choice delight,
> His destin'd from the womb,
> Promis'd by Heavenly message twice descending.
> Under his special eye
> Abstemious I grew up and thriv'd amain;
> He led me on to mightiest deeds
> Above the nerve of mortal arm . . .
>
> (633–9)

---

[16] William Kerrigan, *The Sacred Complex: On the Psychogenesis of* Paradise Lost (Cambridge, Mass.: Harvard University Press, 1983), 54.

[17] The centrality of the covenant in Milton's thinking is emphasized by a number of scholars, notably Joseph E. Duncan, *Milton's Earthly Paradise* (Minneapolis: University of Minnesota Press, 1972), 132–47, and John T. Shawcross, 'Milton and Covenant: The Christian View of Old Testament Theology', in James H. Sims and Leland Ryken (eds.), *Milton and Scriptural Tradition* (Columbia, Miss.: University of Missouri Press, 1984), 160–91, though they both tend to an exclusive emphasis on the evangelical Covenant of Grace. This version is certainly crucial for Milton (as how could it not be for one who had spent seven years at Christ's College, Cambridge, where William Ames and, earlier, William Perkins had formulated their powerful Calvinist theology?). But if less rigid attention is given to the need to make Milton's poetry consistent with the formal positions laid down in his *Christian Doctrine*, and broader attention is given to his writings on politics and society and on his own craft, we shall see him as responsive also to what may without distortion be termed a Covenant of Works. Relations between subject, parliament, and king are ordered by covenant; marriage is a covenant; above all, his work as a poet is the locus of a covenant drama. For an earlier discussion of this topic, see, by the present writer, *Jerusalem and Albion* (London: Routledge and Kegan Paul, 1964), 113, 120–5.

The first line, 'I was his nursling once and choice delight' of course echoes what is said of Wisdom in Proverbs 8: 30–1: 'Then I was by him as a nurseling, and I was daily his delight, playing always before him; playing with the universe, his earth; and my delights were with the sons of men.' But that is not all. The careful reader will recall a parallel echo of the same verse in Milton's invocation to Urania in *Paradise Lost*, Book VII:

> Before the Hills appear'd, or Fountain flow'd
> Thou with Eternal Wisdom didst converse,
> Wisdom thy Sister, and with her didst play
> In presence of th' Almighty Father, pleas'd
> With thy Celestial Song.
>
> (VII. 8–12)

The parallel between Samson and Urania in the echoing of this same verse from Proverbs underlines the metapoetic function of the Samson paradigm. Urania, before the hills appeared, played in the presence of the Almighty Father because she was the muse of sacred poetry ('pleas'd with thy Celestial song'). Indeed this verse from Proverbs has been understood from antiquity as having reference to the sacred writings and their inspired exegesis, Wisdom being a synonym for Torah, for textuality.[18] Seen in this context, Samson's election, his 'special calling' ('I was his destin'd from the womb') not merely suggests his Nazirite vocation, announced before his birth by a heavenly messenger, but suggests through that image the vocation of the sacred poet devoted from birth, indeed before birth, from the very creation of the world, to his visionary task. Samson's high destiny conveyed in the lines, 'I was his nursling once and choice delight, | His destin'd from the womb' has thus the same primordial, covenantal associations that we noted in regard to the figure and function of Urania. Ultimately, the issue is not only the justification of the ways of God to Samson but the ways of God to the poet, to man in general, and to the world. From this point of view the Nazirite bond becomes a metonym for the contractual relation of a Creator God with his creation and indeed for the whole working of providence.

---

[18] Cf. the famous midrashic comment on the first verse of the Bible: 'R. Oshaya commenced: "Then I was by Him, as a nursling; and I was daily all delight" . . . God consulted the Torah and created the world' (*Midrash Rabbah*, ed. H. Freedman and Maurice Simon, *Genesis* I, 1, trans. H. Freedman (London: Soncino, 1939), i, 1).

The continuation of the passage: 'Abstemious I grew up and thriv'd amain; | He led me on to mightiest deed | Above the nerve of mortal arm', exhibits the essential paradox with which I am here concerned, now more clearly formulated than ever before. Samson is controlled, bound by his vow, or by the vows taken on his behalf; he is limited, abstemious, subject to an authority imposed upon him in the past. At the same time, that very vow releases in him extraordinary power, a generative force which makes him capable of 'mightiest deeds | Above the nerve of mortal arm'. We catch the same fundamental rhythm in the opening of Book VII of *Paradise Lost*:

> whose Voice divine
> Following, above th' *Olympian* Hill I soar,
> Above the flight of *Pegasean* wing.

If Urania imposes on the poet the constraining authority of a prior text, she also releases in him an unanticipated surge of power. In the figure of Samson Milton has found the precise paradigm for this phenomenon. And unlike the figure of Urania, whose Pagan name he hesitates to call ('the meaning, not the Name I call'), this paradigm is itself authorized by the Scriptures themselves. Moreover, the Samson model works so extraordinarily well because limitation and release, constraint and unconstraint are joined together by the same covenantal transaction, namely, the Nazirite vow. If he will limit himself in the ways required by his vow, then he will have power without limit! Abstention and what I have termed 'the surge of power' go together; nor is it just a case of the one being a reward for the other; Samson's vocation joins the two modes of existence in an inseparable zeugma: 'Abstemious I grew up and thriv'd amain.' The grant of the free exercise of power, 'above the nerve of mortal arm', and his subjection to the overmastering authority of a particular divine command issue from the same moment of dedication, the same covenantal event. The one is a function of the other.

4

The Hebrew term *nazir* verbally embodies this potent ambiguity and perhaps Milton's knowledge of biblical Hebrew enabled him to sense this. One semantic track joins the stem *nzr* to the cognate *ndr*, thus *lindor neder nazir* (Numbers 6: 2) meaning to separate or withdraw oneself by a vow. This is particularly so in the hiphal and niphal usage: *hazzir* and *hinnazer*, which clearly carry the notion of restriction or self-limitation. Thus: 'He shall abstain from wine and strong drink' (*miyyayin wešekar yazzir*) (Numbers 6: 3). Another track points in the direction of *nezer* which has the fundamental meaning of crown or diadem but comes to signify the actual unshorn head of the Nazirite who has consecrated himself by means of the Nazirite vow. It is this head of hair (*roš nizro*) which would be shaved off and burnt on the altar at the end of the normal term of consecration (Numbers 6: 18). Elsewhere, perhaps by association with the hair of the Nazirite, the wild growth of the unpruned vine, left abandoned in the field on the sabbatical year, is called '*innebe nezireka* (Leviticus 25: 5), i.e. your Nazirite grapes or, as Koehler and Baumgarten render the phrase: your grapes 'left to unfettered growth'. The stem *nzr* thus signifies control and restriction, but also wild growth. The Hebrew language is rich in such semiotic puzzles: *hata't* means both sin and purification, *barek* means to bless; it can also mean to curse, and so forth. But what I think interested Milton was the mystery at the heart of the Nazirite phenomenon intimated by this verbal duality. Here is the very node, the nuclear core we may say, of the covenant as doctrine and life and, we may add that here too, in the symbolism of the unshorn hair of the Nazirite, is the ultimate key, for Milton, of his own vocation as a consecrated poet.

Milton returns in his writings repeatedly to the motif of Samson's hair—'my precious fleece' as it is called elsewhere in *Samson Agonistes*. It had a special fascination for him. In a famous passage of *Areopagitica*, he has a visionary sight of England as a messiah-nation achieving the full promise of her religious and political destiny:

Methinks I see in my mind a noble and puissant Nation rousing herself like a strong man after sleep, and shaking her invincible locks: Methinks I see her as an Eagle muing her mighty youth, and kindling her undazl'd eyes at the full midday beam; purging and unscaling her long abused sight at the fountain itself of heav'nly radiance . . .[19]

---

[19] John Milton, *Works* (New York: Columbia University Press, 1931), iv. 344.

The image is that of Samson rising in the morning with his full strength still preserved in his unshorn locks after one of Dalila's unsuccessful attempts to learn his secret. The extraordinary vigour of this 'puissant Nation' is here seen as seated in its 'invincible locks'. We note how this image gives way to that of height and aspiration. Preserved by 'these locks unshorn, | The pledge of my unviolated vow' as he was later to term them (*Samson Agonistes*, ll. 1143–4), the puissant nation of England can now rise to the height of the eagle's nest and gaze without fear at the sun, the fountain of heavenly radiance. It would seem that with the security afforded by the Nazirite model (as distinct from the Urania model) there is less danger of flying too near the sun and falling like Bellerophon crazed and blind on the Aleian field. It comes as no surprise to learn that the national renewal and strength spoken of in this passage and indeed throughout *Areopagitica* are chiefly a matter of literary creativity. The evidence of new-found power and freedom is, he says, 'this flowery crop of knowledge and new light' with which the inspired writers, and principally one feels Milton himself, greet the dawn of a new age. The sign of the unshorn hair here then seems to guarantee boundless creativity and aspiration.

Some three years earlier, in the concluding chapter of *The Reason of Church Government*, a sustained oration on the theme of law and discipline, he conjured up a vision of Samson with his unshorn locks in which the other semantic option is stressed, i.e. the *nezer nazir* as signifying law and control rather than boundless creativity. The passage is an extended allegory in which the 'person of the king' is Samson, 'his illustrious and sunny locks, the laws, waving and curling about his godlike shoulders'. The bishops who seek to seduce him from the true religion are compared to Dalila. As long as he guards his hair unshorn he is secure,

But laying down his head among the strumpet flatteries of Prelats, while he sleeps and thinks no harme, they, wickedly shave off all those bright and waighty tresses of his laws, and just prerogatives, which were his ornament and strength. . . . Till he, knowing his prelatical rasor to have bereft him of his wonted might, nourish again his puissant hair, the golden beames of Law and Right; and they sternly shook, thunder with ruin upon the heads of those his evil counsellors, but not without great affliction to himselfe.[20]

[20] Ibid., iii. 277.

We note again the 'puissant hair' but the hair of the Nazirite in this passage explicitly stands for laws. These laws the king was to guard but like Samson he surrenders them to flatterers and seducers and as a result he is betrayed and is bereaved of his strength.

But in the passage quoted the locks of hair also suggest another category, which has no basis in the biblical account of Samson's life or in the law of the Nazirite, namely *beauty*. The sunny locks are seen 'waving and curling about his godlike shoulders'. Perhaps in this rather surprising tribute to Charles I (whose long, rich brown tresses are clearly visible in the Van Dyck portraits), he is thinking of Absalom rather than the Nazirite Samson— and Absalsom we remember was betrayed, rather than protected, by his beautiful locks of hair! This stress on beauty would seem therefore to contradict the Samson paradigm. R. Simeon the Just relates the story of a shepherd boy of great beauty whose hair hung from his head in curly locks. Finding himself falling in love with his own image which Narcissus-like he had gazed at in the well, he undertook the Nazirite vow which would require him at the end of a set period to cut off his hair and burn it on the altar. Beauty is involved in this story but the Nazirite vow serves as a guard against the temptations to which it gives rise.[21]

We may note the strongly sexual character of the scene of Samson's betrayal. He is said to lay down his head among the strumpet flatteries of prelates, and whilst his head is lying among them, they cut off his tresses. This scene recurs with some frequency in Milton's writings. In *Samson Agonistes* the sexual aspect is even more explicit:

> At length to lay my head and hallow'd pledge
> Of all my strength in the lascivious lap
> Of a deceitful Concubine who shore me
> Like a tame Wether, all my precious fleece . . .
>
> (ll. 535–8)

The same scene is recalled in *Paradise Lost*, Book IX, where the shame associated with the Fall of Adam and Eve is gathered up under the image of Samson and Dalila:

---

[21] Cf. *Midrash Rabbah*, ed. Freedman and Simon, *Numbers* X, 7, trans. J. Slotki, i. 371–2.

> So rose the *Danite* strong
> *Herculean Samson* from the Harlot-lap
> Of *Philistean Dalilah*, and wak'd
> Shorn of his strength.

(IX. 1059-62)

The Danite Samson, his bright tresses adorning the lap of a harlot, has here become the archetypal sign of post-lapsarian sexuality. The scene gives us beauty fatally flawed through betrayal.

If we seek the equivalent moment in the Urania paradigm we shall find it I think, once again, in the proem to Book VII. After the account of the fatal flight of Bellerophon, the poet begs Urania to preserve him from the opposite danger, that which we may term 'downward transcendence'.[22] It is symbolized by the fate of Orpheus, 'the *Thracian* Bard'. Orpheus of course stands for the enchantments of poetry but he seeks his inspiration in the nether regions—we might want to say, in the depths of the id—and his destiny is to be torn to pieces by the maenads.

> But drive far off the barbarous dissonance
> Of *Bacchus* and his Revellers, the Race
> Of that wilde Rout that tore the *Thracian* Bard
> In *Rhodope*, where Woods and Rocks had Ears
> To rapture, till the savage clamor drown'd
> Both Harp and Voice; nor could the Muse defend
> Her Son. So fail not thou, who thee implores:
> For thou art Heavn'ly, shee an empty dream.

(VII. 32-9)

If Bellerophon represents the Apollonian excess of the poetic vocation—exemplified in the 'upward fall' of Shelley, as Harold Bloom has termed it—then Orpheus here represents the Dionysiac excess. This side of the Romantic inspiration will later on find its expression in De Quincey and in the darker visions of Baudelaire and Edgar Allan Poe. Milton already defines it for us in the fate of Orpheus from which he begs to be saved. The anxiety expressed in these lines addressed to Urania ('so fail not thou, who thee implores') shows how real is the menace and

---

[22] For this term see Gwendolyn Bays, *The Orphic Vision: Seer Poets from Novalis to Rimbaud* (Lincoln, Neb.: University of Nebraska Press, 1964), 4-14; for the trend see also Mario Praz, *The Romantic Agony*, trans. Angus Davidson (London: Oxford University Press, 1988), 15-25.

also the fascination of this 'Orphic quest', this descent into the region of the id.

This 'downward transcendence' or Orphic descent of which we speak finds its most accurate symbolization in *Samson Agonistes* where the image of Samson laying down his unshorn locks in the harlot lap of Dalila marks the nadir of his moral history. Here is the ultimate desertion—Samson laying down the hair of his consecrated head not on the altar of his God but at the very entrance to the abode of instinct and sexuality, the zone which King Lear had so graphically described in his madness:

> But to the girdle do the Gods inherit,
> Beneath is all the fiend's: there's hell, there's darkness,
> There is the sulphurous pit—burning, scalding,
> Stench, consumption . . .
>
> (*King Lear*, IV. vi. 128–31)

Here are the nether regions, the underworld of Orpheus. That way madness lies—that is why the maenads tear Orpheus to pieces. But Samson's descent into the lap of Dalila implies something more than uncontrolled subjection to the id; it is the ultimate scene of betrayal, the violation of his covenant vows. And such violation goes beyond Samson's Nazirite vocation and extends to the vocation of the consecrated poet himself, the covenant which binds him to his source and at the same time authorizes his power and freedom. To surrender to the witchery of Dalila is to forfeit that consecration and that power.

What then is this witchery of Dalila which so appallingly and so disastrously threatens the very foundations of sacred song, so that the scene of Samson's fall links itself to the scene of Adam's Fall and involves no less than the ruin of a world? And in what sense does this episode also intimate the betrayal by Milton of his poetic vocation? We trivialize the pathos of Milton's vision of ultimate loss if we suppose that the issue is sexual vulnerability and temptation as such. Reversing the normal Freudian mode of argumentation, I would wish to argue that the sexual imagery of this scene is merely the index to a profounder problem and a profounder temptation. Samson's sunny locks waving and curling about his god-like shoulders brought together in this scene with the potent charm of Dalila, indeed the very physical centre of that charm, speak to us of the fiercer temptation of beauty itself, the last infirmity we may say of poetic minds—at all events an infirmity of poetic minds dedicated to the interpretation of the Hebrew oracles. For in the end those oracles do not authorize the surrender to the beautiful, even to the beauty of their own language. They bid us beware of treating the prophecies as a performance and they seem to warn us against seeing beauty as an absolute value. From this point of view Dalila not only seduces Samson, she seduces Milton as well, disabling him for the task he had set himself. Hers is a potent beauty. As the Chorus says, 'Yet beauty, though injurious, hath strange power' (l. 1003). She is not merely beautiful, she is something like the principle of beauty itself:

> Like a stately ship
> Of *Tarsus*, bound for th' Isles
> Of *Javan* or *Gadire*,
> With all her bravery on, and tackle trim,
> Sails fill'd, and streamers waving,
> Courted by all the winds that hold them play.
>
> (ll. 714–19)

This description of Dalila's first entry on the stage recalls and is meant to recall the first appearance of Cleopatra to Antony on the river Cydnus in Shakespeare's play[23]—a scene which Shakespeare, following Plutarch, seems to associate with the archetypal image of Aphrodite riding on a scallop-shell after her birth from the foam of the sea.[24] Milton here links Dalila with what we saw earlier as the mythic absolute—Cleopatra in her role as the supreme goddess, wrinkled deep in time, variously manifested as Isis, Venus, and Persephone. Samson may reject her ('Out, out, hyaena') and the poet may seek to do the same. But there is too much involved for the poet wholly to preserve his vow unviolated. There are archetypal forces at work which threaten the hard-won balance of freedom and authority, of constraint and unconstraint which makes a covenantal hermeneutic

---

[23] An echo not always noticed by critics and editors, but see M. Roston, 'Milton's Herculean Samson', *Milton Quarterly* (1983), 91; J. Guillory, 'Dalila's House', in Margaret W. Ferguson, Maureen Quilligan, and Nancy J. Vickers (eds.), *Rewriting the Renaissance* (Chicago: Chicago University Press, 1986), 113–15.

[24] Cf. *Plutarch's Lives*, ed. R. H. Carr (Oxford: Clarendon Press, 1932), 185–7. This may help to explain the imagery of ships and tempests noted by Barbara K. Lewalski as pervasive in *Samson Agonistes* (*Notes and Queries*, 6 (1959), 372–3).

possible. Beauty will threaten all constraints and will impose its own imperious authority. In this context the flower imagery is significant. Thus the Chorus:

> but now, with head declin'd
> Like a fair flower surcharg'd with dew, she weeps
> And words addrest seem into tears dissolv'd,
> Wetting the borders of her silk'n veil.
>
> (ll. 727–30)

Dalila becomes for the moment the heroine of a pastoral idyll in this reminding us of Eve, likened to Persephone in Book IV of *Paradise Lost*:

> Not that fair field
> Of *Enna*, where *Proserpin* gath'ring flow'rs
> Herself a fairer Flow'r by gloomy *Dis*
> Was gather'd, which cost *Ceres* all that pain
> To seek her through the world . . .
>
> (IV. 268–72)

It is not merely the beauty of Eve which had here threatened the accord between the poet and the biblical source: it is the haunting beauty of the verses themselves celebrating their own perfection. And if we think that in 'the fair field of *Enna*' passage with '*Proserpin* gath'ring flowers' we have reached the ultimate celebration of the beautiful, we have still to see Eve as Satan sees her in Book IX of *Paradise Lost*.

> Herself, though fairest unsupported Flow'r,
> From her best prop so far, and storm so nigh.
>
> (IX. 432–3)

It is no wonder that the prophets set their face against the pastoral with its sweetness and nostalgia.[25] There is no resisting such beauty. Not only will a Samson or an Adam lay down his consecrated head in the 'Harlot-lap' of such an Eve. So will the poet and his reader.

The term harlot need not mislead us. Elsewhere it explicitly refers to the fierce temptations of an unhallowed literary culture where beauty, in particular poetic beauty, is the problem

---

[25] Cf. H. Fisch, *Poetry With a Purpose: Biblical Poetics and Interpretation* (Bloomington, Ind.: Indiana University Press, 1988), 60.

rather than sex. In Book IV of *Paradise Regained* the hero's final temptation involves the aesthetic attractions of Greek art and literature. These he rejects as so much 'varnish on a Harlot's cheek' (*Paradise Regained*, IV. 344)—a problematical rejection indeed when we consider that this very poem owes much of its eloquence to the very tradition which is here rejected. The temptation offered by Dalila and the hero's rejection of that temptation have a similar function in *Samson Agonistes* and imply similar tensions at the heart of that poem.

5

One temptation then is the pastoral. The flowers of the pastoral and the pastoral tone borrowed from Dalila will at the close extend to Samson himself, as in Manoa's lines of farewell:

> The Virgins also shall on feastful days
> Visit his Tomb with flowers, only bewailing
> His lot unfortunate in nuptial choice,
> From whence captivity and loss of eyes.

'That strain again!' Milton seems to be saying, 'it had a dying fall.' More often than not the pastoral mode is tinged with elegy. We are reminded of *Lycidas*, another pastoral elegy likewise much concerned with hair—a symbol there of beauty but also of death. We remember 'the tangles of *Neaera's* hair' and we remember Edward King, sunk to his grave beneath the watery floor:

> With *Nectar* pure his oozy Locks he laves,
> And hears the unexpressive nuptial Song,
> In the blest Kingdoms meek of joy and love.
>
> (ll. 175–7)

This puts the hair motif in a perspective very different from that of the book of Judges, for *Lycidas* gives us not the strenuous task of a biblical hero but the sad languors of a Thyrsis in his lament for Daphnis. But there is just enough of this in *Samson Agonistes* to make the Nazirite begin to look from time to time like the hero of a pastoral romance. In such instances, Milton's solemn commitment to the muse of divine poetry—his own particular 'Nazirite vow'—is being threatened by the irresistible beauty of the pastoral.

But of course the issue in *Samson Agonistes* is not so much the seduction of pastoral. It is the even more potent seduction of tragedy. At the risk of stating the obvious, let me say that as well as writing a kind of midrash on four chapters of Judges, Milton is also—as he proclaims in his Preface—trying his hand at 'that sort of dramatic poem which is call'd Tragedy'. This makes it a midrash and not a midrash. The question is: can the genre of tragedy be adapted, in the end, to the kind of discourse to which the term 'covenantal poetics' may be applied? Midrash is open-ended, inconclusive; it is an ongoing dialogue between reader and text. Tragedy by contrast is marked by closure, by roundedness, as in the elegiac lines of Manoa or the summarizing words of the Chorus that follow. But the problem is not so much formal as phenomenological. As we noted earlier in connection with Shakespearian tragedy, the allure of tragedy, like that of the pastoral, has much to do with the allure of death and dying. And this turns out to be a matter also of aesthetic options: the aesthetic of death is challenged by the harsher aesthetic of living, with its untied ends, its trials and errors.

It may still be asked: if midrash is truly dialogic and truly hermeneutic why should it not be possible to read the biblical text as tragedy? The interpreter we have said brings his personal context—cultural, historical, social—to bear on the text to be interpreted. That text retains its authority; the reader or poet—in this case, Milton—retains his freedom. If this is so, why exclude tragedy? Is there in fact a principle of exclusion, or is not everyone authorized to make his own midrash in the light of his own history, his own situation, unloading into it his own cultural baggage, whatever it may be. This would include the religious baggage of the Christian reader who would wish to read *Samson Agonistes* typologically as an allegory of Christian sainthood, and who would wish to persuade us that Milton so read those chapters of Judges. Milton could not have been so unchristian as to want Samson to kill his enemies, so, if he does so, it must be implicitly condemned in the poem itself,[26] or else the killing must mean something else, something more in line with Christian

---

[26] Cf. Irene Samuel, 'Samson Agonistes as Tragedy', in Joseph A. Wittreich, jr. (ed.), *Calm of Mind: Tercentenary Essays on* Paradise Regained *and* Samson Agonistes *in Honor of John S. Diekhoff* (Cleveland, Oh.: Case Western Reserve University, 1971), 235–51.

teaching.[27] The typological readings of *Samson Agonistes* have been much discussed and I will not go over this ground again except to say that Milton's religion as we know it had plenty of room for the expression of human aggressions—it was a matter of what Ezra Pound somewhere called 'Milton's beastly Hebraism'. When he wanted to operate with typology as in *Paradise Lost*, Book XII, he tells us that this is what he is doing. In *Samson Agonistes* he is it seems to me not doing this and the drama he develops is continuous with the biblical narrative in its Old Testament context. It is not metaphor, or figura, but, as we now like to say, metonymy.[28] But the question before us is not whether *Samson* is typological, but whether, if it were, the category of midrash could be stretched to include this kind of reading. Why not Christian typology if that is part of the writer's world of experience and why not an interpretive reading of Samson's life and death as tragedy or pastoral, or the story of Adam and Eve in the Garden as epic if that is the way the interpreter's mind is conditioned by his particular cultural situation? And if not, what is the principle of exclusion?

The question arises in relation to texts of all kinds, not only the Bible. Specifically, it arises as a practical issue in the case of legal texts which are constantly reinterpreted in the light of changing circumstances. In that case we generally have established institutions, accepted as privileged sources of interpretation and as guarantors of continuity. The world of poetry and criticism notably lacks such formal institutions. Many might want to conclude from this that every combination of text and personal context has a prima-facie validity and that there are no criteria of value and significance to distinguish one reading from another.

---

[27] Representative studies of this kind are F. M. Krouse, *Milton's Samson and the Christian Tradition* (Princeton: Princeton University Press, 1949), and T. S. K. Scott-Craig, 'Concerning Milton's *Samson*', *Renaissance News*, 5 (1952), 43–53. Important reservations about the typological understanding of biblical and Renaissance texts have been voiced in recent years, notably by Kenneth Gross, *Spenserian Poetics: Idolatry, Iconoclasm, and Magic* (Ithaca, NY: Cornell University Press, 1985); Herbert Marks, 'Pauline Typology and Revisionary Criticism', *Journal of the American Academy of Religion*, 52 (1984), 71–92; Wittreich, *Interpreting Samson Agonistes*, 57, 244 ff.; and Mary Ann Radzinowicz, *Toward Samson Agonistes: The Growth of Milton's Mind* (Princeton: Princeton University Press, 1978), 283–4.

[28] Cf. Susan A. Handelman, *Slayers of Moses: The Emergence of Rabbinic Interpretation in Modern Literary Theory* (Albany, NY: State University of New York Press, 1982), 76–82.

But if that were so, we would have to include under the category of legitimate hermeneutic the reading of the twenty-third psalm once current among the Tlingit Indians of Alaska: 'The Lord is my goathunter; I don't want him. He knocks me down on the mountain: He drags me down to the beach.'[29] The point is that in the cultural context of this community there are no sheep that go out to pasture; indeed there are no green pastures; there are mountain-goats that are hunted. The only way you can make them lie down is by knocking them over the head. And the only 'still waters' within the experience of these people are those sometimes encountered on the seashore. Here then are two contexts in dialogue with one another. This you may say is an absurd example. The Christian interpretation of Samson which would translate him into an emblem of Christian sainthood is less absurd, but some of us might wish to ask the same question of that kind of interpretation even though it comes naturally to many good scholars and writers, namely, are all examples of dialogue between text and history of equal value and legitimacy?

Bruns gives the basis for an answer in the passage cited earlier, where he speaks of midrash as characterized by a 'mutual belonging of the text and those who hear it' and of 'a common accord between ourselves and what is written'. We might disagree about the conditions for such 'mutual belonging' and 'common accord' and the specific examples they would yield, but the principle of 'mutual belonging' is one that we should welcome. It suggests a pre-existing relation between text and context. From this principle it would follow that not all encounters between the two are what Bruns terms elsewhere in his essay 'modes of participation in the dialogue with Torah'. Where common accord is lacking, the dialogue is presumably no true dialogue and where there is no 'mutual belonging' we are no longer speaking of meaningful interpretive discourse for which the term midrash might be appropriate.

Midrash, grounded as it is in covenantal hermeneutics, is thus open, but it is not that open. There is an *engagement*, a prior belonging which, as the Rabbis saw, took the form of belonging

---

[29] Reported by Constance Naish and Gillian Story in *The Bible Translator*, 14 (1963), 91–2.

to the covenantal community.[30] Milton clearly felt himself to belong to such a community. He had a strong sense not only of his own prophetic vocation but of that of the nation for whom he wrote: 'why else was this Nation chos'n before any others that out of her *as out of Sion* should be proclam'd and sounded forth the first tidings and trumpet of Reformation to all Europ.'[31] And this as I have argued lies behind the special intimacy he enjoys with Urania and the special affinity he finds with the Nazirite Samson. He too is chosen as is the nation whose herald he is. He has prior bonds with the text he is interpreting which go back to the first revealing of that text to 'the chosen seed'.

But there are evidently for Milton other bonds with other texts and other traditions; there are other cultural systems to which he seems sometimes to be no less engaged. It sometimes seems as though before the hills appeared the nurseling Milton was playing in the presence of a different deity or maybe with the tangles of Neaera's hair! All the better you may say for the poetry. The resulting achievement is more beautiful than any midrash. And perhaps it is, for it is questionable whether midrash aims at or achieves the category of beauty. The truth is probably that, whilst the Torah bids us choose life, death is more beautiful.

In the end Milton did not succeed in writing a midrash, but he did not succeed in writing a tragedy either. Samson's death lacks the note of defiant self-assertion of a Lear or a Macbeth. It does not give us the lonely descent into Avernus which tragedy requires; in fact it is not lonely at all, for we are told that the end came 'with God not parted from him, as was fear'd' nor is it really a descent, but rather an upward curve as befits the history of salvation. Manoa says truly, 'Nothing is here for tears, nothing to wail.' If we ask why in this case Milton felt it necessary to turn the narrative of Samson's career from the book of Judges into a tragedy, we would have to say again that it was because such an ambition was integral to his own context, his own world, his own inherited literary culture. It is that context which he brings to bear on the biblical text and between which and the biblical text he seeks an accord. Shakespeare

[30] This would be a special example of what Stanley E. Fish in a different context calls an 'interpretive community'. See *Is There a Text in This Class?* (Cambridge, Mass.: Harvard University Press, 1980), 11.

[31] *Areopagitica* in Milton, *Works*, iv. 340.

does not seek such an accord. What we found in *King Lear* was something else, namely, organized incoherence. Milton aims rather at integration; his ambition is to reinvent the biblical text, to reinterpret it for his generation, to write a midrash doctrinal to a nation. If this aim is in the end defeated, it is because, in spite of his profound understanding of the text he was interpreting, ultimately there can be no accord between the closures of myth and romance and tragedy and the opennesses of biblical narrative and of biblical history.

In the end what we have is a case of 'radical translation', of a brave attempt to 'resituate the text within an alien conceptual framework'.[32] At that point we reach the limits of midrash. Milton's exegetical effort, an effort which often seems to be synonymous with his poetic enterprise as a whole, is therefore doomed, if not to failure, then to something like the partial success which attended the efforts of the Tlingit Indians to translate the twenty-third psalm into their own cultural context, namely, 'The Lord is my goathunter, I don't want him . . .'

---

[32] These phrases are quoted by Bruns, 'Midrash and Allegory', 637, from W. V. O. Quine's *Word and Object* and Donald Davidson's *Inquiries into Truth and Interpretation*.

CHAPTER 6

Paradise Lost: Subtext and Supertext

The descent of Raphael in Milton's poem, to warn Adam and Eve of the trials that awaited them, combines a number of different literary sources. After speeding 'through the vast Ethereal Sky' like a Phoenix, Raphael alights on the eastern cliff of paradise and resumes his proper shape—that of 'a Seraph wing'd' (v. 267, 272, 275, 276):

> six wings he wore, to shade
> His lineaments Divine; the pair that clad
> Each shoulder broad, came mantling o'er his breast
> With regal Ornament; the middle pair
> Girt like a Starry Zone his waist, and round
> Skirted his loins and thighs with downy Gold
> And colours dipt in Heav'n; the third his feet
> Shadow'd from either heel with feather'd mail
> Sky-tinctur'd grain.
>
> (v. 277–85)

This account is clearly based on the mysterious vision of the Seraphim in Isaiah 6: 2. Each of these was said likewise to have six wings: one pair to cover his face, the second to cover his feet, and the third for flying. Milton moves the third (or middle) pair of wings further down on the seraph's body so as decently to shade 'his lineaments Divine'. This is a significant departure from the biblical source where the question of nudity does not arise. But the figure of Raphael as Milton develops it in Book V has more of Baroque amplitude than mystery. He is like a painting by Rubens or Tintoretto. As a consequence we become vividly aware of his physical beauty; but that beauty has to be hidden if Milton is to be true to his vocation as the servant of Urania. There must be decorum and restraint and these are conveyed in the phrase 'to shade | His lineaments divine'. The limbs of the angel, though present in the gorgeous description, are nevertheless shaded.

It is clear that the angel is among other things a figure for the poet himself; it is after all Milton himself who brings us the report of the wars in heaven, of the fall of the angels, and the creation of Man. He is that messenger figured in his poem as Raphael who brings the word from beyond our horizon and strives to make it comprehensible to Adam, that is to say—to us. And in this sense, Raphael is a reflexive image of the poet and his task.

To confirm this we may note that Milton had in fact invoked the image of the Seraph from Isaiah's vision some twenty-five years before the publication of *Paradise Lost* in an autobiographical passage of *The Reason of Church Government*. His great poem still to be written, he says, would not be the result of 'invocation to Dame Memory and her Siren Daughters' but it would be achieved rather

by devout prayer to that eternall Spirit who can enrich with all utterance and knowledge, and sends out his Seraphim with the hallow'd fire of his Altar, to touch and purify the lips of whom he pleases.[1]

Milton is here speaking of his own vocation as a poet/prophet and associating it with the scene in which Isaiah receives his prophetic call (Isaiah 6: 9). Isaiah had felt himself totally unfitted for his task until one of the six-winged Seraphim took a live coal from the altar and laid it upon his mouth, saying 'this has touched thy lips, and thy iniquity is taken away, and thy sin is purged'. Only after that had he heard the divine voice calling out, 'Whom shall I send, and who will go for us?' and he had responded with the words, 'Here I am, send me'. Milton in this prose passage sees himself called in the way that the prophet Isaiah had been called. He too had been burnt with the coal and he would carry the wound and the fire of that burning on his lips to the end of the day. We may properly read the Seraph passage from Book V of *Paradise Lost* in the light of that earlier moment of dedication—a perspective which serves to emphasize the close connection between Raphael and the poet-narrator himself.

In the same passage in *The Reason of Church Government* where Milton speaks of his poetic vocation he also stresses the

---

[1] John Milton, *Works* (New York: Columbia University Press, 1931), III. 241.

enormous intellectual effort, the self-discipline involved in the writing of a major poem, remarking that the performance of his task will require 'industrious and select reading, steddy observation, insight into all seemly and generous arts and affaires'.[2] In short, the knowledge with which the epic poet is charged is not self-generated, nor is it owing to the poetical impulse alone; it is the result rather of a willingness to come to terms with sources, with 'arts and affaires' which are in a deep sense independent of the subjective consciousness. Such knowledge is not spontaneously revealed but has to be acquired with great labour. There is also a time factor. Milton speaks of the great number of years needed for equipping himself for his task. During that time he would 'cov'nant with any knowing reader, that for some yeers yet I may go on trust with him for the payment of what I am now indebted'.[3] The word 'covenant' in this context is extraordinarily suggestive: it suggests the dramatic tension of an undertaking made in the distant past and to be fulfilled (or not fulfilled) in the future. He takes a long forward view into the 'aftertimes' to an audience which he dares to hope 'should not willingly let it die'.[4] The word 'covenant' also suggests partners who retain a certain independence of one another. Milton covenants with the reader, because he and the reader have distinct though complementary roles in the hermeneutic process. They are in a dialogue. The poet is one who is 'sent'—a term crucial to the story of Isaiah's call:

And I heard the voice of the Lord, saying, Whom shall I send, and who will go for us? Then said I, Here am I; send me. (Isaiah 6: 8)

The use of this verb necessarily implies two prepositional relationships. One is sent *by* someone and *to* someone. Milton's awareness of his task is dominated by this sense of being charged by an agent not himself. 'Instruct me, for Thou know'st' he declares in the opening lines of his poem. The I confronts a Thou and, intimate though the bonds between them are, they will not merge or lose their separate identities and functions. Likewise there will be no confusion between the messenger and the addressee. Milton covenants with the knowing reader, their relation being one of debtor and creditor. He is charged with writing a

[2] Ibid.   [3] Ibid.   [4] Ibid. 236.

poem 'doctrinal to a nation'. This consciousness of the audience is strong in him during the writing of the poem.

These prepositional relationships likewise govern the mission of Raphael in Milton's poem. If Raphael is a persona of the poet, then he is, like the poet, the deliverer of a message and as such responsible both to sender and recipient. Such a sense of responsibility is utterly central to Milton's poetics, Raphael in this taking his place alongside Urania and Samson as a reflexive image of Milton's poetic role as he sees it and, indeed, as he carries it out. Raphael is not God and he is not Adam, but someone in between, the mediator who makes communication possible.

In keeping with his role as mediator, Raphael in his descent to Adam's bower, evokes for us another image, not only that of the seraph from Isaiah, but that of Hermes (or Mercury), the messenger of the gods in the classical epic. In case the 'gorgeous wings', the 'downy Gold', and the grand flight of this august messenger from the 'Eternal Father' had not already served to identify him, Milton names him in the continuation of the Seraph passage from *Paradise Lost*, quoted earlier:

> Like *Maia*'s son he stood,
> And shook his Plumes, that Heav'nly fragrance fill'd
> The circuit wide.

> (v. 285–7)

The descent of Hermes (or Mercury) is, as Thomas Greene has shown in a valuable study, a central feature of the epic going back to Homer, almost a key to the whole epic enterprise.[5] Hermes is the essential medium of communication whereby the divine order impinges on the human order—this crossing of boundaries being very much the concern of the epic which has the problem of relating what happens to the hero to the will of the gods. For the Greeks the gods do not reach down to men in their daily lives, nor can Man through his own initiative reach out directly to the gods. To imagine that would be hubristic presumption. In those circumstances, Hermes is a necessary link. His appearance is grand, god-like, and he is provided with golden sandals,

---

[5] Thomas M. Greene, *The Descent from Heaven: A Study in Epic Continuity* (New Haven: Yale University Press, 1963), *passim*.

these being winged like those of Perseus, with whom Hermes is often associated. This gave rise to the changed function of the seraph's lowermost pair of wings in Milton's handling of the motif. His seraph, unlike those mentioned in Isaiah 6, flies with his feet. He thus has mobility as well as grandeur. But, grand though he is, he nevertheless converses freely with men, or rather with the epic hero whose status is sufficiently elevated to enable him to share in this discourse.

Greene emphasizes what he terms the 'executive' function of the messenger in the epic tradition. The gods have plans which need to be executed by human beings. The task of Hermes is to communicate these plans and to see that they are carried out. Aeneas has to move on from Carthage, Priam has to be rescued from Troy. Hermes urges them to their tasks and their journeys; that is why he is the god of travellers. This executive function is much weakened in Milton where Adam is not going to be urged on to act by his angelic visitor. The visit is rather for the purpose of warning and giving information. No action is called for as a result of Raphael's descent; at the most he hopes that Adam will refrain from acting wrongly. Rather than communicating a task, he reads him a lecture! From that point of view, Greene claims, Milton's is a Puritan epic, celebrating the heroism of the inward life.[6] This, however, is to ignore an important aspect of the encounter between Raphael and Adam. If Raphael does not exactly charge Adam with a historical mission, there is nevertheless a kind of transfer of responsibility; a journey is undertaken but it is a hermeneutical journey. It may be suggested that an essential function of Hermes/Raphael in Milton's poem is hermeneutical. And perhaps this is true of the descent of the god in the classical epic also. It is not so much a matter of urging the hero on to his task as of providing an ongoing purpose for the poem. The poem has to go somewhere and Hermes points the way. Aeneas has to cross the sea to build the city of Rome, but more than that Virgil has to recover the Greek forms and carry them forward into the Roman world; past narratives have to be brought into relation with present occasions and future poetic tasks have to be defined. This too is what the descent of the messenger portends.

[6] Ibid. 405.

The messenger represented as Raphael in Book V of Milton's poem is, we may say, the poet as interpreter, engaged in the interpretation of the Scriptures and other remembered texts. He is in this sense a mediator, a messenger, a guide, indeed a traveller. For if Hermes is the god of travellers, he is also the god who gives his name to the interpretive arts and faculties. He crosses boundaries, carrying a message from one sphere of reality to the other; to do so, he binds on the golden sandals with which he speeds through space and time. He thus signifies the principle of communication, making possible the transmission of meanings. But this communicative function is profoundly dialectical; if Hermes brings together the different orders of existence, joining the word of the past to the present, he also makes us aware of the division between them, of the gaps separating different zones of knowledge and different periods, of the necessity and —at the same time—the difficulty of communication. That is why he is not only a messenger or mediator, he is also a marker of limits, the god of boundaries.

According to Van A. Harvey, the Hermes model suggests a triadic structure for the hermeneutic relation: there is a sign or message in the form of a text to be understood; there is a mediator or interpreter of that sign, and there is an audience to which the interpretation is to be communicated.[7] The three factors are markedly independent of one another, as I have noted, but they are nevertheless bound together by mutual responsibility —using that term in the strict sense of an obligation to respond. Interpretation presupposes a sign or message which calls for a response on the part of the interpreter and it also presupposes an audience for whom the interpretation will be meaningful and to whose horizon it will be adapted. The appropriate metaphor is indeed the metaphor of a journey, interpretive fictions like *The Divine Comedy* or *Pilgrim's Progress* being typically cast in the form of a journey.[8] In short, there is a dynamic forward movement as the word from the past is reread and rediscovered. And as the horizon of the audience shifts with the passage of time,

---

[7] Cf. *Encyclopedia of Religion*, ed. Mircea Eliade (New York: Macmillan, 1987), s.v. Hermeneutics.

[8] Cf. Joseph A. Mazzeo, *Varieties of Interpretation* (Notre Dame, Ind.: University of Notre Dame Press, 1978), 65.

new interpretive acts are necessarily called into existence.[9] The movement in time is foregrounded as Raphael relates to Adam the things that occurred before his birth. The situation of Adam as 'reader' is not static either; for Adam and Eve will face their crucial trial in Book IX after the 'lecture' is over. Their changed horizon of knowledge and experience will then necessitate a different series of interpretations to be delivered by another angelic messenger in Books XI and XII.

2

We might consider one further dimension of Milton's account of Raphael's visit to Adam in *Paradise Lost*, Book V. In addition to the explicit echoing of Isaiah 6 and the equally explicit reference to Hermes ('*Maia*'s son'), there is a subtext which refers us somewhat less directly to a third type of messenger, or rather to a third source from which to understand the nature of Raphael's mission. This source is Genesis 18 with its account of the visit of the three 'angels' to Abraham and subsequently to his nephew, Lot. As Milton's commentators have pointed out, a whole cluster of references links Raphael's visit to Adam with this biblical pericope.[10] This link is already hinted at in the speech addressed by the 'Eternal Father' to Raphael prior to his journey:

> Go therefore, half this day as friend with friend
> Converse with *Adam*, in what Bow'r or shade
> Thou find'st him from the heat of Noon retir'd,
> To respite his day-labor with repast,
> Or with repose . . .

(v. 229–33)

'The heat of Noon' connects this occasion with the story of Abraham's visitors who had appeared before him as 'he sat

---

[9] On the temporal aspect of the hermeneutic enterprise see E. S. Shaffer, Introduction to *Comparative Criticism*, 5 (1983), p. xii, with reference to the views of Peter Szondi.

[10] Noted by both Meritt Y. Hughes and Scott Elledge in their editions of *Paradise Lost*.

in the tent door in the heat of the day' (Genesis 18: 1). The reference to the meridian heat will be repeated twice more and with considerable emphasis in the course of Milton's narrative (at v. 300–2 and at v. 369–70). In the Genesis story Abraham would invite his guests to wash their feet from the dust of the journey and rest under the shade of a tree. Later he would set a meal before them which they would eat (18: 4–8). These details are already hinted at in the passage cited above and are elaborated in the sequel after Raphael arrives and is seen by Adam 'as in the door he sat | Of his cool Bow'r' (v. 300). Adam thereupon, echoing the language of Abraham to Sarah (cf. Genesis 18: 6), urges Eve to 'go with speed' and make the necessary preparations for the meal. In the rabbinic tradition, one of Abraham's visitors is in fact identified as Raphael.[11]

There is more than a slight resemblance between the function of the angels who appear before Abraham's tent and that of Hermes in the classical epic. They too have a message to deliver and they too will mediate between the divine and human realms. Moreover, the subtext from Genesis 18 does introduce the idea of an executive mission or something very like it—the visitors are there to announce the birth of Isaac, in other words to point the way forward to the ongoing covenantal history which is the theme of Genesis. Their task is also to rescue Lot and his family from the doomed city of Sodom—again a task of high historical importance; for Lot will go on to become the forefather of the nations of Moab and Ammon (Genesis 19: 37–8). But in the final analysis we are concerned with very different hermeneutic models. When the 'angels' of Genesis 18 and 19 communicate their message they meet a very different response from their audience from that encountered by Hermes when he brings his message from the gods to men. The biblical pericope involves a more dynamic system of relations than the triadic structure implied by the role of Hermes as communicator. Milton's Abraham/Adam is less grand than the Greek epic hero who is favoured with such a visitation; his 'bow'r' with its 'lowly roof'

---

[11] Rashi (R. Shlomo Yitshaqi) on Genesis 18: 2 (quoting *Midrash Rabbah*). Milton would have found Rashi together with other late medieval Jewish commentators in Buxtorf's edition of the Great Hebrew Bible (*Mikra'ot Gedolot*). This, together with Walton's Polyglot (1654), would be standard equipment at this time for a scholarly reader with a working knowledge of the ancient tongues.

under which the bourgeois-seeming couple dine on fruit and cream with their guest begins to look like a contemporary Dutch interior. But in spite of Adam's humble bearing he has a far more independent role than that of the addressee of a message from the Olympians in Homer or Virgil. Human creativity is suspect in much classical poetry and myth; it is felt to be a threat to the gods.[12] The Abraham model on the other hand suggests an extraordinary degree of autonomy on the part of the human auditor.

To illustrate this we should carry the story of Abraham and his visitors a little further. After the meal is over the 'men' depart, Abraham hospitably accompanying them on the first stage of their journey. It is then that they communicate to Abraham the divine plan regarding the destruction of Sodom and Gomorrah, knowing that he will hand it on as an instructive example to his offspring (Genesis 18: 19). It will be communicated to him so that he might adapt it for communicaton to others. So far this resembles the hermeneutic process, or journey, implied in the descent of Hermes. But Abraham, far from passively accepting this arrangement, stands up and expostulates with God, demanding a revision of the plan with the words, 'Shall not the judge of all the earth do right?' Audience response becomes something more like active audience responsibility. Far from submitting to the role of auditor, he seeks to write the text himself! In this amazing confrontation, Abraham, though 'but dust and ashes' (18: 27), raises the stakes again and again, finally making his divine interlocutor agree that he would cancel the planned destruction of Sodom if as few as ten righteous men could be found there. Such presumption on the part of the 'audience' to which the message of the gods is directed is alien to the Hermes model. It is not, however, alien to *Paradise Lost*. Milton represents Adam as precisely this kind of auditor. It is not merely that God makes Adam 'free to fall'; he is also in a way free to write his own story; he does not accept the course marked out for him without question. Echoing the language of Abraham's plea for the doomed victims of Sodom in Genesis 18: 30—'Let not the Lord be angry, and I will speak'—Adam reports to Raphael in Book VIII his demand that a fit companion be provided for him:

---

[12] Cf. R. A. Shoaf, *Milton: Poet of Duality* (New Haven: Yale University Press, 1985), 75–6.

> Let not my words offend thee, Heav'nly Power,
> My Maker, be propitious while I speak.
>
> (VIII. 379–80)

The same note is struck in *Samson Agonistes*. In the previous chapter I discussed the hero's paradoxical combination of power and constraint as a reflexive image of the poet. In particular, Samson seemed to symbolize the relation of the poet with his source. I may now add that like Adam, or Abraham, or Job, he submits and at the same time does not submit to his 'author', expostulating with God and demanding an explanation for his strange and terrible ordeal: 'Why am I thus bereav'd thy prime decree?' Here is the central nerve of Milton's Hebraism. The Chorus, like Job's friends, offers conventional answers, urging patience, reminding Samson of his earlier wrongdoing, and claiming that 'Just are the ways of God, | And justifiable to Men' (ll. 293–4). But Samson maintains his cause, refusing to accept the story as they deliver it to him. Like Job, who is for Milton a major paradigm in this play, and echoing Job's words in chapter 16, Samson demands an explanation, a hearing. How could it be that God has

> led me on to mightiest deeds
> . . . .
> But now hath cast me off as never known,
> And to those cruel enemies,
> Whom I by his appointment had provok't,
> Left me all helpless with th' irreparable loss
> Of sight . . .
>
> (ll. 638–45)

There must be another interpretation which he will have to find out for himself. This is precisely what he does. His final act of self-immolation whereby he also destroys the enemies of his people is essentially his own reading of God's plan, his own independent attempt to make sense of his strange elective destiny. He takes responsibility for the way his story ends. He is like Hamlet in the fifth act, collaborating with providence, but interpreting the signs for himself. He too might have said, 'the readiness is all'! In acting as he does, Samson, like Hamlet, leaves a number of moral questions open; readers and audiences in subsequent generations have to make their own judgements. And a glance at the critical literature devoted to Milton's play shows that the debate continues.[13]

It may be objected that the example of Adam in challenging his 'author' or that of Samson in interpreting his mission in his own independent fashion are at best allegories of the hermeneutic process. They do not really concern the way that a poet responds to his source or the way that we as readers respond to that poem. But Milton in fact has a keen sense of the actual hermeneutic situation implied in these examples. *The Doctrine and Discipline of Divorce* (1643), is a tract devoted to establishing the true meaning of Scripture in the matter of marriage and divorce. Of the author–reader relationship which is called for in the exegesis of the relevant legal texts, he has this to say:

herein he appears to us, as it were, in human shape, enters into cov'nant with us, swears to keep it, binds himself like a just lawgiver to his own prescriptions, gives himself to be understood by men, judges and is judg'd, measures and is commensurat to right reason.[14]

There could not be a clearer hermeneutic statement. In setting before us the word of the Bible for our understanding, God as author covenants with us. That covenant presupposes his independence and ours: he judges and is judged. The text retains its authority but we are given far-reaching interpretive freedom, in particular the freedom to exercise our right reason for its correct understanding. Poetics here bears out the precise pattern of mutuality which we noted in Abraham's pleading for the men and women of Sodom and in the challenge to divine justice that he utters: 'Shall not the Judge of all the earth do right?'

From the point of view created by the Abrahamic model the hermeneutic process set in motion by the descent of Raphael thus gains considerably in dramatic tension. Adam and Eve are in fact embarked on a hermeneutic voyage in which they themselves will largely determine the route and even the destination. Such

[13] John Carey sees the ending as 'morally disgusting' (*Milton: Complete Shorter Poems* (London: Longman, 1981), 333). If so one would have to say the same for all acts of violent retribution against a declared enemy. Not everyone would agree. Moreover, the extrusion of Samson's eyes by the Philistines has to enter the equation somewhere. The narrator in Judges, it should be noted, does not pronounce an authorial judgement.

[14] Milton, *Works*, III. 440.

covenantal hermeneutics has a clear revolutionary potential. It implies among other things a new and enhanced role for Adam, the true hero of the poem, who becomes the decisive persona of the poet.

3

It will be noticed that, epic though it is as an event in the universal history of salvation, the narrative of the angelic visit to Abraham, evoked by Milton at this point, is notably unheroic, compared with the matter of the classical epic. Abraham's angels have neither the grandeur of Hermes, nor the mystery of the Seraphim in Isaiah 6. In fact they are not really angels at all in the sense of supernatural beings but quite simply men or messengers and their meeting with Abraham is correspondingly 'low'.[15] The effect of this subtext in short is to bring about a lurch from grandeur to domesticity, from the world of the epic to something more like that of the novel.[16] As Adam/Abraham acts out this biblical paradigm there is an explicit repudiation of epic magnificence:

> Meanwhile our Primitive great Sire, to meet
> His god-like Guest, walks forth, without more train
> Accompanied than with his own complete
> Perfections; in himself was all his state,
> More solemn than the tedious pomp that waits
> On Princes, when thir rich Retinue long
> Of Horses led, and Grooms besmear'd with Gold
> Dazzles the crowd, and sets them all agape.

(v. 350–7)

In effect this passage rejects and overturns those very qualities of aristocratic grandeur, that very element of display which had marked the appearance of Raphael/Hermes when he first set out on his flight from heaven. It was then said that 'all the Bands | Of Angels . . . to his state, | And to his message high in

---

[15] The term *mal'akim* used here for angels (Genesis 19: 1, 15) denotes simply couriers. The messengers sent by Jacob to Esau (Genesis 32: 3) are also termed *mal'akim*. God employs all kinds of couriers; in Psalm 104: 4 'he makes the winds his messengers (*mal'akaw*)'.

[16] Cf. Greene, *The Descent from Heaven*, 403, 417.

honor rise'. The emphasis was on height and stateliness. Now, in the account of Adam's bearing, there is a specific denial of state in the sense of appurtenances and ornaments of rank. Instead of such externalities, we are directed inward: 'in himself was all his state'. And as the biblical model of Genesis 18 supplants the Hermes model there is instead of height, a repeated emphasis on lowness—the lowness in particular of the human figures who have now moved to the centre of the poem—and the 'lowly roof' under which Raphael vouchsafes to enter (v. 463-4).

Moreover, when Raphael first appeared, gold had been much in evidence—heaven's gate opening on golden hinges, the gold-tipped wings of the messenger (v. 255, 282). But now gold—the 'Grooms besmear'd with Gold'—is singled out for condemnation as part of 'the tedious pomp that waits | On Princes'. From being the distinguishing mark of Raphael in the character of Hermes, gold has now become a sign of emptiness and vanity. In all, there is a radical swerve not only in the value-system or what may be termed the sociological currency, but also in the poetics involved. The shift from the Hermes model to that of Genesis 18 ultimately signifies a shift from the high epic to something more in keeping with the simplicity and directness of the Genesis narratives. This is a poetic option which Milton will explore increasingly from this point on in the poem.[17]

Here then is the measure of the contradiction between the different sources of Milton's inspiration. In this single episode of the descent of Raphael there is a tonal duality as sharp as that which I noted in the Ghost's ambiguous commands in *Hamlet* or in the clear juxtaposition of Cleopatra's grand gestures of immortality in Act V of Shakespeare's play and the Country-man's reductive comments on the worm that will do his kind. In Milton's poem a similar *agon* is played out. We have two opposed ideologies which inevitably yield two competing poetic systems.

This shift in focus that becomes apparent in Book V achieves its full expression in the second half of the poem. What was merely implied in Book V becomes now the subject of a programmatic announcement at the beginning of Book VII. The poem

---

[17] For further comment see Leland Ryken, '*Paradise Lost* and its Biblical Epic Models', in James H. Sims and Leland Ryken (eds.), *Milton and Scriptural Tradition* (Columbia, Miss.: University of Missouri Press, 1984), 50-9.

we are told will now move from the high ground of the epic with its mythological frame and content to the story of Adam and Eve in the garden, their trials, their failures, and their achievements. Here is a more everyday world and it will demand a more everyday Wordsworthian treatment:

> Half yet remains unsung, but narrower bound
> Within the visible Diurnal Sphere;
> Standing on Earth, not rapt above the Pole,
> More safe I Sing with mortal voice . . .

Fom now on there will be a tendency to stress the everyday. After dilating on the mysteries of celestial motion for some one hundred lines, Raphael in Book VIII counsels Adam to 'be lowly wise: | Think only what concerns thee and thy being; | Dream not of other Worlds' (VIII. 173–5). This sounds disagreeably patronizing. Raphael it seems is still conscious of his superior role as Hermes with the golden sandals. But when Adam echoes the same sentiment a few lines later he strikes the right note of dignity:

> But apt the Mind or Fancy is to rove
> Uncheckt, and of her roving is no end;
> Till warn'd, or by experience taught, she learn
> That not to know at large of things remote
> From use, obscure and subtle, but to know
> That which before us lies in daily life,
> Is the prime Wisdom.

> (VIII. 188–94)

The roving fancy and the dream of other worlds have of course a clear metapoetic application. It is Adam steering the poem away from the high epic. Adam's own story will now engage our attention as, at this point until the end of Book VIII, he largely takes over from Raphael the task of narrating the events of the Beginning and he tells them as he himself had lived them. The battles in heaven, and all the mythological apparatus drawn from the hexaemeral tradition which had concerned us in the first half of the poem, will now recede and instead the drama of Adam and Eve, their disobedience and its consequences, will take centre stage. Moreover, in this second half of the poem with Adam as both hero and hermeneut, we are also, as audience, more urgently involved. It is after all our story also that he is telling. To correspond with this hermeneutic shift, there will be a tilt in the direction of the low style, the style of directness and simplicity, which from the Middle Ages on had been associated in the literary tradition of the West with the Gospels and the Genesis narratives.[18] Many of the stronger and more dramatically spare passages in the poem from now on will be found to be close echoes or paraphrases of the biblical text itself:

> I now see
> Bone of my Bone, Flesh of my Flesh, my Self
> Before me; Woman is her Name, of Man
> Extracted; for this cause he shall forgo
> Father and Mother, and to his Wife adhere;
> And they shall be one Flesh, one Heart, one Soul.
>
> (VIII. 494–9)

Those who have generalized about the Chinese Wall of Milton's epic style would do well to ponder such a passage. Its Wordsworthian quality is partly due to the fact that the passage does not contain a single descriptive adjective. The three bare substantives in the last line have the stark revelational quality of the last line of Wordsworth's 'A slumber did my spirit seal':

> No motion has she now, no force;
> She neither hears nor sees;
> Rolled round in earth's diurnal course,
> With Rocks, and Stones, and Trees.

We could almost imagine that Milton is here imitating Wordsworth! It is in fact Wordsworth imitating Milton: 'diurnal' taken from the Proem to Book VII quoted earlier is a give-away. The grand style has of course not disappeared but it will tend to be left to the angels, both fallen and unfallen. From now on Satan ('his words replete with guile', IX. 733) will provide much of the mythological enlargement and the high rhetoric that goes with it. We will accordingly treat both with some suspicion. We return constantly to the region of the domestic and the quotidian. The colloquial note is struck again, for instance, in the

[18] The classic discussion of this *genus humile* is of course in Erich Auerbach, *Literary Language and Its Public in Late Latin Antiquity and in the Middle Ages*, trans. Ralph Manheim, 47–65. For further comment see above pp. 58–9.

whispered urgency of Eve's meditations after eating the forbidden fruit:

> This may be well: but what if God have seen,
> And death ensue? then I shall be no more,
> And *Adam* wedded to another *Eve*,
> Shall live with her enjoying, I extinct;
> A death to think.

(IX. 826–30)

Here Milton is not echoing the biblical text, but he is reproducing practically word for word the motive provided by the medieval Jewish commentator Rashi (quoting a midrash) on Genesis 3: 6: ' "And she gave also to her husband"—Lest she would die, and he live and marry another woman.'[19] Here the midrash is inventing to be sure, but it is reading the biblical text at a human level, providing a realistic human motivation. Not only is the story as drawn from Genesis 3 one of simple life and simple choices, but the accompanying interpretation, the exegetical underpinning, is likewise pitched at a human level and conducted in this-worldly space. The poet-hermeneut, unlike the epic artist of the earlier books is 'standing on Earth, not rapt above the Pole'.

There can be no doubt that the effect of this alternative mode is ultimately subversive; it implies a non-epic universe, and it determines the style of enquiry, of inward dialogue and domestic simplicity, that goes with it. This is a world which has less ceremony, less artifice, and more earnestness than the world of space travel and star wars that occupied the foreground in the first half of the epic. And the move from the one mode to the other is by no means unproblematical. Milton seeks to convince himself and his readers that nothing could be more natural and self-evident at this stage of the poem than to step down into the 'visible Diurnal Sphere'. It may be suggested rather that the effect is to create an unevenness at the heart of the poem. *Paradise Lost* is a poem of profound unrest; there is a continuing uncertainty for instance as to the identity of the hero. In the early books Milton's classical, Renaissance instincts led him to admire

---

[19] And see Louis Ginzberg, *The Legends of the Jews* (Philadelphia: The Jewish Publication Society, 1968), i. 74 and note thereon.

Satan as a symbol of power and self-reliance; in the middle books his Christian preferences pointed to Jesus as the supreme hero; whilst in the later books his Hebrew sources led him to see in Adam (combining as he does the qualities of Lot and Abraham) a figure of meek dignity and human worth. There are in short unresolved contradictions both aesthetic and theological which threaten the coherence and balance of the poem. This was the case in Shakespeare also: the unity of *King Lear*, as I have argued, was only apparent. The twin plots do not in fact harmonize. But Shakespeare both recognizes and seeks to control this incoherence. Milton by contrast seems to believe that Hermes blends perfectly with Raphael and Eve with Proserpin. This is the implicit claim of the poem's marvellous balance and its measured prosody. But the reader may wonder whether this claim is wholly sustained. Could it not be that there is a traitor in the house?

4

Let us consider again Eve's reference to dying in the last quoted extract: 'But what if God have seen, | And Death ensue.' Our attention is momentarily deflected from the notion of death as a cosmic punishment and the sign of a cosmic transformation ('Earth felt the wound, and Nature from her seat | Sighing through all her Works gave signs of woe, | That all was lost' (IX. 782–4)). Instead of that the prospect of death becomes one factor for her to consider and that not the most dreadful. More agonizing for her than the thought of death is the fear lest Adam remain alive to marry another! She has a very human (and, dare one say, very feminine) spasm of jealousy; Eve is here a little like Cleopatra hastening to apply the aspic lest Iras 'should meet the curled Antony' before she does. Except that Eve, we may say, wants to apply the aspic to her Antony.

With the poem operating at this level of realistic portraiture and motivation, it is worth considering a little further the implications this has for the notion of Original Sin which 'brought Death into the World, and all our woe'. In other words what are the doctrinal implications of this hermeneutic and stylistic shift which we are examining? To answer this we may look again at the crucial lines in Book VII announcing the shift:

> Half yet remains unsung, but narrower bound
> Within the visible Diurnal Sphere;
> Standing on Earth, not rapt above the Pole,
> More safe I sing with mortal voice . . .

'Mortal' here in the last line is in apposition with 'safe'. In fact it is in apposition with 'visible Diurnal Sphere' and with the whole cited passage. We have here the acceptance of mortality as appropriate, inevitable, indeed as a condition of our existence. It means something like creaturely. This being so, we may wonder what has happened to the other meaning of 'mortal' enunciated in the opening lines of the poem?

> Of Man's First Disobedience, and the Fruit
> Of that Forbidden Tree, whose mortal taste
> Brought Death into the World, and all our woe.

Could it be that from the point of view announced in the Proem to Book VII mortality is no longer a cosmic catastrophe or a punishment for sin but an event that accords simply with our human nature? This would imply a non-orthodox, non-Augustinian doctrine of the Fall. But it is still biblical. Adam is so called because he was fashioned from the dust of the *adama*, or 'red earth'. Nothing is said in the text of Genesis of his being created so as to live for ever; on the contrary immortality is only mentioned in the text as being a consequence of eating of 'the tree of life' (3: 22) and this must at all costs be avoided! Adam and Eve are thus banished from the garden not because they have forfeited eternal life, but, on the contrary, so as to prevent them from attaining it!

In fact, if we read the first chapters of Genesis in relation to the ongoing narrative of which it is a part, continuing through Genesis, Exodus, and the historical books of the Old Testament —which is basically the way the Hebrew commentators read it[20]—it becomes possible to see the story of Adam and Eve and

---

[20] In the rabbinic sources and more particularly in some of the apocryphal writings, there is mention of an immortal state forfeited by sin. See Ginzberg, *Legends of the Jews*, i. 50, 74; iii. 105. But these notions do not have the force of standard doctrine. The idea that Satan (Samael) embodied himself in the serpent is touched on by Ibn Ezra and the Targum of the pseudo-Jonathan but for the most part the normative Jewish exegesis as set out in the Great Hebrew Bible will have nothing to do with it. Interestingly, the likelier candidate for a Jewish doctrine of Original Sin is the episode of the Golden Calf (Exodus 32) which features the archetypal

their expulsion from the Garden not as a unique event paralleling a primordial fall of the Angels and occurring in a kind of metaphysical space, but as a human story of sin and exile, trial and deliverance yielding a historical pattern which will be repeated throughout the Hebrew Bible. Indeed, the pattern is repeated in the very next chapter of Genesis in the story of Cain and Abel. Rashi links the divine challenge of Genesis 3: 9—'And the Lord God called unto Adam, and said unto him, Where art thou?'—with the question asked of Cain after his transgression —'Where is Abel, thy brother?' There are several other linking phrases. In midrashic commentary the two stories are associated as examples of successful repentance. In both cases the death penalty is commuted to exile. Both are dreadful lapses but neither is the 'mortal sin original', utterly unique and divorced from the normal condition of man.[21]

This of course is not the story that Milton set out to tell. The manifest intention of the poem from the beginning and to its sequel in *Paradise Regained* is to relate the story of 'Man's First Disobedience' as that which 'brought Death into the World' and which would only be set right by the redemptive sacrifice of 'one greater Man' who would make good the sin of Adam. Nevertheless, the other narrative which sees the story of Adam and Eve in its Old Testament context as something in between historical fable and moral exemplum is also present as a counterplot.[22]

---

and ultimate crime, namely, idolatry. (See ibid., iii. 120). The idea of a primordial Fall affecting God, Man, and the World is, however, powerfully expressed in the kabbalistic writings (in particular *The Zohar*, or Book of Splendour); see Gershom G. Scholem, *Major Trends in Jewish Mysticism* (New York: Schocken Books, 1961), 236–51. But these esoteric doctrines find little or no place in the Jewish commentaries that Milton would have used. Denis Saurat's belief that Milton had access to the Kabbalah proper has proved to be untenable. And inter-testamental writings such as the Book of Enoch and the Apocalypse of Moses were scarcely known in Milton's time.

[21] Cf. Ginzberg, *Legends of the Jews*, i. 112, and the hymn 'Thou didst teach the way of repentance' by Benjamin ben Zerach, prescribed for the Fast of Gedaliah. (See *Authorized Selichot for the Whole Year*, trans. Abraham Rosenfeld (London: Labworth, 1962), 202.)

[22] I am borrowing Geoffrey Hartman's term; see 'Milton's Counterplot', in Arthur E. Barker (ed.), *Milton: Modern Essays in Criticism* (London: Oxford University Press, 1965), 386–97, though Hartman is pointing to a somewhat different aspect of Milton's style and imagery, namely, a kind of suspended animation which belongs to the perfection of the pastoral mode. This would seem to represent another non-epic strand in the poem.

I pointed out some years ago that there is a major historical pattern to which the story of the Fall is continuously linked in the imagery of Milton's poem. We could call it again a subtext, but it is more like a supertext, an overarching narrative to which all the other narratives in the Hebrew Bible are seen to be related. I refer to the matter of the Exodus.[23] References to the Exodus are particularly dense in Book I where the fallen angels 'prone on the Flood' are compared with the sedge on the shore of the Red Sea and then, by association, with Pharaoh's chariots and horsemen ('*Busiris* and his *Memphian* Chivalry') drowned in that sea at the time of the Exodus (I. 305–12). But they are also frequent in Book VI where again the account of the casting out of Satan and his hosts from Heaven recalls the overwhelming of Israel's enemies at the Sea.[24]

Nor is the poet drawn to the imagery of the Exodus narrative only in connection with the overthrow of the fallen angels. We are also reminded of the Exodus and what followed when Adam and Eve in Book IX taste the forbidden fruit. Adam declares:

> But come, so well refresh't, now let us play,
> As meet is, after such delicious Fare.

> (IX. 1027–8)

The significance of the word 'play' is revealed by reference to the worship of the Golden Calf in the wilderness: 'And the people sat down to eat and drink, and rose up to play' (Exodus 32: 6).[25] The Jewish commentators, as Milton well knew, had glossed 'play' (*saheq*) as signifying sexual licence following the Israelites' transgression. Here again the corruption of Adam and Eve is related in the language and imagery of the poem to the archetypal frame of the Exodus. Moreover, in so environing the Fall of Adam and Eve, Milton has also implied the possibility of an Hebraic, non-Augustinian conception of the Fall,

---

[23] Harold Fisch, 'Hebraic Style and Motifs in *Paradise Lost*', in Ronald D. Emma and John T. Shawcross (eds.), *Language and Style in Milton*, (New York: Ungar, 1967), 30–51; subsequently taken up by Shawcross in '*Paradise Lost* and the Theme of Exodus', *Milton Studies*, 2 (1970), 3–26, and by Leland Ryken, '*Paradise Lost* and its Biblical Epic Models', 62–8.

[24] e.g. *Paradise Lost*, VI. 810–11 recalling Exodus 14: 13.

[25] Pointed out by James H. Sims, *The Bible in Milton's Epics* (Gainesville, Fla.: University of Florida Press, 1962), 207–8.

i.e. as an offence of great seriousness, but remediable. After due punishment and an act of contrition, the journey to the Promised Land will be resumed.

The Exodus is the master narrative of the Old Testament in the sense that it exhibits the norms governing the ways of God to Man throughout that Scripture. It is also the fundamental story of origins, its Trojan War so to speak, a story of heroic beginnings to which later writers, for instance the authors of Psalms 78, 105, and 114, will constantly look back. For Milton it offered an alternative epic framework for his poem. True, it has no rebellions in heaven, no angels, and no epic heroes to speak of. (Moses is described as 'the meekest man on the face of the whole earth', Numbers 12: 3). Nevertheless, the Exodus narrative functions as a vital, indeed an indispensable, element in the total structure of *Paradise Lost*. To put it very simply, it serves to inject a sense of historical purpose into the poem. Precise geographical and physical notation takes the place of mythological transcendence. We are referred constantly to a solid central region of biblical realism where, instead of incredible journeys through the vast spaces of Chaos, we have the journey of Israel in the wilderness, their triumphs and trials, and the overthrow of the Egptians at the Red Sea. We are in the realm of political action in this-worldly space.

The Exodus is indeed crucial for Milton's purpose; it defines the point of divergence from the classical epic traditon. Michael Walzer has perceptively noted that whilst the *Aeneid* also speaks of a 'divinely guided and world-historical journey to something like a promised land', nothing fundamentally changes. Rome is not going to be that different from Troy. History is seen as part of the natural order governed by the circle of maturity, death, and rebirth. By contrast, Walzer declares:

The Exodus is a journey forward—not only in time and space . . . It is a march towards a goal, a moral progress, a transformation . . . We can think of it as the crucial alternative to all mythic notions of eternal recurrence . . . Biblical narrative generally, Exodus more particularly, breaks in the most decisive way with this kind of cosmological story-telling. In Exodus-history events occur only once.[26]

---

[26] Michael Walzer, *Exodus and Revolution* (New York: Basic Books, 1985), 11–13.

But it is not only that events occur only once; they have a different quality from events in the myth-world of the classical epic; there is a divine challenge and a human response. The covenantal hermeneutic enters into the reading of history. The interpretation of texts opens up into the interpretation of a world. As a result, events are not predetermined; there is an openness; there is room for the reader to make his or her choice. In such a situation, human beings are not doomed either by Fate or by the decree of Original Sin. They are urged to act, to co-operate with providence in the process of salvation. At the beginning of the Exodus the word goes out: 'Speak unto the children of Israel that they go forward!' (Exodus 14: 15). The Exodus narrative has consequently been somewhere near the root of all modern revolutionary movements:

it echoes not only in the literature of the millennium but also in historical and political literature. If we listen closely to the echoes, we can 'hear' the Exodus as a story of radical hope and this-worldly endeavor.[27]

If the Exodus 'as a story of radical hope and this-worldly endeavor' has had a revolutionary impact on European political thinking in the past four hundred years,[28] then it is not surprising that its effect (together with that of the other biblical models I have discussed) on *Paradise Lost* should have been likewise revolutionary. Under these influences the poem veers subtly in the direction of the Pelagian heresy as it takes on a note of Hebraic optimism. This is the ultimate significance of the counterplot that we are discussing as intimated in the episode of the descent of Raphael and more clearly in the Proem to Book VII.

Jason Rosenblatt has recently argued that the Hebraic mode dominates the Edenic world of the early and middle books of *Paradise Lost*; after the Fall, however, and specifically in Books XI and XII, there is a displacement of this in favour of a Christian

---

[27] Ibid. 17.
[28] For an overview of the Hebraic factor in Western revolutionary thought from Hubert Languet, *Vindiciae contra tyrannos* (1579) to the 17th century and beyond, see by the present author 'Le Passage de l'espérance: l'interface du xviie siècle', in Shmuel Trigano (ed.), *La Société Juive à travers l'histoire*, iii (Paris: Fayard, 1993), 116–37.

typological reading of the historical books of the Old Testament.[29] In Michael's discourse to Adam (Eve has fallen asleep, evidently finding this part of the poem a good deal more boring than Raphael's discourse earlier on) the Exodus, for instance, is dehistoricized and given a spiritual interpretation. According to this Pauline hermeneutic, Joshua, instead of being the conqueror of Canaan, becomes the type of Christ who shall 'bring back | Through the world's wilderness long wander'd man | Safe to eternal Paradise of rest' (XII. 312–14). We are reminded of Robinson Crusoe musing on the verse in Psalm 50, 'Call on me in the Day of Trouble and I will deliver thee, and thou shalt glorify me', and weighing up in Pauline, evangelical fashion whether it would not be better to be delivered from sin than from his bondage on the island! He makes himself believe for a time that 'my Soul sought nothing from God, but Deliverance from the Load of Guilt that bore down all my Comfort: as for my solitary Life it was nothing.'[30] But good sense prevails in the end over the radical doctrine of Grace and he pulls himself up with the realization that in his desperate need for material and physical salvation he could not afford to ignore the historical sense of this text and others like it. 'So I stopp'd there.'[31]

In the same way I would argue that in the closing lines of his poem Milton stops there! We have a reinstatement of the Hebrew hermeneutic. Eve now awakes as the two prepare to depart from Eden. There is more than simply acceptance and resignation (the 'meek submission' that Michael had counselled) in Eve's words: 'but now lead on; | In mee is no delay' (XII. 614–15).[32] There is a sense of a new historical purpose to be shared by the man

[29] Jason P. Rosenblatt, *Torah and Law in* Paradise Lost (Princeton: Princeton University Press, 1994), *passim*.

[30] Daniel Defoe, *The Life and Adventures of Robinson Crusoe, &c.*, ed. Michael Shinagel (New York: Norton, 1975), 77.

[31] Ibid. 90. For further comment see Harold Fisch, *New Stories for Old: Biblical Patterns in the Novel* (London: Macmillan, 1998), 31–40.

[32] Rosenblatt recognizes in Eve's final speech with its echoing of Ruth, a reaffirmation of the Hebraic emphasis on human love in 'the field of this World'. But it is a momentary recollection, 'a brief glimpse of an otherwise suppressed alternative to the epic's last books' (*Torah and Law*, 58–60). I am arguing for a different dialectic. The poem, though not neatly divided down the middle, has a stronger Hebraic emphasis in the second half. The closing lines clearly show that the matter of the angelic visits to Abraham and Lot alluded to so centrally in Book V has neither been forgotten nor suppressed.

and the woman—their mutual love now renewed. They are outward bound, not headed exactly for that 'paradise within thee,
happier far' which Michael had urged on them as a substitute
for a this-worldly Eden. It will be for them rather to discover
the road as well as the goal for themselves.

It is important to notice that in these concluding lines of the
poem there is strictly no closure. The poem ends on an upbeat
note with Adam and Eve stepping forward hopefully into their
brave new world. It is emphatically the beginning of a new life:

> High in Front advanc't,
> The brandisht Sword of God before them blaz'd
> Fierce as a Comet; which with torrid heat,
> And vapor as the *Libyan* Air adust,
> Began to parch that temperate Clime; whereat
> In either hand the hast'ning Angel caught
> Our ling'ring Parents, and to th' Eastern Gate
> Led them direct, and down the Cliff as fast
> To the subjected Plain; then disappear'd.
> They looking back, all th' Eastern side beheld
> Of Paradise, so late thir happy seat,
> Wav'd over by that flaming Brand, the Gate
> With dreadful Faces throng'd and fiery Arms:
> Some natural tears they dropp'd, but wip'd them soon;
> The World was all before them, where to choose
> Thir place of rest, and Providence thir guide:
> They hand in hand with wand'ring steps and slow,
> Through *Eden* took thir solitary way.

> (XII. 632–49)

James Sims has drawn attention to the fact that these last lines
of the poem recall the departure of Lot and his wife from the
doomed city of Sodom (Genesis 19: 15–28). It will be seen that
the angel has both Adam and Eve by the hand just as the angels
who rescue Lot and his wife seize them by the hand—the reference to looking back and the reference to the torrid heat of
the place they are leaving make the linkage even firmer. But the
main point is that this is a rescue operation not an expulsion.
Sims makes this point:

[A]lthough the action is associated with the Biblical expulsion from
the Garden, a harsh, punitive, and depriving action by God, Milton has
given overtones of hope to the scene by allusion to the story of Lot,

who was not expelled as a punishment from God but was delivered through His mercy.[33]

This is very true, but I should add that these 'overtones of hope' are not achieved only through this isolated passage. They are part of a continuing, if covert, pattern; the passage takes us back to the episode of the descent of Raphael in Book V. That episode had recalled the visit of the angels to Abraham in Genesis 18 but it had equally recalled the sequel in chapter 19 when those same messengers would visit Abraham's nephew Lot and likewise enjoy a meal 'under the shadow of his roof' (Genesis 19: 3, 8). It was there that the rescue operation had been launched. Lot would be saved for the future. He would be escorted by the angel so as not to be engulfed in the ruin of Sodom and would be spared to found a new line. The shadowy presence of Lot and his wife at this point in the poem thus provides a perspective very different from that which the story of Adam and Eve alone would have provided, especially when read in the orthodox Christian fashion as set out in Michael's neat typologies. The typological mode is no longer entirely relevant at the poem's close. Michael has now we might say assumed the role of Raphael. The issue here is not crime and punishment or the passive accept-ance of inward consolations but salvation and rescue.

But the very last lines of Milton's poem sound an even more emphatic note of salvation and rescue. Behind Milton's words

> They hand in hand with wand'ring steps and slow,
> Through *Eden* took thir solitary way

can be heard the echo of Psalm 107 in the King James Bible:

They wandered in the wilderness in a solitary way; they found no city to dwell in . . .
Then they cried unto the Lord in their trouble, and he delivered them out of their distresses. (verses 4, 6)

This psalm, according to the *Targum*,[34] speaks of a mightier rescue even than that of Lot, namely, the Exodus of the Children

---

[33] Sims, *The Bible in Milton's Epics*, 129.

[34] The Latin version of the *Targum* (Chaldaic paraphrase) is given in Walton's Polyglot as: 'populus domus Israel erraverunt in deserto in desolata via, civitatem habitabilem non invenerunt . . . duxit eos per viam rectem ut ambularunt ad Jerusalem civitatem habitabilem' (verses 4, 7).

of Israel and their wanderings in the wilderness prior to their new life in the Promised Land. As we have seen, this analogy has been with us throughout the poem; it now reveals its revolutionary force. Adam and Eve will endure hardship and struggle, but they are embarked on a journey to a kind of Promised Land. And this applies to the reader also who is clearly invited here and elsewhere in the poem to identify himself with Adam and Eve in their trial, their 'distresses', and their deliverance.

This final picture we have of the pair leaving the Garden has in it a clear element of constraint. They are forbidden to linger as the 'hast'ning Angel' seizes them by the hand. Like Milton himself, subject to the authority of his source, i.e. the fixed canon of Scripture, they too are guided, directed, governed by providence. But they are also given enormous latitude, they are marvellously free to choose:

> The World was all before them, where to choose
> Thir place of rest, and Providence thir guide.

Leslie Brisman, emphasizing Milton's 'poetry of choice', points to the 'openness of option' in this closing scene of *Paradise Lost*. There is, he notes, here and elsewhere a turning towards a future which will be marked by 'continual choice' not simply by a single prohibition which they may choose to obey or disobey.[35] This is well noted. The time, we may say, is free. Author and reader share with the hero and heroine this freedom, or, rather, this combination of freedom and restraint. For what we have again is a covenantal balance. The world and where to choose is all before them, but at the same time they are being driven out of Eden, directed by the hastening angel. There is freedom for sure, but there are also guidance and authority.

Here is the strong central paradox both of Milton's poetics and of his world-view; it will not be maintained by his successors in a later age. The Bible remains as important for Byron

---

[35] Leslie Brisman, *Milton's Poetry of Choice and Its Romantic Heirs* (Ithaca, NY: Cornell University Press, 1973), 171–3. Brisman also lays emphasis on the *stasis* implied in 'thir place of rest' as indicating a space or moment of grace in which 'temporality is redeemed'. I am not sure that I know what this means; if it means that historical time is abandoned or transcended, then I would want to say that whilst this is often true of the Romantic poets, it is not true of Milton. (And see below, Chapter 9, sect. 1.)

in *Cain* as it was for Milton in *Paradise Lost* and he will also
echo Milton throughout. But significantly Byron chooses the
defiant Cain ('Am I my brother's keeper?') as the hero of his
drama of the Fall. For like Cain and unlike Adam, Byron is in
rebellion against his author. His hero demands to know why
he is punished for Adam's sin and why indeed it was regarded
as a sin in the first place. 'The tree was planted, and why not
for him?' In effect Lucifer expresses the play's main thrust. He
is one who dares

> look the Omnipotent tyrant in
> His everlasting face, and tell him that
> His evil is not good!
>
> (I. i)

Byron thus, whilst drawn powerfully to his biblical source, reverses its direction, denying it any normative authority. Instead
of addressing his Muse like Milton with the words 'still govern
thou my Song', he says in effect with Cain, 'That which I am,
I am' (III. i). It is the new posture of the children of the Enlightenment. The chapters that follow will explore the radically new
hermeneutic that this yields and its implications for the poetry
of William Blake and other poets of the Romantic period.

PART III

BLAKE

CHAPTER 7

Mock on Voltaire Rousseau

Milton's poetry represents for Blake a model so total, embracing both the grand design of his prophecies as well as the minute particulars of their language, that critics have too readily located Blake in the same interpretive tradition as Milton. For Leslie Tannenbaum Blake's project as a poet of biblical inspiration is essentially continuous with that of Milton;[1] Joseph A. Wittreich, Jr., includes Spenser in the same continuum: 'For the Renaissance and for Blake, the creator and the interpreter are one . . . in this respect, the poet is also like the prophet who proclaims a new vision and who serves simultaneously as an interpreter of it.'[2] All three, he claims—Spenser, Milton, and Blake—lean on the Bible in fundamentally the same way, arriving at their own meaning and vision by a process akin to allegory or typology. Both Milton and Blake use a symbolic design which has the effect of transforming their audience 'from a theatre of readers into a house of interpreters'.[3]

As we have seen, Milton truly and earnestly sought to interpret the biblical text, whether it was that of Judges or Genesis, and he invited the reader to perform the same acts of recognition and understanding. Wittreich properly emphasizes this aspect of Milton's poetry.[4] But does Blake relate to the Bible in the same way? This is hardly the impression that his prophecies make on us when we set them beside *Paradise Lost* or *The Faerie*

[1] L. Tannenbaum, *Biblical Tradition in Blake's Early Prophecies: The Great Code of Art* (Princeton: Princeton University Press, 1982), 24, 86–99, 119–28.

[2] J. A Wittreich, Jr., 'Sublime Allegory: Blake's Epic Manifesto and the Milton Tradition', *Blake Studies*, 4 (Spring 1972), 29.

[3] Ibid. 38. Further elaborated by the same author in *Angel of the Apocalypse: Blake's Idea of Milton* (Madison, Wis.: University of Wisconsin Press, 1975), 177–9, with some nuancing of the differences between Spenserian allegory and that of Milton and Blake (180–6). For a contrary view, see Robert J. Gleckner, *Blake and Spenser* (Baltimore: Johns Hopkins University Press, 1985), 149–50.

[4] See above, Chapter 5, pp. 161–2.

Queene. Blake seems rather to affirm a radical freedom from any pre-existing authority, both that of his Renaissance precursors as well as that of the biblical texts on which they had so deeply pondered.[5] Blake himself made the distinction with perfect clarity. His own visions, including his drawing of the Last Judgement, were owing to 'the daughters of Inspiration', whereas allegorical interpretations and the like were he said 'formed by the daughters of Memory'.[6] Urania was, of course, like the other muses, a daughter of Memory (Mnemosyne) and Milton's submission to her governance was therefore an artistic limitation. Blake's own inspiration would be of a different order, freed from the bondage of memory and precedent.

The Bible is present everywhere in Blake's writing, and yet it would seem to have no independent authority; it does not stand over and against him. There is no evident struggle, no exegetical tension such as we found in Milton. His vision is essentially unmediated, the Bible yielding not the Word which governs his song, but the outlines of a new myth, fragments of a greater whole which would be generated by the transcendent power of the new poet's own imagination.[7] This is not strictly biblical interpretation but rather the assumption by the poet of the powers of the biblical writers themselves. He draws from them the power to write a new Bible, unchecked by any constraints exercised on him by the old. 'I know of no other Christianity and of no other Gospel,' Blake declares, 'than the liberty both of body & mind to exercise the Divine Arts of Imagination' (*Jerusalem*, Pl. 77). This stance presupposes a system of intertextual relations quite different from that which we have termed covenantal hermeneutics. There is no covenant, no bond entered into, no acceptance of a command delivered from the past and still valid in the present. We have here some other category which has yet to be defined. The twofold, Nazirite form of Milton's poetics has here given way to something more unitary, more holistic, and, I would

---

[5] Cf. M. Roston, *Changing Perspectives in Literature and the Visual Arts, 1650–1820* (Princeton: Princeton University Press, 1990), 290.

[6] 'A Vision of The Last Judgment' from Blake's Notebook, pp. 68–72, in *The Poetry and Prose of William Blake*, ed. David W. Erdman (New York: Doubleday, 1970), 544, 545. Quotations from Blake will be from this edition, hereinafter cited in parentheses in the text either by Plate number where this is applicable, or by page in Erdman (to be referred to as E).

[7] Cf. Gleckner, *Blake and Spenser*, 117–18, 150, 308.

add, more monologic.[8] Instead of the dialectic of power and constraint, we would seem to have power alone, that of the triumphant individual voice which has annihilated, or attempted to annihilate, all constraints of system and language.

Of course this is a gesture, an ideal, rather than a purpose actually accomplished. For we may doubt whether the poet's Imagination can operate with total freedom from the 'mind-forg'd manacles' of law, reason, and poetic precedent. 'Reason', Blake says himself in *The Marriage of Heaven and Hell*, 'is the bound or outward circumference of Energy' (Pl. 4) and the Sons of Los set 'bounds to the Infinite putting off the Indefinite' (*Milton*, Pl. 28: 4).[9] But the gesture of self-liberation is what counts. It is that which determines the direction of the new hermeneutic.

2

We may consider briefly the genetic question. What had supervened between the age of Milton and that of Blake to make possible so radical a development? To answer in one word, one would have to say that the Enlightenment is what had changed the world. Blake was to attack the Age of Reason and all that it stood for, in particular the abstract, mathematical reasoning of Locke and Newton which came to sum up for him, especially in his last prophetic books, the false Urizenic 'philosophy of the five senses'. But, as Jean H. Hagstrum has perceptively noted, the Enlightenment values which Blake so categorically rejected 'had in fact invaded the deepest recesses of his being'.[10] Blake is as much the child of the Enlightenment as he is the poetic offspring of Milton. His annotations to Bishop Watson's *Apology for the Bible* written in 1798 in which he defends Thomas

---

[8] I find myself in disagreement on this point with Harold Bloom (in several places) and also with Aaron Fogel (see the latter's 'Pictures of Speech: On Blake's Poetic', *Studies in Romanticism*, 21 (1982), 217).

[9] On this aspect, see Milton O. Percival, *William Blake's Circle of Destiny* (New York: Columbia University Press, 1938), ch. 4 *passim*. And see below, p. 269.

[10] Jean H. Hagstrum, 'William Blake Rejects the Enlightenment' (From *Studies on Voltaire and the Eighteenth Century*, 25 (1963), 811–28), reprinted in Northrop Frye (ed.), *Blake: A Collection of Critical Essays* (Englewood Cliffs, NJ: Prentice-Hall Inc., 1966), 142–55 (p. 143). And cf. Denis Saurat's still useful *Blake and Modern Thought* (London: Constable, 1929), 17–36.

Paine's iconoclastic approach to the Bible against the Bishop's strictures are an obvious indication of this:

The Bible or ⟨Peculiar⟩ Word of God, Exclusive of Conscience or the Word of God Universal, is that Abomination which like the Jewish ceremonies is forever removed & henceforth every man may converse with God & be a King & Priest in his own house. (E 605)

Milton had, in his Puritan fashion, violently attacked the priestly code of Leviticus as no longer binding for Christians,[11] but Blake's words suggest much more than this, namely, the jettisoning of the whole notion of a revealed word. It would seem from his Notes to Watson that there is no divine command made known exclusively in the Bible and, that being so, it is questionable whether the text calls for an interpretative effort aimed at elucidating its (non-existent) commands. In *Paradise Lost*, Book XII, the angel Michael had explained to Adam how the Jewish ceremonies might be reinterpreted for Christians using the time-honoured devices of typology. Such Christian commentary leaves the biblical commands in place but translates them into a new language. Blake for his part calls on Bishop Watson to face up to Paine's argument that 'all the Commentators on the Bible are dishonest Knaves who in hopes of a good living adopt the State religion'. Exegesis in the strict sense has become irrelevant. Also in the spirit of the Enlightenment, Blake raises the question of authenticity and authorship: 'If Moses did not write the history of his acts, it takes away the authority altogether . . .' (E 606). We are in an intellectual climate very different from that of Milton and his generation.

Though Milton had not been aware of this, the signs of the new dawn (or the new twilight—depending on one's point of view) were already visible before his death in Spinoza's *Tractatus Theologico-Politicus* (1670). Here the Enlightenment finds its first major voice—a voice which will continue to echo through the eighteenth and nineteenth centuries to become a diffused influence in the thinking of the time. Blake would probably not have read Spinoza's text, but he could have heard its echo, 'the daughter of his voice', as Milton might have said, in many contemporary writings, most obviously in Paine's *Age of Reason*

---

[11] See *The Reason of Church Government*, Book I, chs. 3 and 5.

(1794, 1795) the book which Blake was to defend against the attacks of Bishop Watson, Paine's book being in many ways no more than a simplified and somewhat vulgarized version of the *Tractatus*.[12]

Spinoza's fundamental criticism is of breathtaking simplicity: he approaches the question of the authority of the text from the angle of epistemology. Do the biblical records give us true knowledge? His answer is that they do not. Such narratives cannot give us knowledge; knowledge can only be derived from 'general ideas in themselves certain and known'[13]—in other words from philosophy. And this includes the knowledge of God— what had till then been called Divine Philosophy. Following Maimonides and his principle of 'accommodation' but carrying this way of reading to a much more radical extreme, Spinoza will treat all biblical references to God's interventions in human affairs as figures of speech, accommodated to human understanding.[14] Revelation thus affords us no certain knowledge of God and his doings.

If then the Bible does not give us the Truth either of God, Man, or Nature, what, according to Spinoza, does it teach? His answer is, Obedience. It commands. But then with an intellectual sleight of hand which will be the mark of Enlightenment thinking, he adds that such obedience can equally be achieved by the path of Reason and Nature (chapter 8). And the suggestion

---

[12] Paine echoes nearly all Spinoza's arguments regarding the authorship of the Pentateuch, the nature of prophecy, and the truth-claims of the Bible. But, unlike Spinoza, Paine has no deep feeling for the biblical text; down to the publication of the second part of *The Age of Reason* in 1795, he tells us that he 'kept no Bible'. In the preface to that volume, he notes, with a touch of sardonic humour, that he has now acquired 'a Bible and Testament; and I can say also that I have found them to be much worse books than I had conceived' (*Age of Reason: Being an Investigation of True and Fabulous Theology*, by Thomas Paine (New York: Willey Book Co., n.d.), 97). This is more like the tone of Voltaire and the Deists. On Blake's closeness to the radicalism of Paine, see generally David V. Erdman, *Blake: Prophet Against Empire* (New York: Doubleday, 1969), 298–305; he takes him to be the model for Tharmas in *The Four Zoas*. And see S. Foster Damon, *A Blake Dictionary* (Providence, RI: Brown University Press, 1965), s.v. Paine. See also E. P. Thompson, *Witness Against the Beast: William Blake and the Moral Law* (Cambridge: Cambridge University Press, 1993), 60–3, 125–8.

[13] Benedictus de Spinoza, *Tractatus Theologico-Politicus*, ch. 4, trans. R. H. M. Elwes (New York: Dover Publications, 1951), 61.

[14] Ibid., ch. 2, 37–40. And cf. Amos Funkenstein, *Theology and the Scientific Imagination from the Middle Ages to the Seventeenth Century* (Princeton: Princeton University Press, 1986), 241–3.

is that for the thinking man and woman this path to obedience, based not on the text of the Bible but on 'the intellectual love of God', is to be preferred. The road to Deism and to all that followed after is now open.

What then, we may ask of Spinoza, gives the Bible so great an influence on human affairs? Why does the social and political turmoil of his own century, including the violent controversy surrounding his own teaching, turn out to be to so great an extent a matter of conflicting interpretations of the biblical text? What was the secret of its power? It would seem that the hint of an answer is provided in his discussion of prophecy. Unlike Maimonides who had pointed to the prophets as being primarily distinguished by an intellectual endowment superior to that of other men[15]—in short greater knowledge—Spinoza sums up their achievement in the word 'imagination'. He claims that

prophetas non fuisse perfectione mente praeditos, sed quidem potentia vividius imaginendi.[16]

Prophets are endowed with 'unusually vivid imaginations'. But by elevating imagination to first place, making it indeed the single defining characteristic of prophecy, Spinoza need not be supposed to be here awarding particularly high marks to prophecy. He was probably no more impressed by their *potentia imaginendi* than Hobbes was impressed by what he called Fancy. The notion of a powerful imagination simply served to explicate prophecy as well as to distinguish it from more rational pursuits aimed at the acquisition of true knowledge.

Now Blake performs his own sleight of hand with all this. Agreeing with Spinoza and with Thomas Paine, who here as elsewhere echoes Spinoza's argument, he identifies the 'Spirit of Prophecy' with 'Poetic Genius',[17] but, unlike Spinoza and Paine,

---

[15] Maimonides, *The Guide for the Perplexed*, Part II, ch. 36, trans. M. Friedlander (London: George Routledge, 1947), 225–7.

[16] *Tractatus*, ch. 2, in Benedictus de Spinoza, *Opera*, ed. Carl Gebhart (Heidelberg: Winter 1925), iii. 15. Maimonides had likewise stressed the image-making faculty of prophets, but this was for him secondary to their rational and intellectual powers (*Guide for the Perplexed*, 225).

[17] 'The Religeons of all Nations are derived from each Nation's different reception of the Poetic Genius which is every where call'd the Spirit of Prophecy': from Blake's etching of 1788 entitled 'All Religions are One' (E 2).

he sees that as the prophet's mark of distinction.[18] More than that, in a reversal as breathtaking as that of Spinoza himself, he will found a new epistemology based on the claims of the poetic/prophetic imagination. For Blake it is the poet who through his *potentia imaginendi* gains access to true and certain knowledge, to those 'minute particulars' which are he says 'the jewels of Albion' (*Jerusalem*, Pl. 45: 17), whilst the reasoning spectre of the Enlightenment philosophers can provide us only with meaningless abstractions:

What is General Knowledge is there such a Thing[?] [*Strictly Speaking*] all Knowledge is Particular. (*Annotations to the Works of Sir Joshua Reynolds*, E 637)

Where Spinoza had denied that prophets are endowed with superior mental gifts ('non fuisse perfectione mente praeditos'), Blake sees the prophet/poet as gifted with the higher intelligence which comes from the 'four-fold vision'—a cognitive system which includes the sensory, imaginative, and visionary powers of the mind. The term 'mental' as in 'mental fight' or 'the Mental Traveller' always carries for Blake this wider reference. It suggests the activity of the whole mind and also the indivisibility of subject and object in the processes of perception and cognition.[19]

Mental Things are alone Real what is Calld Corporeal Nobody Knows of its dwelling Place ⟨it⟩ is in Fallacy & its Existence an Imposture. ('A Vision of The Last Judgment', E 555)

He proceeds to give his famous example of such 'mental' perceptions of the Real:

[What] it will be Questiond When the Sun rises do you not see a round Disk of fire somewhat like a Guinea O no no I see an Innumerable company of the Heavenly host crying Holy Holy Holy is the Lord God Almighty. (ibid.)

It will be noted that we have here a powerful volte-face. Accepting the Enlightenment's view of prophecy as mere poetry, he turns poetry—and supremely the poetry of the Bible—into a mode of cognition more absolute than that which had been

[18] Cf. Tannenbaum, *Biblical Tradition*, 14, 294 (n. 35); Morton D. Paley, *Energy and the Imagination* (Oxford: Oxford University Press, 1970), 21.

[19] Cf. Northrop Frye, *Fearful Symmetry: A Study of William Blake* (Boston: Beacon Press, 1965), 19, 23–6.

assumed by devout readers of an earlier age. Spinoza had left to the Bible the attenuated role of commanding obedience—it expressed in some sense the will of God. Blake, like Paine and the Deists, goes further than Spinoza along the path of secularization, abandoning that role also. The text does not command obedience; it is pure myth, pure poetry. But as such it becomes paradoxically a source of true knowledge—the role which Spinoza and the Deists had explicitly denied to it.[20] In the passage just quoted, the biblical vision of the Seraphim from Isaiah 6: 3, which Spinoza through his critical lens would have viewed as mere figure, becomes for Blake a literal truth. The real sun is an innumerable company of the heavenly host crying Holy Holy Holy. The fallacy was that of the unfortunate friend who could only see a yellow disk about the size of a guinea; he was suffering from an atrophy of the organs of perception, from single vision and Newton's sleep.

Thus the Bible is for Blake both less than revelation and more than revelation. It has the special authority which comes, not from its supposed divine origin as the Word of God addressed to Man, but from its origin within the human Imagination, the Imagination being the only source of divine knowledge which Blake recognized. Wordsworth we may remember likewise gave unmistakably divine honours to the Imagination—it is to that 'awful Power' that he owed his moment of revelation when he and his friend understood that they had crossed the Alps:

> That awful Power rose from the mind's abyss
> Like an unfathered vapour that enwraps,
> At once, some lonely traveller. I was lost;
> Halted without an effort to break through;
> But to my conscious soul I now can say—
> 'I recognize thy glory:' in such strength
> Of usurpation, when the light of sense
> Goes out, but with a flash that has revealed
> The invisible world, doth greatness make abode,
> There harbours.
>
> (*Prelude*, VI. 594–603)

[20] E. S. Shaffer discusses a similar shift from a radical questioning of the Bible as revealed truth to its reinstatement as sublime myth, in the writings of Herder and Coleridge at about this same time. See '*Kubla Khan*' and *The Fall of Jerusalem: The Mythological School in Biblical Criticism and Secular Literature* (Cambridge: Cambridge University Press, 1975), ch. 2 *passim*.

But Wordsworth here not only wraps the traveller with a vapour; he also wraps the reader in a misty language which half conceals and half reveals the astounding shift to which the passage testifies. The source of revelation and the locus of the numinous are now the mind of man himself. The mistiness of the imagery and the obscurities of the syntax in the passage quoted and in the sentences which follow it are themselves a sign of the numinous, the poet reverentially veiling his meaning in the presence of the holy—'that awful Power'. But they are also a sign of the hesitancy which marks the acknowledgement by the poet of the new source of power and holiness. Blake knows no such hesitancy and no such inhibitions. He makes his statement with a bold literalness and a sharpness which befit the art of an engraver:

The Eternal Body of Man is THE IMAGINATION, that is God himself.[21]

3

This stress on the transcendent powers of the individual mind is naturally not a product of the Enlightenment considered in its more rational forms, but it has its origin in the same revolutionary ferment and questioning of tradition which marked the age as a whole. For Wordsworth and Coleridge it was evidently nourished by Kant, especially in his discussion of the Sublime.[22] In Blake's case we may point to the eighteenth-century resurgence of interest in gnosticism and other Christian and pre-Christian heresies. Blake was caught up by all this. Paradoxically, his sources of information included the writings of such sceptical observers as Pierre Bayle and Joseph Priestley who, in spite of their incredulity, showed enormous interest in such esoteric currents![23] Here

[21] This is among the mottoes he inscribed on the Laocoon engraving (E 271, 454). Blake did not give Wordsworth full credit for his imaginative vision; his poetry had in it too much of Man and Nature. He claimed moreover that 'Imagination has nothing to do with Memory' (Annotations to Wordsworth's Poems, E 654–5).

[22] Critique of Judgement, Part I, Book 2.

[23] Joseph Priestley, An History of Early Opinions Concerning Jesus Christ (1786), and Nathaniel Lardner, The History of the Heretics in the first Two Centuries after Christ (1780), were evidently known to Blake. These and other materials are investigated by Stuart Curran in his valuable essay, 'Blake and the Gnostic Hyle: A Double Negative', in Blake Studies, 4: 2 (1972), 117–33. With somewhat less probability Saurat points to Johann Lorenz von Mosheim's two-volume Latin De rebus Christianorum ante Constantinum Magnum Commentarii (1753) as a source for Blake's knowledge of gnosticism (Saurat, Blake and Modern Thought, 3–10).

is another example of how Blake's enthusiasms were stimulated, dialectically, by Enlightenment thinkers opposed to enthusiasm.

Central to gnosticism in all its forms is the conviction that man's inmost self is related to the godhead. The *gnosis* that the gnostics taught was above all the knowledge of the self. 'He who knows himself knows all', said Hermes Trismegistus. And as a corollary to this they violently rejected the outer world of material phenomena as fallen and corrupt. The witness to God is in the soul; his signature is not to be sought in the created universe or in the design of history. There an anti-god held sway. In effect the gnostics gave exaggerated prominence to a dualism which is inherent in the orthodox forms of Christianity— in the Pauline epistles, in Augustine, and later in Puritanism. There was the union with the Saviour on the one hand achieved in the inwardness of the soul (cf. 1 John 4: 13) and, on the other, there was the negation of the things that are seen, World and Flesh being blighted by Original Sin. But where such extreme evangelical positions were concerned, the Church in its wisdom had learned to exercise compromise and moderation. Our this-worldly concerns would be brought into the circle of the religious life; significance, beauty, and even holiness would be discovered in the physical creation. Glory would be given to God for dappled things. The Christian gnostics rejected such wisdom, they were dualists on principle. Matter was the source of evil and the God who had brought the material world into existence— specifically the Creator God of the Hebrew Bible—was an evil Demiurge whose laws were so many commands from Satan's kingdom!

It followed that the gnostics had little or no use for typology and for textual exegesis generally.[24] Nor were they much concerned with the harmonizing of Scripture; such programmes were undertaken most often by those who sought to refute the teachings of the gnostics and the Manicheans. Like Blake the gnostics drew upon elements of the Scriptures and of other sources also, but in order to construct their own myth. According to this myth, Jesus, stripped of his physicality, becomes the supreme God, known through the inwardness of the self. Thus they made little or no attempt to come to terms with the narrative of Jesus'

[24] See Gleckner, *Blake and Spenser*, 308.

life on earth as presented in the synoptic Gospels. As far as the Old Testament was concerned, that Scripture was basically not profitable for salvation and no amount of interpretation would make it so.

From this point of view Blake's *The Everlasting Gospel* is an essentially gnostic poem. In it we see Jesus tearing the seam between the two testaments in a radical rereading of the Gospel:

> He laid his hand on Moses Law
> The Ancient Heavens in Silent Awe
> Writ with Curses from Pole to Pole
> All away began to roll
> The Earth trembling & Naked lay
> In secret bed of Mortal Clay
> On Sinai felt the hand Divine
> Putting back the bloody shrine . . .
>
> (E 512–13)

The anti-Judaic thrust of this poem is matched frequently in the prophetic books. In *The Four Zoas* Blake gives us his version of the confrontation between the Jewish God and the Christian Saviour:

> Urizen calld together the Synagogue of Satan in dire Sanhedrim
> To judge the Lamb of God to Death . . .
>
> (*Night the Eighth*, E 363)

Behind this opposition of the Synagogue and the Lamb, based of course on Revelation 2: 9, we have a cosmic struggle between Darkness and Light, between Urizen, representing Elohim, Law, and Reason on the one hand, and the divine power of the Imagination on the other. For closely associated with the 'Lamb of God' in the context of this 'Night' of *The Four Zoas*, stand Los and Enitharmon, signifying the highest principle of all, namely, Imagination as expressed in Art and Poetry. In a parallel passage a little earlier on we hear of Urizen communing

> with the Synagogue of Satan in dark Sanhedrim,
> To undermine the World of Los & tear bright Enitharmon
> To the four winds . . .
>
> (E 359)

All this might seem to be a straightforward revamping of early Christian gnosticism, but Blake is never as simple as that. He radically revises the Gospel in accordance with the gnostic heresy but he ends by radically revising the gnostic model as well; it is, as Stuart Curran has cogently argued, a case of subversion from within,[25] and much the same as the strategy he used in reference to the notion of prophecy inaugurated by Spinoza. There Blake had performed a kind of conjuring trick, adopting his opponents' principle and using it to overturn them. Here he carried out a twofold reversal of the same kind.

Thus *The Everlasting Gospel* exhibits the shape of the gnostic dualism, but we have only to consider the figure of Jesus in that poem to see that he has become something like the polar opposite of the spiritual, unworldly deity of the gnostics whose worship is based on 'the negative perfection of denial'.[26] Each section of the poem opens with a startling rhetorical question meant to demolish this image: 'Was Jesus humble . . . Was Jesus chaste . . . Was Jesus gentle?' Jesus it appears was none of these things. 'He acts', says Blake, 'with honest, triumphant Pride' (E 510). The emphasis is on the verb. In striking contrast to the Gospel record as normally understood and in even more striking contrast to gnostic beliefs, we have here an active, even demonically active hero. The mark of Jesus is Energy, that Energy which according to *The Marriage of Heaven and Hell* 'is Eternal Delight' (Pl. 4). He violently binds Satan in a Chain:

> And bursting forth, his furious ire
> Became a Chariot of fire.
>
> (*The Everlasting Gospel*, E 515)

It is clear that Blake has done more than contradict the gnostic image of Jesus; he has carried out an exchange across the lines marked out by the gnostic dualism, transferring to the figure of Jesus the demonic energy of the Creator-God of the Old Testament, rejected though he was by the gnostics as the evil force in the universe. As though to make this transference clear, Blake's hero speaks in a voice 'Loud as Sinai's trumpet sound' (E 514). Blake's self-contradictions are patent; the same hero who laid violent hands on Moses' Law so that the earth 'on Sinai felt the hand Divine, | Putting back the bloody shrine', here issues his own law in the voice of Sinai!

---

[25] Curran, 'Blake and the Gnostic Hyle', 130.   [26] Ibid.

Coherence is not to be sought amid such confusions; all that one might want to say by way of explanation is that in *The Everlasting Gospel* Blake agrees with the gnostics in identifying the Creator-God of Sinai with the Devil—this is the ground of the strong anti-Judaic and anti-nomian current in this poem and elsewhere in his writings. At the same time, being a poet, Blake is of the Devil's party. He needs energy, the demonic energy of the divine 'man of war' (Exodus 15: 3) who, in the prophet's vision (echoed also in Revelation 14: 18–20) strides from Bozrah after the slaughter of his foes (Isaiah 63: 1–2), his garments stained with blood, 'like him that treads in the winepress'. Several times in his prophetic writings Blake will recall this image of the God who has 'trodden the winepress alone; and of the peoples there was none with me; for I have trodden them in my anger, and trampled them in my fury' (Isaiah 63: 3).[27]

Faced with such a text, Blake seems to anticipate Nietzsche. 'Good & Evil are no more!', he declares (E 513). The moral categories whether of approval or disapproval disappear—in fact the entire dualistic system of the gnostics melts away. Instead there is an exchange of energy between the divided sections of the divine order. Power comes to the aid of Spirit as the Lamb takes on the ferocity of the Tyger; at the same time Spirit comes to the aid of Power as the satanic God of Sinai is seen to be the source of imaginative vision. Los who signifies Imagination, the poetic principle, is in *The Four Zoas* fundamentally associated with Jesus and threatened by the same 'Synagogue of Satan' and the same 'dark Sanhedrim'. And yet the winepress, which is the quintessential locus of the wrathful God of Hebrew prophecy, becomes in Blake's *Milton* 'the Wine-press of Los'. And he goes on:

This Wine-press is call'd War on Earth, it is the Printing-Press
Of Los; and here he lays his words in order above the mortal brain

(Pl. 27)

The energy and warlike fury associated with the winepress are here a precondition for poetic activity—there Los lays his words in order. It represents Imagination nourished by violence.

[27] In *Milton*, Plate 27, and *The Four Zoas, Night the Ninth* (E 389).

Blake does not escape contradictions any more than Shake-speare and Milton; his universe is riven by the primordial divi-sions affirmed by the gnostics, so that it is never by any means certain that he who made the Lamb also made the Tyger. But there is a short-circuit effect too, so that the poet, his faculties roused by Isaiah's images of terror and beauty or by the lyric intensity of the Song of Solomon, recognizes in these texts the highest form of art, namely, the Sublime:

The Stolen and Perverted Writings of Homer & Ovid: of Plato & Cicero, which all Men ought to contemn: are set up by artifice against the Sublime of the Bible. (*Milton*, Preface, Pl. 1)

Hebrew Law and Prophecy, their teaching condemned in gnos-tic fashion as the work of Antichrist, are now reinstated as the supreme work of the Imagination. Longinus himself had first pointed to the opening verses of Genesis as an example of the Sublime and this perception had been developed by Robert Lowth in his *Lectures on the Sacred Poetry of the Hebrews* (1753) to become received doctrine in the latter half of the eighteenth century.[28] Blake goes further, declaring in effect that the Bible is the exclusive model for sublimity. In his prophetic books he will abandon 'the modern bondage of Rhyming' in favour of the greater vehemence and liberty of biblical poetry. God, indeed the God of Sinai, again speaks in him:

> that God from whom [*all* books are given,]
> Who in mysterious Sinais awful cave
> To Man the wond'rous art of writing gave,
> Again he speaks in thunder and in fire!

> (*Jerusalem*, Pl. 3)

In these prefatory lines to *Jerusalem* addressed 'To the Public' Sinai has become not the place where the Law was given to a chosen people but the place where the wondrous art of writ-ing is granted to the chosen vessels of poetic inspiration. The thunder of Sinai will again be heard in the 'terrific parts' of his

---

[28] Lowth's lectures were a major factor in preparing the ground for Blake's empha-sis on prophecy as the work of the poetic imagination. On this see M. Roston, *Poet and Prophet: The Bible and the Growth of Romanticism* (London: Faber, 1967), *passim*, and for a more recent discussion, see Stephen Prickett, *Words and the Word: Language, Poetics and Biblical Interpretation* (Cambridge: Cambridge University Press, 1986), 116–17.

own poems, the art of the engraver who inscribes his images on plates finding its essential prototype and warrant in the divine engraving of the Word on the tablets of stone given to Moses (Exodus 24: 12).

4

The priority here given to Hebrew models for poetry and the corresponding rejection of classical art forms as 'Stolen and Perverted', i.e. plagiarized, is a notion which Blake had found in Milton. In *Paradise Regained*, Book IV, Milton's hero rejects the offer of Attic wisdom and with it a command of the arts of classical poetry and oratory. He insists instead on the superior quality of Hebrew art:

> All our Law and Story strew'd
> With Hymns, our Psalms with artful terms inscrib'd,
> Our Hebrew Songs and Harps in *Babylon*,
> That pleas'd so well our Victors ear, declare
> That rather *Greece* from us these Arts deriv'd;
> Ill imitated, while they loudest sing
> The vices of thir Deities . . .
>
> . . . .
>
> Remove their swelling Epithets thick laid
> As varnish on a Harlot's cheek, the rest,
> Thin sown with aught of profit or delight,
> Will far be found unworthy to compare
> With *Sion*'s songs, to all true tastes excelling . . .
>
> (IV. 334-47)

But Blake, though adopting Milton's stand on the priority of Hebrew poetry, makes it clear in the continuation of *Milton*, Plate 1, that he is also using this argument against Milton himself: 'Shakespeare and Milton were both curbd by the general malady & infection from the silly Greek and Latin slaves of the Sword.' Moreover, Blake was clearly correct in pointing to Shakespeare's inconsistency and in setting off Milton's principle against his practice. After all, the form and language of this very poem of Milton, i.e. *Paradise Regained*, indicate the invincible attraction that the classical models had for him. Milton is condemning the literary arts of the ancient world and doing so in an epic poem which testifies—especially in the eloquent account of the temptations which the hero withstands—to the unallayed fascination of a poetic tradition which stems directly from Greece and Rome! In short the hero only appears to withstand these temptations. Milton could no more do without his classical inheritance than he could do without the last infirmity of fame or the realm of political action, both likewise included among the temptations to which the hero of *Paradise Regained* is subjected. Virgil's 'thick Epithets' are condemned as 'varnish on a Harlots cheek' but this is a convenient slur. As noted earlier (above, p. 173), what is really involved here, as with the 'harlot lap' of Dalila, is the inescapable fascination of poetic beauty, in particular of those forms inherited from Greece and Rome. For Milton such a fascination could not to be taken lightly.

Blake's rejection both of the charms and the restraints of classical art would seem to be more radical and more complete. He even rejected the half-way house of blank verse which Milton had adopted in compliance with the examples of Homer and Virgil,[29] as being 'as much a bondage as rhyme itself' (*Jerusalem*, Pl. 3). He himself in his prophetic writings will strike out for greater freedom ('Poetry Fetter'd, Fetters the Human Race') basing himself on the Hebrew model of loose-limbed parallelism 'uncurbed' by any rules derived from classical prosody.

Blake's sublimity thus involves a degree of freedom from classical sources which Milton never achieved and indeed never aimed at. And we would surely not be wrong in seeing this turn in Blake's poetry as representing a new irruption of Hebraism— or of something that can only be understood in the context of Hebraism—into Western art and culture. If we think of the spiritual history of the West as marked by a continuing struggle between Jerusalem and Athens (an approach supported by Blake's own dialectic), then a good case could be made out for seeing the period of the Enlightenment as characterized by the temporary dominance of one model, namely, the Graeco-Roman, whilst, in Blake's typical poetry, this dominance is challenged, even, it would seem, violently overthrown. In restoring the Bible to first

---

[29] In his note on 'The Verse' added to the 1668 edition of *Paradise Lost*. See *John Milton: Complete Poems and Major Prose*, ed. Merritt Y. Hughes (New York: The Odyssey Press, 1957), 210.

place he is reversing the clear trend of the Enlightenment towards denying any special importance to the Bible.[30]

We can illustrate how complete this reversal is by setting Blake's remarks on 'the Stolen and Perverted Writings of Homer & Ovid' which are he says 'set up by artifice against the Sublime of the Bible' beside a passage written by Voltaire in 1769 under the heading 'Des plagiats reprochés aux Juifs':

Si on voulait se donner la peine de comparer tout les évènements de la fable [biblique] et de l'ancienne histoire grecque, on serait étonné de ne pas trouver une seule page des livres juifs qui ne fût un plagiat.[31]

Everything of any value in the Bible it seems has been stolen from the Greeks! Two views on the worth of the literature of ancient Israel so diametrically opposed to one another could not be imagined.

Yet curiously enough, Blake, in spite of taking a position directly opposed to Voltaire on the question of the value of Hebrew poetry, shares the pronounced anti-Judaic animus of Voltaire, Holbach, and the English reformers whom they influenced, such as Tom Paine.[32] The Chapel on the Green is offensive because of 'Thou shalt not writ over the door!'—again the hated voice of Sinai—and because of 'the Priests in black gowns' who bind with briars our joys and desires. Blake will write a gospel freed at last from Jewish repressiveness. Blake had acquired these attitudes from latter-day gnostics and from antinomian fringe groups among the radical dissenters of his time.[33] But Voltaire

[30] H.-G. Gadamer makes the important observation that the religious tradition of Christianity (and specifically the Bible) was the primary target of Enlightenment criticism. See his *Truth and Method* (New York: Seabury Press, 1975), 241–5.

[31] 'Dieu et les hommes', in *Œuvres complètes de Voltaire*, xxviii (Paris, 1879), 190.

[32] On Blake's close affinities with the English Jacobins Thomas Paine and Joseph Priestley, whom he almost certainly knew personally, see Erdman, *Blake: Prophet Against Empire*, 152–63; also Thompson, *Witness Against the Beast*, 126–8.

[33] As several critics have recognized, Blake picked up many of his radical notions less from books than from his association with fringe groups in London such as the Behmenists and the New Church of the Swedenborgians set up in Great East Cheap in 1788. There is good historical evidence for Blake's association with these movements. England in the late 18th century had a rich sectarian undergound. See Désirée Hirst, *Hidden Riches* (London: Eyre and Spottiswoode, 1964), 180–211; Thompson, *Witness Against the Beast*, 35–40, 129–35. Thompson (ch. 6, pp. 65–101, and *passim*) has argued for a special link between Blake and the 'Muggletonians', successors of the 17th-century Ranters, a radically antinomian group who held their meetings in public houses. However, whilst Blake clearly shared many of their notions, there is no evidence of his ever having actually associated with them.

was a powerful collateral influence. Not only does Voltaire speak with contempt of biblical poetry and narrative as second hand, but he loses no opportunity to attack biblical Jews for their barbarity, their absurdity, and (worst of all for the classically minded) their lack of culture and taste.[34] In an exegetical essay entitled 'La Bible enfin expliquée' written in 1776, his comment on Isaiah's denunciation of human sacrifice (Isaiah 57: 5) is that this in itself shows that the Jews practised infanticide at all periods![35] Peter Gay believes that these constant attacks are at bottom an expression of Voltaire's hostility to Christianity which he hated even more than he hated Judaism.[36] However, to the reader of the *Dictionary*—starting with the article on Abraham—it seems to be the other way round. It is because of the Jew that we have the burden of the commandments—hence the need for a kind of Freudian revolt against the Jewish father who represents the authority of the past. In the new climate of freedom and with the proclamation of the Rights of Man, such authority is now to be overthrown.[37] Blake regularly echoes these judgements. In his defence of Paine against Bishop Watson

[34] Voltaire reviewed the second edition of Robert Lowth's lectures *On the Sacred Poetry of the Hebrews* in the *Gazette Littéraire* for Sept. 1764. It was on the whole a favourable review, with some approval given to the imagery of the prophets, but he took care to note that the ancient Jews 'lacked taste, delicacy, and proportion' (*Œuvres complètes*, xxv. 204).

[35] Ibid., xxx. 35. On this strain in Voltaire, see Leon Poliakov, *The History of Anti-Semitism*, iii, trans. Miriam Kochan (London: Routledge, 1975), 86–99, and A. Herzberg, *The French Enlightenment and the Jews* (New York: Columbia University Press, 1968), 301–11. Voltaire owed much evidently to the anti-Jewish current in the writings of some of the English Deists, in particular Conyers Middleton and the 3rd Earl of Shaftesbury (see Paul H. Meyer, 'The Attitude of the Enlightenment Towards the Jew', *Studies on Voltaire and the Eighteenth Century*, 26 (1963), 1176–7).

[36] Peter Gay, *Voltaire's Politics* (Princeton: Princeton University Press, 1959), 245, 351–4 (Appendix on Voltaire's anti-Semitism).

[37] The complex we are discussing is most clearly displayed in Paine's writings. *The Age of Reason* shows the anti-Judaic strain of the newly enlightened in all its virulence. The ancient Israelites were he says 'a nation of cut-throats and ruffians . . . corrupted by and copying after such monsters and imposters as Moses and Aaron, Joshua, Samuel and David' (139). His opening attack on the conservatism of Burke in his epoch-making *Rights of Man*, Part I (1790) is essentially a rejection of any authority, political or otherwise, derived from the past and imposed on the present: 'Every age and generation must be as free to act for itself, in all cases, as the ages and generations which preceded it. The vanity and presumption of governing beyond the grave, is the most ridiculous and insolent of all tyrannies' (*The Political Works of Thomas Paine* (London: Dugdale, 1844), 285).

mentioned earlier he speaks out as clearly as Voltaire against Jewish barbarities, condemning in much the same language as Voltaire 'the Wickedness of the Israelites in murdering so many thousands under pretence of a command from God' (E 604).

Blake abandoned much of the philosophy of the Enlightenment in his later poetry, condemning Voltaire as a Urizenic figure to be likened to Bacon, Locke, and Newton,[38] but he continued to the end to echo Voltaire's violent antipathy to the God of Sinai. From this point of view, The Everlasting Gospel, probably one of his latest poems, is as Voltairian a production as one can imagine. And yet at this same time in Milton and Jerusalem he was finding his deepest inspiration in the prophetic voice of Sinai. Where Voltaire is consistent, Blake is profoundly inconsistent. If Voltaire hated Jews and Judaism, he also hated Jewish poetry. 'Les collines qui bondissent comme des agneaux', he declared, 'forment une image qui passe toutes les limites de la licence.'[39] For Blake the little hills that skip like lambs adapt themselves perfectly to his notions of the Sublime and the Beautiful. More than that, other literary models are merely weak imitations of this one strong aesthetic standard. How are we to resolve or even to define this contradiction?

What needs to be emphasized is that this is a contradiction which belongs to the interiority of the poetry itself. It is not a matter simply of thematics. The result of this simultaneous affirmation and rejection of the values of the Enlightenment is a dual focus which involves tone, language, and imagery. With the movement towards secularization and with the questioning of the authority of the Bible which Blake shared, go a certain

---

[38] During the 1790s, Blake found himself on the side of Voltaire who appears as a kind of Orc figure accompanied by a 'fiery cloud' in The French Revolution and other early prophecies. Ironically, the great traducer of the Bible is here defined by a powerful biblical image (see Exodus 13: 22) associating his revolutionary leadership with the journey of the Children of Israel through the wilderness to the Promised Land! At about the turn of the century there is a change; from now on Blake regularly ranks Voltaire, Rousseau, and the Deists with Locke and Bacon as personae of Satan. On this change and its historical background, see David W. Erdman, Blake: Prophet Against Empire (New York: Doubleday, 1969), 416–20, and Hagstrum, 'William Blake Rejects the Enlightenment', sect. iii (149–53). It seems to me that the shift is above all bound up with the instatement of Los (in place of Orc) at this time as the central mythological character and the promotion of Milton as the chief representative of the revolutionary idea. (See below, pp. 260–2.)

[39] Œuvres complètes, xxv. 204.

tone, even a certain prosody, which do not accord with the
poetics of the Sublime—that biblical mode which Blake so passionately embraced in his prophecies. Consider the following
passage from *The Everlasting Gospel*:

> Was Jesus Born of a Virgin Pure
> With narrow Soul & looks demure
> If he intended to take on Sin
> The Mother should an Harlot been
> Just such a one as Magdalen[40]

We hear the precise note of Voltairian mockery in these witty
and irreverent couplets. Paradoxically, even when he is attacking the scepticism of Voltaire and the *philosophes* we hear the
voice of Voltaire:

> He who Doubts from what he sees
> Will neer Believe do what you Please.
> If the Sun & Moon should doubt,
> Theyd immediately Go out.
>
> ('Auguries of Innocence', E 483)

Here are the urbanity, the gift of epigram, and also the rapier-
like polemical skill which we associate with Voltaire and with
such earlier English writers as Gay, Pope, or Swift. These octo-
syllabic couplets come as naturally to Blake as do 'the terrific
numbers' as he termed the loose, parallelistic verses of the prophetic poems. But the two modes represent ideological and poetic
opposites, as Blake surely recognized.

Blake tells us in *The Marriage of Heaven and Hell* that he
dined with Isaiah and Ezekiel; but he also told Crabb Robinson
on another occasion that he regularly conversed with Voltaire![41]
Here in these lines we may hear the voice of Blake communing
with Voltaire, engaging with him in the discourse of wit and
irony; but this does not combine with the voice in which he com-
munes with Isaiah and Ezekiel. To maintain such varied social
relations ultimately implies a measure of contradiction as marked
as that which we found in the double structure of *King Lear*,
or in the opposed styles of *Paradise Lost*. Like Shakespeare

---

[40] From Blake's Notebook, 120 (E 794).
[41] See Mona Wilson, *The Life of William Blake*, newly edited by Geoffrey Keynes
(London: Oxford University Press, 1971), 331.

moreover Blake is reflexively aware of his own dual focus. But, unlike Shakespeare, he is also intent on overcoming it; he aspires to a state—psychological, metaphysical, and poetical—in which contraries are made one. But that integration, whilst it is Blake's professed ideal, is rarely achieved in practice.

It should be noted that in the lines quoted above from 'Auguries of Innocence', Blake assumes the ironic voice of the eighteenth-century sceptics in order to demolish doubt! Irony is here deconstructed. But the deconstructive inversions and loops operate in both directions—if scepticism is undermined by showing the doubtfulness of doubt, then that which is to replace scepticism, namely faith and vision, can in this ironic discourse only be defined by negatives: 'If the Sun & Moon should doubt, I Theyd immediately Go out.' World creation and the image of divine providence upholding the fabric of the universe are not here directly invoked; we get closest to them through the image of world extinction, but that image is immediately dissolved through the play of wit, the last words of the couplet calling attention to their own absurdity, 'Theyd immediately Go out'! Irony it seems can take nothing seriously, not even the extinction of the universe.[42] Irony, we should remind ourselves, is not merely a mode of discourse, a matter of technique. It is nearer to being an ideology, or rather a kind of anti-ideology, for, more than it upholds a particular mode of thinking, it sets out to demolish other modes of thinking. No one understood these implications better than Blake, for Blake both identified with the spirit of the Enlightenment and found his most passionately held convictions threatened by that spirit.

The clearest and subtlest statement of this situation is his poem, 'Mock on Mock on Voltaire Rousseau'. Here Blake actually foregrounds the dual focus that we are considering, making it the very matter of the poem. He presents the duality itself, the fundamental *agon* within himself and within the spiritual history of his time with such lucidity that he comes as near as anywhere in his writing to overcoming it. Blake here brilliantly combines the two voices of which we have spoken by a kind of

---

[42] Cf. Friedrich Schlegel, 'Über die Unverständlichkeit', in *Kritische Ausgabe*, ii, ed. Ernst Behler *et al.* (Zurich: Thomas Verlag, 1967), 369–70; Søren Kierkegaard, *The Concept of Irony*, trans. Lee M. Capel (New York: Harper and Row, 1965), 298.

dialogic interplay, with the poet-narrator taking both sides in the dialogue:

> Mock on Mock on Voltaire Rousseau
> Mock on Mock on tis all in vain
> You throw the sand against the wind
> And the wind blows it back again
>
> And every sand becomes a Gem
> Reflected in the beams divine
> Blown back they blind the mocking Eye
> But still in Israels paths they shine
>
> The Atoms of Democritus
> And Newtons Particles of light
> Are sands upon the Red sea shore
> Where Israels tents do shine so bright

(E 468–9)

This poem makes clear what we may term the hidden agenda of the Enlightenment, the ideology which its irony negates. For this irony is aimed at discrediting a seriousness which is at bottom Hebraic. If Bayle and Voltaire went out of their way to attack the Hebrew Bible and the supposed barbarity of the Old Testament prophets, they did so because they had correctly identified those writers as their chief antagonists. The object of the mocking eyes was 'Israels tents'.[43] Blake's perception goes deep into the spiritual history of the West. It would hardly be an exaggeration to say that the scepticism, the irony, the classical decorum of the period of Voltaire were called into existence by way of reaction to enthusiasm, to the moral intensities which had been so heavy a burden on the culture of the West since the Reformation and before. It was time for the play of wit which would finally liberate us from the burden and exaltation of the biblical covenant. Athens would offer a better ground of happiness than Jerusalem, even if it meant giving up the glorious vision of the heavenly host crying Holy, Holy, Holy. After all, Zion's best songs were all borrowed from the Greeks! Freedom was the cry and that meant freedom above all from the God of Sinai!

[43] This does not really apply to Rousseau who, like Diderot and unlike Voltaire, did not write disparagingly of Jews or their religious traditions. Blake seems to have linked Rousseau with Voltaire in this poem for no good reason except that they were the chief philosophers of the Enlightenment.

Here again in these neatly turned quatrains of 'Mock on Mock on Voltaire Rousseau' we have the paradox of the mocker mocked. The poet-narrator is a mocker no less than Voltaire whom he is attacking. His verses have all the elegance, the incisiveness, and the compression that we associate with the age of wit. They may not have the playfulness of the lines quoted earlier from 'Auguries of Innocence', but they have a biting satiric edge. The irony of the sands that become gems and the mocking eye that is blinded is an irony aimed at the supreme ironists of the age. He will outdo them in this poem. Blake is not only employing the weapon of irony here—he is also showing how truly he understands its negative nature; its denials invite counter-denials—the sand is blown back again into the eye of the mocker. Wayne C. Booth, commenting on the self-destructive nature of irony, has shown that, after the onion skins of discredited truth are peeled off, the ironist is left seeking in vain for a stable ground and discovering 'no core of truth, nothing but nothingness itself'.[44] This annihilation of vision is brilliantly caught by the image of the blinding of the mocker's eye by the sand which he has himself thrown against the wind.

But the ironic voice is countered by another voice, that of biblical prophecy. The figure of the mocker who comes to curse but whose curses (sand) are against his will turned to blessings (gems) owes much evidently to the story of the heathen prophet Balaam (Numbers 22–4). Balaam we may remember gazes down on 'Israel's paths' as the People of Israel make their way through the wilderness from the Red Sea to the Promised Land; he has been summoned by Balak, the King of Moab, to curse the Israelites and thereby arrest their progress. 'Israels tents' are of course those which Balaam sees in Numbers 24: 2: 'And Balaam lifted up his eyes, and he saw Israel abiding in his tents' (Authorized Version). When he sees the shining tents of Israel, we are told that the Spirit of God comes upon Balaam and instead of mocks and curses he utters a series of inspired poems, the third of which opens with the words: 'How goodly are thy tents, O Jacob, and thy tabernacles, O Israel!' (Numbers 24: 5).

[44] Wayne C. Booth, *A Rhetoric of Irony* (Chicago: University of Chicago Press, 1974), 244.

Balaam describes himself as 'the man whose eyes are open' (Numbers 24: 3, 15) but in the margin of the King James Bible Blake would have read that the phrase *shetum ha'ayin* could bear the opposite sense, namely, 'the man whose eyes are shut'. In Blake's poem it is the sand turned into gems which 'blind the mocking Eye'. The dialectic of vision and lack of vision is an essential feature of this biblical pericope. In Numbers 22: 23–31 Balaam fails to see the adversary angel who stands in his path; instead his ass sees the angel and, stopping in a narrow path, crushes Balaam's foot against the wall. It is not until God 'opened the eyes of Balaam' that he was able to see his adversary (verse 31). One would want to say that as a would-be mocker and sceptic Balaam is blind, but when truly inspired he is open-eyed. His poetic praise of the goodly tents of Jacob is prefixed by the announcement of his clear sight—'the saying of him who hears the words of God, who sees the vision of the Almighty, falling down, but having his eyes open' (Numbers 24: 4)—here not the ambiguous *shetum ha'ayin* but the unambiguous *gelui 'enayim*, i.e. 'clear-seeing'. The same formula precedes Balaam's final oracle (Numbers 24: 16–24), the two poems constituting a peak of sublimity in the Pentateuch as a whole.

Blake is not actually interpreting the text of Numbers. The source text is not confronted; it has become transformed through what Coleridge called the 'esemplastic power' of the Imagination, recycled at what seems to be a preconscious or unconscious level. It is, if anything, the biblical text which is interpreting the poet, organizing his imaginative discourse.

What emerges is a multifaceted use of the figure of Balaam, the would-be mocker who is blind and also clear-eyed. Voltaire and Rousseau are the supreme figures of the Enlightenment, the era of clarity, but they are also in a special degree blind. They are like the man who, looking at the sun, could only see a yellow disk the size of a guinea. But they are not the only Balaam figures in the poem. The poet-narrator is also a mocker in the Enlightenment fashion: he is mocking Voltaire and Rousseau, using witty inversions, compression, and irony to point his mockery. At the same time he is, like Balaam, a prophet figure 'who sees the visions of the Almighty, falling down and having his eyes open'. Voltaire and Rousseau do not share this capacity for vision; their eyes are shut. The poet-narrator is the truer

Balaam who sees the shining tents of Israel and, seeing them, is inspired to utter his poem. It is within his aroused imagination that the sand thrown into the wind becomes gems. Gems in Blake have special reference to the treasures of poetry, in particular, biblical poetry. In 'The Mental Traveller' we hear of the 'gems of the Human Soul I The rubies & pearls of a lovesick eye'— in *Jerusalem*, the significance of these same gems is elaborated:

In silence the Divine Lord builded with immortal labour,
Of gold & jewels a sublime Ornament, a Couch of repose,
With Sixteen pillars: canopied with emblems & written verse.
Spiritual Verse, order'd & measur'd, from whence, time shall
  reveal.
The Five books of the Decalogue, the books of Joshua & Judges,
Samuel, a double book & Kings, a double book, the Psalms &
  Prophets
The Four-fold Gospel, and the Revelations everlasting

(Pl. 48)

The sneers of the wits (we remember Voltaire's derisive comment on the 'little hills [that] skip like young sheep' from Psalm 114) light up for us the authentic gems of biblical poetry. This is what Blake's poem is about. 'And every sand becomes a Gem I Reflected in the beams divine.'

The image of the grains of sand, three times repeated in the poem, was also, it seems, suggested by the Balaam pericope. Balaam's first oracle (Numbers 23: 7–10) closes with the exclamation:

Who can count the dust of Jacob, and the number of the fourth
  part of Israel?
Let me die the death of the righteous, and let my last end be like
  his!

A frequent variant for 'the dust of Jacob' is the comparison of Israel to 'the sand of the sea which cannot be numbered for multitude' (Genesis 32: 13, Genesis 22: 17, Hosea 1: 10). These grains of sand are in the poem transformed into gems and are then linked in the final stanza with the atoms of Democritus and Newton's particles of light.

> The atoms of Democritus
> And Newtons Particles of light
> Are sands upon the Red sea shore
> Where Israels tents do shine so bright

It will be seen that the alchemy of the poem has converted these atoms and particles into magical poetic properties, visions of truth. The Urizenic errors and deceptions of the Enlightenment have been mastered and redeemed, they have become the 'dust of Jacob' shining brightly on the Red Sea shore. As in 'Auguries of Innocence', Imagination has seen a world in a grain of sand!

This transformation, or something very like it, had already occurred in the lyrical verses of the poet-prophet Balaam who first spoke of 'the dust of Jacob' and ended by envisioning a star which comes forth from Jacob and a sceptre from Israel (Numbers 24: 17). Blake is in short acting out the Balaam paradigm: the biblical text is reading him, in particular it is reading his self-divisions. Like Balaam and like Voltaire and Paine he comes to curse: to condemn the Druid barbarities of the Genesis narratives, the dark chapel on the green symbolizing state religion, the Law of Sinai which fetters the free spirit of Man, and the Jewish Scriptures which 'were written as an Example of the possibility of Human Beastliness in all its branches' (E 604). Balak could not have wished to hear better curses than these from the eloquent Balaam. But like Balaam and unlike Voltaire, Blake stays to bless. For when the poetic power of that same Scripture seizes him, the dark chapel becomes a shining tent, the dust of the serpent's curse becomes a gem, the very trumpet of Sinai echoes in 'the voice of the Bard who Present, Past & Future sees', whilst the dread tablets of stone become the model for the 'wondrous art' of the engraver, 'who sees the visions of the Almighty, falling down, but having his eyes open'.

CHAPTER 8

Cognition and Re-cognition

Though little noted by critics, the paradox of his intense pre-occupation with the poetry of the Hebrew Scripture and his traumatic recoil from the entire doctrine and discipline of the Law which forms the substance of that Scripture, is a paradox quite central to Blake's writing. A similar pattern may be found (though less centrally) in Shelley; he too classes Hebrew poetry with the greatest known to men and remarks in *A Defence of Poetry* that it would be impossible to conceive the moral condition of the world without it. And yet in the spirit of the Enlightenment (and the gnostics) he denounces the Lawgiver and Creator-God of the Old Testament as an evil tyrant.[1] Here it may be suggested is the key to the profound change which takes place in the status of poetry in general for Blake and many of his contemporaries. Poetry becomes a self-justifying value. We do not attend to any message that it communicates or any other truth it serves. 'What the Imagination seizes as Beauty must be truth', Keats would say in a famous letter to Benjamin Bailey (22 November 1817). This notion of the autonomy of the imagination is no doubt related to many other current developments in philosophy and literature. But it would appear that the hermeneutic and epistemological shift to which it gives rise was first enunciated in reference to the biblical text. As noted in the previous chapter, Spinoza pointed in this direction in the *Tractatus*; prophecy becomes purely and simply the work of the imagination. Blake and others of his generation will seize upon this notion and give it a startling new emphasis. From now on the Bible and indeed other powerful texts received from the past will tend to be read

---

[1] Cf. his account of Solomon's Temple in 'Queen Mab': 'There an inhuman and uncultured race | Howled hideous praises to their Demon-God' (Part II, ll. 149–50). Many of Prometheus' speeches in *Prometheus Unbound*, Act I, are of a similar tendency but more veiled, the 'Demon-God' being masked as Jupiter.

for their poetry alone, not for any message which might have reference to a world outside the poem. This is clearly how Blake read the Balaam chapters. The speaker in 'Mock on Mock on Voltaire Rousseau' has thrilled not to the shining tents of Israel out there but to the image of those tents in the Balaam oracles. The vision is a poetic vision, the imaginative event occurring in the intertextual space between Balaam and Blake; it does not involve any revaluation of the Israel of history, or of the bearing that the praise of Israel might have for Christian society or Christian beliefs in the nineteenth century. Even after writing the poem Blake could continue to believe that the Jewish Scriptures were 'only an Example of the wickedness & deceit of the Jews' (*Annotations to Watson*, E 604).

Indeed, one can go further than this. The Balaam paradigm itself, unlike other examples of Old Testament poetry, could serve to define just such a separation between the Word and the World. In the way the story is told, we can imagine Balaam returning to the denunciation of Israel just as soon as the poetic fit has left him. What he speaks is 'the word that God puts in his mouth' (Numbers 22: 38)—any connection with outward evidences is minimal. Balak places him on a high spot where he can see 'but the utmost part of them' (Numbers 23: 13) but in fact Balaam does not remain with Balak at this observation post. On the occasion of the first two oracles he removes himself and finds his inspiration in a lonely meeting with YHWH, returning to Balak and to the sight of the Israelites only after the word has been put in his mouth (Numbers 23: 4–5, 16). The King James Bible emphasizes this apartness of Balaam and his immersion in a kind of inner world, by adding the words 'into a trance' to the account of his prophetic experience: 'which saw the vision of the Almighty, falling *into a trance*, but having his eyes open' (Numbers 24: 4 and 16). Read in this light, the Balaam narrative and the four poems comprised in the pericope may be said to mirror perfectly Blake's self-divisions as well as his concept of the autonomy and power of the imagination. The poetic word does not require the evidence of things seen. On the contrary, it controls and shapes the world. Curses have power and so do blessings. Blake too knew nothing of greater moment than the poetic word which makes and unmakes the world and does so without moving beyond its own sovereign domain.

Poetry has thus become all-sufficient, self-validating, and self-signifying. Poems will tend to be about poets writing poems. Wordsworth's epic poem has as its subject 'Growth of a Poet's Mind'. There is now nothing it would seem of greater moment. Giving epic value to the things that occur in the poet's mind suggests of course an enormously enhanced role for poetry, but in another sense the inward turning of the poet can mark a withdrawal—an escape from responsibility. Something like this double movement seems to take place at a dramatic moment in *The Prelude*. In Miltonic fashion and with much echoing of Milton, Wordsworth had been speaking of his involvement as a young man in the great revolutionary movement of his time in France. But as the result of a crisis which he underwent about the year 1795, the details of which are not altogether clear, he mentally withdrew from history and politics and 'yielded up moral questions in despair'. His recovery coincided with the move to Racedown in Dorsetshire where his sister Dorothy taught him to find salvation in poetry itself:

> She, in the midst of all, preserved me still
> A Poet, made me seek beneath that name,
> And that alone, my office upon earth.

> (Book XI, 346–8)

But what is meant by speaking of a vocation that is sought in poetry 'alone'? Clearly, the aim will not be just the technical mastery of the medium. The continuation of this passage in *The Prelude* makes clear that what we have here is nothing less than a new epistemology. Wordsworth goes on to say that to seek one's office upon earth by writing poetry and communing with other poets is to have access to 'genuine knowledge'. Once Dorothy had shown the way, he was brought back with the assistance of Nature

> To those sweet counsels between head and heart
> Whence grew that genuine knowledge, fraught with peace,
> Which, through the later sinkings of this cause,
> Hath still upheld me . . .

> (ibid. 353–6)

This insistence on the cognitive aspect of poetry in its new, inward-turned role is shared by all the Romantic poets. Wordsworth himself in the famous Preface to *Lyrical Ballads* declares that 'Poetry is the breath and finer spirit of all knowledge'.[2] As we saw earlier, for Blake it was axiomatic that the Imagination afforded us true knowledge. Shelley in *A Defence of Poetry* makes the point with great emphasis, declaring that poetry 'is at once the centre and circumference of knowledge; it is that which comprehends all science, and that to which all science must be referred.'[3] Coleridge seems to echo the same notions and the same high-pitched rhetoric when he writes,

For poetry is the blossom and the fragrancy of all human knowledge, human thoughts, human passions, emotions, language.[4]

But Coleridge, leaning on the German transcendental philosophers, also offers something nearer to a precise definition.[5] All knowledge, he maintains, is knowledge of the self and is grounded in the self (*BL* 136)—as with the Delphic oracle which proclaimed 'Know thyself' as the final truth. The absolute principle of certainty, Coleridge declares, is 'the SUM or I AM'.

[2] *Wordsworth and Coleridge: Lyrical Ballads 1798*, ed. W. J. B. Owen (Oxford: Oxford University Press, 1969), Appendix, 168.

[3] *Peacock's Four Ages of Poetry, Shelley's Defence of Poetry, Browning's Essay on Shelley* (Percy Reprints, No. 3), ed. H. F. B. Brett-Smith (Oxford: Blackwell, 1921), 53.

[4] S. T. Coleridge, *Biographia Literaria*, with an Introduction by Arthur Symons, in Everyman's Library (London: J. M. Dent, 1906), 171. Hereafter referred to as *BL* and cited in parentheses in the text.

[5] Kant in *Critique of Judgement*, Part I, Book 2, sects. 23–9, 49, explicitly refers to the creative aspect of the imagination and, somewhat more ambiguously, to its cognitive function: 'The imagination (as a productive faculty of cognition [*als produktives Erkenntnisvermögen*]) is of course very powerful in creating another nature as it were [*Schaffung gleichsam einer andern Natur*], out of the material that the real world of nature supplies her with.' Further down in the same section he offers a more qualified formulation: imaginative representation, he says, does not express definite concepts but nevertheless brings to them a kind of 'inexpressible supplement, the feeling of which quickens the cognitive faculty [*dessen Gefühl die Erkenntnisvermögen belebt*]' (I. Kant, *Werke*, x, ed. Wilhelm Weischedel (Frankfort on Main: Suhrkamp Verlag, 1968), 414, 417). Friedrich Schelling a little later on (in *Philosophie der Kunst*, 1802) is much more emphatic as regards the cognitive powers of the Imagination. It could give us access to absolute knowledge. (See *Werke*, iii, ed. Otto Weiss (Leipzig: Fritz Eckardt Verlag, 1907), 33, 277). On Coleridge's links with both Kant and Schelling, see Dorothy M. Emmet, 'Coleridge on the Growth of the Mind', in *Bulletin of the John Rylands Library*, 34: 2 (1952), repr. in Kathleen Coburn (ed.), *Coleridge: A Collection of Critical Essays* (Englewood Cliffs, NJ: Prentice-Hall Inc., 1967), 161–78.

In this, and in this alone, object and subject, being and knowing, are identical, each involving and supposing the other. (*BL* 144)

In this sentence the Self is perceived as its own object; elsewhere he speaks of the Self as subject confronting Nature as object. But even when the world of phenomena is involved, an 'intimate coalition' or merging of subject and object takes place. In fact 'all knowledge rests on the coincidence of an object with a subject'. Whilst a 'necessary antithesis' is here involved, that antithesis is overcome in the cognitive process:

During the act of knowledge itself, the objective and subjective are so instantly united, that we cannot determine to which of the two the priority belongs. There is here no first, and no second; both are coinstantaneous and one. (*BL* 137)

Elsewhere in *Biographia Literaria* he applies this concept of the fusion of opposites to the work of the poet. The Imagination 'dissolves, diffuses, dissipates . . . struggles to idealize and to unify', the poet uniting idea with image, Nature with mind. Poetry in this merely provides a crucial example of the cognitive process in general. For all knowledge, he tells us, ultimately resolves itself into a response to the supreme directive 'Know Thyself' (*BL* 136). The poet who 'brings the whole soul of man into activity' (*BL* 166) by uniting every outside referent with the interiority of the mind is the one who, above all others, learns to know himself. In this he echoes in the finite mind 'the eternal act of creation in the infinite I AM' (*BL* 159).[6]

If we try to establish Coleridge's epistemology from these scattered and not always lucid definitions, we shall come to the conclusion that for him cognition always means re-cognition—the recognition of the correspondence and even identity between the mind and that which is outside the mind. The mind as object marvellously fuses with the mind as subject—that is the moment of gnosis. The World as object suddenly and marvellously reveals its essential congruence with the Self as subject. At that moment knowledge is born. All cognition is thus the re-cognition of sameness or correspondence.

[6] I am ignoring the distinction Coleridge makes here between the 'Primary' and 'Secondary' imagination—a distinction that may have been widely misunderstood. The poet clearly has need of both. See on this, J. R. de J. Jackson, *Method and Imagination in Coleridge's Criticism* (London: Routledge and Kegan Paul, 1969), 110–18.

This mode of experience would seem to be fundamental to an understanding both of the philosophical theories of the Romantics and their poetics. Wordsworth is an eloquent exponent and practitioner of Coleridge's ideas. After the crossing of the Alps in Book VI of *The Prelude*, already referred to, Wordsworth notes how in spite of the overwhelming power of the outer scenery, the mind ('not prostrate, overborne') reasserted itself, by the processes of recognition:

> Finally, whate'er
> I saw, or heard, or felt, was but a stream
> That flowed into a kindred stream; a gale,
> Confederate with the current of the soul.
>
> (Book VI, 742–5)

The antithesis of inner and outer, subject and object is overcome as what was thought to be outer is recognized as a 'kindred stream'. After this recognition the two streams can flow together to become a unity, that of the soul or Self. In Book XIV of *The Prelude* he reverts to the same image of the stream in defining the source of the Imagination and its mode of operation. In this poem he has, he says, traced the stream

> From the blind cavern whence is faintly heard
> Its natal murmur; followed it to light
> And open day; accompanied its course
> Among the ways of Nature, for a time
> Lost sight of it bewildered and engulphed;
> Then given it greeting as it rose once more
> In strength, reflecting from its placid breast
> The works of man and face of human life.
>
> (Book XIV, 195–202)

The origin of the Imagination is here thought of as a natal (or we might say, prenatal) murmur. It belongs to a state of pre-consciousness beyond language and 'beyond the possibility of our knowledge', (*BL* 147), somewhere before the Self becomes conscious of itself.[7] Thereafter, its progress is defined by the image

---

[7] Jackson locates 'Primary Imagination' in this region of the unconscious (ibid. 116).

of the stream which is lost sight of and then discovered again and joyfully *recognized* as it emerges from the undergrowth. It will be noticed that the image of the stream calls forth by association that of the mirror—the stream 'reflecting from its placid breast | The works of man and face of human life'. As M. H. Abrams has demonstrated, these are two fundamental metaphors of the mind to be found in this period: the mirror with its passive reflective function is characteristic of the thinking of Locke and his followers—the mind mirrors impressions of the outer world, recording sensations, as we might say, on a photographic plate—whilst the later Romantic writers, and specifically Coleridge and Wordsworth, preferred the image of the overflowing fountain or the radiant lamp to suggest a more active, creative role for the mind.[8] For as Coleridge writes in 'Dejection', 'I may not hope from outward forms to win | The passion and the life, whose fountains are within.'

But in fact it would seem that the two images are reciprocal; the passage from *The Prelude* just cited is built on both images; the water is at one and the same time a reflecting mirror and an overflowing stream or fountain. We have the introjection of outer experience in the interiority of the soul and we have the forceful projection of the mind on that which is outside. The image of the stream 'as it rose once more | In strength' comes to express this more dynamic character of the Imagination. A little earlier he had said of the Imagination that it was 'but another name for absolute power' (line 190). But both metaphors—the one dynamic, the other passive—are necessary; the world of eye and ear is made up of 'what they half create and what perceive'.[9] What counts is the mutual recognition of identities, that of the face in the mirror, that of the confederate stream which joins the flow of our own existence. In such recognitions we have glimpses of knowledge—ultimate gnosis in fact, the knowledge of the All.

We may add that the stream and the mirror are both components of the legend of Narcissus and that the kind of thinking that we are here concerned with is in a deep sense narcissistic

---

[8] M. H. Abrams, *The Mirror and the Lamp: Romantic Theory and the Critical Tradition* (New York: Norton, 1958), 57–8.

[9] 'Lines Composed Above Tintern Abbey', ll. 106–7.

thinking.[10] The mind gazes at its own reflection in the pool or fountain and as it does so the boundary between inner and outer is abolished and we have an unbroken unity of the Self. But not only does the world disappear; as the Self becomes absorbed in its own self-contemplation its objective reality seems to dissolve and it is in danger of being lost in its own shadow. In the legend of Narcissus this is expressed by saying that Narcissus, after falling in love with his own image, pines away and dies. The boundary between self-knowledge and self-annihilation is precarious indeed.[11]

The Narcissus legend comes to tell us one more thing, namely, that there is a deep connection between gnosis in the sense of self-knowledge and eros; for it is a story about the Self falling in love with its own Selfhood (or with a fractured part of that Selfhood, as Freudian psychologists would argue). Knowledge sought in these terms is the knowledge of the soul's hidden partner who is ever at our side and with whom we seek union. In the magic moment of recognition, or, to use Coleridge's formulation, in the coinstantaneous 'act of knowledge', when the identity of the self and its mirror-reflection are marvellously discovered, ecstasy is attained and we have access to 'the passion and the life whose fountains are within' ('Dejection: An Ode'). The other name for such passion and such ecstasy, as the love-poets have always known, is death. There is a point where both gnosis and eros are one with *thanatos*.[12]

The most complete account of this ecstatic mode of cognition is to be found in Shelley's poem 'Epipsychidion' which is in every way a key text for our purpose. This of course is first and foremost a love-poem but Emilia Viviani, the object of the poet's love, is explicitly identified with the 'soul of the soul'. Hillis Miller points out that eyes are a constant symbol in Shelley's

[10] Cf. Barbara A. Schapiro, *The Romantic Mother: Narcissistic Patterns in Romantic Poetry* (Baltimore: Johns Hopkins University Press, 1983), 19 and *passim*. Cf. also Kathleen Coburn, 'Reflexions in a Coleridge Mirror: Some Images in his Poems', in F. W. Hilles and H. Bloom (eds.), *From Sensibility to Romanticism: Essays Presented to Frederick A. Pottle* (New York: Oxford University Press, 1965), 415–37. Without any evident dependence on Freud or Lacan, Ms Coburn amazingly arrives at similar notions to theirs. Her perceptions regarding the 'breast-mirror' (pp. 427–33) are particularly striking.

[11] Schapiro, *The Romantic Mother*, 63, 130.

[12] Cf. Diana Hume George, *Blake and Freud* (Ithaca, NY: Cornell University Press, 1980), 95 (in reference to *The Book of Thel*).

love-poetry; they are the eyes of the beloved 'and also, at the same time, the protagonist's own eyes reflected back to him'.[13] The love to which his poetry points is typically incestuous; it is the love of Narcissus for his lost twin. But whilst the poem celebrates the Platonic love of the soul for its own essence, the erotic nature of this union cannot be doubted:

> To the intense, the deep, the imperishable,
> Not mine but me, henceforth be thou united
> Even as a bride, delighting and delighted.

(ll. 391–3)

To the frequent images of fountains and lamps Shelley adds that of chords of music making a harmony:

> I love thee; yes, I feel
> That on the fountain of my heart a seal
> Is set, to keep its waters pure and bright
> For thee, since in those *tears* thou hast delight.
> We—are we not formed as notes of music are,
> For one another, though dissimilar;
> Such difference without discord, as can make
> Those sweetest sounds, in which all spirits shake
> As trembling leaves in a continuous air?

(ll. 138–46)

As Coleridge had pointed out, true knowledge involved the abolition of 'necessary differences' and their harmonious resolution. Shelley is here saying the same thing. The Mediterranean setting (real or imaginary) provides another confederate stream of harmony:

> And every motion, odour, beam and tone,
> With that deep music is in unison:
> Which is a soul within the soul—they seem
> Like echoes of an antenatal dream.

(ll. 453–6)

Shelley insists on the cognitive aspect of this unison, declaring that 'her spirit was the harmony of truth'—truth being identified with 'that best philosophy' of Plato (ll. 216, 213). Nevertheless

[13] See John Hillis Miller, 'The Critic as Host', in Harold Bloom *et al.* (eds.), *Deconstruction and Criticism* (London: Routledge and Kegan Paul, 1979), 238.

the image of music, so central to this poem, suggests that the harmonious union of psyche and epipsyche takes us beyond the sphere of cognition pure and simple and, we may add, beyond the sphere of language. In the passage just quoted the 'deep music' of the soul and the chords of which it is composed become 'like echoes of an antenatal dream'—a perception shared by Wordsworth, as we noted earlier. Shelley applies himself again and again to this twilight zone of the unconscious and the incognizable, where the soul is lost in its own shadow. At that point language fails as 'thought's melody I Becomes too sweet for utterance'. At the same time, the images of fountain and lamp reach a climax of intensity:

> And we will talk, until thought's melody
> Become too sweet for utterance, and it die
> In words, to live again in looks, which dart
> With thrilling tone into the voiceless heart,
> Harmonizing silence without a sound.
> Our breath shall intermix, our bosoms bound,
> And our veins beat together; and our lips
> With other eloquence than words, eclipse
> The soul that burns between them, and the wells
> Which boil under our being's inmost cells,
> The fountains of our deepest life, shall be
> Confused in Passion's golden purity,
> As mountain springs under the morning sun
> .   .   .   .
> One hope within two wills, one will beneath
> Two overshadowing minds, one life, one death,
> One Heaven, one Hell, one immortality,
> And one annihilation. Woe is me!
> The winged words on which my soul would pierce
> Into the height of Love's rare Universe,
> Are chains of lead around its flight of fire—
> I pant, I sink, I tremble, I expire.

> (ll. 560–72; 584–91)

Remarkably, Shelley's language becomes most precise as he reaches the threshold of annihilation or linguistic dissolution and defines it for us. This is Shelley's fundamental *aporia*. His poetry focuses on the point where poetry itself is eclipsed. Hillis Miller has well defined Shelley's poetry as 'the record of a perpetually renewed failure . . . The words . . . remain on the page as the unconsumed traces of each unsuccessful attempt to use words to end words.'[14] But this need not be seen as a failure; he rises to his height of eloquence to speak of the inexpressible, of 'thought's melody | Become too sweet for utterance'. Here is the final ecstasy of gnosis where objective, conceptual knowledge is dissolved and the mind becomes part of the ground of Being itself. It is a mode of experience cultivated at this same time in the poetry of Hölderlin. Shelley communicates this mode to us with special clarity, at the same time establishing a clear link between gnosis and eros. The ecstasy of the supreme knowledge of the Self, the union of the psyche and epipsyche, reveals itself as an erotic ecstasy—a kind of orgasm. And as such its proper analogy is death. It is not entirely inappropriate to remark that shortly after writing this poem, Shelley found the literal fulfilment of his dream of annihilation in the Gulf of Spezzia, 'under the quick, faint kisses of the sea' (l. 547).

It may be, as Geoffrey Hartman has suggested, that the Romantic poets were seeking an escape from self-consciousness, a path through gnosis to the unconscious life of the mind of Man and with it a release from mere Selfhood.[15] But if they sought such liberation what they more often found at the end of the road was despair. The true gain has been that of the reader: he has heard the word of power, he has thrilled to the poetry and the passion whose fountains are within; or to borrow Shelley's biblically inspired metaphor, he and his beloved have become an 'expanding flame . . . ever still | Burning, yet ever inconsumable' (ll. 576, 579) which issues from the soul's 'buried lamp' (l. 477). The burning bush had signified for Moses a transforming encounter between the Self and the Other and with that a call for redemptive action; for Shelley it comes to signify the intensity of the inner life, a candle within doors. But the reader, responding to the poetry, is not called upon to pay the price of this diminution; he hears the word of power and rejoices. Taking with him the 'winged words', he can mount upwards in a 'flight of fire', leaving the 'chains of lead' behind.

[14] Ibid. 237.
[15] Geoffrey H. Hartman, 'Romanticism and Anti-Self-Consciousness', in Harold Bloom (ed.), *Romanticism and Consciousness: Essays in Criticism* (New York: Norton, 1970), 48, 55.

2

Blake makes his own special contribution to these definitions of the working of the mind and in particular to the account of what may be termed the intra-sexual life of the Imagination. He does it by means of an elaborate symbolic structure, that of the Four Zoas—the visionary components of Albion, who is Universal Man or the Divine Humanity. Albion is a cosmic figure, including in himself the whole of reality, temporal, physical, and spiritual. In their ideal state the Zoas combine the male and female principles, but these principles are constantly splitting apart only to be marvellously rejoined 'in dreams of bliss among the emanations'. Every such coupling is in the strict sense an act of recognition, as an integral part of the Zoa, temporarily alienated, is restored to its primordial unity. True perception and knowledge are a function of the harmonious integration of the Zoa system—this is the 'fourfold vision' referred to in Blake's letter to Butts (E 693). Another ideal representation is the building of Golgonooza. This is the city of Art and Imagination, but it is also an essentially erotic landscape, its architecture of 'Spires & Domes of ivory & gold' (*Milton*, Pl. 35: 25) representing male and female sexuality. The northern gate of the quadrilateral structure leads to eternity (Eden).

Blake in effect makes the modalities of romantic self-consciousness the very subject of his poetry. Notions and processes which are only hinted at in the imagery of Wordsworth and Shelley are here projected on a large mythic canvas. Moreover, Blake gives them the distinctness of an organized system. His great strength comes from the fact that whilst notions of the all-embracing character of the Self and of the universal power of the Imagination had found expression hitherto in the lyric of romantic subjectivity, Blake's voice is not that of romantic subjectivity.[16] *Songs of Innocence and of Experience* are of course lyric poems but they do not speak of the loves and sorrows of their author or implied author. They are nearer to dramatic lyrics. 'The Sick Rose' communicates the pathos of the 'rose' and the 'worm' in their 'dark secret love' and in their unappeased and

[16] As perceptively noted by Leopold Damrosch, Jr., 'Burns, Blake, and the Recovery of Lyric', *Studies in Romanticism*, 21 (1982), 637–60. He defines this mode by the term 'non-expressive symbolism' (p. 655).

deadly hostility. What we have is a kind of mythic mini-drama. Whatever subjective contents are involved have been projected outward into a dynamic structure or symbolic language, which in the longer poems takes the form of an elaborate mythology.

Thus where Shelley gives us mere hints of the mythic drama of the psyche and the epipsyche, attention being mainly focused on the personal passion of the poetic speaker, Blake gives us a detailed and graphic account of the erotic union between the Imagination (Los) and his female emanation (Enitharmon), where the word 'harmony' is embedded in the name of the female partner to this union. Los, as Imagination, not only creates the world but also frequently stands for Blake himself in whose consciousness all these events and processes occur. But again they occur over there and can be beheld and represented in clear outline. Thus Blake has invented a precise mythological language or shorthand for speaking of cognition and recognition, defining the ground of romantic inwardness without being himself engulfed in the abyss of that same inwardness.

Blake goes a stage further: he uses the same dramatic language of symbols to define the system of intertextual relationships on which his poetics is founded—in other words to spell out the hermeneutic mode which governs his response to the writings of his precursors. This was the issue we raised at the beginning of our discussion of Blake. He has, it will be recalled, dismissed the Daughters of Memory and proclaimed exclusive allegiance to the Daughters of Inspiration. But is such denial of memory compatible with the manifest indebtedness of Blake to Milton? Ironically, this very proclamation of his freedom from anterior voices and examples is itself an echoing of Milton who had, in a famous passage in *The Reason of Church Government*, promised his readers a poem of divine inspiration not to be raised from the vapours of wine 'nor to be obtained by the invocation of Dame Memory and her Siren daughters'. The truth is that indebtedness is a weak word: Blake is in thrall to Milton. He is as haunted by the power and personality of Milton as Keats was haunted by Shakespeare. But how is such text-hauntedness to be related to the narcissistic mode, to the transcendent I AM of romantic self-consciousness? Do not these recognitions of power and presence inevitably involve an otherness, an intrusion, a message so to speak, from outside the circle of the Self?

It is this very dialectic which Blake explores in his poem *Milton* —a poem which, as Robert F. Gleckner has pointed out, tells the story of Blake's final 'regeneration of himself' as *the* poet.[17] This makes it the equivalent of Wordsworth's *Prelude*, recounting the growth of the poet's mind. But in this case it is the growth of the poet's mind observed as a function of the mythic drama being enacted between himself and his precursor, Milton. Exhibited in this fashion, the hermeneutic process becomes the main theme of this poem.

As though to emphasize this, the central event in this poem and one which has epic portentousness, is the vast journey of Milton, 'the immortal Man', from the invisible to the visible world through 'the Sea of Time & Space' to arrive in Blake's garden in Felpham, there to become one with the poet. The union with the poet is recounted twice, both occasions echoing different episodes from Milton's own *Paradise Lost*. On the first occasion Milton's journey and descent recall in numerous verbal echoes the fall of his own Satan from Heaven, his appearance in Hell, and his subsequent voyage over the vast spaces of Chaos to Paradise. In Plate 14 Milton explicitly identifies himself as the Satan of his own poem: 'I am that Evil One! | He is my Spectre.' And then comes the actual arrival of Milton in Blake's garden:

> so Milton's shadow fell,
> Precipitant loud thundring into the Sea of Time & Space.
> Then first I saw him in the Zenith as a falling star,
> Descending perpendicular, swift as the swallow or swift;
> And on my left foot falling on the tarsus, enterd there;
> But from my left foot a black cloud redounding spread over Europe.

> (Pl. 15: 45–50)

Milton is imagined entering into Blake's left foot, but this is a hermeneutic event, not a surrealistic psychodrama. What really enters into Blake here, to become part of himself, are the marvellous lines from *Paradise Lost*, Book I, linking the builder of Pandemonium with Mulciber who, in Homer's *Iliad*, is cast out of heaven by Zeus:

---

[17] Robert F. Gleckner, 'Most Holy Forms of Thought: Some Observations on Blake and Language', *English Literary History*, 41 (1974), 556.

> from Morn
> To Noon he fell, from Noon to dewy Eve,
> A Summer's day; and with the setting Sun
> Dropt from the Zenith like a falling Star,
> On *Lemnos* th' *Aegean* Isle . . .
>
> (*Paradise Lost*, I. 742–6)

Blake has appropriated the language of this passage of Milton in his account of Milton's descent, making it an integral part of his own poem. But he not only appropriates Milton's text; by an extraordinary feat of reflexive virtuosity he makes this very appropriation also the matter of the episode described. In the passage quoted he dramatizes the encounter with Milton's text, representing it not as a meeting with an anterior voice or presence but as physical coalescence, *incorporation*. In other words, Blake has found Milton's poetry, especially the line 'dropt from the Zenith like a falling Star', to be an irresistible fascination. It joins him by a process to which we might give the term *homoousia*, entering into his left foot to become an inseparable part of himself.

And yet viewed from another angle, this episode of 'coinstantaneous' union (to use Coleridge's word) takes place against the background of a fierce contention with Milton and all that he had stood for. He is represented as the Satan of his own poem because he is a fundamentally Urizenic figure closely linked for Blake with the cruel, Lawgiving God of the Old Testament:

> He saw the Cruelties of Ulro, and he wrote them down
> In iron tablets: and his Wives & Daughters names were these
> Rahab and Tirzah, & Milcah & Malah & Noah & Hoglah.
> They sat rang'd around him as the rocks of Horeb round the land
> Of Canaan: and they wrote in thunder smoke and fire
> His dictate; and his body was the Rock Sinai . . .
>
> (Pl. 17: 9–14)

All this is just about the worst thing one can say about anyone's body in Blake's world. Here Milton, dictating his poems to his wives and daughters who acted as his amanuenses, becomes the evil demiurge of the gnostics inscribing a cruel law on iron tablets. In this he signifies for Blake all that is negative in institutional religion. Not only that, but it would seem that all that is bad in the Europe of Pitt and George III, all its social tyrannies and moral distortions, may be traced back to the evil authority of the past, with Milton as the dark Urizenic figure looming up out of the centre of that past. This is the paradox of Blake's bond with Milton. At the very moment when Milton's sublime poetry literally possesses him and is possessed by him, he gazes at his left foot and sees 'a black cloud redounding spread over Europe'.

In short, we have again a maximum of attachment to the poetry together with a maximum of distancing from the message of that poetry—from the doctrine and discipline which were so basic an ingredient of Milton's covenantal faith. Blake joins with Milton to divide. But what stands out most is the startling reflexive clarity with which he discerns this very dialectic and defines it for us.

Blake's poem will from now on be devoted to the redemption of Milton. He must be cured of his attachment to law and morality—in a word his Puritanism must be purged away. In the end he will 'bathe[s] in the Waters of Life, to wash off the Not Human'. He will cast off Albion's filthy garments and 'clothe him with Imagination', thus 'cast[ing] aside from poetry, all that is not Inspiration' (Pl. 41: 7). When that happens the 'black cloud' will no longer interpose between Milton and Blake; Milton will have become pure poet, knowing no gospel other than the Divine Art of Imagination and thereby his assimilation to Blake will be complete. It is a process rather like that recorded in *The Prelude*, Book XI, whereby Wordsworth abandoned history and revolution to devote himself to poetry 'alone'. But that move had followed a normal logic of cause and effect; here the redemption of Milton and his regeneration as 'pure poet' takes place some one hundred and thirty years after that poet's death! Time is transcended as the irreversibilities of history are abolished and the past becomes plastic and malleable. Indeed it would seem that there is no longer any past. Recognitions have become so total that not only has the boundary between subject and object disappeared, as Coleridge said it should, but that also between past and present. We are in a state of simultaneity where the object of knowledge—in this case the text which fertilizes the poet's imagination—has become continuous with the Self. We would thus seem to have a hermeneutics without memory and thus without the need to invoke the 'daughters of Memory'! The sense of temporal distance or difference has it seems been abolished and perhaps at this point the question should be raised as to whether such a relationship belongs to the category of hermeneutics at all as originally understood.[18]

It is instructive to compare the relation of the two poets to their respective precursors in the passages quoted. If Blake is recalling the precipitous descent of Satan in Milton's *Paradise Lost*, Milton, as noted above, is recalling some lines from the end of Book I of Homer's *Iliad*. There Hephaestus (Mulciber) relates how once his father Zeus in a pet of anger had sent him flying from heaven to land at sunset on the island of Lemnos. The assembled gods are delighted and amused by the story and also by the present somewhat ridiculous appearance of Hephaestus as he bustles about serving them with nectar and tries to keep the peace in Olympus so as to prevent a recurrence of the same unpleasantness. If we ask what is involved in bringing this classical source to bear on Milton's biblical epic theme, we have to answer that Milton too is fascinated here as in so many other places by the affinity between the two, the fall of Satan and his crew marvellously paralleling the fall of Mulciber 'thrown by angry Jove | Sheer o'er the Crystal Battlements'. So much so that in reading the passage we come to identify the unnamed architect who builds Pandemonium—if only for a moment—with Vulcan/Hephaestus, the builder of the towers and palaces of Olympus.

But if Milton and his readers are fascinated by the parallelism they are no less fascinated by the differences. One can go further: in contrast to the epistemology outlined by Coleridge, the pleasure experienced by Milton's reader is derived from the recognition of difference as much as from the recognition of sameness. True knowledge, we might say, involves the acknowledgement of the distinction between subject and object, past and present, self and that which is outside of the self, and finally, as in our present instance, the distinction between the voice of the precursor and our own. Milton keeps these differences before

---

[18] Joseph A. Mazzeo argues that traditional Christian interpretations of the Old Testament preserve the historicity of the text being interpreted. There is a sense of temporal distance. Characteristically, allegorical fictions are often cast in the form of a journey; see *Varieties of Interpretation* (Notre Dame, Ind.: University of Notre Dame Press, 1978), 49, 65.

us in a fruitful tension in the Mulciber passage. Hermeneutics has to do after all not only with establishing links but also with establishing boundaries. If Mammon (or, by association, Satan) is like Mulciber, he is also subtly but clearly differentiated from him. In the languorous charm and beauty of the lines describing Mulciber's flight, 'from Morn | To Noon he fell, from Noon to dewy Eve, | A Summer's day', we have the evocation of a whole literary culture utterly different from that to which the fall of the angels belongs. In fact the image of Mulciber arriving in Lemnos on a lovely summer's evening constitutes something like the cultural antithesis of the figure of Satan in the infernal pit shorn of his beams and shedding disastrous twilight on half the nations. Mulciber has never been in that pit, he has never built in hell. That antithesis is what is emphasized in the continuation of the passage:

> Men call'd him *Mulciber*; and how he fell
> From Heav'n, they fabl'd, thrown by angry *Jove*
> Sheer o'er the Crystal Battlements: from Morn
> To Noon he fell, from Noon to dewy Eve,
> A Summer's day; and with the setting Sun
> Dropt from the Zenith like a falling Star,
> On *Lemnos* th' *Aegean* Isle: thus they relate,
> Erring; for he with his rebellious rout
> Fell long before; nor aught avail'd him now
> To have built in Heav'n high Tow'rs; nor did he scape
> By all his Engines, but was headlong sent
> With his industrious crew to build in hell.

> (*Paradise Lost*, I. 740–51)

The words 'thus they relate, | Erring' establish the difference between the two records—the word 'Erring' receiving special emphasis from its position at the beginning of a run-on line. To attribute what is told of Mulciber in Homer to the builder who constructed Pandemonium is to err. There is also a sharp insistence on temporal distance. In contrast to the simultaneity assumed in the Blake passage where the two poets meet in a kind of timeless present as the past loses its pastness, we have here a triple time-scheme. There is the time of the poet-speaker himself as he looks back ('thus they relate, | Erring') giving to the recalled narratives a legendary character; then there is the time of Greek myth and, carefully differentiated from it, the greater antiquity of the biblical record ('for he with his rebellious rout | Fell long before'). Milton seems to be here making a statement about historical precedence, but the situation is even more complex for it would appear from the earlier part of the passage that Mulciber, unlike Satan or Mammon, never fell at all: 'how he fell | From Heav'n, they fabl'd'. It was all a fable. Moreover, as Milton well knew, the hexaemeral tradition relating the fall of the angels was in fact later than Homer's epic. The confusion would seem to be deliberate: legend or history? earlier or later? And then there is the confusion as to the identity of the builder of Pandemonium: Mammon or someone else? Could it be Mulciber after all, as the syntax at one point seems to require, thus making the story told in Homer a kind of apocryphal addition to the 'true' story of the building of Pandemonium?

These questions are not resolved in Milton's text. We are left instead with a certain opacity as of optical images which are imperfectly aligned. There is an absence of that transparency of vision which enabled Wordsworth to 'see into the life of things'. The different time-levels, the different levels of truth, above all the discontinuities of tone which prevent the two recalled narratives from totally blending with one another—all this contributes to the opacity. The last words of the cited passage with their emphatic closure, 'but was headlong sent | With his industrious crew to build in hell', harshly contradict the sunlit beauty and charm as well as the marvellous undulating rhythm of the description of Mulciber's flight: 'from Morn | To Noon he fell, from Noon to dewy Eve, | A Summer's day'. By superimposing one image on the other, Milton makes us vividly aware of their affinity but also of their separateness from one another. Both effects are essential to Milton's poetics.

In short, we are confronted with sources which blend and yet do not blend; they do not form a confederate stream among themselves, nor do they flow together to unite with the inner fountain of the poet-speaker's consciousness so as to create a continuity. The temporal differentiation so pointedly insisted upon serves to create a respect for boundaries; it also provides the distance needed for what we may term the hermeneutical perspective. Milton's poetic enterprise derives much of its authority from his ability to recapture ancient voices and ancient scenes and from the joy of those recognitions. But his power is due no less to the sense of a gap, an inevitable newness thrust upon him, a temporal distance which obliges him to say that which has not been said before. True acts of interpretation—and this includes interpretive fictions—have this paradoxical quality; they testify both to the knowability and the unknowability of the ancient word. That word is familiar, but it will always contain something unfamiliar, unfathomed. It communicates with us but it communicates over a great distance and, that being so, parts of the message will inevitably remain problematical. In Blake's incarnational hermeneutics, this paradoxical quality is lost. The past word is totally knowable, its pastness abolished as the dead poet becomes one flesh with the living poet. The distance on which the hermeneutic perspective depends has been collapsed.

3

We now come to the second account of Milton's entry into, and union with, Blake; it occurs in Plate 21 of Blake's poem:

> But Milton entering my Foot; I saw in the nether
> Regions of the Imagination; also all men on Earth,
> And all in Heaven, saw in the nether regions of the Imagination
> In Ulro beneath Beulah, the vast breach of Milton's descent.
> But I knew not that it was Milton, for man cannot know
> What passes in his members till periods of Space & Time
> Reveal the secrets of Eternity: for more extensive
> Than any other earthly things, are Mans earthly lineaments.

> And all this Vegetable World appeard on my left Foot,
> As a bright sandal formd immortal of precious stones & gold:
> I stooped down & bound it on to walk forward thro' Eternity

(Pl. 21: 4–14)

There is a temporary loss of cognitive self-awareness as the Self is momentarily eclipsed by the shadow of its own processes ('for man cannot know | What passes in his members till periods of Space & Time | Reveal the secrets of Eternity') but clarity of vision reasserts itself and when the Self is again perceived, it has expanded to include the whole 'Vegetable World'.

This passage too is based on an episode in *Paradise Lost*. Milton in his descent into Blake's garden here assumes the role of the angel Raphael who in Book V of *Paradise Lost* had descended into the Garden of Eden to give Adam an account, spread over four books, of the battles in Heaven and the Creation of the World, including the creation of Man himself—a moment beyond the range of Adam's self-awareness—'for who himself beginning knew?' (*Paradise Lost*, VIII. 251). This phrase evidently suggested the loss of self-awareness noted in the passage from Blake describing the poet's rebirth or regeneration brought about through a union with his predecessor. The story of the Creation is also hinted at in Blake, but in Blake's version the whole Creation reveals itself as an extension of Adam's (or Blake's) own body, the 'lineaments' of which include 'all this Vegetable World'. Raphael's detailed account of the Creation of the World and the events that preceded it—his revealing to Adam of 'the secrets of Eternity'—is thus collapsed into half a dozen lines; instead of the birth of Adam as the end-point of a long process, we have the whole process taking place within the 'nether regions of the Imagination' and viewed as part of the total and inclusive self-consciousness of Adam/Blake/Milton.

It will be recalled that Raphael, alighting on the 'Eastern cliff of Paradise' preparatory to his meeting with Adam, had assumed his proper shape, that of 'a Seraph wingd'. As I noted in an earlier chapter (above p. 179), Milton departed from the wing-arrangement of the Seraphim (or 'fiery angels') of Isaiah 6: 2 by disposing the middle pair in such a way as decently to conceal the angel's nudity:

> six wings he wore, to shade
> His lineaments Divine; the pair that clad
> Each shoulder broad, came mantling o're his brest
> With regal Ornament; the middle pair
> Girt like a Starry Zone his waist, and round
> Skirted his loins and thighs with downy Gold
> And colours dipt in Heav'n; the third his feet
> Shadow'd from either heel with feather'd mail
> Sky-tinctur'd grain.
>
> (*Paradise Lost*, V. 277–85)

The word that most excited Blake in this passage was 'lineaments'. These had been shaded by Raphael's wings. The word reappears in Blake's poem as the 'earthly lineaments' of the Divine Albion (who here merges with Blake). The lineaments are now displayed in their cosmic extent: 'for more extensive | Than any other earthly things, are Mans earthly lineaments'. Nothing is shaded, nothing concealed; Milton's 'lineaments', now unconcealed, become the focus of Blake's own totally liberated invention.

Blake returns to the word obsessively: often with a strong sexual emphasis as in the phrase, 'the lineaments of Gratified Desire'.

> What is it men in women do require
> The lineaments of Gratified Desire
> What is it women do in men require
> The lineaments of Gratified Desire

> (E 466)

Towards the end of *Milton* this Miltonic word which so haunted Blake becomes the key term in a direct, frontal assault upon the notion of restraint and regulation whether in poetry or in the moral life:

> These are the Sexual Garments, the Abomination of Desolation
> Hiding the Human Lineaments as with an Ark & Curtains
> Which Jesus rent . . .

> (Pl. 41: 25–7)

Thus Milton's poetic invention becomes the very instrument with which Blake seeks to demolish the Urizenic restrictions of Milton's universe! Never again will the wings of the angel modestly conceal his 'lineaments divine'. Jesus/Blake/Los has finally revealed the angel's naked limbs, or, to put this more accurately, he has finally liberated the naked beauty of Milton's poetry. As Milton comes to bathe in the waters of life, all the 'filthy garments' are cast aside, all moral purposes and ideas, and we are left with the word of pure Imagination. We might want to say that the erotic pleasure which Blake celebrates in the phrase 'the lineaments of Gratified Desire' is the 'pleasure of the text' itself which is here echoed, the near-coital *jouissance* which the later poet experiences when he makes the earlier poet's word his own, whilst rejecting all other messages and meanings.

There is another aspect of the Seraph figure in Milton which Blake makes his own and that is the reflexive aspect. As noted above in Chapter 6, the figure of Raphael as Seraph-angel in Book V of *Paradise Lost* needs to be related to Milton's autobiographical digression in *The Reason of Church Government*. There he had spoken of his own poetic vocation in terms of the call received by Isaiah when a Seraph had seared his lips with a burning coal taken from the altar. Sensing this connection, Blake went further and claimed for himself a like inspiration, identifying himself—indeed uniting himself here—with Milton/Raphael/Seraph. The union with this aspect of Milton's imagination, the burning or Seraph aspect, is vividly represented in Plate 22 where we have a third version of the supernatural visitor who descends into Blake's garden. In this version it is Los, god of Poetry and the Imagination, and specifically, the spirit of biblical poetry, who is seen to unite with Blake:

> Los descended to me:
> And Los behind me stood; a terrible flaming Sun: just close
> Behind my back; I turned round in terror, and behold.
> Los stood in that fierce glowing fire; & he also stoop'd down
> And bound my sandals on in Udan-Adan; trembling I stood
> Exceedingly with fear & terror, standing in the Vale
> Of Lambeth: but he kissed me and wishd me health.
> And I became One Man with him arising in my strength.

> (Pl. 22: 5–12)

Blake's lips too it seems have been kissed with the burning coal and something of Isaiah's terror at the sight of the fiery angel is conveyed in this passage (cf. 'Woe is me, for I am undone', Isaiah 6: 5). Blake thus shares Milton's inspiration as well as Milton's proximity to this biblical source.

But that is where the likeness ends. Blake's sense of himself as an inspired poet/prophet is in fact radically different from that of Milton. The prophet is one who is 'sent' (Isaiah 6: 8). As I have suggested, that same verb was prominent in Milton's recalling of this scene. 'The eternall Spirit', he says, 'sends out his Seraphim with the hallow'd fire of his Altar, to touch and purify the lips of whom he pleases.'[19] Intimate though the bonds

---

[19] John Milton, *Works* (New York: Columbia University Press, 1931), iii. 241.

are between the 'eternal Spirit' and its messenger, they do not merge or lose their separate identities. One of them knows, the other needs to be instructed; one of them sends, the other is sent. In Blake's case such distinctions are lost, or—more correctly speaking—they are jettisoned. The messenger is himself transformed into Los who is the god, the ultimate authority behind the text, the creator not only of poetry but of Man and the World. He is thus no longer a mediator. Nor is the poet. Self-sent and self-elected, the poet now merges his identity with that of Los himself to become one with him: 'And I became One Man with him arising in my strength.'

The deliverer has become one with the recipient of the message. The result is an indistinguishable unity of Los/Milton/Raphael/Blake. Dialogue in short has given way to monologue. Instead of the dialectical tension between the parties to the hermeneutic encounter, we have a continuity, a flow of confederate streams into one mighty channel. There are now it would seem no messages or constraints or boundaries, but only power and freedom without limits. Why then would Blake need a messenger, even a vestigial one? Why would he return to Milton's language and patterns of imagery, including the image of the descent of Raphael? Is there not in the very power which this paradigm exerts over him a kind of constraint? These are questions which we will yet need to ponder.

CHAPTER 9

The Golden Sandal of Hermes

We have yet to note another striking image which Blake introduces into his account of the descent of Milton/Raphael into his garden at Felpham. It is the image of the golden sandal bound on the foot of the poet-speaker as the bearer of a continuing mission. 'As a bright sandal formd immortal of precious stones & gold: | I stooped down & bound it on to walk forward thro' Eternity' (Pl. 21: 13–14). In Plate 22 this detail is repeated but now it is Los who performs the symbolic transference. Los had earlier on (Pl. 8: 11) removed his own left sandal; he now binds the sandals on the feet of the terrified poet: 'Los stood in that fierce glowing fire; & he also stoop'd down | And bound my sandals on in Udan-Adan' (Pl. 22: 8–9).

Now this golden sandal which Blake has so wonderfully made his own (in more than one sense) is also related to Milton's account of the dispatch of Raphael to Adam in Book V of *Paradise Lost*. It is of course the golden, winged sandal of Hermes, the messenger of the gods, whom Milton had conflated with the figure of Raphael. Blake, too, well understood the significance of Hermes in the epic tradition as a whole.[1] He is remembering not only the description of the messenger and his accoutrements in *Paradise Lost* but also the descent of Mercury in Virgil's *Aeneid*:

The god made ready to obey his mighty father's bidding, and first binds on his feet the golden shoes which carry him upborne over seas or land, swift as the gale.[2]

And Virgil in his turn is echoing Homer where Hermes is sent by Zeus to escort Priam to the tent of Achilles. The messenger promptly obeyed:

---

[1] Cf. Thomas M. Greene, *The Descent from Heaven* (New Haven: Yale University Press, 1963), *passim* (and see above pp. 182–3).
[2] *The Aeneid*, IV. 238–41, in *Virgil*, i, trans. H. Rushton Fairclough, The Loeb Classical Library (London: Heinemann, 1947), 413.

Straightway he bound beneath his feet his beautiful sandals, immortal, golden, which were wont to bear him over the waters of the sea and over the boundless land, swift as the blasts of the wind.[3]

In spite of his rejection of 'the Stolen and Perverted Writings' of the Greeks and Romans, Blake vividly encapsulates in this detail the whole epic tradition beginning with Homer and implicitly claims a place in that tradition for his own poem. For in the Homer passage the winged sandals of Hermes which enable him to mediate between heaven and earth clearly stand in a metonymic relation to the tradition as a whole, suggesting the grandeur, height, and the inspired character of the epic poem as a transaction involving men and gods. Blake's visionary project defines itself as an epic poem in this sense. But the winged sandals suggest something more than this: above all, they signify movement. Hermes is on the move and his business is to urge the hero to move also; cities have to be built, journeys have to be made. There is also a sense of time passing—the time of nations. The individual life, that of the hero, must be made to beat to that greater rhythm. Aeneas has to be urged on to his historic task and Mercury comes to remind him of this. For there are promises to be kept, promises which have their beginnings in Troy and which will have their fulfilment in Rome.

Is Blake's hero similarly urged forward? Does Los/Milton/Blake have a heroic task to perform for which the winged sandals are the appropriate symbol? Read in one way, *Milton* exhibits, indeed fulfills, the greatest of such epic ambitions. Los who is the poetic Imagination, is also seen as the force behind revolutions, in particular that spiritual revolution to which Milton had dedicated himself in *Areopagitica* and which had aimed at transforming the face of England and the world: 'that out of her as out of Sion, should be proclam'd and sounded forth the first tidings and trumpet of Reformation to all Europ.'[4] From this point of view, what is signified by the union of Los with Blake is that Blake is now inspired in like fashion, made capable of continuing Milton's messianic task and of carrying it to

---

[3] *The Iliad*, XXIV. 340–2, in *Homer's Iliad*, ii, trans. A. T. Murray, The Loeb Classical Library (London: Heinemann, 1967), 587.

[4] John Milton, *Works* (New York: Columbia University Press, 1931), iv. 340.

completion. That is what the poem is about; it is the good news that it announces:

> I will not cease from Mental Fight,
> Nor shall my Sword sleep in my hand:
> Till we have built Jerusalem
> In Englands green & pleasant Land
>
> (Pl. 1: 13–16)

The revolutionary idea had been personified in Blake's earlier prophecies, such as *America*, *Europe*, and *The French Revolution* by Orc. But Orc, the son of Los, had been a 'naked babe', a god of war and blood rather than of the religious spirit. Los would now take his place, redeeming Orc from his secular limitations; his coming would signify the principle of revolution in its higher, biblical character:

> He recollected an old Prophecy in Eden recorded,
> And often sung to the loud harp at the immortal feasts
> That Milton of the Land of Albion should up ascend
> Forwards from Ulro from the Vale of Felpham; and set free
> Orc from his Chain of Jealousy.
>
> (Pl. 20: 57–61)

The descent of Milton and his union with Blake which immediately follow this recollection by Los thus represent the fulfilment of a prophecy which would have the most momentous consequences for the history of the world. The spirit of revolution and prophecy as found in Elijah and Ezekiel and again in seventeenth-century England in the work of Milton would now be recovered, its true promise now, and only now to be fulfilled. Earlier revolutions would be seen as merely a prologue to this ultimate revolution! From this point of view the poem is epic in the highest degree. Even though the heroic deeds which it records all take place inside the poem and are so to speak poetic events, they do have reference none the less to the historical process. History would respond by a kind of occult sympathy to the word of the poet. Thus he would not need to step outside the poem in order to mediate the cosmic change which is here intimated. Unlike Milton Blake would not have 'to go on trust' with his readers for sixteen years whilst he abandoned poetry and exercised his left hand in political debate. Blake's would be a 'Mental Fight', taking place within the space of the

Imagination, but it would be an epic fight just the same. The hero of this latter-day poem, no less than the hero of the *Aeneid*, is charged with building a city, namely, Jerusalem, and thereby altering the course of history. The lines just quoted point clearly to the epic, not only by their tone of epic solemnity but by the patently Homeric setting that they evoke as the narrator pictures the rhapsodist singing the words of the prophecy 'to the loud harp at the immortal feasts'. It is like the reference to the sandals with golden wings. No clearer signal of epic intent could be devised.

Los comes to express this poetic direction: conceived as the spirit of biblical prophecy and revolution he has a dynamic role. He is the god of time, or rather, as Foster Damon puts it, 'he is Time itself'.[5] In a celebrated passage in the first Book of *Milton*, Blake envisions the sons of Los at work: 'the Sons of Los build Moments & Minutes & Hours | And Days & Months & Years & Ages & Periods; wondrous buildings.' He proceeds to develop an image of the vast constructions of history: 'And every Age is Moated deep with Bridges of silver & gold.' Minutes, hours, days, months, and years all have their instrinsic significance defined by the architectural imagery of tents, gates, walls, terraces, and towers. Time mounts upwards like a turreted building, unique and balanced, every part supporting the rest. A creative and purposive structure, the six thousand years' span of human history is the supreme achievement of Los. Time-extension is here given solidity by the imagery of spatial extension and 'the Guard are Angels of Providence on duty evermore' (Pl. 28: 44–61). This would do also to define the sense of time and opportunity created by the last act of *Hamlet*.

But then comes a startling reversal; after the lines on time and providence, epic vision gives way suddenly to what we can only term the anti-epic. Like Prospero, the poet abolishes the vision he has just set forth and reveals the cloud-capp'd towers, the whole universe of space and time, as an illusion. Truth is embodied not in the vast unfolding plan of providence with its days, months, years, ages, and periods, but in 'a Moment, a Pulsation of the Artery':

---

[5] S. Foster Damon, *A Blake Dictionary* (Providence, RI: Brown University Press, 1965), s.v. Los, 247.

For in this period the Poets Work is Done: and all the Great
Events of Time start forth & are conciev'd in such a Period,
Within a Moment, a Pulsation of the Artery.

(Pl. 29: 1–3)

The key word is not time but eternity: 'every Space smaller than
a Globule of Mans blood opens | Into Eternity of which this
vegetable Earth is but a shadow' (Pl. 29: 21–2). As in so much
Romantic poetry there is a narcissistic movement inwards, a turning away from the dust and struggle of history to some more
interior source of knowledge, some more transcendent aim. In
Blake we have a more traumatic version of a movement which
may be matched also in Wordsworth or in Keats. Keats in his
early poetry had sought to portray the gigantic ages of history in
its progressive evolution, but his final poetry for the most part
reveals him too as abdicating this aim. The Grecian urn begins
by being 'the foster child of silence and slow time' but in the end
it 'teaze[s] us out of thought | As doth eternity'. It comes to
represent a transcendent moment of love, a transcendent chord
of music, and a transcendent moment of devotion.

Blake, in *Milton*, has written an epic to end all epics. He proclaims that the epic, which would seem to be the poet's attempt
to give meaning to our journey through space and time, our
ongoing struggle to build the city of the future, is really a lyric,
conceived and bodied forth in an ecstatic moment of vision. Los
is the god of history, but he is also paradoxically the god of
that poetic inspiration which in a timeless moment renders all
history nugatory. Blake assumes the mantle of the prophet, but
here is his radical departure from the mode of biblical prophecy.
Los and the poet do not stand over against one another in the
challenging posture of dialogue as do Milton and his Muse, or
Samson and his God. Blake never challenges Los to explain 'Why
am I thus bereav'd thy prime decree?' On the contrary, there is
a blending of their identities. Los and Blake fuse into one: he
is Blake's own inspiration raising him above the flux of time
and its frustrations. And we may add that it carries him into
a region where the epic, with its commitment to the diachronic
structure of narrative, would seem to have no further work of
that kind to do; instead we have pure synchrony. For just as
persons blend so events lose their distinctiveness, as all history

is collapsed into the infinitesimal moment of vision, the pulsation of the artery.

Some critics have concluded that this is Blake's ultimate statement in this poem: diachrony is in the end subordinated to synchrony.[6] But others have disagreed; they have found in the imagery of apocalypse the sign of Blake's continuing commitment to change and revolution. Peter Butter draws attention to the sense of historical crisis still created in the very last lines of the poem, lines which resemble the closing lines of *Europe*:

> Rintrah & Palamabron view the Human Harvest beneath
> Their Wine-presses & Barns stand open; the Ovens are prepar'd
> The Waggons ready: terrific Lions & Tygers sport & play
> All Animals upon the Earth, are prepard in all their strength
> To go forth to the Great Harvest & Vintage of the Nations

(*Milton*, Pl. 42: 36–43: 1)

The grand narrative of world salvation is here reaffirmed in spite of earlier denials.[7] Clearly, if in reading the poem we give full weight to the tone and imagery of these lines, we will have to conclude that, unlike Wordsworth, Blake has not given up moral questions in despair and withdrawn to Dorsetshire to cultivate his private muse. Nor has he given up his sense of judgement here in favour of a cosmic forgiveness of sin. He still sees himself as the poet of revolution.

Which of the two readings is then finally correct? Logically, the one excludes the other. Or is there perhaps some synthesis that we have missed? The answer is that neither reading is correct or rather that the poem pulls powerfully in both directions and there is no synthesis. The contradictions in its vision and structure are not resolved. The folly is to suppose with so many critics that they necessarily are. Northrop Frye entitles his marvellous study 'Fearful Symmetry' and its last section, 'The Final Synthesis'. Both titles indicate what devout Blakeians want

---

[6] Cf. Morton D. Paley's comment on the narrative element in *Jerusalem*: 'There is a story in *Jerusalem*, consisting of many episodes, but this diachronic aspect of the work is for the most part subordinated to its synchronic aspect' (*The Continuing City: William Blake's Jerusalem* (Oxford: Clarendon Press, 1983), 303). This could be argued equally in reference to *Milton*.

[7] Peter H. Butter, '*Milton*: The Final Plates', in Michael Phillips (ed.), *Interpreting Blake* (Cambridge: Cambridge University Press, 1978), 162–3.

to believe rather than what the poetry itself finally illustrates.[8] This is one of the Idols of the Tribe which we noted also in the common view that *King Lear*, in spite of its manifest contradictions, must somehow, somewhere be unified! It is not. Likewise, *Paradise Lost*, in spite of its order and balance betrayed a tension, an unevenness in the heart of the poem which Milton was unable to overcome. Blake's contradictions are even less capable of resolution. His final long poems are and are not, epics. One can go further: they are supremely epic and anti-epic at the same time. Rather than seek to persuade ourselves that such inconsistencies cannot be present, we would do better to try to relate them to the fundamental dilemmas of our culture. This does not exclude the private madness of the artist, but it may reveal the public context for such aberrations.

With regard to *King Lear* I suggested that a kind of *agon* is enacted between two mutually exclusive viewpoints and between two sharply different structural principles operating within the fabric of the same play. There is no resolution, but if we are perceptive enough we may draw profit and instruction from watching the puppets dallying. And this may have been what Shakespeare intended. Blake clearly does not calculate the effect of his contradictions and confusions in the same fashion. He is not a dramatic writer who can detach himself to that extent from his plot and allow the different ideological currents free play. He is more involved, more committed to finding answers, for world salvation will depend on his finding the right answers. His grand symbolic-mythological scheme is in effect a mighty attempt to organize his universe in such a way that its contradictions, poetic and philosophical, will be resolved, that its fragments will be organized into a mythic whole.[9] But it fails in this. The meanings of the symbols constantly shift and reform

---

[8] Cf. Denis Saurat's equally reverent conclusion to *Blake and Modern Thought* (London: Constable, 1929): 'Blake's peculiar usefulness in our time is in his power of synthesis', but Saurat cautiously adds the words, 'or at least in his desire for synthesis' (p. 198).

[9] Cf. Thomas McFarland's view of Romantic poetry as combining an essential fragmentariness with a 'yearning for larger, more comprehensive unity'. His paradigm is Shelley's 'Ozymandias' (*Romanticism and the Forms of Ruin* (Princeton: Princeton University Press, 1981), 15, 31, 343 ff.). McFarland's important thesis is in some sense anticipated by A. C. Bradley, 'The Long Poem in the Age of Wordsworth', in *Oxford Lectures on Poetry* (London: Macmillan, 1941; first published, 1909), 177–205.

themselves anew. But if Blake cannot resolve his contradictions and cannot turn them to dramatic account, he can do one other thing which Shakespeare and Milton could not do: he can, through the power of his intellect, give us a near total understanding of the nature of the contradictions themselves. His incomparable reflexive virtuosity enables him to explore them, or, at least, provides us with the light we need for exploring them ourselves.

2

If the central event of Book I of *Milton* was the union of Milton, Blake, and Los, that of Book II is the apocalyptic self-annihilation of Milton. This, as we would expect, involves the poet-speaker also who, at the climax of terror, falls down lifeless in his garden to rise after a moment 'to Resurrection & Judgment in the Vegetable Body'. The figure whose arrival had provided the occasion for the central event of Book I had been Raphael/Hermes, the messenger of the epic tradition; for Book II it is the virgin Ololon, the Emanation of Milton, whose descent accompanies Milton's self-annihilation and who herself undergoes a catastrophic self-division at the same time.

> Before Ololon Milton stood & percievd the Eternal Form
> Of that mild Vision; wondrous were their acts by me unknown
> Except remotely; and I heard Ololon say to Milton
>
> I see thee strive upon the Brooks of Arnon. there a dread
> And awful Man I see, oercoverd with the mantle of years.
> I behold Los & Urizen. I behold Orc & Tharmas;
> The Four Zoa's of Albion & thy Spirit with them striving
> In Self annihilation giving thy life to thy enemies

(Pl. 40: 1–8)

If Blake is seen uniting with Los in Book I ('Los had enterd into my soul: | His terrors now posses'd me whole! I arose in fury & strength' (Pl. 22: 13–14)), here in Book II Milton is seen striving with 'Los & Urizen'. Los is now an antagonist explicitly associated with Urizen, i.e. with those aspects of life and society which stand in the way of imaginative freedom. Those aspects are summed up in the word 'Selfhood'. Milton in his reply to Ololon speaks of 'a Selfhood which must be put off & annihilated'. It should be noted that what has to be destroyed is not selfishness;

we are not speaking merely of Puritan self-righteousness or of the narrowness and pretensions of the Age of Reason, but of the actual autonomous Self, that which for Wordsworth and Coleridge as well as for Blake guaranteed integrity and wholeness. That is what Selfhood ultimately implies. It expresses itself typically in the Sublime mode as in the triumphant closing passage of Book I, beginning: 'The Sky is an immortal Tent built by the Sons of Los.' For if Los is Poetry, he is that poetry which arrogates to itself the power of creation! 'Both Time & Space obey my will', he had declared when uniting with Blake in Book I. Here is the final reach of Selfhood, and here also is Blake's poetry at its most magnificent and its most audacious. But we should remember that if Creation is the work of Los who is the poetic Imagination, it is also for Blake, especially in his gnostic moods, the work of an evil demiurge. The 'winepress of Los', the terrors of which are set out in Plate 27, is a primary expression of Los's powers. And the image, as we noted earlier, recalls the Old Testament God of Battles coming from Bozrah, his garments stained with blood after treading the winepress alone (Isaiah 63: 1–3). Here is an image to stir the heart, but it represents the Satanic antithesis to the rule of Jesus; it represents Selfhood. Here is the Blakeian *aporia* once again. The Imagination creates the world, but such world creation is the work of Satan. As a result, the Sublime itself ('the Sublime of the Bible') acquires an inevitable Urizenic undertow. The poetic word when uttered—elevated and triumphant though it is—performs, through its very power and authority, its own act of treason. 'Both Time & Space obey my will', is the poetry of power but also of Selfhood. And that Selfhood so magnificently displayed in such lines from Book I is going to be annihilated in Book II.

Blake has here projected on to his large mythological canvas the most fundamental of his own contradictions. Alongside the enormous emphasis on the Self as the focus of all knowledge and the all-important scene of adventures, is self-annihilation, the denial of Selfhood. This it would seem is the ever-besetting danger which threatens the narcissistic personality. Self and Self-loss come together in the poetry of Hölderlin,[10] of Shelley, and indeed in a greater or lesser degree, of all the Romantic poets.

[10] Cf. Stanley Corngold, 'Hölderlin and the Interpretation of the Self', in *Comparative Criticism*, 5 (1953), 192–3.

We may leave aside Freudian explanations which would relate this phenomenon to a 'divided and unresolved inner condition' resulting from a 'self-destructive attachment to the mother',[11] except to say that if Los and the sons of Los, the authors of time as we know it, are the principal agents in Book I, acting as a kind of all-male Chorus, then this role in Book II belongs to 'the daughters of Beulah'. It is their voice we now chiefly hear. And on the first Plate of Book II Beulah—significantly enough for this Freudian thesis—appears 'as the beloved infant in his mothers bosom round incircled | With arms of love & pity & sweet compassion' (Pl. 30: 11–12).

Such hints could lead to interesting speculations, but our concern here is not with psychological causes but rather with the way that this split manifests itself in the poetry. To take Blake's term 'annihilation' in all seriousness is to recognize that we are not concerned only with a division between two kinds of poetry, e.g. epic versus lyric, or two structural principles, e.g. the diachronic versus the synchronic. It is more like form versus formlessness, where formlessness implies a radical threat to poetic expression as such. What is at stake is the very possibility of structure, of genres of any kind (whether epic or lyric), indeed the very possibility of language itself as a signifying system.[12] Robert Gleckner draws attention to the 'self-transcendence of language' in the poetry of Shelley and other Romantic poets; John Hillis Miller had made a similar point.[13] But transcendence

[11] Barbara A. Schapiro, *The Romantic Mother* (Baltimore: Johns Hopkins University Press, 1983), 19, 130–1.

[12] On the connection between narcissism and language, see Jacques Lacan's rereading of Freud in 'The Mirror-Stage as Formative of the Functions of the I as Revealed in Psychoanalytic Experience' (1949), in Hazard Adams and Leroy Searle (eds.), *Critical Theory since 1965* (Tallahassee, Fla.: Florida State University Press, 1986), 734–48. Lacan speaks of 'primary narcissism' as belonging to a stage of development before language (p. 735). In a later seminar he emphasizes that it is with the emergence from the mirror-stage and the discovery of 'radical heteronomy' in 'the self's radical ex-centricity to itself' that language and signification are born ('The Agency of the Letter in the Unconscious or Reason Since Freud' (1958), ibid. 754). These essays are reprinted from Jacques Lacan, *Écrits*, trans. Alan Sheridan (New York: Norton, 1977). For a somewhat different reading of Lacan see G. H. Hartman, *Pychoanalysis and the Question of the Text* (Baltimore: Johns Hopkins University Press, 1985), 92–4.

[13] Robert F. Gleckner, 'Romanticism and the Self-Annihilation of Language', *Criticism*, 18 (1976), 178–85, and cf. John Hillis Miller, 'The Critic as Host', in Harold Bloom et al. (eds.), *Deconstruction and Criticism* (London: Routledge and Kegan Paul, 1979).

is merely a euphemism. When Shelley writes in *The Defence of Poetry* that 'poetry is a sword of lightning ever unsheathed, which consumes the scabbard that would contain it', he is talking about poetic self-annihilation.[14] Never was the end of poetry, its threatened extinction, so poetically expressed! Moreover, what we have is not merely a threat to poetry, but rather to articulate speech of any kind. Communication gives way to silence. 'Heard melodies are sweet, but those unheard | Are sweeter', Keats declares, the point being that music consists of events in time, whereas unheard melodies are timeless, or eternal. But eternity and silence are simply, once again, euphemisms. What we are talking about in the end is poetic self-annihilation. Blake with his unmatched clarity spells it out for us.

Blake has the merit of supplying us not only with an accurate term for this phenomenon but with a detailed map of its working. Los we recall is (like Hermes) the god of eloquence, poetry, and articulate speech. In *Jerusalem*, Plate 36, he is said to have 'built the stubborn structure of the Language'. There is a like emphasis in Book I of *Milton* where the sons of Los are observed marking out the limits of Golgonooza. And Golgonooza is, in Hazard Adams's apt definition, 'the city of verbal form'.[15]

Some Sons of Los surround the Passions with porches of iron & silver
Creating form & beauty around the dark regions of sorrow,
Giving to airy nothing a name and a habitation
Delightful! with bounds to the Infinite putting off the Indefinite
Into most holy forms of Thought: (such is the power of inspiration)

(*Milton*, Pl. 28: 1–5)

Golgonooza is Los's masterpiece, representing the integration of Man as an amalgam of soul and body who finds his highest expression in the works of Imagination. The echoing of *A Midsummer Night's Dream* in the third line of this passage points to Shakespeare as the ultimate master of words. But even Shakespeare's creations are it seems menaced by nothingness. The sons

---

[14] Gleckner, 'Romanticism and the Self-Annihilation of Language'; also id. 'Most Holy Forms of Thought: Some Observations on Blake and Language', *English Literary History* 41 (1974), 559.

[15] Hazard Adams, 'Blake and the Philosophy of Literary Symbolism', *New Literary History*, 5 (1973), 142.

of Los are, in the imagery of this passage, rather like King Canute trying to control the ocean. From the lines quoted it is clear that the control exercised by the naming power of the poet is threatened from within by the 'Passions' and from without by the 'Indefinite'. We wonder how long such bounds can hold. Even if the Passions also supply the necessary content for the creative activity of the sons of Los ('Some . . . surround the Passions with porches of iron & silver | Creating form & beauty') there can be no doubt of the danger they represent; it is that of formlessness. In an earlier passage (Plate 24) Blake had particularized this internal region of formlessness, relating it to the instinctual life of the human body itself (the region we might say of the id) including the genitalia and the bowels (Bowlahoola). Here is the underground source of the poet's inspiration but it is ominously wordless. Filled with the sounds and movements of the physical organism itself, it also enfolds lurking images of horror:

> In Bowlahoola Los's Anvils stand & his Furnaces rage;
> Thundering the Hammers beat & the Bellows blow loud
> Living self moving mourning lamenting & howling incessantly
> . . . .
> Loud sport the dancers in the dance of death, rejoicing in carnage
> The hard dentant Hammers are lulld by the flutes lula lula

> (Pl. 24: 51–3, 62–3)

The *Walpurgisnacht* atmosphere recalls 'the barbarous dissonance | Of *Bacchus* and his Revellers' from which Milton prays to be defended in the Invocation to the Muse at the beginning of Book VII of *Paradise Lost*.[16] Milton had dreaded the fate of Orpheus who, after descending into the underworld, was torn in pieces by the Maenads. Here were the lower reaches of the Imagination from which only Urania could guard him. Blake is here describing that same region; his dancers, 'rejoicing in carnage', are the same 'wilde Rout that tore the *Thracian* Bard | In Rhodope'. But Blake's tone is less censorious; unlike Milton he seems to accept this savage spectacle as natural—a necessary evil (like rock concerts). At the same time there is no doubt of its Urizenic tendencies; Tharmas founded Bowlahoola we are

---

[16] See above, p. 169.

told 'because of Satan' (Pl. 24: 49).[17] It may simply reflect the life of the organism but there is menace there none the less, the menace of disintegration. The poetic word, indeed articulate speech as such, is threatened.

As for the threat from without, the city of Golgonooza, as we are told in *Jerusalem*, is surrounded by the 'land of death eternal' (Pl. 13: 30), a main feature of which is the lake of Udan-Adan, the region of the Indefinite, situated to the east. This is part of the Ulro, or death-in-life. The elaborate description of this dreary landscape in *Jerusalem* owes much to the account of Hell in *Paradise Lost*, Book I, as well as to Job 10: 21–2. It is, Blake tells us, 'the land of darkness flamed but no light, & no repose'. The emphasis is on the absence of order: it is 'Chasmal, Abyssal, Incoherent!' (*Jerusalem*, Pl. 13: 53). In the account Blake gives in Book I of *Milton*, Udan-Adan again is essentially form-less, or rather it is formlessness itself:

The Lake of Udan-Adan, in the Forests of Entuthon Benython
Where souls incessant wail, being piteous Passions & Desires
With neither lineament nor form but like to watry clouds

(Pl. 26: 25–7)

There can be no doubt that in these lines from Book I of *Milton* the lack of form symbolized by Udan-Adan is lamented. The norm, the preferred standard, is the limitary design of Los and his sons, symbolizing order, power, and symmetry, and, we may add, Selfhood. In Book I, Milton had descended into the region of Udan-Adan (Pl. 21), but, obedient to the prophecy recorded in Eden and remembered by Los, he had not remained there but had 'up ascend[ed] | Forwards from Ulro' (Pl. 20: 59–60). Here in Book II, however, we remain for the most part in Ulro; the reader and the poet-narrator now seem to be them-selves located in the 'nether regions of the imagination in Ulro beneath Beulah'. This is the important change; the Indefinite has become the norm, supplying the perspective from which 'high' art and literature are judged. The Cherubim and Seraphim, asso-ciated with Milton's epic and the 'bright Paved-work' from the epiphany in Exodus 24: 10, suggesting a biblically inspired art, are now beheld as belonging to Satan:

---

[17] And see *The Four Zoas*, Night the Fourth, where Los builds anew 'the Ruind Furnaces of Urizen' (E 328).

Loud Satan thunderd, loud & dark upon mild Felpham's Shore
Coming in a Cloud with Trumpets & with Fiery Flame
An awful Form eastward from midst of a bright Paved-work
Of precious stones by Cherubim surrounded . . .

(Pl. 39: 22–5)

What had generally been conceived in Book I as the supreme achievement of Los is now condemned as the work of Urizen. Allowing for some inconsistency and confusion, this broad distinction may stand. A different set of values and symbols now supervenes. A terrible beauty is born but the message it mediates is the necessary annihilation of the standard affirmed earlier, a consummation which is also a 'consumation', the consuming of language and form in a poetry without words, a harmony of silence without a sound. This is Shelley's phrase and Shelley, like Blake, is never more eloquent than when he points to the void where eloquence—his own eloquence, that is—is at an end.

3

Book II introduces a number of symbolic figures which have the seemingly impossible task of signifying unsignifiability, or at least of saying that which normally lies beyond or beneath the threshold of the sayable. In terms of Blake's larger system they are all associated with the states of Beulah and Ulro. The first of these figures is of course Ololon herself. Her name seems to stand for a wordless ululation, something like the sound of the flutes ('lula lula') in Bowlahoola—another wordless region. Thomas Vogler perceptively remarks that what is suggested is the incoherent infant cry. Along with the daughters of Beulah, Ololon points us to a region beyond meaning, that of the 'preverbal maternal symbiosis'.[18] Specifically, she is Milton's 'Emanation' in that she is the challenge, the antithesis to the Miltonic *logos*, 'the suppressed gap in his own discourse'. She is the denial of the hermeneutic, not a meaning that Milton (and the reader) must discover, but a space, 'an internal void that must be entered'.

---

[18] Thomas A. Vogler, 'Re:Naming MIL/TON', in Nelson Hilton and Thomas A. Vogler (eds.), *Unnam'd Forms: Blake and Textuality* (Berkeley: University of California Press, 1986), 145.

To enter it is to be liberated from Selfhood, but also to be dis-joined from 'the signifying chain of the symbolic order'.[19]

Blake is here caught in an inevitable web of contradictions. This is the case with Udan-Adan itself, the region of the Indefinite. Udan-Adan represents the deconstructive principle; it calls in question the mighty constructions of the sons of Los, the forms of beauty to which they give 'a name and a habitation', whilst here in Udan-Adan souls have no names and no repose. And yet in his dialectical fashion, Blake deconstructs his own deconstruc-tion, *defining* the Indefinite by giving to it the name Udan-Adan and locating it precisely in relation to Golgonooza. Similarly, as an antithesis, Ololon is necessarily part of the symbolic order; she figures in a narrative. Her descent, paralleling that of Milton, takes on meaning within a poetic system—even if her meaning is the absence of meaning. Blake cannot escape this contradic-tion, but again he can light it up for us with brilliant mythopoetic clarity. Thus in the poetic narrative Ololon is constantly being constructed and deconstructed. She is at different times a cloud, a shadow, a 'moony ark'. As such she is part of the landscape of Beulah ('Beulah's moony shades and hills'), a geographical, or psychological, or climatic state rather than a person. As a state she is pronominally 'we' or 'they', i.e. a collectivity—'into this pleasant Shadow, all Ololon descended'. But when she has to enter the 'vegetable World' and confront the poet-narrator (or later, engage in a dramatic exchange with Milton), she is momentar-ily individuated and she materializes as 'One Female, Ololon . . . a Virgin of twelve years':

> Walking in my Cottage Garden, sudden I beheld
> The Virgin Ololon & address'd her as a Daughter of Beulah
> Virgin of Providence fear not to enter into my Cottage
> What is thy message to thy friend?
> . . . .
>   but pity thou my Shadow of Delight
> Enter my Cottage, comfort her, for she is sick with fatigue
>
>   (Pl. 36: 26–32)

In this hypostasis Ololon will perhaps remind the reader of the story of the angels appearing to Abraham in Genesis 18.

---

[19] Ibid. 154, 162.

(There is incidentally a similar ambiguity in that passage as the angels change from plural to singular and back again to plural in the course of a few verses). Sarah we remember was in the tent listening to the conversation; the mention of Catherine Blake in the cottage, 'sick with fatigue', enforces the same domestic note. Characteristically, this scene is again mediated by Milton's *Paradise Lost*, Book V, where Raphael, now a domesticated divine messenger, at Adam's urging 'vouchsafes to enter' his bower there to partake of a midday meal. We may imagine Ololon responding to the poet's invitation in the above passage by entering his cottage and there sitting down with Catherine to discuss their household affairs. But the defining of the Indefinite in this fashion is only temporary. After her confrontation with Milton in Plate 40 Ololon throws off her female identity and, so to speak, self-destructs:

> So saying, the Virgin divided Six-fold & with a shriek
> Dolorous that ran thro all Creation a Double Six-fold Wonder!
> Away from Ololon she divided & fled into the depths
> Of Milton's Shadow as a Dove upon the stormy Sea.
>
> (Pl. 42: 3–6)

The six parts of Ololon (representing Milton's three wives and three daughters) are cast off and together with that her history, her selfhood, and her virginity. She becomes again a kind of floating signifier, without any clear shape, individuality, or number. The annihilation of the *logos* is here represented as a kind of primordial Fall—hence the dolorous universal shriek—but also as an apocalyptic moment of renewal, the dove upon the stormy sea being the sign of a Second Coming for which Ololon's disastrous self-division gives the signal. History is collapsed as the Fall and the ultimate Redemption occur in immediate sequence or more probably at the same instant.

Vogler has suggested that Ololon represents the denial of the hermeneutic. Yet paradoxically these metamorphoses, including her final dissolution, all have strong literary associations. Even when suggesting through the figure of Ololon a poetic freed entirely from the 'daughters of Memory',[20] Blake is inevitably

---

[20] The daughters of Beulah, with whom Ololon is closely linked, stand for inspiration; by contrast, the daughters of Albion stand for memory. Cf. Milton O. Percival, *William Blake's Circle of Destiny* (New York: Columbia University Press, 1938), 45.

echoing earlier voices. Specifically, we may note that his very grasp of formlessness and the non-verbal seems to have been learned from a somewhat obscure remembered source. When first introduced by that name in Plate 21, Ololon is described as 'a sweet River, of milk & liquid pearl | . . . on whose mild banks dwelt those who Milton drove | Down into Ulro'. The 'river of pearl' is a phrase found in the writings of Thomas Vaughan, the seventeenth-century alchemist, to describe the *prima materia*. He found it to be a formless substance, of constantly changing qualities, 'with a thousand miraculous colours'.[21] The *prima materia*, itself indefinable, is yet the matrix of all forms. That would seem to be one meaning of Ololon. All things dissolve in her to be miraculously reborn in a mystic union at the end of days. 'Watch over this World,' she is told, 'and with your brooding wings, | Renew it to Eternal Life' (Pl. 21: 55–6). We cannot miss the association with the holy spirit in the opening lines of *Paradise Lost* who 'with mighty wings outspread | Dovelike satst brooding on the vast Abyss | And mad'st it pregnant'. There is an extraordinary density of allusion as the 'Spirit of God' of Genesis 1: 2 joins with Milton's Muse and with the *prima materia* of the alchemists to become the literal matrix of creation, with the pregnancy in question having strong reference to poetic creation.

But it is poetic creation of a particular kind. We are speaking of a monologic mode of inspiration, an instantaneous fusing of differences. It is this moment which Blake has been seeking to define throughout this poem. We noted earlier that Blake had startlingly reversed the account he had given of the grand architecture of Space and Time constructed by the sons of Los, declaring that

---

[21] *Lumen de Lumine: Or A new Magicall Light discovered, and Communicated to the World*, by Eugenius Philalethes [Thomas Vaughan] (London, 1651), devotes six pages to 'The River of Pearl' (sigs. F6ᵛ–G1ʳ); the description includes a reference to 'wine, oile, and milk'. The possible link between Ololon and Thomas Vaughan's 'River of Pearl' was first noted by S. Foster Damon, who termed it a 'psychological curiosity' (*William Blake: His Philosophy and Symbols* (first edn., 1924; Gloucester, Mass.: Peter Smith, 1958), 417). In light of C. G. Jung's interpretation of alchemy as expressing archetypal symbols, however, Blake's use of this source makes perfect sense. (Cf. Jung on the *prima materia* in *Psychology and Alchemy*, trans. R. F. C. Hull, vol. xii of *The Collected Works of C. G. Jung*, ed. Herbert Read, Michael Fordham, and Gerhard Adler (London: Routledge and Kegan Paul, 1953), 304–26).

Every Time less than a pulsation of the artery
Is equal in its period & value to Six Thousand Years.

(Pl. 28: 62–3)

For in this Period the Poets Work is Done
. . . .
Within a Moment: a Pulsation of the Artery.
. . . .
And every Space smaller than a Globule of Mans blood opens
Into Eternity . . .

(Pl. 29: 1, 3, 21–2)

Here was the lyric antithesis to the epic mode, the Dionysiac
versus the Apollonian, Blake in this anticipating Nietzsche's
insights by some seventy years. Nietzsche too would brilliantly
perceive that the Dionysiac mode of inspiration involves 'a mystical process of unselving', a dissolution of the principle of individuation so essential to the serener art of Apollo, 'the god of
individuation and just boundaries'.[22] It is this Dionysiac state
or condition that Blake explores in this second part of the poem;
here the boundaries of Space and Time melt away and eternity
is collapsed into the instant when the poet's work is done. All
of Ololon's appearances in Book II occur in this moment; or
perhaps it would be truer to say that the various appearances
of Ololon are a way of talking about this moment.

There is a Moment in each Day that Satan cannot find
. . . .
In this Moment Ololon descended to Los & Enitharmon
Unseen beyond the Mundane Shell Southward in Miltons track.

(Pl. 35: 42, 46–7)

Naturally enough, since she belongs to the instantaneous moment
of vision, her mark is suddenness.

---

[22] Cf. *The Birth of Tragedy*, sects. v, i, ix, in *The Birth of Tragedy* and *The
Genealogy of Morals*, trans. Francis Golffing (New York: Doubleday, 1956), 39, 22,
65. Nietzsche's notion of the matrix of Nature addressing us through Dionysiac
art (ibid., sect. xvi, p. 102) also reminds us of what is said of Ololon in Blake's
poem. It may be argued that Nietzsche was no more able than Blake before
him to achieve a resolution of the conflict represented by these two opposed
principles in life and art. But he claims that in ancient Greece a kind of integration and harmony was momentarily achieved by the tragedians of the age of Pericles
(see sect. x).

> nor time nor space was
> To the perception of the Virgin Ololon but as the
> Flash of lightning but more quick the Virgin in my Garden
> Before my Cottage stood, for the Satanic Space is delusion.
>
> (Pl. 36: 17–20)

Ololon thus represents infinitesimal time and infinitesimal space, everything larger than which is Satanic (or from the perspective of Book I, is 'created by the Hammer of Los' (Pl. 29: 20)).

4

The moment which Satan cannot find and in which Ololon makes her various apearances in Book II is also the signal for the entry into the poem of two other images or figures closely associated with her which likewise point to the lyric mode. They are the Lark and the Wild Thyme. The Lark's nest is 'at the eastern Gate of wide Golgonooza' and the Wild Thyme is a small purple plant growing in the grass above that nest. They are thus close to, if not part of, the region of the Indefinite. Not only do these images signify the lyric mode but the passages devoted to their appearance are the lyrical climaxes of the poem, the moments of maximum poetic intensity. The Wild Thyme makes it possible for us to conceive the minute space which opens up into eternity, 'within that Center Eternity expands' (Pl. 31: 48); by means of a 'prophetic pun' as Erdman calls it,[23] it also suggests the dimension of time, but 'wild', that is, transcended and liberated from its bondage to the clock and the historical process. The mounting Lark stands for the single, passionately aspiring voice of the poet sounding out in a world devoid of other presences; he suggests inspiration—'his little throat labours with inspiration' (Pl. 31: 34)—a lyric purity in which language as well as place and time are all but transcended. Seemingly alone high up in the sky, 'mounting upon the wings of light into the Great Expanse' (Pl. 31: 32) and singing there for himself like the Solitary Reaper, he suggests above all a poetics of pure monologue. And yet it should be noted that, in the symbolic grammar of the poem,

---

[23] David V. Erdman, *Blake: Prophet Against Empire* (New York: Doubleday, 1969), 431.

Blake's Lark is not alone. He is emphatically linked to another bird, namely, the Nightingale. The great passage at the beginning of Book II celebrating the Lark's flight and song begins and ends with the image of the Nightingale from whose song the Lark, so to speak, takes his cue! The passage should be quoted at length:

Thou hearest the Nightingale begin the Song of Spring;
The Lark sitting upon his earthy bed: just as the morn
Appears; listens silent; then springing from the waving Corn-field! loud
He leads the Choir of Day! trill, trill, trill, trill,
Mounting upon the wings of light into the Great Expanse:
Reecchoing against the lovely blue & shining heavenly Shell:
His little throat labours with inspiration; every feather
On throat & breast & wings vibrates with the effluence Divine
All Nature listens silent to him & the awful Sun
Stands still upon the Mountain looking on this little Bird—

(Pl. 31: 28–37)

until presently all the other singing birds join in, the sun resumes its circuit, and finally 'the Nightingale again assays his song'

& thro the day,
And thro the night warbles luxuriant; every Bird of Song
Attending his loud harmony with admiration & love.
This is a Vision of the lamentation of Beulah over Ololon!

(Pl. 31: 42–5)

The Nightingale thus frames the reference to the Lark, forming a kind of *inclusio*. Harold Bloom is surely right in detecting in the Nightingale reference a tribute to the blind poet Milton, who had in the Proem to Book III of *Paradise Lost* compared himself to 'the wakeful bird' which 'Sings darkling, and in shadiest Covert hid | Tunes her nocturnal Note'.[24] Anne Ferry has argued that the Nightingale is more than an isolated image in *Paradise Lost*; it is a metaphor for the narrative voice itself, that of the inspired poet-prophet who is hidden in darknesss and yet gifted with celestial light. The nightingale symbol thus comes to embrace the world of Milton's poem in its totality.[25] Not

[24] Harold Bloom, *Blake's Apocalypse* (New York: Doubleday, 1963), 380.
[25] Anne Davidson Ferry, *Milton's Epic Voice: The Narrator in Paradise Lost* (Cambridge, Mass.: Harvard University Press, 1963), 25, 176, 179.

surprisingly therefore nightingales for the Romantic poets often come to stand for Milton.[26] But in Blake's case this is more than a mere tribute to Milton; rather what Blake gives us is a precise map of his own poetic enterprise in relation to that of Milton, much as he does in the Zenith passage from Book I discussed earlier. According to this map the Lark is a self-image for Blake, as he is for Shelley, for Wordsworth, and so many Romantic poets. The Lark, listening silent to the Nightingale's Song of Spring and then taking his higher flight and singing his own intenser song, is Blake drawing his inspiration from Milton's prophetic poetry and yet claiming to go beyond him, 'casting aside from Poetry all that is not Inspiration'.

It is easy to see which side of Milton's poetry the Nightingale comes to symbolize. Milton's name for her was Urania, the spirit of sacred song, who visited his slumbers nightly. Blake recognizes in Milton's poetry the quality of a premeditated and continuing illumination: 'thro the day, | And thro the night [he] warbles luxuriant.' His 'loud harmony' is that of Los, of the Apollonian, epic tradition, whilst the clear, keen joyance of the Lark suggests a more Dionysiac rapture. He feels the surge of transcendence as, not content with the earth-bound character of the Nightingale, with 'sitting upon his earthy bed', he mounts into the 'lovely blue & shining heavenly Shell'.

It would thus seem that we have here not a monologue but an exchange between two voices, even a kind of confrontation. Should we not therefore revise the position we had arrived at regarding the essentially monologic character of Ololon and the symbols associated with her, namely, the Lark and Wild Thyme? Would it not rather be a case of dialogue—the Lark answering the Nightingale and enacting in this the hermeneutic dialogue between Blake and Milton? The answer is that though two voices are heard there is no genuine dialogue between them; what we have instead is a kind of antiphonal utterance. The passage we are discussing is in this respect parallel to the account in Book I of the descent of Milton and his incorporation into the body of the later poet. This was literally an *incarnation*. Similarly,

---

[26] This is obviously so in Coleridge's 1798 poem 'The Nightingale' in which Milton is explicitly invoked and challenged. Keats's 'Ode to a Nightingale' invokes Milton likewise in the phrase 'Darkling I listen', but less explicitly.

Blake's marvellous Morning-Song of the Birds—surely one of the great lyrical passages in the English language—is literally a *concert*. But neither incarnation nor concert is dialogue; rather they represent the process of blending, of osmosis. The two parties to the hermeneutic encounter do not (as in Milton's poetics) retain their independence. Here in Blake's poem the Lark listens to the Nightingale and responds with a wordless 'trill, trill, trill, trill'.

A key term in the cited passage is 're-echoing'. The Lark's song is spoken of as 'reecchoing against the lovely blue & shining heavenly Shell'. Echo we remember was the lover of Narcissus, but Narcissus, incapable of a genuinely interpersonal relationship, i.e. of dialogue, reduces his partner to a mere echo. Another key term is 'effluence': 'every feather | On throat & breast & wings vibrates with the effluence Divine'. 'Effluence' like 'lineaments' is a Miltonic word. It comes from the Hymn to Light which opens Book III of *Paradise Lost* (the same pericope from which Blake had remembered the Nightingale passage).

> Hail, holy Light, offspring of Heav'n first-born,
> Or of th' Eternal Coeternal beam
> May I express thee unblam'd? since God is Light,
> And never but in unapproached Light
> Dwelt from Eternity, dwelt then in thee,
> Bright effluence of bright essence increate.
>
> (III. 1–6)

It is easy to see why Blake seizes upon the word 'effluence' in this passage; it captures the notion of flowing or emanation. Divinity overflows into the bird; the separation of the Creator and his Creation is lost; inspiration flows from the Nightingale to the Lark; voices blend and flow together, the Nightingale from *Il Penseroso* blending with the Lark from *L'Allegro* in this landscape of Beulah 'where Contrarieties are equally True'. As Nietzsche was to point out, the Dionysiac vision naturally seeks a kind of mystical oneness where differences disappear, including the difference between the Self and that which is outside the Self. We can call this zone 'the maternal womb of being' or we can call it self-annihilation.[27] The Lark no less than the figure of Ololon points us in that direction.

---

[27] See Nietzsche, *The Birth of Tragedy*, sects. i, xvi, pp. 23, 97, 101.

Above all, the Lark passage exemplifies the removal of barriers between the later poet and his source, the poem of the precursor poet being so totally absorbed that its separate identity is abolished. From this point of view 'effluence' becomes a kind of pun on influence—but influence carried to the point where there is a total effacing of differences. And as though to illustrate this, Blake's poem enacts such 'effluence' by its appropriation of this very term from Milton's poem! In taking it over, Blake has effaced the reservations and distinctions which marked its original use in Milton's poem.

If we look again at the Miltonic context of 'bright effluence' we shall see that in these lines of his 'Ode to Light' which open *Paradise Lost*, Book III, Milton has carefully balanced two conceptions. According to one, Light is a created entity 'offspring of Heav'n first-born'. According to the other, Light is uncreated, i.e. pre-existent and eternal, like a Platonic Idea—a possibility supported by the phrase 'God is light' from 1 John 1: 5. The first leans on a Hebraic theology of Creation going back to Genesis 1: 3 and presupposes a Creator independent of the world he creates and capable also of endowing that creation with a measure of independence from himself. The other presupposes a radical theology of Incarnation and Emanation—light as an emanation or effluence coeternal with divinity itself. Here, as Milton well knew, is poised the weight of two opposite world-views; the two options are suspended before us with an awareness of their crucial difference from one another and the consequent risk involved in choosing between them. Hence the self-admonitory phrase, 'May I express thee unblam'd?' Hence also the calculated ambiguity regarding the antecedent of 'increate' in line 6 (light or the creator of light?).[28] Blake throws such caution to the winds, giving exclusive emphasis to that way of thinking, strongly tinged with hellenism, according to which things flow

[28] The passage has been much debated by the critics. Merritt Y. Hughes suggested ('Milton and the Symbol of Light', *Studies in English Literature*, 4 (1964), 21–2), that Milton accepts here the Augustinian distinction between created and uncreated light: the former is what we see, whilst the latter, which is invisible to mortal sight, is part of the godhead. This would accommodate both the first epistle of John and Genesis 1 in a kind of two-tier system. It seems to me that Milton's language is more essentially *ambiguous* than that, the passage reflecting an unresolved conflict in Milton's mind and a tension between the sources which he had inherited.

into and out of one another from eternity. This is the force of the term effluence in Blake's poem.

The tension and ambiguity which marked Milton's text have thus disappeared. The feathers of the bird vibrate with 'the effluence divine'. A motion and a spirit rolls through all things, nullifying any distinction between Creator and Creation, enabling us to see a world in a grain of sand and heaven in a wild flower (or a wild bird). Ironically, Milton's 'effluence' will serve to remove all the barriers and boundaries which characterize Milton's universe. The effect of such effluence/influence is that, as with lineaments, a term derived from Milton can in the end be used as a weapon against Milton himself.

The image of the Lark is charged with a like irony. Blake's Lark too is out of Milton, but radically altered. In his Morning Song of the Birds Blake was remembering not only the Lark from *L'Allegro* but also that from Book II of *Paradise Regained*. Again the context merits close examination. After withstanding the first temptation of Satan, Jesus spends a restless and hungry night in the wilderness dreaming of Elijah being fed by the birds:

> Thus wore out night, and now the Herald Lark
> Left his ground-nest, high tow'ring to descry
> The morn's approach, and greet her with his Song.
> As lightly from his grassy Couch up rose
> Our Saviour, and found all was but a dream . . .
>
> (ll. 279–83)

This is a good example of the control exercised by the epic poet over the separate parts of his images. The 'Herald Lark' is clearly linked with the Saviour, but as simile; this mode does not legitimate confluence. The conjunction 'as', prominently positioned at the beginning of the fourth line of the passage cited, brings the two figures together but it also keeps them apart. What we have is a kind of compressed epic simile which, extended, would read: '*as* lightly as the Lark rose from his grassy Couch, *so* uprose our Saviour'. The compression has the important effect of making the 'grassy Couch' apply jointly and simultaneously to both bird and Saviour. (In Blake it becomes the Lark's 'earthy bed'.) But the details which here unite the two figures are carefully differentiated from those which keep them separate. The Herald Lark does not dream of Elijah and Daniel, nor is he tested.

The mechanism of the simile demarcates the human region of testing from the natural region of spontaneity. By the same token, when the Lark is said to 'leave his ground-nest, high tow'ring to descry | The morn's approach, and greet her with his Song', this description applies to the bird but not to the Saviour. The figures do not combine and do not blend. Quite the contrary. The man, of whom it is said, 'Fasting he went to sleep, and fasting wak'd', is in no mood to greet the morning with a song. The bird's joy and the elevation of its flight are a measure of the ironic distance between the two. They join as we have said only in the following line: 'As lightly from his grassy Couch up rose | Our Saviour'. Even there, whilst they both share the 'grassy Couch', the ambiguity of 'up rose' preserves the distance between the two figures. Whilst the bird will fly up into the empyrean, Jesus will merely in human fashion 'rise up' from his couch and his troubled slumber. Indeed, later in the poem (Book IV, lines 541–95), the last temptation, which Milton's hero naturally overcomes, involves being carried aloft to the 'highest Pinnacle' of the Temple and being invited to attempt a Daedalus-like feat of space travel. But Jesus firmly declines to go along with this and instead is rescued by angels who safely set him down on a green bank (IV. 586–7). In ironic contrast to the bird (and to all the Greek high-fliers from Bellerophon to Hercules), Milton's hero is emphatically earth-bound, the 'greater Man' who makes good the lapse of the first Adam, rather than 'the greater Sun' of the Nativity Hymn.

Blake does not merely iron out these distinctions; he actually reverses Milton's dialectic of proximity and distance. The Lark sits on 'his earthy bed' just long enough to hear the Nightingale begin his Song, and then, taking the poet and the reader with him, he springs from the 'waving Corn-field . . . Mounting upon the wings of light into the Great Expanse'. As with all typical Romantic treatments of the skylark, the poet identifies himself with the vertical flight of the bird and the rapture of its song, its 'harmony divine'. It becomes an object of aspiration and wonder as it separates itself from the earth and the things of the earth, defining the point where men become like gods through the action of the high imagination.

And here we arrive at the ultimate irony of Blake's misreading of Milton. He had prefaced his great poem with a dissuasive

against 'the general malady & infection from the silly Greek &
Latin slaves of the Sword', an infection which had, he claimed,
marred the work both of Shakespeare and Milton. True inspiration should be sought in the Bible alone rather than in 'the Stolen
and Perverted Writings of Homer & Ovid: of Plato & Cicero'.[29]
Here, however, in the example we are considering, Milton keeps
close to the model of Luke's Gospel, with its 'Hebraic' emphasis
on salvation in worldly space and time. His hero thus literally
refuses to take wing and soar aloft and shares only his 'grassy
Couch' with the Lark; whereas Blake, 'mounting upon the wings
of light', points towards a more spiritual doctrine of divine transcendence, one mediated perhaps by Plotinus, but having its
origin in Plato! For it is surely in Plato's 'Phaedrus' that the true
original of all Romantic skylarks is to be found:

The soul . . . when perfect and fully winged . . . soars upward, and
is the ruler of the universe. . . . The wing is intended to soar aloft and
carry that which gravitates downwards into the upper region, which
is the dwelling of the gods; and this is that element of the body which
is most akin to the divine.[30]

Central to Plato's teaching here is the emphasis on the upward
and downward directions. Time is intersected by the perpendicular line of eternity. Likewise, instead of the horizontality of
earthly space we have a vertical line or point, what T. S. Eliot
was to term 'the still point of the turning world'. For Blake, the
Wild Thyme is the point from which 'Eternity expands'—it is
the annihilation of space. For in the world of pure spirit there
is neither space nor time; and language too reaches its ultimate
sublimation in the wordless 'trill, trill, trill, trill' of the Lark. Here
we arrive at the denial of textuality. A mere syllable separates
inspiration from expiration. And when the word has expired,
what else, one wonders, is there left for the poet to do?

A like significance attaches to the 'spots of time' which Wordsworth speaks of in a famous passage in *The Prelude*, Book XII.

---

[29] Characteristically, this attack on the Greek and Roman classics (with the side-
swipe at Milton) is itself inspired by Milton's own *Paradise Regained*, IV. 334 f.!
See above, p. 223.
[30] *The Works of Plato, Translated . . . by B. Jowett* (4 vols. in 1) (New York:
The Dial Press, n.d.), iii. 404. And cf. Plotinus, *Enneads*, I. 3. 3, and IV. 8. 1. I am
grateful to Edna Sharoni, a colleague at Bar-Ilan University, for pointing out the
line of imagery connecting Plato, Plotinus, and the Romantic poets.

They provide a glimpse ('as far as words can give') of a reality beyond growth and change. Like Blake's Lark, their sign is perpendicularity; they are special moments which intersect the linear course of our existence, enabling us 'to mount, | When high, more high' (XII. 217–18). Wordsworth has several larks also. The one he introduces at the end of *The Prelude* functions in a manner very like that of Blake's Lark in the passage I have been considering, where the bird springs from the waving Corn-field to lead the Choir of Day. Wordsworth had given us an epic account of his life and times extending over fourteen books; the impress of Milton's great epic can be felt on every page of that account, the story of the 'Growth of a Poet's Mind' taking on a religious solemnity almost equal to that of Milton's 'great Argument'. But now as his labours come to an end, Wordsworth sums up the whole of his poetic journey, viewing it from the position of transcendence. He has retired into the countryside and can no longer quite affirm the substantial reality of his earlier pilgrimage through time and space ('I said unto the life which I had lived, | Where art thou?'). It is then that he defines his poetic voice in terms of the song of the lark:

> Anon I rose
> As if on wings, and saw beneath me stretched
> Vast prospect of the world which I had been
> And was, and hence this Song, which like a lark
> I have protracted, in the unwearied heavens
> Singing . . .

> (XIV. 379–84)

As he gazes back over the 'vast prospect of the world which I had been | And was', we have the same sense of a horizontal journey through time intersected by the vertical line of the bird's flight. For Wordsworth too this symbolic geometry graphically illustrates the supplanting of the epic design by the lyric impulse. But it does more than that; it lights up the fundamental tension in the poetry of the West between the Greek and Hebrew modes of inspiration. Both Blake and Wordsworth bear witness to this tension. Blake firmly insists on the priority of the Hebrew mode but in this instance his practice betrays him. With other poets it is sometimes the other way round. What stands out in all cases is the tension itself. Blake takes wing like the soul of Plato's philosopher 'into Eternity of which this vegetable Earth is but a shadow' (*Milton*, Pl. 29: 22). But the lapse cannot be long maintained. After the Lark is heard, Milton's Nightingale resumes his song '& thro the day, | And thro the night warbles luxuriant'. The onward journey will be resumed and with it the pilgrimage through the wilderness of this world and the search for salvation and renewal. 'Watch over this World', Ololon is told in Book I, 'and with your brooding wings, | Renew it to Eternal Life' (Pl. 21: 55–6). Ololon here realigns herself with the Holy Spirit of Genesis 1: 2 as interpreted by *Paradise Lost*, I. 20–2.

5

We return to the winged sandals of Hermes. Here as befits a Greek god, is the image of flight once again; Hermes descends vertically from heaven to earth in order to link the lives of men with the gods. But in addition to the upward and downward movement, there is also the sense of an onward hermeneutic journey, a task and a communication. That too is what the name Hermes implies. The poet-speaker in Blake's *Milton* performs the gesture implied by the Hermes role in the marvellous lines in which he binds on

> a bright sandal formd immortal of precious stones & gold:
> I stooped down & bound it on to walk forward thro' Eternity

Is this walking forward anything more than a gesture? Is there a message that Los/Blake/Milton will carry from the past into the future, a responsibility that the poet has to his source on the one hand and to his audience on the other, with the sense of historical perspective that goes with it?[31] As the three persons—Los, Milton, and Blake—join, eternity is already with us and there would seem to be no need to walk forward at all, for eternity is by definition the point where journeys end, where the perpendicular line meets the horizontal plane and seemingly abolishes it.

---

[31] On the necessary relation between hermeneutics and history consciousness see above Chapter 8, n. 18, and cf. also R. F. Gleckner, *Blake and Spenser* (Baltimore: Johns Hopkins University Press, 1985), 149, and Gerald L. Bruns, 'Midrash and Allegory', in Robert Alter and Frank Kermode (eds.), *The Literary Guide to the Bible* (Cambridge, Mass.: Harvard University Press, 1987), 644.

But do Los, Milton, and Blake really join? Can such fusion be maintained? The answer is implicit in much of what I have been saying. Incarnational hermeneutics has its own self-contradictions. Los does not in the end fuse with Blake, nor Blake with Milton; the second Book of the poem shows how very problematical these unions become as annihilation threatens the 'bright Paved-work' of Milton's poetic vision and the 'Daughters of Beulah' take the place of the 'Sons of Los'. Whilst Blake appears to make the past entirely malleable, altering it so as to cure Milton of his Puritanism and make him a fit contemporary of Shelley and Tom Paine, the truth is that Time will not be mocked. History has its irreversibilities.

In short, the diagram that we attempted to draw is too simple or, rather, it contains its own antithesis. There can surely be no vertical line without a horizontal line to define it, no eternity without time, and, we may add, no Lark without a Nightingale. When these latter join there is a concert. But we do well to listen attentively to the discords also.

CHAPTER 10

The Poetics of Incarnation

Ololon, I have suggested, comes to signify unsignifiability, the annihilation of the *logos*. Thus she fittingly presides over the self-annihilation of Milton at the triumphant close of Blake's poem. At the same time, and by a typical Blakeian paradox, she is the focus of multiple significations. The 'sweet river of milk & liquid pearl' connects her not only with the *prima materia* or the Philosophers' Stone of the alchemists, but also with the 'pearl of great price' to which the Kingdom of Heaven is compared in Matthew 13: 46, an image often associated with the Bride of the Lamb from Revelation 21. The Bride is in that same chapter identified with 'the holy Jerusalem descending out of heaven' whose 'light was like unto a stone most precious'. Ololon's final role in fact is that of the Bride of the Lamb. After she seemingly self-destructs in Plate 42, she is seen resurrected as part of the unity of 'Jesus the Saviour':

> round his limbs
> The Clouds of Ololon folded as a Garment dipped in blood
> Written within & without in woven letters: & the Writing
> Is the Divine Revelation in the Litteral expression . . .

In this last metamorphosis there is an astonishing reversal of much that we have been saying so far. After we have passed the lake of Udan-Adan, i.e. the region of formlessness, and after we have undergone the crisis of annihilation, it seems that the forms and formalities of *écriture* become possible once again. Ololon is here transformed into a text 'written within and without'—a text to be interpreted. Our attention is drawn not only to Revelation 21 but also to Revelation 1: 13 (with its vision of 'the Son of Man clothed with a garment down to the foot') and most particularly to the scene in Exodus where Moses descends from the mountain bearing in his hands the two tablets of stone 'written on both their sides, on the one side and on the other were they written' (Exodus 32: 15). Here indeed in the last lines of Blake's poem we have not only a text interpreted, but a celebration of textuality itself. After all, the reference is to that most fundamental of texts, the *script-ure* inscribed on the tablets of stone, the actual *Ur-text* from which the practice of hermeneutics takes its rise. Ololon is transformed into this text, now woven into a garment! As Vincent De Luca aptly points out, it is 'less a vision of the Word made Flesh than one of the Flesh made Word'.[1] But such a formal inscribing of words, the weaving of such a garment, will only be possible with the mystic union of the Lamb and his Bride. It is 'a manifestation that is simultaneously incarnational and textual'.[2] And as such it involves a dissolution of separate identities, a consummation which is also a consuming of the world and its boundaries as we have known them.

The text from Exodus 32 interestingly provides the hint for such an annihilation. For these tablets referred to as having been 'written on both their sides' were those which Moses would shatter at the foot of the mountain four verses further down. (The tablets which replaced them in chapter 34 do not have this special feature.) Their revelational force would thus be short-lived. The implication is that the scene of writing, the Incarnation which accompanies the union of Ololon and Jesus in Blake's poem ('the Writing | Is the Divine Revelation in the Litteral expression'), will be equally short-lived. There will be a moment of clarity but the clouds of Ololon will supervene and we will find ourselves once again in the region of the Indefinite.

The mark of what I am calling incarnational hermeneutics would then be its suddenness, as well as the transitory nature of its incandescence. By contrast, covenantal hermeneutics which I suggested was the mode represented in Milton's poetry by Urania and the Nazirite Samson is predicated on the notion of a prior and continuing relationship between the parties to a dialogue: Urania was present from the first and she will be present to the last; and in the time between she visits the poet's slumbers nightly. She belongs we may say with the unbroken tablets.

[1] Vincent A. De Luca, *Words of Eternity: Blake and the Poetics of the Sublime* (Princeton: Princeton University Press, 1991), 217.
[2] Ibid. 216.

2

This helps to explain why Blake did not produce a poem as systematically and continuously related to the Bible as *Samson Agonistes* or *Paradise Lost*. He claims to enjoy a greater degree of biblical inspiration than Milton and indeed there are biblical echoes everywhere in his poems, but the poetic interpretation of particular passages tends to be spasmodic—as in the instance just quoted where he glances for a moment at the divine writing on the tablets—or elusive, as in the reinvention of the Balaam pericope in 'Mock on Mock on Voltaire Rousseau' discussed in an earlier chapter. There we have an indirect use of the biblical narrative; persons and historical background are indistinct, in fact all but effaced, but what remains is the *mise-en-scène*, picked out by the vivid details of the prophet's mocking eye (seeing or blinded) and the bright tents of Israel spread out before him on the Red Sea shore.

Indeed if we look for examples of biblical exegesis in Blake's poems, we shall find most often pictures of 'minute particulars' rather than plots. In *Milton* we have a number of such sharply etched, but essentially discontinuous episodes—the confrontation of Milton and Urizen in Plate 19 'on the shores of Arnon' re-enacting (as all the commentators have pointed out) the struggle of Jacob and the Angel at Peniel (Genesis 32); or the sons and daughters of Luvah at the winepresses as they tread the Last Vintage of the nations (Plates 25, 27) recalling both Revelation 14 and Isaiah 63; or Ololon fleetingly manifested at the end of the poem as a 'moony Ark' or 'a Dove upon the stormy Sea', details which serve to associate the story of the Flood with this landscape of apocalypse. The shape of the Flood narrative has all but disappeared; instead Blake gives us a tableau that implies disaster and salvation simultaneously—which is what the ending of the poem is about.

In brief, Blake's 'interpretations' of the Bible tend to be visions in the sense of arrested scenes. It is thus not surprising that his most memorable reinventions of Bible scenes and poems are to be found in his actual paintings rather than in literary narrative. As already noted, Blake, unlike Milton, did not write any longer poem based on a biblical text. *The Everlasting Gospel*, in spite of its title, is not shaped by the Gospel form or the Gospel narrative; it is essentially a loose parody. By contrast, the numerous Gospel scenes which Blake painted or engraved at different times add up to something like a systematic exegesis of those texts. Indeed, taken together, his drawings, engravings, and water-colours contain a reading of the Bible—its narratives, poems, and prophecies—more extensive and detailed than that to be found in any other English poet or painter.[3] It is of course his own inversive reading that is here represented but the figures and their doings have explicit reference to the Bible. Among books of the Old Testament, Blake gave special and continued attention to the Genesis narratives, whilst his scenes from Psalms represent something like a sustained christological reading of that book.[4] But above all his illustrations to Job, done first in water-colour in 1805–6 and then engraved on Plates with surrounding texts towards the end of his life, are in every sense a major work and will enable us to summarize the nature of his engagement with the Bible and indeed his hermeneutic praxis as a whole.

3

The first remark that needs to be made concerns the genre to which this set of engravings belongs. Whilst the 21 engravings are accompanied by quotations (and sometimes misquotations) from the Bible, these verses are secondary to the pictures. The weight of meaning belongs to the pictures. They are in this different from the engraved plates of his lyrics and prophecies earlier on where the texts are on the whole the main vehicle of signification. The viewer of the Job series is invited to read the biblical texts provided, as a comment on the pictures, rather than to read the pictures as a comment on the texts. If any analogy to this uniquely Blakeian genre is possible, one could suggest the relationship between Coleridge's 'The Rime of the Ancient Mariner' and the accompanying gloss. The gloss is important but secondary, giving us, on the whole, doctrine, whilst the ballad itself gives us imaginative vision. Something like this balance is presupposed in Blake's illustrations to Job and this has implications for his whole enterprise. He is here writing or, rather, painting his own bible; the words of the Bible itself are secondary.

[3] For the scope and variety of this achievement, see *William Blake's Illustrations to the Bible*, ed. Geoffrey Keynes (London: Trianon Press, 1957).

[4] Cf. Mary Lynn Johnson, 'David's Recognition of the Human Face of God in Blake's Designs for the Book of Psalms', in David V. Erdman (ed.), *Blake and His Bibles* (West Cornwall, Conn.: Locust Hill Press, 1990), 117–56.

FIG. 1. Job and his Family

Coming to the first of these tableaux (Fig. 1), we have a picture of Job's family before the onset of his troubles, in a scene of pastoral innocence.[5] Literally so, for Job's sons are shepherds

[5] From *Illustrations of the Book of Job: Invented & Engraved by William Blake* (1825). The corresponding water-colour illustrations (the Butts set) are numbered 550 1–21 in Martin Butlin's magisterial catalogue, *The Paintings and Drawings of William Blake*, 2 vols. (New Haven: Yale University Press, 1981). The paintings themselves are reproduced in vol. ii, plates 697–717. (Hereafter, Butlin is followed by plate number, in parentheses, in the text.)

FIG. 2. By the Waters of Babylon

and their sheep, lying down in green pastures, fill the foreground and part of the middle-ground of the picture. It would do almost as an illustration to Psalm 23. But our attention is immediately arrested by an odd detail: whilst the figures are grouped at the foot of an oak tree in attitudes of tranquil piety, the musical instruments, intended evidently to accompany their pious devotions, are hanging on the tree above their heads, unused. This makes us think not of Psalm 23 but of Psalm 137, where the exiles 'by the waters of Babylon', refusing to sing the Lord's song in a strange land, are said to have hung their harps on the willow trees. In fact, at about the same time that Blake was painting the Butts set of Job water-colours (Butlin 697–717), he also produced a painting (Butlin 541) to illustrate Psalm 137 (Fig. 2).

Here a family of exiles, their faces not unlike those of Job and his wife and children, are seen seated on the ground in chains, with their musical instruments suspended above them on the branches of a willow tree. The Job picture embodies a clear reference to this other scene.

What does this cross-referencing imply? Blake's *By the Waters of Babylon* clearly suggests the opposite of pastoral ease and tranquillity; it is a scene rather of tragic alienation. By quoting this painting and this psalm in the Job picture Blake is making a statement which calls in question the image of pastoral fulfilment which the picture otherwise conveys and which is emphasized by the first verse of Job quoted in the lower margin of the engraving (Fig. 1): 'There was a Man in the Land of Uz whose Name was Job; & that Man was perfect & upright & one that feared God & eschewed Evil.' If this doctrinal gloss is saying that all was well with Job before his trials began, then the picture is saying that all was not well—Job and his family were, so to speak, in exile, alienated from their true good, as symbolized by the unused instruments of their art. These will be restored to use only in the last engraving of the series where Job and his family, now standing upright under the same tree, are seen joyfully performing on those same instruments (Fig. 3).[6]

The cross-referencing in fact tells us more than this—not only that Job, even before his trials began, was alienated from his true good, but what has brought about this alienation. For in *By the Waters of Babylon*, illustrating Psalm 137, the exiles are not alone. In the left forefront of the painting and dominating the seated figures, are the persecutors, chief among them the King of Babylon himself, crowned, clothed in scarlet, his gaze directed scornfully at the captives. The painting thus speaks not only of alienation, but of subjection. It is because they are subject to the power of a tyrant that the exiles cannot freely exercise their art. Here, unspoken in the Job illustration but clearly inscribed in the Babylon painting, is the explanation for the silenced instruments

---

[6] A parallel to this is provided by the painting of 1805 entitled *The Hymn of Christ and the Apostles* (Butlin 546) where the Apostles and the two Maries are pictured with the musical instruments in their hands under a willow tree. This picture balances the Babylon painting (Butlin 541) in the same way as the last of the Job series balances the first. See also Johnson, 'David's Recognition of the Human Face of God', 144–6.

FIG. 3. Job and his Family Restored to Prosperity

of Job and his family. They are also subject to tyranny. If Job is 'one that feared God & eschewed Evil' then it is clear that the fear which his God arouses is not morally different from that aroused by the Babylonian tyrant in the picture illustrating Psalm 137.

Here in this detail is in fact the key to Blake's fundamental rewriting of the Job story. The God whom Job obeys is no other than Urizen, the founder of churches and the author of laws and prohibitions—hence the free hand which he gives to Satan to roam the world and harass men and women.[7] The story that will unfold in these pictures will thus not be that of a man perfect and upright whose rectitude is finally vindicated, but of one who had lent himself to an evil system and must now learn to free himself from the Synagogue of Satan and embrace the gospel of the Divine Humanity. And at the heart of that gospel will be, not duty and obedience, but 'the liberty both of body and mind to exercise the Divine Arts of Imagination'. Thus the sign of redemption will be the instruments taken down from the trees in the last picture of the series for the purpose of exercising those divine arts. Here is all the vision we know on earth and all we need to know.

But now comes the major paradox. The series of Job illustrations is justly praised for its power and beauty. Most admirers of Blake's paintings, if asked to name his greatest artistic achievements, would put some of the Job plates very near the head of the list: Plate 11 (Fig. 4) for instance ('With Dreams upon my bed thou scarest me & affrightest me with Visions') or Plate 16 with its hint of the Vision of the Last Judgement ('Thou hast fulfilled the Judgment of the Wicked'). Above all they would point to the fearful symmetry of the divine Creation of the stars in Plate 14 (Fig. 5) and of the great sea-monsters, Leviathan and Behemoth, in Plate 15 (Fig. 6), as suggested to the artist by God's speech out of the whirlwind (Job 38–41). Moreover, it is these images of power and splendour which surely drew Blake to Job in the first place as the subject of his great series of paintings. Nevertheless, if we press the implications of the final plate we must conclude that in principle such representations belong to the unredeemed world, one in which the instruments of art are still hanging on the trees. The truly liberated imagination which in the final plate discovers the 'human form divine'[8] has no place for the tyrant-god of Plates 11 and 16 or

[7] Cf. Jean H. Hagstrum, *William Blake: Poet and Painter* (Chicago: Chicago University Press, 1964), 127–9.

[8] Cf. Anne K. Mellor, *Blake's Human Form Divine* (Berkeley: University of California Press, 1974), 254.

FIG. 4. Job's Evil Dreams

the Urizenic creator of the sea-monsters in Plate 15. In fact to follow this contradiction to its logical extreme, we would have to say that the truly liberated imagination has no room for the Book of Job as a whole, since the instruments of art, signifying the life of the Imagination, are only taken down from the trees in the last Plate, i.e. when the series is already complete.

FIG. 5. When the Morning Stars Sang Together

The true achievements of poetry, music, and painting are thus essentially beyond the boundary of the work offered, whilst the wonders that are actually offered to our view are at the same time implicitly condemned as lacking in final artistic significance!

It may be worth noting that Psalm 137 which was clearly in Blake's mind during the composition of these paintings,

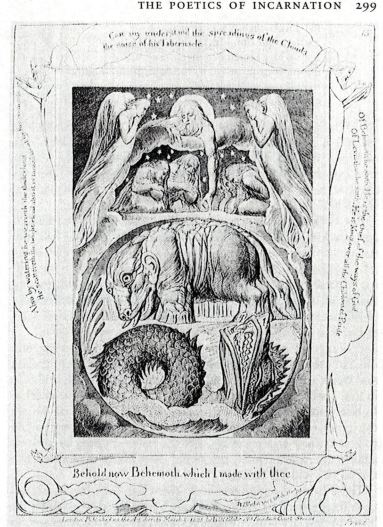

FIG. 6. Behemoth and Leviathan

incorporates a contradiction similar to the one just noted in relation to Blake's Job series. On the one hand, the poem speaks
of the impossibility of singing the 'songs of Zion'. 'How shall
we sing the Lord's song in a foreign land?', it asks. And the
exiles proceed to enforce this by an oath, abjuring the pleasure
of song in favour of the graver duty of memory:

> If I forget thee, O Jerusalem,
> let my right hand forget her cunning!
> If I do not remember thee,
> let my tongue cleave to the roof of my mouth;
> if I do not set Jerusalem
> above my highest joy!

And yet, on the other hand, these very verses of the psalm have become a love-lyric, indeed a true song of Zion regularly sung at festive recitals. More than that, like Psalms 84 or 122 they have become a paradigm for subsequent songs of Zion! The same declaration is a denial of art and an example of art at its most eloquent![9]

But though it deconstructs itself in this way, the psalm is nevertheless sharply focused and this is owing to the fact that we are hearing two or more voices engaging one another along a historical axis. We hear the voice of the exiles in Babylon calling a curse down on their captors and forswearing all joy and singing until they are restored to Zion. But we also hear the voice of the poet of the Return, looking back on the remembered scene in Babylon ('By the waters of Babylon, | there we sat down . . .') and recapturing the love-longing of the exiles. It is he who mediates the earlier scene for us. If the captives remember Zion and weep, the later poet remembers their remembering and finds in that a stimulus for a song celebrating the ageless love of Zion. In like fashion, the prophet Ezekiel (33: 30–3), residing among the exiles in Babylon, rebukes his audience for coming to him to gratify their literary tastes. But the more strongly he protests against the role of poet, the richer does his language become, the more vivid his imagery.[10]

These biblical paradigms and others like them had evidently been internalized by Blake and may have helped to give him the basis for an art which flourishes even as it is condemned. In spite of ideological restraints poetry will break through. But there is in Blake's case no such clearly evoked social and historical context as in the Ezekiel passage, nor is there an external point of reference as in Psalm 137 where the geographical polarity of

---

[9] Cf. Gabriel Josipovici, *The Book of God: A Response to the Bible* (New Haven: Yale University Press, 1988), 165–6.

[10] For further comment see Harold Fisch, *Poetry with a Purpose: Biblical Poetics and Interpretation* (Bloomington, Ind.: Indiana University Press, 1988), 43–7.

Babylon and Jerusalem provides the poem with an ultimate coherence. We are left instead with a radical discontinuity, as in the two books of *Milton*, between a poetics of the Sublime and a poetics of Annihilation ultimately directed against the Sublime. This contradiction, which Blake does not resolve, lies at the base of the Job series also.

4

Plate 11, 'Job's Evil Dreams' (Fig. 4), constitutes a climax of sublimity. Burke had chosen Job as his primary text to illustrate what he regarded as the essential qualities of the Sublime, namely, terror, power, and darkness.[11] Blake's engraving would serve as a graphic accompaniment to Burke's essay. Here Job, laid out on his bed in the darkness of the night is 'affrighted with visions'. The quoted text reads: 'With Dreams upon my bed thou scarest me & affrightest me with Visions' (Job 7: 14). Hellish demons from below threaten to seize him, whilst stretched out horizontally above him is a demon-god, his right hand pointing to the tablets of the Law and his left leg displaying a cloven-hoof. Blake is here quoting from his earlier, even more famous picture, *Elohim Creating Adam* of 1795 (Butlin 388) (Fig. 7). There Elohim, dominating with his awful power the whole centre space of the picture, stretches his hand over an affrighted Adam whom he is moulding out of the clay, the two figures being likewise disposed in a horizontal axis one above the other. And yet there is a basic difference: although the serpent is already entwined round the lower part of Adam's body, suggesting that he will be born subject to the law of sin, the earlier picture is not as ideologically determined as the Job illustration.[12] In the earlier picture we surrender to the Sublime in a simpler and more direct fashion; we are caught up in the majesty of the vision of Urizen as Creator. Adam is fearfully and wonderfully made but

[11] Edmund Burke, *A Philosophical Inquiry into the Origin of Our Ideas of the Sublime and Beautiful* (1756), Part II, sects. iv and v; see *Burke's Writings and Speeches*, i (London: Oxford University Press, 1906), 114–18.

[12] There is a similar contrast between the figure of Satan in the 1795 painting of *Satan Exulting over Eve* (Butlin 389) and his depiction in the Job series (Plates 3 and 6). In the former he is a beautiful and graceful athlete; in the Job pictures he is a malevolent demon.

FIG. 7. Elohim Creating Adam

there is no hint of rebellion against his Maker. In the later picture, there is sublimity to be sure, but the full adversarial force of the vision is developed. Urizen is here an evil incubus and Job's only hope is to free himself from his domination.

Blake's emphatic linking of 'Job's Evil Dreams' with *Elohim Creating Adam* shows us that Blake had in one respect at least correctly read the text of Job. For Job is not only a theodicy; it is also a great creation poem. One modern scholar, N. H. Tur-Sinai, has suggested that many sections of the poem 'stem from an elaborate poetic account of the creation and the first steps of Man'—an early *Liber Adami* that is now lost to us.[13] Job creates an image of a world fresh from the hand of its Creator, as yet unsubdued by Man who stands in awe before it. From this point of view the great speech of God from the storm in

[13] N. H. Tur-Sinai, *The Book of Job: A New Commentary* (Jerusalem: Kiryath Sepher, 1957), 409, 558–9. Milton had the same intuition when, in the first two books of *Paradise Lost*, he drew heavily on the book of Job in seeking to define the dark anti-creation which is the subject of that part of his poem.

THE POETICS OF INCARNATION 303

chapters 38–41 represents a poetic alternative to Genesis 1 and 2, more elaborate and more lyrical; above all it introduces the dimensions (less conspicuous in Genesis) of power and mystery. Here is also the true ground of the Sublime in Job, as Blake and others before him had recognized. Blake does full justice to this aspect of the poem not only in Plate 11 but also in Plates 14 and 15 (Figs. 5 and 6) based on the Creation imagery in God's speech from the storm. Plate 14, 'When the Morning Stars Sang Together' recalls the magnificent opening of that speech, whilst in the margin, the six days of Creation from Genesis 1 are introduced as a pictorial subtext. Plate 15 pictures the great sea-monsters Behemoth and Leviathan. In the right margin, Blake quotes Job 40: 19: 'He is the chief of the ways of God' where 'chief' translates *reshit* (literally 'beginning') which is also the first word of Genesis. Thus Behemoth becomes for Blake, as he had been also for the author of Job, a key figure in a Creation myth parallel to, but different from, that intimated in the first chapters of Genesis. Here the dynamics of the painting imply not a timeless Platonic vision, but the purposeful forward movement of a created universe. It is this biblical vision rather than the perpendicular line of the Lark's flight (as in *Milton*) which here stirs the imagination.

But the Creator of the stars and of the wonders of the deep, whether in the version of Genesis or that of Job, is for Blake a profoundly ambiguous figure. These images of the Sublime contain their own antithesis. Behemoth and Leviathan of whom the Creator-God of Plate 15 seems so proud, represent, as Foster Damon has noted, 'the unredeemed portion of the psyche . . . these are terrible forces within man, against which he seems helpless'.[14] Northrop Frye stresses the political aspect: Behemoth and Leviathan are for Blake in this picture 'the power in man that makes for tyranny'.[15] They remind us of Nebuchadnezzar, King of Babylon. And as I observed earlier such tyranny stands for all that is opposed to the free life of the Imagination. Blake notes in the margin that Leviathan is 'King over all the Children of Pride' (Job 40: 34). That pride belongs to Elohim, Creator of

---

[14] *Blake's Job: William Blake's* Illustrations of the Book of Job, Introduction and Commentary by S. Foster Damon (New York: Dutton, 1969), 40.
[15] Northrop Frye, 'Blake's Reading of the Book of Job', in Alvin H. Rosenfeld (ed.), *William Blake: Essays for S. Foster Damon* (Providence, RI: Brown University Press, 1969), 233.

the World, who is for Blake also the demiurge of the gnostics. It is he who utters the unforgettably sublime verses of the speech in chapters 38–41. Nevertheless, paradoxically, he must be overcome if true vision is to be attained. For he is ultimately the same God whose frightfulness dominates Plate 11 as he points to the commandments and at the same time reveals his cloven hoof.

We may note an additional parallel to Plate 11. As Foster Damon correctly notes, Job's God here is identical with the God of Eliphaz.[16] In chapter 4 Eliphaz had also spoken of 'the visions of the night' when a spirit had passed before his face and the hair of his flesh had stood up. This had been the subject of Plate 9. The deity that Job worships clearly inspires those same terrors. He is a punishing God like that of the friends. And both for Job and the friends, he is the God of institutional religion. Thus the moral distinction between Job and his friends, so decisive for his vindication in Job 42: 7, is here annulled. The story does not demonstrate Job's integrity and moral independence as compared with the more conventional piety of the friends, but levels them all under the same rubric. Like theirs Job's error is to fear God and keep the commandments written on the stone tablets. He must be purged of that unworthy tendency.

All this will involve radically altering the shape of the fable. Job's great oath of clearance in chapter 31 in which he declares his innocence of the crimes of adultery, deceit, idolatry, and exploitation, usually regarded as a dramatic climax, a high point in Job's contention with God, will become merely one more example of his puritanical narrowness and selfhood. He must give up that selfhood and learn true liberty, which means liberty from the law. ('I tell you, no virtue can exist without breaking these ten commandments.'[17]) Indeed there can be no true contention with God—such as that expressed in Job's repeated demands for a hearing (10: 1–7; 13: 22–7; 31: 35–40)—since it is clear from Plate 11 that Job's fear of God and God's diabolical capacity for instilling fear are merely reflections of one another. God, as critics have noted, is created in Job's image—he has no independent existence. Job simply projects upon him his own hidden fears.[18] This may be in line with modern psychological

---

[16] *Blake's* Job, 32.   [17] *The Marriage of Heaven and Hell*, Plate 23 (E 42).
[18] Cf. Andrew Wright, *Blake's Job: A Commentary* (Oxford: Oxford University Press, 1972), 9.

notions but it is one of Blake's most crucial departures from the biblical system: it takes away any possibility of a genuine dialogue or confrontation—which for many is the heart of the book's meaning—replacing this with a theology of emanation. In this picture flames rise up from below towards the outstretched figure of Job whilst the terrifying figure of God presses closely upon him from above with an intolerable weight of fear. Far from addressing, questioning, or answering, Job is turning away his face and holding up his hands in a gesture of helplessness as the waves of fear envelop him.

We do not need to use great interpretive insight to detect here the swerve from dialogue to monologue. Demonstrating once again his amazing ability to represent his own hermeneutic processes in clear outline, Blake has defined the swerve for us (in this picture and in the rest of the series) by giving God and Job the same face—a doubling which has been often noted though its full significance has perhaps not always been spelled out.[19] Job, down to Plate 17 (Fig. 9), is not aware of this phenomenon; he thinks of his God as over there beyond his reach, as a being up in the sky, separable from himself. Hence the terror which his visitor inspires in him in Plate 11. He still has to learn that the object of his fears is in his own mind.[20]

> Thou art a Man God is no more
> Thy own humanity learn to adore.

> (*The Everlasting Gospel*, E 511)

In the meantime, the viewer has already acquired this knowledge because the artist has quite conspicuously and deliberately made God the mirror-image of Job, starting with Plate 2 and until he disappears from sight after Plate 17, thus overwriting the Job story with the myth of Narcissus, or something very like it.

This monologic pattern represents Blake's endorsement of the Coleridgian thesis which, as we noted earlier, maintains that 'the act of self-consciousness is the source and principle of all our possible knowledge'. And Coleridge had gone on to say that

---

[19] But see J. Wicksteed, *Blake's Vision of the Book of Job* (London: Dent, 1924); Milton O. Percival, *William Blake's Circle of Destiny* (New York: Columbia University Press, 1938), 139; Hagstrum, *William Blake*, 129.

[20] Cf. Frye, 'Blake's Reading of the Book of Job', 228–9.

'the true system of natural philosophy places the sole reality of things . . . in the absolute identity of subject and object'.[21] But such identity, if logically pursued, he points out, would lead to one of two results—either we would see all things in God as Malebranche had taught ('we proceed from the self, in order to lose and find all self in God' (*BL* 146)) or else we would see all things in the Self which he says 'is groundless, but only because it is itself the ground of all other certainty' (*BL* 140). Coleridge indicates that in general he prefers the second solution.

Translating Coleridge's argument into the pictorial terms of Blake's Illustrations to Job, we may say in reference to Plate 11, that the identity of subject and object (Job and the figure of God) will eventuate either in the figure of Job dissolving into the being of God or in God dissolving into the being of Job. In other words, the assumption of identity involves the disappearance of one side of the subject/object dichotomy. This is in fact what happens in the last four plates of the series where God disappears. But the deeper result is a poetics of annihilation which leaves us neither with God nor with any true ground on which to base a knowledge of the Self. For the attempt to say anything meaningful about the Self involves standing apart from the Self and thus restoring the subject/object antithesis. But this has been ruled out because of the perceived identity of the two. It follows in Coleridge's words

that we can never pass beyond the principle of self-consciousness. Should we attempt it, we must be driven back from ground to ground, each of which would cease to be a ground the moment we pressed on it. We must be whirled down the gulf of an infinite series. But this would make our reason baffle the end and purpose of all reason, namely unity and system. (*BL* 147)

Coleridge gets over this difficulty after a fashion by invoking the principle of the will, but the baffling vision of the infinite series is not really eliminated; it comes to haunt him in his poetry.[22]

---

[21] S. T. Coleridge, *Biographia Literaria* (1817), with an Introduction by Arthur Symons, in Everyman's Library (London: J. M. Dent, 1906), 148–9 (hereafter *BL* in parentheses in the text).

[22] Especially 'Dejection: An Ode' the mood of which is emphasized by such reflections as 'O Lady! we receive but what we give, | And in our life alone does Nature live'; and see also 'Human Life: on the Denial of Immortality' from *Sibylline Leaves* (1817), ending with the line: 'Thy being's being is contradiction'.

This Romantic notion of the sovereignty of the Self together with the frustrations and contradictions to which it gives rise have been received with a good deal of equanimity by the critics, as though they were self-evident propositions, or even, in the case of Blake, as though they were visionary insights. But other attitudes are possible. A more sober judgement might relate these notions to the mirror-stage of the newborn child as described by Jacques Lacan. In normal development, we are told, the mirror-stage, or 'primary narcissism', in which the I thrills with the recognition of its own reflection, comes to an end in early infancy and the child learns to relate to an *Umwelt*, to link itself to 'socially elaborated institutions'.[23] Above all, the knowledge that comes to us from our unconscious depths in the course of maturation, is not, as Coleridge thought, the knowledge of the Self but rather 'the discovery of the other'.[24] Paul Ricoeur, drawing on traditional Christian ways of thinking, insists likewise on a ground beyond the Self. We make a gesture of communication reaching out to that which is not ourselves.[25] But the most powerful philosophical perception of the Other as actually *preceding* the consciousness of the Self is set out in the work of Emmanuel Lévinas. Truth is not discovered by the 'coinciding of self with self', he says, but by bearing witness on behalf of the Other. This primary awareness of alterity involves responsibility, where that word carries the notion of answering as well as moral obligation. We are addressed, challenged, by the Other and we *respond* to that challenge by saying 'Here I am'.[26] Lévinas might almost seem to be directing his words to Coleridge and Blake. In fact he is addressing a whole trend in Western philosophy, from Plato onward, but especially that of the Enlightenment, according to which all knowledge is essentially self-knowledge.

[23] 'The Mirror-Stage as Formative of the Functions of the I as Revealed in Psychoanalytic Experience', in Hazard Adams and Leroy Searle (eds.), *Critical Theory Since 1965* (Tallahassee, Fla.: Florida State University Press, 1986), 737, and see Chapter 9, n. 12, above.

[24] Id., 'The Agency of the Letter in the Unconscious', ibid. 754.

[25] Paul Ricoeur, *The Conflict of Interpretations: Essays in Hermeneutics* (Evanston, Ill.: Northwestern University Press, 1974), 81–5.

[26] Emmanuel Lévinas, *Otherwise than Being or Beyond Essence*, trans. Alphonso Lingis (The Hague: Martinus Nijhoff, 1981), ch. IV, sect. 5 (p. 119) and ch. V, sect. 2(e) (p. 149); and see id., *Difficult Freedom: Essays on Judaism*, trans. Sean Hand (Baltimore: Johns Hopkins University Press, 1990), 7–8.

Pope was merely uttering the generalities of his age when he declared:

> Know then thyself, presume not God to scan,
> The proper study of Mankind is Man—

or when he noted that by a happy coincidence self-love and social were the same.[27] For Rousseau narcissism was, we may say, a way of life. Again, it becomes apparent that here as in other characteristic positions, Blake is much more an Enlightenment figure than has been thought. Pierre Bayle, Voltaire, and the Deists would have eagerly applauded the notion that the God whom Job feared was simply a projection of his own mind. To give them both the same face would have seemed to them a witty and original way of making this point. For Blake himself his discovery was not a matter of wit but rather of prophetic vision, revelation! That is the amazing anomaly. He utters Enlightenment views with the zeal of the *evangelos*, the inspired messenger. But he is self-dispatched and the good news he brings to his audience is that the kingdom of God is within them and therefore, strictly speaking, there will be no more messages.

In Plate 13, 'The Lord Answering Job out of the Whirlwind' (Fig. 8), God and Job are being whirled round in an endless circle or, rather, ellipse. Their faces are again identical and the lines of the whirlwind emphasize their inseparability. The 'whirlwind'— a popular mistranslation, going back to the King James Bible, of the Hebrew *sa'arah* (lit. 'storm-wind')—gives Blake the key to the circular pattern of this painting with the divine figure at the centre and Job included in the circle of energy created by that figure.[28] It might almost serve to illustrate Coleridge's account, quoted above, of the vortex of self-consciousness in which the Self is 'whirled down the gulf of an infinite series'. But the discovery of identity, which implies the collapsing of the distinction between subject and object, does not here bring dismay or bafflement to the parties. God and Job have the same face, but Job is now evidently aware of this and rejoices at it. Instead of turning away in terror as in Plate 11, he now directly faces God, gazing at him with open-eyed wonder. Both faces have a benign

---

[27] Alexander Pope, 'Essay on Man', Epistle II, 1–2, and Epistle III, 318.
[28] Cf. Wright, *Blake's Job*, 33–5.

Fig. 8. The Lord Answering Job out of the Whirlwind

expression. Damon speaks of the 'mystical ecstasy' of the picture and of the 'serene joy' of Job and his wife.[29] The reason for this is that this moment does not merely mark the abolition of the subject/object dichotomy—it is the beginning of the epiphany of God as Christ.

[29] Damon, *Blake's* Job, 36.

Here then is a major transformation.[30] The God of Plate 11 has now disappeared and a new deity has taken his place. Or, to put this in more Blakeian terms, the Selfhood which gave rise to the vision of Plate 11 has been, or is about to be, annihilated and another vision will be glimpsed. Here is an annihilation which is also a rebirth, as in the self-destruction of Milton and Ololon which accompanies the resurrection of Jesus at the end of *Milton*. As a sign of this, the deity in this picture is portrayed with arms outstretched in the form of the cross, indicating an emphatically Christian soteriology. The joining of the two figures by means of the circle follows from this. God is about to take on the nature of Man and, by the same token, Man is about to take on the nature of God. It is Blake's way of portraying the Incarnation.

This situation is further confirmed in Plate 17 (Fig. 9), another design based on the image of circularity (supplied here by the shape of the moon or sun behind the figures with beams of light radiating from the centre of the circle). Here Job and his wife again face God in a mood of serenity. Job is not simply brought near to God by the force of the whirlwind as in Plate 13; he is now in heaven and the distance between Man and God is abolished. They not only have the same face but they occupy the same world of light. It is equivalent to the moment when Los enters into Blake's left foot and they become one Man. The important quotation in the lower margin is from the Gospel of John: 'At that day ye shall know that I am in my Father & you in me & I in you' (14: 20). Here is a key to the whole series of illustrations. God and Man are consubstantial and co-eternal. For according to Blake's radical reading of the Gospel, Incarnation signifies nothing less than the abolishing of all distinction between Man and God; God dissolves in Man and no otherness is left to command us, to question us, or to affright us. Instead, Man himself—not merely Jesus, but every man and woman— is potentially endowed with divine glory and even divine power! This is no longer Christianity in any of its orthodox or even less orthodox forms but something more like what we are told of certain Far Eastern religions. Instead of a single, unrepeated, and unrepeatable event, we encounter multiple incarnations, men

---

[30] This is the view of Damon and others; Frye agrees but locates the final stage of regeneration in Plate 17 (see his 'Blake's Reading of the Book of Job', 230).

FIG. 9. The Vision of Christ

becoming gods as 'an almost routine affair'.[31] In fact Blake goes
further even than this, universalizing the fusion of God and Man
so that the boundary between them disappears. Incarnation is
now not an event so much as a state achieved by the awakened

---

[31] R. J. Z. Werblowsky, 'Some Reflections on Two-Way Traffic or Incarnation/
Avatara and Apotheosis', *Japanese Journal of Religious Studies*, 14 (1987), 281–4.

Imagination whereby God becomes Man and Man becomes God.[32] This is what Blake termed the religion of the Divine Humanity.[33]

Many distinguished Blake scholars have reacted to these ideas of Blake with a surprising lack of critical reserve, some even with unconcealed enthusiasm. Blake criticism has not in the end benefited by this tendency. The pattern that I have traced has been seen as a supreme visionary achievement, leading to a recovery of the unfallen Edenic state.[34] Northrop Frye speaks of Blake's presentation of the book of Job as an 'epitome of the whole Bible'.[35] It would seem to me that in an age which tends to treat more sober systems of belief with unalloyed scepticism, a little scepticism might be spared for these eccentricities also, without prejudice to our admiration for Blake's poetry. But leaving aside the issue of Blake's beliefs and how we relate to them, and leaving aside also such a compendious entity as 'the whole Bible', could we not all—sceptics and devotees alike—perhaps agree on the essential hermeneutic question, namely, that these illustrations are not in the strict sense an exegesis of the biblical book of Job, not even a typological exegesis? Christian typology is based on the persuasion that an Old Testament source may be reinterpreted to bear a Christian sense, without losing the concrete force of its own context.[36] Blake does not practise such

[32] Leslie Tannenbaum finds an analogue, or possibly a source, for Blake's ideas in the writings of a contemporary sectarian preacher, Jacob Duché, who strongly affirmed that 'through Jesus, God became man to show the process whereby man may become God'. This led to a belief in 'the continual recreation of God in human form' (*Biblical Tradition in Blake's Early Prophecies* (Princeton: Princeton University Press, 1982), 113–16, 122–3). Blake evidently knew Duché; they were both interested in the teachings of Swedenborg and they were neighbours for some time in Lambeth where Duché had a chaplaincy and where the Blakes resided from early 1791. (See D. Hirst, *Hidden Riches* (London: Eyre and Spottiswoode, 1964), 207–12; David V. Erdman, *Blake: Prophet Against Empire* (New York: Doubleday, 1969), 290 n. 18).

[33] Cf. Wicksteed, *Blake's Vision of the Book of Job*, 183–91; Mellor, *Blake's Human Form Divine*, 253–4.

[34] Cf. Frye, 'Blake's Reading of the Book of Job', 226; Percival, *William Blake's Circle of Destiny*, 139–42, 289–92.

[35] Frye, 'Blake's Reading of the Book of Job', 234.

[36] Augustine, *The City of God*, Book XVII, ch. 3, insists that when references to the heavenly Jerusalem (i.e. the New Testament) are discovered in Old Testament sources, such readings may 'not contradict the truth of the history', i.e. that of the earthly Jerusalem. (See *The City of God*, trans. John Healey (London: Dent, 1945), ii. 146–7.) Erich Auerbach's famous essay on typology in Dante ('Figura', in *Scenes from the Drama of European Literature*, trans. R. Manheim (New York:

interpretation. The pictures are much rather, it would seem, an attempted refutation of Job. They comment on the text of Job for the purpose of contradicting its belief system and reversing its narrative direction.

I return to Plate 13 (Fig. 8) as the clearest example of such a deliberate overturning of his source. God's speech from the storm is the ostensible subject of this painting ('The Lord Answering Job out of the Whirlwind'). But if we look at the contents of God's speech in the text of Job (chapters 38–41), we will find that what is stressed from first to last is the unbridgeable distance between Man and the Creator of the vastness of the universe. This is clearly expressed in the rhetorical question with which the speech opens: 'Where wast thou when I laid the foundations of the earth? declare if thou knowst' (38: 4). Job cannot possibly declare. This message is enforced again and again in this great catalogue of images of primeval splendour and power in the face of which Man is reduced to insignificance. That God and Man can address one another in spite of the great abyss which divides them is the fundamental paradox of the book. But here in Blake's engraving that paradox is lost. There is no dialogue (God does not appear to be speaking at all) and, on the other hand, God's appearing to Job in the whirlwind, far from suggesting an abyss of separateness, signals as we have noted the closing of a circle and prepares us for the coming fusion of Man and God in which their separate identities will be lost. Blake was clearly aware of this contradiction and he was not trying to find a way round it by interpretation.[37]

Nor is this a matter of an isolated detail or a single tableau; the overall design of the series of paintings represents a radical reversal of the thrust of the biblical book not merely as we might understand it but also as Blake himself surely understood it. We have already referred to the two visions of Creation, Plates 14

Meridian Books, 1959)) has a like emphasis. Dante, he insists, in his vision of the Inferno and the Purgatorio does not abandon the dimensions of the earthly and the realistic. Other positions have been taken at different times (see J. S. Preus, *From Shadow to Promise: Old Testament Interpretation from Augustine to the Young Luther* (Cambridge, Mass.: Harvard University Press, 1969), *passim*), but Augustine's two-tier system has commanded a broad assent down to the Reformation and beyond.

[37] For some refreshingly direct comment on Blake's subversion of his biblical sources, see Murray Roston, *Changing Perspectives in Literature and the Visual Arts, 1650–1820* (Princeton: Princeton University Press, 1990), 286, 290.

('When the Morning Stars Sang together') and 15 ('Behemoth and Leviathan') (Figs. 5 and 6). In the biblical context these references had immediately followed the verse just cited ('Where wast thou when I laid the foundations of the earth?') to enforce the utterly immeasurable distance between God and Man, between what God had done and what Man could barely grasp, far less control. Where was Job when the morning stars were created, what can he know about them? How can Man measure himself against God when he cannot even approach the dreaded Leviathan? 'Will he make a covenant with thee? wilt thou take him for a servant for ever?' (41: 4). It is this terrifying contrast between divine power and human frailty developed over four chapters which had driven Job to his ultimate submission in Job 42: 1–6. In Blake's illustrations, we have the precise reversal of this movement. Job is seen moving nearer to God as the scene of the Creation is unfolded; in Plate 14 (Fig. 5) he is still with his wife and friends in a kind of concave enclosure at the base of the picture; but in Plate 15 (Fig. 6) Job and God occupy the same space at the top of the picture, both of them looking down at the lower world of Behemoth and Leviathan as though indeed Job had shared with God the creating of these monsters! God's left hand with the index-finger pointing downwards divides the space between Job and the friends, thus elevating him even further. In Plate 17 (Fig. 9), as I remarked earlier, Job is joined to God in the same heavenly circle of light. There is no further distance between them to be bridged. It is the achieved Divine Humanity.[38]

As a logical consequence of all this, God now disappears from view like the Ghost of Hamlet's father after Act III. He is not seen again in the concluding plates. The reason for this, as Blake's commentators have noted, is that Job himself has now become the incarnate Christ! There is no other. He will also assume the cruciform posture in Plates 18 and 20 (Fig. 10) to make this startling transformation even clearer. In keeping with all this, Blake totally ignores Job's repentance and submission in Job 42: 1–6, retaining only verse 5 which reads: 'I have heard thee with the hearing of the Ear but now my Eye seeth thee', as the subscript for Plate 17 (Fig. 9). For Blake these words come to signify

[38] Cf. Wright, *Blake's Job*, 42–5.

not the I/Thou of dialogue which makes possible the meeting of the covenantal partners even as it confirms their separateness, but rather the mystic moment of recognition in which the I encounters its own reflection in the mirror. That, as the picture with its doubling of the faces makes clear, is how Blake understands the words 'my Eye seeth thee'. What ensues is a thrilling monologue in which the distinction between subject and object is dissolved ('you in me & I in you') for both the I and the Thou have been annihilated. Job has become one with God. A more complete antithesis to the biblical book of Job could not be imagined and yet, amazingly, Blake is drawn to the book by the power of the great argument that he is seeking to confute— the sublimity that goes with terror and distance. And it is that fascination also which he communicates to his audience.

Plate 20, 'Job and his Daughters' (Fig. 10), the strangest of the illustrations, is also the one which stands at the greatest possible distance from the text of the biblical book. Job, no longer a hero who is morally tested, is the God-Man incarnation. (Again we note the cruciform posture as he holds his hands in blessing over his daughters.) This incarnation has now reached its ultimate form as the Human Imagination, Imagination being synonymous, we are told, with the Divine Humanity.[39] According to another formulation, the Human Imagination is 'the Divine Body of the Lord Jesus' (*Milton*, Pl. 3: 3–4). This accords precisely with the picture. Job in this picture becomes the fully awakened artistic and poetic Imagination. Two features of the picture illustrate this. First, in the water-colour version the three daughters are represented as the three arts of Painting, Poetry, and Music.[40] It is this world of renascent art which Job embraces as he stretches out his arms over the daughters in the sign of the Cross. That is the sign of the triumph and salvation to which the story in Blake's version had been moving, not any worldly change in Job's fortunes which might stand in a metonymic relation to the historical and political process. The triumph and salvation will be consummated in the final plate where, as already noted, the musical instruments are finally taken down from the tree. It is the triumph of art itself which is here celebrated.

[39] See *Jerusalem*, Plate 70: 19–20 (E 222).
[40] The water-colour (Butlin 716) was painted in 1821. This feature does not appear on the corresponding engraved plate (Fig. 10).

FIG. 10. Job and his Daughters

But there is in the picture a second, more remarkable inversion (literally) of the Job story. Job is also revealed as himself the artist who has painted or engraved these very pictures which constitute the series that we are considering. In the panels on the wall behind him we see his work, including the design of Plate 13 ('The Lord Answering Job out of the Whirlwind') and an impression of Plate 3 on the catastrophe which had overwhelmed

the sons of Job. Job is revealed as the author of these illustrations, including this selfsame illustration in which this statement
is now being made! It is the final word in poetic reflexivity. We
have here a work of art which, like the pastoral, eternally echoes
its own origins and processes.

Up till now the story of Job as set out in the picture series
had involved two levels of representation. First of all Job had
figured as a person undergoing a process of error, tribulation,
and salvation. From this point of view, his transformation from
a God-fearing conformist, a worshipper of Urizen, to becoming
himself the incarnate Christ represented Blake's idiosyncratic
rereading of the book as salvation-history. But Job also enacted,
almost by way of allegory, this very process of radical reinterpretation. That is to say, he was a figure in a hermeneutic drama.
In the abolition of distance between himself and God first by
their having the same features, then by the collapsing of the space
between them, thereby cancelling the subject/object dichotomy,
and finally by the fusion of the two figures, Job served to illustrate a new hermeneutic model. According to this model, the text
over there disappears and the dialogic confrontation characteristic of covenantal hermeneutics gives way to a hermeneutics of
monologue. But in Plate 20 (Fig. 10), Job is revealed not merely
as a paradigm, an example of the process of hermeneutic transformation, but as the hermeneut himself, the artist who generates
this very mythic design out of his own inspired imagination. In
this third level of representation, Job, we may say, becomes the
author of his own history, or rather of the artwork which has
now become his spiritual achievement and which is, in fact, all
the history that we need be concerned with.

The paintings on the wall thus have no reference to anything
beyond themselves. Moreover they all exist in the same moment
of time; history has been nullified and with it, salvation-history.
Most important of all, the original text of the book of Job as
an object of interpretation has been eclipsed. It has no longer
any independent authority. A new Bible, the inspired work of
the new artist, self-referential and self-justifying, has now taken
its place. The pictures 'on the walls of Job's mind' are what
we are now invited to interpret as 'the creative Word of God'.[41]

---

[41] Northrop Frye, *Fearful Symmetry* (Boston: Beacon Press, 1965), 434 ('Notes
on the Illustrations', n. 6).

They are not a commentary on something else but rather the original revelation now displayed as imaginatively prior to the biblical text.

5

It will be seen that in the last two illustrations discussed there is the ultimate working out of a poetics of annihilation as in the final plates of Milton. Commenting on the picture of 'Job and his Daughters' just considered, Northrop Frye remarks that the objective order from which Job's calamities came has been annihilated.[42] Job, we may add, has been in a sense annihilated also. He no longer bears the weight of his tragic ordeal; his self-hood, indeed his individual existence, has been abolished and he re-emerges as general principle, i.e. the Divine Humanity, or a collectivity, like Ololon. We could, if we wished, use Frye's more positive formulation and say that in the last two plates he dies to be resurrected as a community, represented here by his family.[43] But essentially we have here a poetics of annihilation and denial—a denial not only of Selfhood as such, but of what often goes with it, namely, the power and wonder and rebellion associated with the Sublime.

But Blake, as I have noted, cannot escape the fascination of the Sublime, nor can his readers. That is the built-in paradox of the series. Plate 20 gives us (and gives Blake) a temporary resolution of that difficulty. The Sublime is present but placed, so to speak, in quotation marks. It is there in the scenes recalled on the panels, the circle of energy recalled and quoted from Plate 13 where God had spoken out of the whirlwind, the terror and darkness of Satan's destructiveness recalled from Plate 3. These framed examples give us a Sublime gathered into the artifice of eternity, a Sublime of the second order, one in which the violence and creative wonder are only symbolically recalled—in a word, a sublimated Sublime! For we now behold the arrested symmetry of art rather than the violence of the storm itself. The great works of time, all passion spent, have now become a pattern on the wall of the Interpreter's House. They will continue

---

[42] Frye, 'Blake's Reading of the Book of Job', 231.   [43] Ibid. 230–1.

to stir the imagination but as objects of aesthetic contemplation rather than as historical paradigm or testimony.

There is one other work of Blake in which the Sublime is a central feature as well as a central issue and that is 'The Tyger'. Blake is here producing a textbook example of the Sublime, exaggerated, according to Harold Bloom, to the point of parody.[44] Moreover it is generally agreed that the image of the tiger in this poem was suggested by the war-horse and the sea-monsters in Job 38–41.[45] There are many linking features. Leviathan and Behemoth are in Job described as arousing fear and wonder in the observer; God draws attention to the muscles of the belly of Behemoth, the sinews of his thighs, and his iron-like limbs. This is followed by a series of questions about Leviathan: 'Canst thou draw out Leviathan with a hook? or press down his tongue with a cord? would you put a hook through his nose, or bore his jaw through with a bridle ring?' and finally: 'Try to lay your hand upon him, you will no longer think of fighting' (Job 41: 1–2, 8). Blake likewise builds up the impression of the fearfulness of the tiger by a series of very similar rhetorical questions.

> What the hand, dare sieze the fire?
> And what shoulder, & what art,
> Could twist the sinews of thy heart?

It would seem at first sight that we have to do with the same God who inspires terror into Job and his friends in the first part of the Job series and that the poem is grappling once again with the ambiguities of Creation as in the middle plates of the Job series—its majesty and its menace. According to Kathleen Raine, the answer to the question, 'Did he who made the lamb make thee?' is No![46] The creator of the tiger is Urizen, Elohim, the Old Testament God of judgement, not Jesus who made the lamb and is called by its name. This would make the poem into one more example of the ongoing and unresolved conflict—as in *Milton* and as in the Job illustrations—between a poetics of the Sublime and a poetics of Incarnation in which Selfhood is lost and power has been rendered powerless.

---

[44] Harold Bloom, *Poetry and Repression: Revisionism from Blake to Stevens* (New Haven: Yale University Press, 1976), 44–6.

[45] Id., *Blake's Apocalypse* (New York: Doubleday, 1963), 147; Morton D. Paley, *Energy and Imagination* (Oxford: Oxford University Press, 1970), 47–9.

[46] Kathleen Raine, 'Who made the Tyger?', *Encounter* (June 1954).

This, however, is not quite the impression the poem creates. It does not suggest a Manichean tension between two principles but, much rather, an achieved synthesis. When the force of the tiger is invoked in this poem, the instruments of music are not hanging on the tree awaiting some other time and place in which to make their music heard. We do not have the sense that praise and wonder are held back. On the contrary, 'The Tyger' has the perfection and harmony of Blake's lyric art at its best—an art not inhibited by the self-denying ordinance of the exiles in Psalm 137! And yet it is, as I have said, not only sublime but pointedly so, with a sublimity that is foregrounded throughout and rendered unmistakable by the parallel with Job!

How can this be? What has made the tiger almost of a kin with the Lark and the Wild Thyme of *Milton*, Part II—a lyric tiger? What I would want to say is that while Blake's tiger certainly derives from the Leviathan of Job, we do not have to do with a created tiger, the work of a God who might be Urizen or Elohim or even Yahweh, but with a framed tiger like the pictures on the wall in Plate 20. From the opening apostrophe in the first line of the poem—

> Tyger Tyger, burning bright,
> In the forests of the night

—it is already beheld as a work of art, a tiger produced by the human Imagination which, for Blake, 'is God himself' ('The Laocoon', E 271). In so far as it has a mythic origin, it is perhaps the work of Los (who is a blacksmith, hence the hammer and the furnace of stanza 4), but Los after he has entered the poet and become one flesh with him. In other words this Leviathan is not directly out of the biblical Book of Job, but one sired by the poetics of incarnation—the Leviathan that Job himself might have created after he had undergone the transformation which is the subject of Blake's Job series. Job then, by union with Christ, is regenerated as the Divine Humanity. He also becomes the supreme artist who does not merely name the creatures, as the Bible teaches, but creates the world in his inner space, on the walls of his mind!

From this point of view a key term in the poem is 'fearful symmetry' appearing both at the beginning and at the end to form an *inclusio*:

> What immortal hand or eye,
> Could frame thy fearful symmetry?

There is terror in the poem but it has been rendered harmless by symmetry, by art. The tiger of Blake's poem is, from the beginning, not a beast in the jungle but a beast in a picture. He is a Memorable Fancy, existing in the creative imagination of the artist and there alone. There too in that inner space are to be found the 'forests of the night' and the 'distant deeps or skies', for there is no other world. Poetry has now, for Blake and others among his contemporaries, made the decisive shift: it no longer faces the world, but turns inward to face itself.

In *The Marriage of Heaven and Hell*, Blake had spoken in a Memorable Fancy of seeing 'among the fires of Hell' (i.e. his artist's workshop) 'a mighty Devil folded in black clouds' (meaning himself—'devil' signifying its opposite), writing 'with corroding fires' (i.e. engraving on plates) the following sentence:

> How do you know but ev'ry Bird that cuts his airy way,
> Is an immense world of delight, clos'd by your senses five?

> (E 35)

From this perspective, the Sublime and the Beautiful, however high their flight, however broad their sweep, tend to be confined solipsistically to our interior consciousness. There 'imagination bodies forth the shapes of things unknown'. At the end, this is a fundamental difference between Blake's visionary poetry and that of the Bible which testifies, however indirectly, and however unscientifically, to a world outside the poem, to a history; a voice addresses us and to it we respond. This in a way is also the difference between Blake's Sublime and that of the classical theorists from Burke onwards. For Burke and Lowth, the Sublime awakens our sense of human inadequacy and ignorance. It reminds us of the limits of our humanity. For Kant as for Wordsworth, the Absolute, to which our sense of the Sublime points, has its seat in the mind—that is Kant's great innovation —nevertheless it transcends our power of representation. As Vincent De Luca points out, it is precisely here that Blake departs from classical theorists of the Sublime. There is for Blake no transcendental standard before which Imagination is muted. For

Blake the Imagination has access to the infinite; the absolute is attainable.[47]

In this connection we may consider the interrogative mode in this poem. The critics have properly noted that the rhetorical questions of which the entire poem is made up, echo those of God's speech in Job.[48] But what has not been noted is that those questions have now entirely changed their character and they now have a reverse effect. When Job was addressed out of the storm and bidden to 'gird up thy loins like a man; for I will demand of thee, and thou answer me', we knew already that precisely because he was a man he would never be able to answer. Rhetorical questions such as 'Where wast thou when I laid the foundations of the earth?' carry their own answers with them. As I have already suggested, the answer to this question is that Job is merely a creature and cannot even begin to grasp the mighty works of the Creator. It is the wonder of his creatureliness as well as the awareness of his appalling insignificance which will bring Job to his final submission:

I have heard of thee by the hearing of the ear: but now my eye sees thee. Wherefore I abhor myself and repent in dust and ashes.

The questions in Blake's poem likewise carry their own answers with them, but they are different answers:

> In what distant deeps or skies
> Burnt the fire of thine eyes!
> On what wings dare he aspire?
> What the hand dare sieze the fire?
>
> And what shoulder, & what art,
> Could twist the sinews of thy heart?

The aspiring wings are those of the poet at the height of his vision; the hand that dare seize the fire is that of the inspired poet and engraver. For the questions have reference not to world-creation but to the human daring of artistic creation. As a result, these lines do not challenge the reader's or speaker's presumption, forcing him to acknowledge his human limitations. On the contrary, they are a paean, a celebration of the wonder, the incredible, unbounded reach of the poet's imagination. And we may

---

[47] De Luca, *Words of Eternity*, 38.
[48] Paley, *Energy and Imagination*, 48–9; Bloom, *Blake's Apocalypse*, 147.

add—the poet's imagination as expressed in this very poem! They point to the 'fearful symmetry' of the poem itself as the supreme demonstration of the all-sufficiency of the artwork. In fact, the quoted phrases, in spite of the frequent use of the mark of inter-rogation, are not true questions. They might equally appear as: 'On what wings dare he aspire!' 'And what shoulder, & what art!' 'what dread hand! & what dread feet!'—making them exclamations. Essentially these questions do not challenge the reader; rather they draw attention reflexively to the poem's own demonstrated achievement. Hence the circular shape provided by the *inclusio*. The poem begins and ends with its own fear-ful symmetry.

Art, therefore, and the artist are the true subjects of the poem. 'And what shoulder, & what *art*', the poem declares, 'Could twist the sinews of thy heart?' The sublime artist measures himself against the creation. He ascribes to himself the power, the terror, and the creative energy of the maker of lambs and tigers. Here in this determined elevation of the artist to divine rank, we also have the answer to the question: 'Did he who made the Lamb make thee?' If in the physical universe, the answer is No, in the poetic world of pure vision the answer would seem to be Yes. For the seeming contraries of innocence and experience, larks and leviathans, lambs and tigers, melt away as the poet's 'immortal hand or eye' makes all things one. Poetry, Coleridge said, recon-ciles opposite or discordant qualities (*BL* 166); Blake goes a step further: poetry reconciles opposite and divided worlds. That answer too is implied in the poem's questions.

And yet, in spite of the exalted status granted to the artist, what we have nevertheless is a poetics of annihilation. Critics have wondered who is the speaker in the poem. It is hard to say. The poet, or the implied speaker, has essentially disappeared; there is no 'I' in the poem, no first-person pronouns or references of any kind. It is easier to talk about the implied author of the tiger! He is, I have suggested, something like the figure of Job/Christ/Blake in the final plates of the Job series. The creator of tigers has now become one with the artist who, as Sidney had said, makes things better than Nature brings forth. But here again his figure cannot be clearly discerned. The 'he' of the second and fifth stanzas ('On what wings dare he aspire?' 'Did he smile his work to see?') is too elusive to be a persona; he becomes rather a way of talking about the process of imaginative creation. For the 'he' to become a persona, there would have to be a history, a dramatic plot in which creator and creature address one another, as they do in the great climactic chapters of the book of Job. Here in the incarnational process of poetic imagining, we have rather a dissolving of persons, a ceaseless flow of energy between the author and his work, so that we cannot know the dancer from the dance.

In this fluid state in which a mythology is created—or rather in which it seemingly creates itself—we find a radical fragmentation, indeed a dissolution of the human figure. Instead of a person or a figure, we discern a dismembered 'hand or eye', a hand that 'dare sieze the fire', an eye that might frame a symmetry, a shoulder that might twist a sinew, hands and feet severed from the rest, but no entire figure or shape. Whilst in this poem, the image of the tiger is created through the mode of apostrophe—created indeed by language—there are no equivalent rhetorical gestures which might serve to evoke a speaker or author in his human singularity and integrity, one that might then stand over against the tiger. It would seem that such singularity has been lost; as in the case of Ololon, the final aesthetic achievement, the word beyond the word, involves self-destruction, or at least fragmentation. What is at stake is the viability of the human person.

Blake has again remarkably anticipated developments of which we have become painfully aware during the one hundred and seventy years since his death. Michel Foucault pointed out that with language and the autonomy of language now carried to their utmost limit

what emerges is that man has 'come to an end,' and that by reaching the summit of all possible speech, he arrives not at the very heart of himself but at the brink of that which limits him; in that region where death prowls, where thought is extinguished, where the promise of the origin interminably recedes.[49]

The symmetry of which the poem speaks and which it so magnificently realizes through its structure and language, ultimately rests on the abolition of boundaries—between religion

---

[49] Michel Foucault, *The Order of Things: An Archaeology of the Human Sciences*, trans. of *Les Mots et les choses* (New York: Random House, 1970), 383.

and poetry, between man and the universe, between God and Man—distinctions which up to the time of Blake seemed to be central to human self-perception, indeed to human existence. 'The Tyger' is from this point of view a poem of crucial significance. It succeeds for the space of twenty-four lines in blending these contraries, achieving at the same time an aesthetic perfection of which very few writers in English have been capable. From this point of view, it may justly stand as Blake's masterpiece. But to use his own interrogative mode: At what fearful cost?

Index

Abraham:
   visit of angels to 185–8, 189–91,
      203, 273–4
Abrams, M. H. 241
Adelman, Janet 41
Aeneid 199
Antony and Cleopatra (Shakespeare)
      35–74, 86, 171, 191
   biblical perspective in 58–62, 64
   cult of Bacchus in 72
   typical images 42–8
   mythological patterns 41–2, 50–6,
      59
   language of theatrical performance
      in 56–7
Areopagitica (Milton) 166–7, 260
Aristotle 7, 35
   his *Physics* 69–70, 77
Assmann, Jan 85, 87
Auden, W. H. 141–2
Auerbach, Erich 58–9, 193 n., 312 n.
'Auguries of Innocence' (Blake)
      228–9, 231, 234
Augustine:
   City of God 312 n.
   Confessions 77–9, 82–3, 84, 103–5,
      281 n.
   importance of Psalms in 84
   as model for meditation-writers
      103–4

Bacchus, *see* Dionysus
Bakhtin, M. M. 65, 156
Balaam 231–4, 236, 290
Barber, C. L. 8 n.
Barr, James 88
Battenhouse, R. W. 60 n., 62 n.
Bellerophon 169, 283
berit, *see* covenant
Bethell, S. L. 42, 43
Blake, William:
   and the Enlightenment 211–14,
      224–30, 232, 308
   as epic poet 259–66
   and gnosticism 217–23, 225, 242

identifies with Isaiah 257
incarnation in 249, 254, 279, 287,
      289, 310–12, 314–15, 317, 324
his irony and wit 228–30
as lyric poet 277–86
his mythological system 246,
      260–3, 265, 269–72, 277
as painter and engraver 290–318
and prophecy 214–16
see also under individual works
Blayney, Peter W. M. 143
blood ritual 3, 4, 5, 8, 9, 11, 12–13
   see also human sacrifice
Bloom, Harold 85, 109, 123, 124,
      154 n., 157, 278, 319
Booth, Wayne C. 231
Bowersock, G. W. 72 n.
Bradley, A. C. 17, 120, 132
Brisman, Leslie 204
Bristol, Michael D. 8 n.
Bruns, Gerald 158–9, 176
Burke, Edmund 301
Burton, Robert 94
Butter, Peter 264
By the Waters of Babylon (Blake)
      293–4
Byron, Lord:
   Cain 204–5

Carey, John 189 n.
Carr, Archie 81 n.
Cavell, Stanley 57 n., 121
Chapman, George 25–6
Coburn, Kathleen 242
Coleridge, Samuel Taylor 122
   'The Ancient Mariner' 77, 291
   Biographia Literaria 238–41,
      305–7, 323
   Table-Talk 155
covenant:
   as biblical pradigm 86–8
   as divine drama 89–90
   Oral Law based on 159
   as rupture 87, 89
   see also Hamlet; Milton

Cullman, O. 88
Curran, Stuart 220

Damon, S. Foster 262, 275 n., 303, 304, 309
Danby, John F. 62 n.
De Luca, Vincent A. 289, 321–2
Defoe, Daniel:
    Robinson Crusoe 201
Dionysus 8 n., 39, 55, 91, 114–15, 276
    feast of 64
    and Hercules 51–2, 72
    as represented in 3rd century mosaic 72 n.
Doctrine and Discipline of Divorce (Milton) 189
Donne, John 94
Duché, Jacob 312 n.

Edwards, Philip 94 n.
Elohim Creating Adam (Blake) 301–2
Empson, William 106
Erdman, David V. 277
Everlasting Gospel, The (Blake) 219–21, 227, 228, 229–34, 290, 305
Exodus:
    paradigm of, in Paradise Lost 198–204
    as revolutionary idea 199–200

Felperin, Howard 62 n., 122, 135, 136
Ferry, Anne Davidson 278
Flinker, Noam 157 n.
Foucault, Michel 324
The Four Zoas (Blake) 219, 221
French Revolution, The (Blake) 227 n.
Frye, Northrop 79, 264, 303, 312, 318

Gadamer, H.-G. 225 n.
Gay, Peter 226
genus humile, see sermo humilis
Gleckner, Robert F. 248, 268, 269
gnosticism 217–19
    see also Blake
Golden Calf, sin of 196 n., 198
Goshen-Gottstein, Alon 159 n.
Granville-Barker, Harley 121
Greene, Thomas M. 182–3, 190, 259 n.

Hagstrum, Jean H. 211, 296
Hall, Joseph 25, 26, 90, 100–2
Hamlet (Shakespeare) 32, 48, 61, 74–115, 116–17, 131
    covenant paradigm in 84–90, 92
    drinking rituals in 74, 75–6
    image of circularity in 131
    repudiation of Dionysiac mode in 76–7
    and Senecan revenge-play 79–80, 106, 114
    soliloquies 102–5
    suicide a central issue in 94–8
    theatre-images in 90–2, 110–13
    the weight of Christian allusion in 93–5, 98–100
hand-washing ceremonies 10–12, 13–16, 23
Hartman, Geoffrey 141, 197 n., 245
Harvey, Van A. 184
Heilman, R. B. 121
Henry IV, Part I (Shakespeare) 15
Hermes 155, 182–4, 192, 259–60, 286
    and hermeneutics 184
Hölderlin, J. C. F. 245, 267
Holland, Norman N. 122–3
Holland, Philemon 64 n.
Holloway, John 57
Homer 251, 259–60
Hughes, Merritt Y. 281 n.
human sacrifice 5–7, 11, 12
    rejected in Deuteronomy 16
    replaced by animal sacrifice 14
hyperbole 36, 38, 40, 41, 42

Illustrations of the Book of Job (Blake) 291–325
incarnation see Blake
Isis 50–1, 53–4

James, D. G. 118
Jerusalem (Blake) 222–3, 233, 269, 271
Job, see Julius Caesar, King Lear, Illustrations of the Book of Job (Blake)
Joseph, Miriam 116
Josipovici, Gabriel 300
Julius Caesar (Shakespeare) 3–34, 35–6, 67, 107
    biblical antithesis evoked in 23–8, 34
    echoes Job 34

statues in 19
typical images 17–20
Jung, C. G. 275 n.

Kafka, Franz:
  The Trial 148
Kant, I. 217, 238 n., 321
Keats, John 235
Kermode, Frank 123, 161–2
Kerrigan, William 162–3
King Lear (Shakespeare) 30, 116–49,
  265
  echoes blessing of Isaac 137–9
  double-plot in 132–7, 144–5
  Folio and Quarto versions 142–9
  images of circularity in 130–1
  and Job 123–9
  kneeling in 118, 139–40
  echoes parable of Prodigal Son
    118
  and Prometheus 123, 126–7
  and salvation 117–19
  suicide in 128–30
King Leir, see *The True Chronicle
  Historie of King Leir*
Kirschbaum, Leo 5, 6
Knight, G. Wilson 19, 28, 31
Kott, Jan 123
Kuriyama, Constance Brown 46

Lacan, Jacques 268 n., 307
Lactantius 25
Lévinas, Emmanuel 30–1, 307
Lévi-Strauss, Claude 80
Lewis, C. S. 116
Lipsius, Justus:
  Two Books of Constancy 25
Longinus 21, 222
Lowth, Robert (bishop) 222
Luis de Granada 100–1
Lyons, Bridget G. 136

Macbeth (Shakespeare) 13, 14, 15,
  110
Maccoby, Hyam 7, 11
McFarland, Thomas 265 n.
Maimonides, Moses 214
Marriage of Heaven and Hell (Blake)
  211, 220, 228 304, 321
Martz, L. L. 100–1
Mazzeo, Joseph A. 251 n.
meditation, practice of 100–2,
Mellor, Anne K. 296

Mercury:
  see Hermes
met-agon 9, 28, 63, 123, 149
midrash 158–9, 161–2, 174–8, 194,
  197
Midrash Rabbah (Genesis) 164
Midrash Rabbah (Numbers) 168
Miller, John Hillis 242–3, 244–5,
  268
Miller, Jonathan 121
Milton (Blake) 221, 248–51, 254,
  255–8, 260–4, 266–87, 301
  sandal of Hermes in 259–60
Milton, John 25, 95, 153–205
  and covenant 159, 163–5, 181,
    189
  identifies with Isaiah 179–80, 181
  linked with the nightingale 278–9
  and midrash 158–9, 161–5, 174–8,
    194
  and Original sin 195–205
  see also individual works
Mishnah 14 n.
'Mock on Mock on Voltaire
  Rousseau' (Blake) 229–34, 236,
  290
Momigliano, Arnaldo 79 n., 84–5
Montaigne, Michel de 83, 96, 105
More, Henry 25–6, 31, 90, 91
Moses ben Maimon, *see* Maimonides,
  Moses
Muggletonians 225 n.
Muir, Kenneth 140 n.
Mulciber 251–3
Murray, Gilbert 55 n., 131

narcissism:
  in Greek culture 28, 29 n.
  in Romanticism 241–2, 247, 263,
    267–8, 305, 307
Narcissus, legend of 241–3, 280, 305
nazirite vow 165–7, 168
  see also *Samson Agonistes* (Milton)
Nietzsche, Friedrich 72–3, 74, 221,
  276, 280
North, Thomas, *see* Plutarch
Nuttall, A. D. 3–4

Ololon 266, 272–7, 280, 286, 288–9
Orpheus 169–70, 270
Osiris 6, 53–4
Otto, Walter F. 72 n., 115 n.
Othello (Shakespeare) 16

Paine, Thomas 211–12, 225–6
Paley, Morton D. 264 n.
Paradise Lost (Milton) 179–205, 248–9, 251–4, 255, 280, 281
  descent of Hermes in 155, 182–4, 192
  Hebraic optimism of 200
  Urania in 156–8, 182
Paradise Regained (Milton) 173, 223–4, 282–4
Peat, Derek 122
Pilate, *see* Pontius Pilate
Pirke d'Rabbi Eliezer 162
Plato 28–9, 38, 284, 285
  his *Timaeus* 69, 77
Playboy of the Western World, The (Synge) 4–5
Plotinus 284 n.
Plutarch:
  Lives 8, 20, 21, 22, 24, 33 n., 37–9, 40–1, 64, 153, 171
  Moral Essays 64
Pontius Pilate 10–12, 14–15, 23
  and see hand-washing ceremonies
Pope, Alexander 308
Prickett, Stephen 222 n.
Prometheus 123
Prosser, Eleanor 94 n., 108 n.

Raine, Kathleen 319
Ralegh, Sir Walter 90, 112
Rashi 186 n., 194, 197
Reason of Church Government, The (Milton) 167–8, 180, 257
Reibetanz, John 122
Ribner, Irving 116, 121
Richard II (Shakespeare) 10–14
Ricoeur, Paul 81–2, 307
Romeo and Juliet (Shakespeare) 55
Rosenblatt, Jason 200–1
Roston, Murray 313 n.
Rousseau, J. J. 230 n., 308

Samson Agonistes (Milton) 95, 124, 153–78, 188–9
  as Christian typology 174–8
  and Job 124, 186
  and *Lycidas* 173
  and pastoral 172–3
  suicide a problem in 95
  as tragedy 174–8
Saurat, Denis 265 n.

Schelling, Friedrich 238 n.
Schlegel, Friedrich 229
Schwartz, Regina M. 157 n.
Seaford, Richard 8 n., 55 n.
Seaton, Ethel 61–2
Seltzer, Daniel 121, 146
Seneca 23, 25
Seraphim 179–80, 216
sermo humilis 58–9, 193 n.
Shaffer, E. S. 216 n.
Shakespeare, William:
  Freudian interpretations 46
  ghosts in 32, 95
  met-agon in 9, 28, 63, 123, 149
  and myth 50–8
  'primal scenes' in 8, 15, 56, 63, 86
  and providence 108–10
  and religious meditation 100–2
  and the revenge play 79–80
  and tragedy 15–16, 35, 55–6, 63, 113, 125–6
  see also individual plays
Sharoni, Edna 284 n.
Shawcross, John T. 157 n.
Shelley, Percy Bysshe 235, 238
  'Epipsychidion' 242–5
Shlonsky, Abraham 137
Sidney, Sir Philip 147, 153
Sims, James H. 198 n., 202–3
Songs of Innocence and Experience (Blake) 246–7
  see also 'The Tyger'
Spenser, Edmund 117, 209
Spinoza, B. 212–16, 235
Steiner, George 40
stoicism versus Christianity 24, 25, 26, 95–6
Stoll. E. E. 121
Sublime (literary category) 217, 222, 228, 301–3, 318–19, 321–2
super-*agon* see *met-agon*

Tannenbaum, Leslie 209, 312 n.
Taylor, Gary 143
Tate, Nahum 120–1, 125 n.
Thompson, E. P. 225 n.
Toplady, Augustus 12 n.
Toulmin, Stephen 89
tragedy 7–8, 55, 174
  and see Shakespeare
Traversi, D. A. 48–9

True Chronicle Historie of King Leir,
  The 118, 134, 139, 153
Tur-Sinai, N. H. 302
'Tyger, The' (Blake) 319–25

Urkowitz, Steven 143

Vaughan, Thomas 275
Vernant, Jean-Pierre 29 n.
Virgil 199, 259
'Vision of the Last Judgment' (Blake)
  210, 215
Vogler, Thomas 272–3, 274
Voltaire 225–8, 230
Vyvyan, John 117

Walzer, Michael 199–200
Wandering Jew, legend of 13
Warren, Michael 143, 145
washing of the hands
  see hand-washing ceremonies
Watson, Richard (bishop) 211–12, 226
Wells, Stanley 143, 148
Werman, Golda S. 162 n.
Wilson, Richard 8 n.
Wittreich, Joseph 161, 162, 209
Wordsworth, William 88–9, 155,
  193, 216–17, 237–8, 240–1,
  284–5

Yitshaqi, Rabbi Shlomo *see* Rashi
Yuval, Israel J. 16 n.